Your Move

Your Move

second edition

Ann Hutchinson Guest
Tina Curran

Routledge
Taylor & Francis Group
New York   London

Routledge
Taylor & Francis Group
270 Madison Avenue
New York, NY 10016

Routledge
Taylor & Francis Group
2 Park Square
Milton Park, Abingdon
Oxon OX14 4RN

International Standard Book Number-13: 978-0-415-97892-7 (Softcover)

Library of Congress Cataloging-in-Publication Data

Guest, Ann Hutchinson.
  Your move : the language of dance approach to the study of movement and dance / Ann Hutchinson Guest, Tina Curran ; illustrations by Ann Hutchinson Guest. -- 2nd ed.
      p. cm.
    Includes index.
    ISBN 0-415-97892-0 (pbk. : alk. paper)
    1. Movement education. 2. Dance. 3. Movement education--Study and teaching. 4. Dance--Study and teaching. I. Curran, Tina. II. Title.

GV452.G83 2007
372.86--dc22   2006100340

Visit the Taylor & Francis Web site at
http://www.taylorandfrancis.com

and the Routledge Web site at
http://www.routledge.com

Acknowledgments

So many people gave me encouragement and assistance on the first edition of this book that it is difficult to give adequate credit and expression of appreciation to each one. Long before it reached final production, many had contributed to its growth at the working typescript stage. As my assistant in the Language of Dance® classes, Michelle Groves contributed many suggestions to the original version developed from use at the Teacher Training College of the Royal Academy of Dance.

Teachers in many different countries and fields of movement study generously took the time to read the typescript of the first (1983) edition and send in thoughtful comments and criticisms. My grateful thanks go to:

Ann Kipling Brown	Rhonda Ryman	Muriel Topaz
Meg Abbie Denton	Sheila Marion	Lucy Venable
Irene Glaister	Peggy Hackney	Joan White
Patty H. Phillips	David Henshaw	

For the much revised present edition I have welcomed the valuable input and teamwork from Tina Curran, whose experience in presenting Language of Dance at many different courses illuminated what changes and developments were needed. We in turn are much indebted to Jane Dulieu, Valerie Farrant, Susan Gingrasso, Oona Haaranen, Jimmyle Listenbee, Inez Morse, and Heidi Wiess for pinpointing the many details in the book that needed correction, clarification, or improvement.

The "'nurturing'" and production of the book would have been impossible without the devoted and patient work of the staff at the Language of Dance Centre: Lynda Howarth, Lauren Turner, Carolyn Griffiths, and Shelly Saint-Smith each of whom contributed to the production of the Calaban notation, and to assembling, checking, correcting, and compiling.

Not to be forgotten is my expression of appreciation to the resident dance historian, my patient husband, Ivor Guest, who ever gives encouragement.

Contents

Reading Studies and Reading Practices

Introduction

by Ann Hutchinson Guest

Your Move is a book about *movement*. Its aim is to provide an exploration of move-ment based on a fundamental, universal approach applicable to all movement study. *Your Move* was chosen as the title of this book because it states directly and simply that the focus is on movement, and that each individual should make each move-ment his or her own. No movement study has achieved its ultimate goal until each particular movement is understood intellectually and experienced kinetically. The spirit of the movement, the content (intent) and the physical act must be blended into a unified whole.

In this book, the progression in exploration leads to dance. Movement is "distilled" to its elements, which form a basic movement "alphabet." This alphabet is composed of the prime actions, movement concentrations, and aims. These actions, concentrations and aims are: flexion, extension, rotation, direction and level, traveling, change of support, absence of support, balance, loss of balance, and relationship to the environment. Each of these elements has subdivisions, the various possibilities of which are combined to produce movement sequences. Progression develops from the simplest of examples to the more intricate. For example, a prime action such as flexion is explored first as any form of flexion for the body-as-a-whole; later the specific forms of contracting, folding, and adduct-ing (joining) are explored as they relate to various parts of the body, such as the torso, arm, or hand. The focus in this book is on combining "what to do," the basic movements, the "verbs" and their derivatives with the "how to do it," the "adverbs" of timing and dynamics.

ORIGIN AND MEANING OF LANGUAGE OF DANCE®

From experiences as a dancer and dance educator, I recognized that no logical list of prime actions had ever been codified on which all dance (and other movement) is based. In painting there are three prime colors, in western music the octave—

what exists for dance? This question led into an investigation lasting many years. My background of study in ballet, modern dance (European and American), and various ethnic forms provided me with a broad view of dance, and my work with the system of recording movement, Labanotation, provided the tool through which findings could be pinned down. The results of this research were the establishment of the Prime Actions and Movement Concentrations presented in the Language of Dance Movement Alphabet and the development of the Movement Family Tree.

All movement can be seen to be composed of a specific selection and combination of the many variations of these prime actions. What better way to begin education in movement study than by investigating this raw material?

For dance such introduction to the raw material of movement offers a greater understanding of dance as a language in both the expressive and communicative sense. How do the parts of a movement relate to the whole? To perform with conviction one must understand the content of a sequence and the "value" to be placed on each component part. To interpret a passage of choreography one must have a concept of the meaning of movement, its "kinetic sense," or its dramatic intent. Such understanding of movement is also necessary for the mastery of technique.

And what better basic education can be devised than combining the physical experience of movement with the written form, the visual aid which provides clarification. Any serious educational study in other fields automatically incorporates some form of notation—what better way to pin down the seemingly intangible aspects of movement than through this visual aid? Consider music. Music notation is introduced as an aid to understanding pitch, time structure, time values, and manner of performance—the basis of the art. Music notation provides the means to memorize and practice without the presence of a teacher. Learning to read music also provides access to the literature of music and facilitates a professional career. The same is true of the use of notation in connection with movement studies.

The act of dancing is a physical one, but behind it must be an intelligent awareness of what one is doing. Communication requires clarity based on a comprehensive understanding of the nature and facts of movement. The Language of Dance, like all languages, has the purpose of communication, communication through a common terminology and vocabulary supported by the written form. Full communication in dance should occur at all levels, at all stages, and at all locations. Communication across the oceans of the world requires a common language, the use of symbols to represent the many "building blocks" of movement on which all dance cultures are based.

PURPOSE OF THIS BOOK

Your Move provides the Language of Dance (LOD) framework for learning about movement. The approach presented in this book can be a first introduction to movement exploration given to beginning movers of all ages as well as being used for deeper study by advanced movement practitioners. Language of Dance also offers a completely fresh look at movement to those already trained in one or more movement styles. The knowledge gained in understanding what one is doing and why, can help further mastery of technique as well as enriching quality of performance. In addition, Language of Dance provides an excellent basic introduction to movement composition and thence to choreography. It opens the eyes to a "store cupboard" of movement possibilities. This framework can also be used as an analytic lens through which to compare choreographic styles and movement genres.

Your Move presents a way of looking at and learning about movement which, to our knowledge, has never before been published. Both practical facts and expressive ideas are covered. The chapters first explore each new element through a consideration of how this prime form of movement or basic concept appears in the world around us. Starting with familiar examples, movement exploration then concentrates on how the body can make use of each basic form or idea. Introductory work concentrates first on the physical experience, a guided exploration of the material with direct interaction between teacher and students. Discussion of the movement experience and reinforcement of the concept through introduction of the appropriate symbols provide clarification. Improvisation leading to composition of movement sequences gives the opportunity for readers to make this material "their own" and to demonstrate the degree to which the material and logical variations of it have been understood mentally and physically. Exploration and performance of the Reading Studies for each chapter can be introduced before or after compositional ideas are developed.

The Language of Dance framework clarifies, organizes, supports, and enhances the work and aims of movement educators leading to movement/dance literacy. The first part of the book, chapters 1 to 11, starts with the most basic elements listed in the Movement Alphabet. Part Two, Chapters 12 to 22, of the text develops these concepts further as well as introducing additional information. This book concludes with the transition from detailed Motif Description into the Structured Description of Labanotation. The serious student can progress toward structured movement description and thus, like a student of music, benefit from the available recorded literature.

APPLICATION TO MOVEMENT PRACTICE

The Language of Dance approach, though not limited to these, has four important applications:

1. as a first introduction of movement leading to dance for young children and beginners of all ages. At first the discipline of only a single factor is presented so that freedom in interpretation is allowed. While experiencing this basic action, the students may find their own way to express the given concept. Gradually as physical coordination and understanding develop, the factors of time, space, part of the body, relationship, and dynamics are combined and refined to provide the challenges needed. Although this book is designed for use by older students and does not concentrate on application of the material to teaching children, its basic approach and ideas allow the material to be used fruitfully in that area.
2. as an enriching and deepening experience for advanced movement practitioners.
3. as material for movement composition leading to choreographic study.
4. as material for educators who desire to expand their conscious knowledge of the elements of movement to make implicit instruction explicit through enhanced understanding and a clearly defined vocabulary.

TRAINING THE EYE

Movement literacy includes the ability to observe and identify the multiple factors of which movement is composed. Mastering physical skills does not necessarily include skills in movement observation. Movement contains so much detail that it can be difficult to know where to start unless some guidelines are given. Should one be aware of the spatial pattern, or of what parts of the body are in action? Should the rhythm, the use of time, be the point of focus, or is concentration to be on the dynamic pattern, the movement qualities used? As visual aids, the Motif Notation symbols provide a means of clarification and communication. If one can write down what one wants to say about a movement, then one can communicate this information to others. Analyzing the component parts of movement helps to observe and to understand. The eye must be trained to see, the mind to comprehend, and the vocabulary developed to communicate.

UNIVERSAL APPROACH TO MOVEMENT

The Language of Dance material in *Your Move* is not based on any one form or style of movement, but itself provides a basis for movement of all kinds. After the first general exploration of the prime actions, however, further investigation which advances toward structured movement is bound to be directed toward one or another movement discipline. In *Your Move* the development is intentionally directed toward dance, dance of all kinds; no preference is given to any particular type. The exploration in this book does not involve structured forms; therefore there is still much freedom. The Language of Dance® also embraces movement terminology as universal as possible to support its wide application and provide a method of clear communication for all.

ORGANIZATION OF THIS BOOK

In Part One of this book, that is Chapters 1 to 11, we deal with the first general prime actions of the Movement Alphabet. In embodying this material much freedom in interpretation and leeway in performance is allowed as long as the basic movement concept is understood and portrayed.

In Part Two, Chapters 12 to 22, exploration builds on this foundation while layering new information and becoming increasingly specific, thus leading toward a more structured movement description. Although many specific details are introduced, such as further development of relating, paths for gestures, use of parts of the body, specific forms of flexion and extension, and variations in interpreting direction, the movement exploration continues to be creative and comparatively free; it is still presented and described on paper through Motif Notation.

The Appendices provide additional details, including the transition from Motif Notation to Labanotation, the Structured Description in which details are specifically stated, given in Appendix B. Reference to the Family Tree of Verbs is provided in Appendix E. This chart will help in relating new material presented in Part Two to that covered in Part One.

Movement Alphabet
of Verbs

The prime actions ("verbs") and concepts of which movement is comprised.

PRESENCE OR ABSENCE OF MOVEMENT

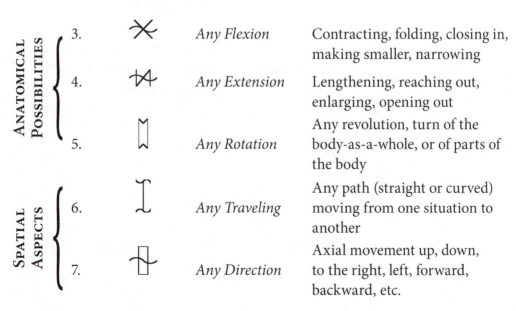

INITIAL STATEMENTS

1.   *Any Action*   Movement of some kind, a change

2.   *Stillness*   Suspension of motion, sustainment of an arrested activity

An action may be concerned with or may focus on:

ANATOMICAL POSSIBILITIES

3.   *Any Flexion*   Contracting, folding, closing in, making smaller, narrowing

4.   *Any Extension*   Lengthening, reaching out, enlarging, opening out

5.   *Any Rotation*   Any revolution, turn of the body-as-a-whole, or of parts of the body

SPATIAL ASPECTS

6.   *Any Traveling*   Any path (straight or curved) moving from one situation to another

7.   *Any Direction*   Axial movement up, down, to the right, left, forward, backward, etc.

SUPPORTING	8.	*Support*	An action ending in a new support, transference of weight, a step
	9.	*A Spring*	Any aerial step leaving the ground and returning to it
CENTER OF GRAVITY	10.	*Balance*	Equilibrium, centering of center of gravity over a static or moving support
	11.	*Falling*	Center of gravity moves beyond base of support

MOTION, DESTINATION

MOVEMENT INTENTION	12.	*Motion Toward*	Approaching, moving toward a person, object, direction, or state of being
	13.	*Motion Away*	Leaving, withdrawing from a person, object, direction, or state of being; a gesture away from a person
	14.	*Destination*	Statement of ending situation, position or state to be reached, designated aim

RESULTS OF ACTIONS

	15.	*Any Still Shape*	The movement aims to produce a shape
	16.	*Any Form of Relating*	The aim of the movement is to produce a relationship of some kind

THE MOVEMENT "FAMILY TREE"

Movement consists of an action (the **verb**) performed by a particular part of the body or by the body-as-a-whole (the **noun**), with a particular dynamic quality or other manner of performance attribute (the **adverb**).

The **nouns** include a partner, a prop, or a part of the room (stage). In this book nouns and adverbs are not dealt with in great detail; focus is mainly on exploring and understanding the verbs, the actions, the range of basic movement possibilities.

CHAPTER ONE
Movement; Stillness; Timing; Shape; Accents

What is movement? There can be dozens of answers to that question depending on the context in which the question is presented. Are we concerned with electric impulses from the brain which trigger muscular responses and thus produce physical movement? Or do we anticipate the reply "Movement is life!"? We need a simple, practical investigation of human movement which leads to recording the outcome of muscular responses. In this book, the viewing and experiencing of movement progresses from an initial broad introduction to a focus specifically on dance.

MOVEMENT

Perform one movement, then follow it with a rest, a moment of inactivity. Move again. Find variations without seeking a specific structure. Just move. Whatever the movement, it may have arisen from a thought (an idea which came to mind), or from a physical impulse (an out-flowing from the center of the body). A movement may be just a simple spatial displacement rather than an arrival in a particular pose. As we are starting with the most basic, elementary movement concepts, let us take spatial displacement. From whatever position you are now in, make a change, move a limb, making a gesture with, perhaps, the right arm, or move the torso into a different situation. Move the head and arms away from where they were. If sitting or kneeling, change by rising or lowering, or by transferring the weight to another part of the body. If you focus on leaving the situation where you were, rather than on moving to a predetermined new spatial placement, the action is more likely to reflect true motion performed for the sake of moving, of enjoying the process, rather than of achieving a particular "picture."

We need to consider the difference between movements which are just "done" (such as those that are purely functional), and movements that are performed, such as those in gymnastics, skating, swimming, or dance. What is "performed" movement and what is not? In turning on the television one can distinguish in a moment between a panel discussion on some current topic and a comparable discussion occurring in a play. The difference lies in the manner of presentation. Practical, everyday movements, such as putting a book on a table, when performed by a mime artist or a dancer, are presented with a heightening, be it ever so slight, of intensity in the manner of execution. In dance, one may "walk through" the motions, marking them for memory, but for full benefit and enjoyment of the experience, the innate expressive content of each movement has to be found and presented fully.

INDICATION OF AN ACTION

The simplest statement regarding movement is that an action, a movement of some kind, occurs. For such a basic statement, an equally basic notation indication is provided, 1.1a. This vertical line, called an action stroke, makes no statement about the movement other than that it occurs.

An
Action

1.1a

So we have one movement. What could it be? Start with a simple action. Simplicity can often be more difficult than complexity. What should that first action be? The first action can be ANYTHING! Turn, bend over, lower to the floor, wave the arms, reach for the ceiling, twist to one side, or just take a deep breath and allow another movement to emerge. A swaying of the torso can be the start, developing into a larger movement.

Depending on the context, the accompanying music, the dramatic situation, the proximity of and relationship to other persons, an action (1.1a), could be an appropriate, expected movement (appropriate to the context in which it occurs), or it might be **any** kind of movement at all, the performer having total freedom of choice. The sign for ad libitum, 1.1b, is placed at the start of the action stroke, as in 1.1c, when **total freedom of choice** of movement (versus an expected or appropriate movement) is allowed. The range of such movement can be from a general fluent spatial displacement of the body-as-a-whole to a single finger movement. Begin by using general, overall body movement, each part moving in harmony as it supports the main movement idea.

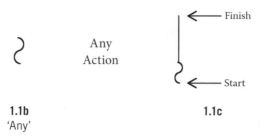

1.1b
'Any'

1.1c

The Basic Staff

Motif Description, that is, expressing a basic movement idea or intention, is represented on paper through Motif Notation. This notation uses no staff, as such. The column which runs vertically up the page from the double horizontal starting line to the end, as in 1.2a, represents the body-as-a-whole. No distinction is made yet regarding use of one body part or another. Later on, movements of the right or left side of the body will be indicated as well as actions of specific parts of the body. Note the use of a double line: ══════, to indicate both the start of action and the end of the example. In the space immediately before the double starting line is written the starting position, if any. In 1.2b this space is outlined with dotted lines. The dotted lines, used in 1.2a are as a visual aid to delineate the staff, are not drawn in a score.

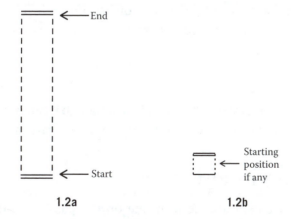

1.2a

1.2b

Simultaneus Actions

Two or more actions may occur at the same time; one part of the body may perform an action at the same time as another part. Double or triple actions may have occurred in your previous movement exploration; now simultaneous actions are consciously being performed as such. Experiment with different body part possibilities, perhaps both arms, or one arm and one leg. Try moving the torso with both arms performing a different action in unison. Many possibilities can be explored.

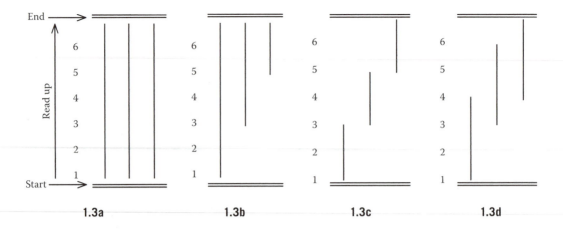

1.3a   1.3b   1.3c   1.3d

The reading sequence for movement is up the page, i.e., from the bottom of the page up. Actions which occur at the same time are written side by side. Example 1.3a illustrates three separate actions occurring at the same time, starting on count 1 and extending through count 6. Use a tempo which suits you. Three actions occur in 1.3b but starting at different times. The first action extends through the 6 counts; the second starts on count 3 and the third on count 5. All finish at the same time. In 1.3c the three actions are completely separate; each takes two counts and start two counts apart. Quite similar but more difficult to perform is 1.3d. Here the actions start in a similar way but overlap by one count each. The sense of overlapping actions is not difficult, but precise performance may take practice.

TIMING

Timing is such an integral part of movement that, although it can be ignored and a neutral attitude to time can be taken, we want early on to be aware of it and to enjoy it.

SUSTAINED MOVEMENT

Choose a simple movement and concentrate on the passing of time. If a gong is played, begin moving at the moment the gong is struck and continue until the sound dies away or someone stops it. Find a movement which the sound inspires. You may think of a word to say inwardly which supports your movement idea: for example, the word "S-T-R-E-A-M-I-N-G" being sustained for as long as needed. The question will arise: "How long is that?" No statement has been made yet of specific length; you still have freedom in the choice of duration. Now try a contrasting movement, but still very sustained; indulge fully in time, enjoy the slowness of it, relish the sustainment, the feeling of never wanting it to stop.

INDICATION OF SUSTAINED ACTIONS

The **extension in time** of a movement is represented on paper by the length of the vertical line, the action stroke. In 1.4a the action extends in time from the start of this symbol to the end. As we all have slightly different innate attitudes toward time, each person will have a different idea of the duration 1.4a should represent. This does not matter as long as we are solo performers; it is when unison movement is needed that a basic beat must be established and kept constant. Music provides just such control; in a ballet such as Jerome Robbins' *Moves*, which is performed without music, the dancers must count inwardly to maintain a regular beat or must take visual cues from each other.

For 1.4a the chosen movement may cover a long or a short distance spatially. Length of time is quite separate from spatial length or distance, that is, space measurement.

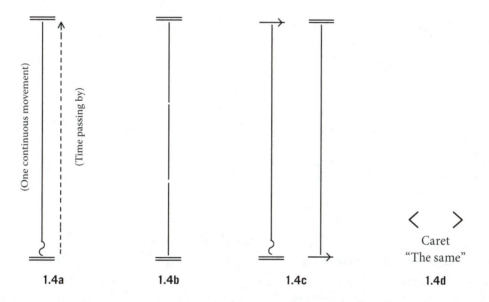

| 1.4a | 1.4b | 1.4c | 1.4d |

Caret
"The same"

Only one movement is stated in 1.4a. Example 1.4b provides three sustained actions one after the other without a break. Note that the three are separate actions, not one very slow movement.

For movement exploration, 1.4b provides greater scope than 1.4a in that it offers a choice of three slow movements which follow one another and can be linked together. If moving so slowly seems difficult, find an image which will support each movement, for example, underwater plants slowly swaying through the gentle motion of the water.

When a movement sequence continues beyond the top of the page, a single horizontal line is used to conclude the staff and a new staff is started to the right with another single horizontal line at the bottom of the page. In 1.4c the continuity of one movement over two staves is shown. The end of the first action stroke and the beginning of the second are linked through use of a caret, shown in 1.4d. This sign means "the same," thus stating that it is the same movement.

CONTINUITY OF MOVEMENT

While experimenting with performing 1.4b, it will be clear to you that these are three separate movements. The first movement might be a gesture moving out into space, the second might be the same gesture returning on the same path. If the second action happens immediately after the first with no break, have you performed one movement or two? When a break between actions occurs, even a slight pause, then it is quite clear that two separate actions have taken place. When no break occurs, a slight modification in the path of the gesture, the space pattern, can produce one movement, rather than two.

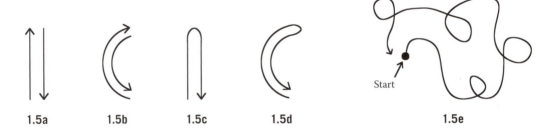

| 1.5a | 1.5b | 1.5c | 1.5d | 1.5e |

Example 1.5a illustrates a space pattern of two movements. You follow a straight line path and then reverse direction, a "there and back." Example 1.5b shows two similar movements using an arc; but 1.5c and 1.5d show only one action. The curved transition produces one continuous line of movement. Example 1.5e represents one long continuous line of movement. If one part of the body is being used, try involving the whole body for an overall harmonious effect.

SUDDEN MOVEMENTS

It is now time for a complete change of mood, of intent, of inner experience into the world of no-time-to-spare, of haste, speed, quickness, suddenness. Choose an action and execute it at the fastest possible speed. It could be the same movement which you chose before, but the chances are that something quite different will be more suited to the speed now demanded of you. Try one very fast action, then another and another. Continuous performance of sudden actions can become very tiring. You and the audience long for a break; allow pauses of different lengths between.

INDICATION OF SUDDEN ACTIONS

A sudden action is shown by a short line, 1.6a. The movement has barely started before it is ended. Example 1.6b shows a brief movement phrase composed of three very quick actions, one immediately after the other. A suitable accompaniment could be three percussive sounds such as three drumbeats; the movement could be claps, stamps, jabbing actions in the air, twitches, or dabbing motions.

When no movement takes place, there is no action. A blank space indicates no movement, i.e., no change. In 1.6c an action is followed by no change (remember to read from the bottom up). Example 1.6c provides the most rudimentary movement theme—an action followed by inaction.

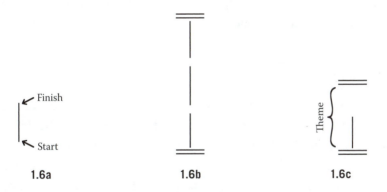

Finish

Start

1.6a　　　　**1.6b**　　　　**1.6c**

The "theme" of three sudden actions will be more interesting if combined with absence of action. In 1.6d, between each set of three quick actions, there is a gap. Note that this gap is of the same duration as that of the three actions. In complete contrast to this, 1.6e shows three quick actions, but with a considerable separation between each one. These could be the same three actions used for 1.6d, but how different the effect now that they are so separated in time!

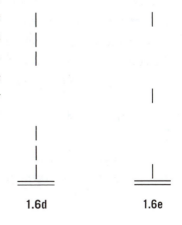

1.6d　　　　**1.6e**

The time pattern of 1.6f is interesting since it starts like 1.6d but develops differently. The movement pattern progresses from three swift actions one after the other, then two actions, then one. The total number of actions in 1.6f is the same as in 1.6d but they are presented differently in time. From such simple material many interesting variations can result, involving various parts of the body in smaller or larger spatial displacements. Try performing actions each of the same duration but each using greater or lesser physical space.

In performing sequences, focus needs to be on the movement patterns, or the sequence of events. Take, for instance, the simple example of 1.6f. This pattern could be accurately counted into 12 beats, but more important is to sense that the first three actions are followed by a gap of an equal duration. Two actions come next, followed by a gap of the same duration. The ending is a single action with a one beat gap following. There is no music for this example; the tempo, the speed of the beats, is left open. The value of this pattern lies in sensing the durations, experiencing the actions and absences of actions, rather than meticulously counting out each one.

1.6f

Spatial Continuum

Have you ever thought of how we move in space—the wonderful range of choice, and yet the limitations involved in never escaping the spatial continuum? It is impossible to move from point "x" to point "y" in space or on the paper here without going through all the points between. Music can jump octaves, intervals of all kinds, but movement is by nature chromatic: we must pass through the intervening space.

By the **manner** in which we perform the movement we can give an impression of "jumping" from point "x" to "y," as in 1.7a. A swift, unemphasized transition and a clear arrival, which is held momentarily, will produce this effect. Thus by speed and intensity we can give the impression of darting from point to point, position to position, without intervening links. This impression of darting can deceive the eye, thus creating an illusion of escape from the spatial continuum. Example 1.7b illustrates the picture that a very sudden, sharp rising will produce in the viewer's eye.

A very different effect is achieved by the deliberate use of chromatic movement—movement which consciously progresses through all the intervening spatial points. Such movement cannot be extremely fast; by moving more slowly, indulging in time, one has the opportunity to enjoy the passage through space. This passage

1.7a
A Spatial Leap

1.7b

is now often captured by rapid photography in multi-image pictures or in slow-motion filming. Moving with a chromatic image in mind, as depicted in 1.7c and illustrated in 1.7d, produces a fullness, a richness of gesture in motion that is missing in actions designed to move swiftly to distant destination points. Full awareness of the passage through space happens naturally in swimming where the resistance supplied by the water provides a consciousness of the fact that there can be no sudden darting from point to point. Only by eliminating frames in cinematic manipulation can the illusion be created of cutting to a destination.

1.7c
Awareness of
passage through space

1.7d

ORGANIZATION OF TIME

In this book we are concerned with the nature of movement and its different forms, with a general investigation of time. An exploration of time as used in dance is a study on its own. But even in this first exploration of movement, time cannot be ignored. We cannot move without involving time, without using it in some way. For our purposes here we deal with the basic organization of time.

How much time is actually taken for these examples? No indication has as yet been given regarding counts, beats, seconds, or other time-measuring devices. We have been dealing with free, unmeasured time. Within the span of time indicated on the paper between the double horizontal lines, the movements are proportionally spaced. For 1.6d, 1.6e, and 1.6f, the same overall amount of time was allowed so that the contrast between the three examples could be seen. If relative timing is understood and performed, it does not matter if one person's choice for the overall timing is longer than another's. Some forms of dance use time freely; only at key moments do all performers have to coordinate. For many actions no formal organization of time is needed. In many sports, time can be personal; its use centers on what functionally produces the desired result. In dance it is common for time to be strictly organized, largely because of the physical enjoyment of a rhythmic beat, but also because of the organization of the accompanying music or sound.

LENGTH OF PAUSE, GAP

A break between movements may range from a very slight pause to an extended gap. Such pauses or gaps are important in that they can significantly affect the expression of the series of movements. A very expressive stop in the flow of movement is the breath pause. This brief hesitation before continuing is used in speech as well as in movement. Such a brief breath pause can be like a suspension, an intake of breath before launching into the next movement. Note the timing progression in 1.8a–1.8h.

In 1.8a there is no separation between the action strokes, only enough of a break to show that the movement is not one continuous line. These tiny gaps only separate the actions; they have no time significance. Example 1.8b shows slight pauses between the sustained movements; they produce an effect not unlike commas in a sentence, very slight breath pauses. In the absence of these pauses, movement flows on without any "punctuation" as in 1.8a. When sentences are completely devoid of punctuation, the listener or reader loses the meaning of what is being said.

The meaning in spoken or written words can be altered by placement and length of pauses, and so it is with dance. If movement flows on endlessly it is like cooked spaghetti; you can't find the beginning or the end. The breath pause provides a fleeting moment of rest during which the audience can see a clear image, an arrival point, and thus it is essential for good phrasing in performance. This moment of arrival is the point at which the photographer snaps the picture.

A longer pause can also provide needed punctuation. A gap, a clear separation, can be important in separating movement ideas, as in 1.8c. A gap may be just a cessation of movement, a wait before the next action, no change taking place. The end of the gap may be used as an anticipation of what is coming next, a minor preparation such as a shift of weight, an anticipated change of direction. Such preparations are minor and are not emphasized, they occur in the normal course of moving without being pinpointed or highlighted.

In performing 1.8a, take a three-part circular arm pattern starting with the arms down. Raise them forward for the first action, open sideward for the second, then lower to the starting position for the third. Perform this simple arm pattern without any pauses at all, as is illustrated in 1.8a. Then introduce breath pauses, as in 1.8b. Then introduce slightly longer gaps, as in 1.8c, followed by the version of equal time for moving and for waiting, as in 1.8d. As the movements quicken and the gaps become longer, you will be performing 1.8e and 1.8f. In 1.8f the movements to each point are as swift as possible: sudden, staccato actions.

How will accompanying music affect these movement examples? Each of the sequences takes the same amount of space on the page, so each takes the same overall span of time, the same amount of music. But within this time span (between ===== and =====) the organization of the actions and the breaks between have provided much variation. If you still use the same arm pattern, how would 1.8g come to life? Bear in mind that the overall time is still basically divided into three parts; therefore 1.8g shows the forward and sideward part of the previous movement pattern occurring within the first third of the time span. A gap of the same length follows; the lowering of the arms then occurs on the last third. In 1.8h the arms are raised forward swiftly, then there is a gap. The arms then open to the side during all of the second part of the time span, and then are lowered during all of the last time span. These examples could also be interpreted as full body actions.

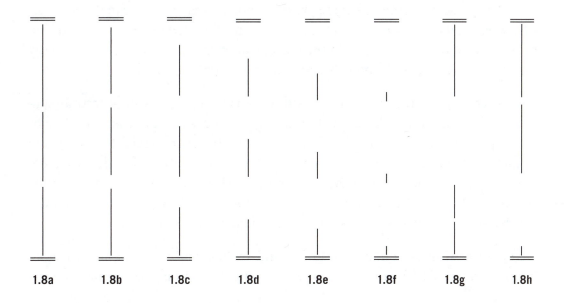

1.8a   1.8b   1.8c   1.8d   1.8e   1.8f   1.8g   1.8h

Many choices for musical accompaniment could be made; obviously something flowing would be suitable. The music need not "spell" out the timing of the movement; it is more interesting if your movement relates to the music but retains its own rhythmic independence. There is also the challenge of your movement being independent and yet occurring simultaneously with the music.

STILLNESS

What is stillness? Basically it is the passage of time when external physical movement action does not occur. It is absence of movement, absence of action, but with an active inner alertness, energy, and intention. It is not "stop"; it is not a "blankness," a "deadness," a "minus" (though these may be wanted at times for special effect). As Agnes de Mille has observed, "A tacit in music is not a silence. It is a suspension. In a play, that tacit is called a pause, and all too often, God knows, the pause in question is a dead, dulling silence, a break in the continuity, a gap, an on-stage nap, empty air. Unless a pause can make tension, it's sheer dereliction of duty."

During an absence of movement, a stillness should be enjoyed by both performer and viewer; it should be a positive experience. Stillness provides a "frame" for an interesting sudden action, making it memorable. It should have its own meaning or significance equal in importance to that of an action. In stillness there may be repose, not the blankness of people sitting still waiting for a bus, but rather the active stillness of listening as in listening to a symphony. Such stillness catches the eye. Because so much emphasis is placed on actions, on techniques of moving, it seems important to give full value here to the concepts behind stillness. If there is a significant gap between actions, the previous movement must terminate in a position of some kind, but the line of the previous motion still projects into the stillness, a fragment of it lingers on beyond the arrival point. The movement is "arrested" but the energy flow escapes as though the movement intended to continue. The energy continues even though the body has arrived at a spatial destination.

The energy and the quality of the stillness may vary significantly according to the mood being expressed. Despite the ending position, a sense of transience exists. This is particularly true of a stillness of shorter duration, comparable to a comma in a sentence; a longer stillness can relate to a full stop, a cessation of outer movement that can express the idea of arrival: "Here I am. This is where I belong." Arrested action may be intended, a strong positive statement, or it may be a stillness from which a new movement emerges, the result of a new movement idea.

Because stillness contains meaning and expression, a special sign is used. The sign for "hold," 1.9a, is used in many contexts to retain or maintain a state or condition. For the special state of stillness with a sustained active inner sense, the sign for out-flowing, 1.9b, is added to form the sign for stillness, 1.9c. Note the difference in meaning for the examples in 1.9d–1.9g. In 1.9d there is a definite gap between movements, nothing happens, there is a cessation of movement, no particular intent is evident. In 1.9e, a hold sign is added, expressing the idea of a held position, as in the game of making statues. In 1.9f stillness fills the gap; the reverberation, the movement expression "sings on"; there is intent. Stillness cannot exist when there are other actions taking place, one cannot move and be still at the same time. Note that the duration of the stillness encompasses the **stillness symbol plus the amount of blank space following it**, as in 1.9g.

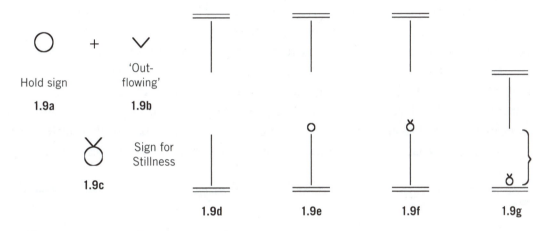

GENERAL TIMING, MEASURED TIMING

In describing movement patterns through Motif Notation, how much need is there to be very accurate in timing? This question often comes up. Specific timing is usually reserved for the Structured Description in Labanotation; there the elements of space, specific form, degree of movement, and part(s) of the body used are carefully described. However, in Motif Description, the freedom of performance of the Motif symbols indicated often needs a general, comfortable indication of timing.

Care has been taken with the timing shown in the examples given here in order to provide a general statement. Precision should not be looked for; instead a comfortable rendition should be sought. While the studies and the accompanying music were composed in collaboration, in the recording session some leeway occurred so that there is not always a total "one to one" relationship. When the timing is not obvious, the reader should find his/her way of relating to the music.

INDICATION OF REGULAR TIME SPANS (MEASURES)

The passage of time is always read from the bottom of the page up. Double horizontal lines are placed at the bottom left of the page to indicate the start of organized time. Placed at the top of the page (or at the end of a phrase or dance, if longer than one staff), a double horizontal line indicates the end of this time span, illustrated in 1.10a. As you read up the page, single horizontal lines, called bar lines, mark the measure of time, thus providing an organized time structure. The starting double line also often incorporates a bar line. In 1.10b, the time span is divided into three measures (bars), each of equal length. In 1.10c, four measures are indicated.

In 1.10d the measures (bars) are numbered for reference, the number being placed immediately after the bar line on the left. The span of time covers two staves, eight measures being indicated. When a movement sequence continues beyond the top of the page, a single bar line is used and a new staff is started to the right with another single bar line at the bottom of the page. A double bar line at the end indicates the conclusion of the piece. For this basic structure, the tempo (speed) and the number of beats for each measure have been left open. Any piece of music or drumming in spans of eight measures can be used and any tempo can be set for this structure.

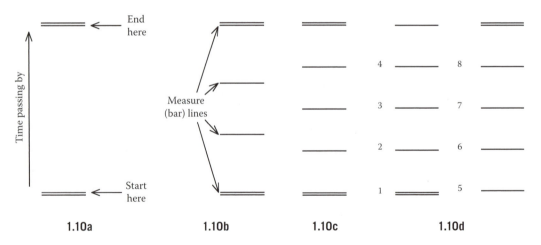

1.10a   1.10b   1.10c   1.10d

INDICATION OF METER

The next step in organization of time is to specify meter (the measure of the time units). The indication is also known as the Time Signature, however, "meter" more directly states its function. The meter states the number of beats (basic pulses) in each measure and the time value of each. This specification of the meter (the measure of each span) is indicated at the start of the staff, on the left, before the movement sequence begins. In 1.11a the meter is 4/4, the number of beats (4) is placed at the top and the value for each beat, here a quarter note (crotchet) indicated by 4, is placed at the bottom. Although written here in the text as 4/4, in music it is written with a 4 above a 4 with no line between. In 1.11a, the four counts (beats) within the measure have been indicated with smaller numerals, larger numerals being used for the numbering of the measures (bars).

Other familiar meters are 3/4, shown in 1.11b, and 6/4, illustrated in 1.11c. In each of these, the counts have been indicated for the first measure. If the same unit on paper is used for each beat, then a measure of 4/4 covers more space (time passing by) than one measure of 3/4.

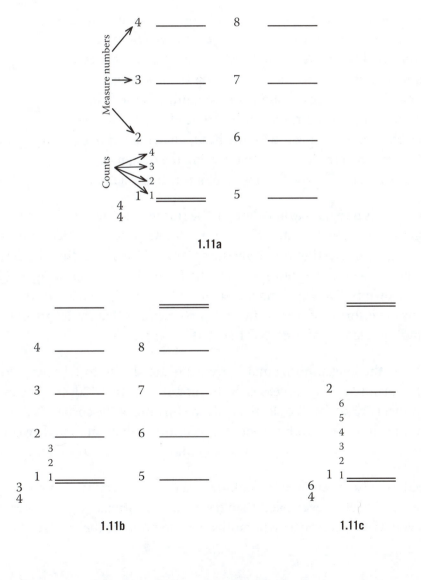

1.11a

1.11b   1.11c

In Motif Notation, the individual beats in each measure are not usually indicated, as some freedom in timing is allowed. Statement of tempo (speed) is still left open. In the early stages of exploring movement patterns, ample time is needed to experience the material and so a slower tempo is advised. The above first specifications about time, the statement of meter, are only a general guide as to what music may be used as accompaniment.

Listen to the 3/4 music for Reading Study No. 1. As it is being played, run your finger up this movement score, following the passage of time and coordinating the music measures with those marked in the study. Do the same with the next Reading Study, No. 2, which is in 4/4 meter.

TIME DIVISION OF A SPATIAL DESIGN

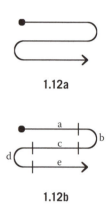

1.12a

1.12b

The speed at which the body-as-a-whole or a gesture moves through space can vary. As a first exploration we will be concerned only with a simple example. Example 1.12a illustrates a gestural pattern moving to and fro, starting at the left and ending at the right. The black dot shows the beginning of the design. Try this pattern with the right arm in front of the body, then with the left arm. Then try it with the head, allowing the body to participate. Then try it with a foot, tracing the design on the floor. Example 1.4a could be the notation of this single action.

Though this design, one long line can be traced at an even pace with no change in the speed of the movement; different time durations for its different sections will produce a more interesting result. By the simple device of dividing the design with cross lines, we separate it into segments. In 1.12b, the same drawing as 1.12a, the design is shown in five segments identified as "a," " b," "c," etc. Now the following variations in performance can be indicated. Remember that the length of the action stroke indicates length of time, NOT spatial distance.

In 1.12c, the longer, horizontal movements are shown to take very little time, while the turning of the corners is performed slowly. In 1.12d, the longer lines of the movement are performed slowly while the turning of the corners is done swiftly. The rendition in 1.12e introduces equal motion and stillness at first, then continuous motion, becoming slower with each action. Many other variations may be tried.

Speed can also be enjoyed in walking and running. Try the same space pattern as above walking at an even pace; then try it with variations in speed, breaking into a run if you wish. Find movement motivations to underlie the change of pace.

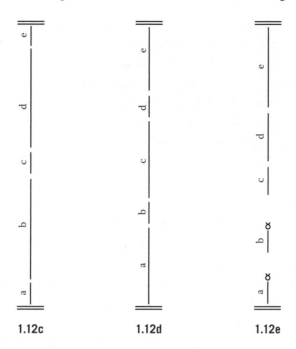

1.12c   1.12d   1.12e

INTERPRETING A READING STUDY

There are unlimited ways to dance the two simple Reading Studies (Nos. 1 and 2), but a few suggestions may help get you started. These studies can be performed while sitting, kneeling, or standing. Flowing arm gestures with body accompaniment may be used, hence the suitability of sitting or kneeling where concern with balance is absent. It could be a "dance" just of the hands, with the body reacting in some way to augment the hand patterns. Other possibilities may be a single arm performing the first phrase of four measures, or the arms may alternate for each new action. Basic movement actions may also be used. If the performer is standing, then a sustained transference of weight (a step) might be a choice. However, for a very sustained slow step, a transference of weight may not be easy, hence other action ideas or gestures may be chosen. Should traveling be chosen, this should be seen and experienced as a **one-action idea**, one intention, and not a series of individual steps, i.e., individual actions. After a first general exploration, experiment with one or more of the above ideas to produce more inventiveness, perhaps contrast Reading Study No. 1 with Reading Study No. 2, making Reading Study No. 1 focus on the whole body and Reading Study No. 2 feature individual body parts.

Use the points in the following list to actualize Reading Studies Nos. 1 and 2, that is, to interpret the symbols into dance. Apply this strategy to all Reading Studies.

1. Recognize general similarities or differences between the movements written.
2. Look for phrases, groupings, patterns; look for the main ideas.
3. Notice the timing, the meter of the reading.
4. Listen to the music and count each measure and beat.
5. Visually follow the score, listening to the music as it is being played and running your finger up the staff, following the passage of time, thus coordinating the music measures with those marked on the page.
6. Be aware of the duration of each action and stillness.
7. Visualize your choice of how you will perform the notation; "talk" through the movement.
8. Physicalize the notated movement.
9. Interpret a short phrase—perhaps four measures at a time—embody it, then put the book down and perform from memory, transferring written movement into kinesthetic experience. Then move on to the next phrase (four more measures in this first reading), working in the same way before linking these two phrases together.
10. Practice the movement phrases, seeking fluidity, logical transitions between main movement ideas, and appropriateness of timing.
11. Add change of front when such freedom is allowed and bring in dynamics and qualitative coloring.
12. Find movement meaning in the sequences to make them your own.

MOVEMENT PATTERNS IN TIME

Two studies in actions of different time values producing specific patterns in time.

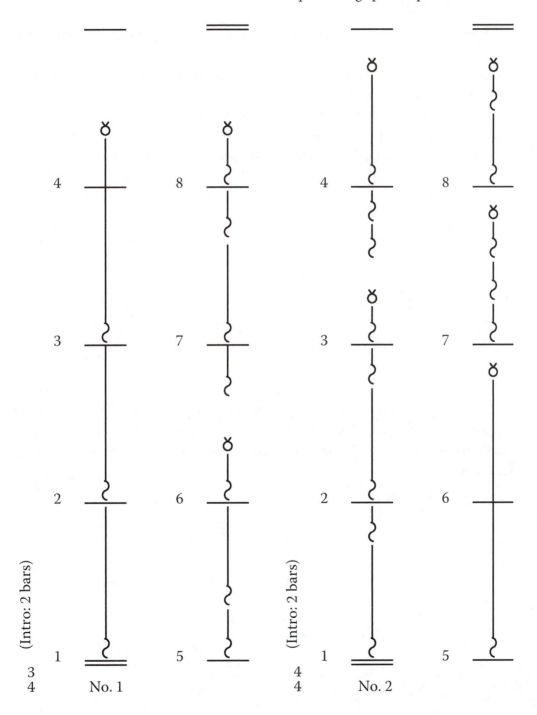

ARRIVAL AT A SHAPE

The intention of a movement may be to arrive at a specific static body shape. To produce a shape, the person has to stop moving, thus the action is destinational. Exploration of body shapes and the range of possibilities will be dealt with later; here only the basic idea is presented.

Example 1.13a is the sign for "a shape." It is composed of the diamond representing aspects of space crossed by a horizontal line. In 1.13b an action has the aim, the destination, of producing a shape. The length of the action stroke gives the duration of the movement into that shape. The small vertical bow links the action to the shape, thus indicating that this is the ending, the aim, the destination. Example 1.13c indicates any action arriving at a shape, followed by stillness. Because nothing is specified, how this shape is realized is left open to interpretation; much freedom is allowed. A stillness following the arrival at a shape allows the shape to be alive, rather than a stone statue, as would be produced in 1.13d.

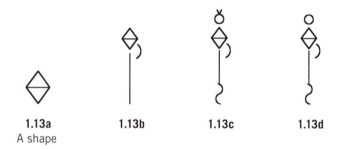

| 1.13a | 1.13b | 1.13c | 1.13d |

A shape

Reading Study No. 3 is similar to Reading Study No. 1 with the added element of arrival in a shape. Notice when the shape is achieved at the end of a slow movement or more swiftly on one count. The meter is now 4/8 instead of 3/4. The study is repeated, as indicated by the marks: ⦂— placed on the left at the start and on the right at the end of the score.

READING STUDY NO. 3

ACTION ARRIVING AT A SHAPE

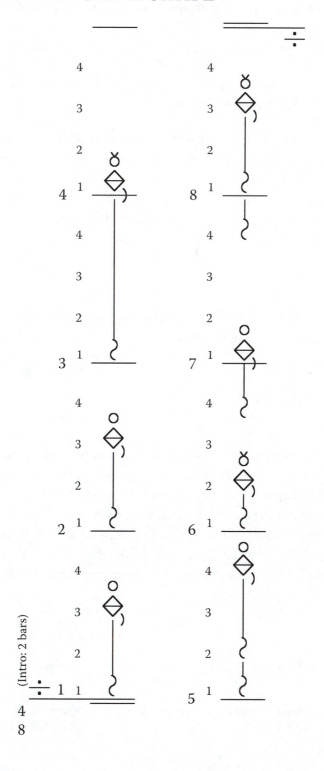

INTRODUCTION OF DYNAMICS

Dynamics are an essential part of all movement. Movement cannot occur without some degree of energy, and dynamics are concerned with the ebb and flow of energy, how energy is used, and to what degree. We will be concerned with the kind of movement to be performed, the "what" action, but we must also be concerned with "how" that action is presented, the quality, the texture, i.e., the dynamic content.

A movement can be made more interesting by placement of accents. An accent is always sudden, a brief burst of energy.

A movement can have an accent at the start, it may occur at the end of the action, or somewhere during the movement. An accent is a momentary stress (increase in energy); it is familiar in movement, in speech, and in music. A sharp rise in energy and a slight increase in speed, both of which disappear immediately, are easy to produce; at this stage the performer need not analyze exactly what ingredients are needed to produce an accent.

ACCENTS

An accent may be slight (light), as in 1.14a, using a slight rise in energy, or it may be strong, 1.14b, involving marked energy.

1.14a
A slight accent

1.14b
A strong accent

Placed at the start of a movement, an accent may give an impulse to that movement, sending it on its way, as in 1.14c and 1.14d. Such initiation may be slight or with greater energy. It gives an emphasis to the start of the movement, as does an impulsive action in everyday life. This added energy level and change in speed immediately dissipates, and the movement continues at the previous or the contextually appropriate energy level and speed. Note that the "tail" of the accent sign always points in toward the movement indication it enhances or modifies.

1.14c
A slight accent
at the start

1.14d
A strong accent
at the start

Placed at the end of the action, an accent provides a clear finish, an ending "flourish," as in 1.14e and 1.14f. A strong accent provides an ending with an impact, a firm concluding movement statement.

1.14e
A slight accent
at the end

1.14f
A strong accent
at the end

When an accent occurs during a movement it is as though the extra energy gives a momentary push, sending the movement on its way. The movement should not stop but should continue at the previous energy level.

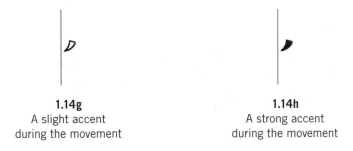

1.14g
A slight accent
during the movement

1.14h
A strong accent
during the movement

READING STUDIES NOS. 4 AND 5

DYNAMICS: ACCENTS

Reading Studies Nos. 4 and 5 are structurally the same as Reading Studies Nos. 1 and 2, but made more lively by the introduction of accents. Here the accent signs have all been placed on the right of the movement indications; they could equally have been placed on the left. As there is only one action at a time, placement of accents makes no difference.

Note that in Reading Study No. 5, accents in the middle of the movement are featured. In measures 5 and 6 of Reading Study No. 4 the sustained movement has two accents, the second stronger than the first, propelling the movement on its way.

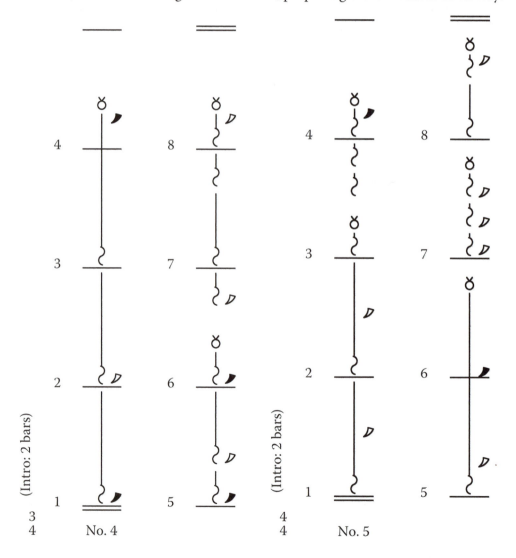

REVIEW FOR CHAPTER ONE

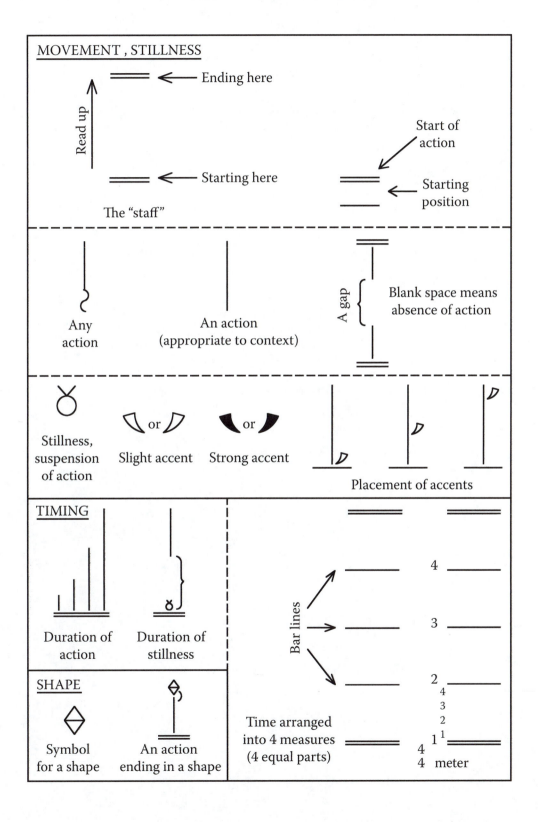

MOVEMENT , STILLNESS

Read up

Ending here

Start of action

Starting here

Starting position

The "staff"

Any action

An action (appropriate to context)

A gap

Blank space means absence of action

Stillness, suspension of action

Slight accent   Strong accent

Placement of accents

TIMING

Duration of action   Duration of stillness

Bar lines

4

3

2

SHAPE

Symbol for a shape

An action ending in a shape

Time arranged into 4 measures (4 equal parts)

4
3
2
1

4
4   meter

CHAPTER TWO
Traveling

Traveling! A familiar activity, but what exactly does it mean in movement terms? How much are everyday meanings carried through into dance? The dictionary states, "To journey, to proceed from place to place, to move from point to point, to be transported, to pass by, pass along, passage from one location to another, to move in a given direction or path, or through a given distance; to traverse, to travel across, to cross over (as over a river); to advance or retreat, to run back and forth." More important is the sense of going, which, in time, leads to being aware of how you are going—discovering the kind of path taken.

Two main ideas emerge from the above: (1) that of "passage," the act itself of traveling, and (2) that of location, a particular place away from or toward which one moves. Both ideas apply directly to dance, but in addition dance is concerned specifically with the nature of the path traveled, i.e., whether it is generally straight or curved, the sense of directness, or of a more three-dimensional curving through space. Also to be considered are the speed of traveling and the mode of locomotion. Note that locomotion is defined as "locus" (Latin for place), plus "motion" (progressive movement), hence travel. Locomotor steps are steps which travel.

What initiates traveling? It could be said to be "Get up and go!" The aim may be to leave where you are, to put as much distance as possible between you and the point from which you started. The next point of arrival may also be undesirable, and off you go again—away, away! Or the motivation may be the reverse: to arrive somewhere, trying one place after another, searching endlessly for the right one. Or the motivation may be neither of these, but simply the sheer joy of traveling through space, across the room or stage wherever empty space is waiting—the simple enjoyment of the "going."

2.1a   2.1b

When does one travel for the sheer joy of it? Such travel is rare in classical ballet since the feet are usually busy performing "steps" of some kind. I on-ce saw Irma Duncan perform and imagined the use which Isadora must have made of such free flow surging through space. Nadia Chilkovsky Nahumck composed for a ten-year-old an exquisite dance based only on running with variations in speed and dynamics. Paul Taylor captured this special feeling of exuberance in a dozen different patterns, all fleeting and traveling, in his ballet *Esplanade*. It is exhilarating to watch, and both exhilarating and exhausting to do for it is never ending, there is always more space to conquer.

If the emphasis is on departure, there may be a dramatic reason, perhaps an escape from imaginary alien space creatures, or inner demons as in Anna Sokolow's *Rooms*. A dramatic reason for emphasis on arrival at a destination may be reunion with a loved one. Who has seen Ulanova in *Romeo and Juliet* flying to Friar Lawrence for help? Or seen Rudolf Nureyev in the ballet *Marguerite and Armand* running swiftly like the wind when he finally discovers that Marguerite really loves him and is dying? It was so beautiful a run because an emotional impetus carried his limbs, thrusting him forward.

2.1c

He, his center, had to be there. There was no thought of his feet stepping, of how his arms were held. These things were not important. An inner force swept him across the stage; there was only one aim, one thought which propelled him forward.

Despite the prevalent use of traveling in dance, its full potential as an expressive movement is seldom realized. The body prepares itself differently according to (1) whether a goal is to be reached, an intention communicated, or (2) traveling is embarked upon for its own sake, i.e., the pure enjoyment of going, or (3) what type of path is to be performed. Try traveling for different reasons and on different pathways and notice what happens in your body or how you feel.

Every room has "awaiting space" to be filled. It is there to be used, and, as we use it, the awaiting space changes, it calls, challenges. Lucky is the performer who is alone on the ice rink with the chance for gliding, skimming, traveling at will. The solo dancer on stage has similar freedom of spatial choice, but the presence of other performers makes the use of space more interesting because of changing patterns of relationship.

Does traveling have to be fast? Must it be a run? What of a walk? A crawl? The slower the kind of action used, the less the idea of traveling is directly expressed. Walking occurs for many reasons and can be a means of expressing several movement ideas, amongst which is traveling. That traveling is the focus of a walk must be expressed by the carriage of the body. The intention to travel may be expressed clearly even though travel itself is barely achieved. An exhausted person crawling expresses both the desire to travel and a limitation in doing so. On the other hand we see babies crawling at amazing speeds.

2.1d   2.1e

Improvise on traveling using changes in speed, distance covered, and energy, and also variations in the general carriage of the body, use of arms, head, etc. Since traveling is the theme, all complementary movements must be merely "coloring," embellishment for the main theme; they must not become important in themselves.

Too easily the accompanying music can call forth a variety of steps, foot patterns which embellish the path to the point of diminishing the awareness of traveling.

FORM OF THE PATH

Pure enjoyment of passage through space, of the act of traveling itself, requires neither a sense of destination nor a need for departure, only a wish to go, to explore freely the space available. Such is the feeling of the open road, of the wanderer setting off on his travels with no planned route. In dance, such freedom of traversing space is often enjoyed through running, but other modes of locomotor steps which allow ground to be covered may be used. Just as in daily life the traveler stops to rest, so in dance there will be pauses, shorter or longer moments of stillness, "punctuations" in the "sentences" of traveling. Such rests may occur because the momentum or energy has temporarily been spent, not because this spot, this location, was a destination chosen beforehand.

The path taken while traveling may range from a random progression, as occurs when one is uncertain, drifting or day-dreaming, to paths resulting from specific goals or from the desire to experience specific path designs. In traveling, there may be no awareness of the shape of the path or the choice may be intentional. Absence of motivation may result in meandering, free form or random pathway, but focus on reaching a goal will require a straight path. Between these two extremes lie several variations.

Freedom of choice is shown by the sign of 2.2a, the ad libitum sign drawn horizontally. This sign placed at the top and bottom of a path sign, 2.2b, means "any" form of path. The length of the vertical line indicates how much time is spent in traveling; 2.2b shows a longer duration than 2.2c. The interpretation of 2.2b may be either a choice of one specific type of path only, expressed in 2.2d by the number one in a circle placed within the path sign, or the performer may choose to follow a series of different types of paths without a break, this choice being indicated by a vertical ad lib. sign within a circle, the statement for "any number," as in 2.2e. Thus 2.2f states any number of different paths may be used.

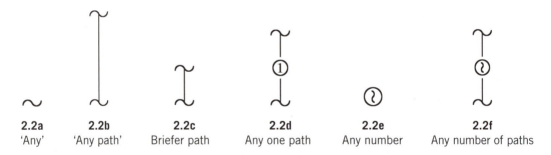

| 2.2a | 2.2b | 2.2c | 2.2d | 2.2e | 2.2f |
| 'Any' | 'Any path' | Briefer path | Any one path | Any number | Any number of paths |

FLOOR PLANS

Paths traversed across the floor can be shown on a floor plan, 2.3a. This plan shows a bird's-eye view of the performance area, room, or stage, the open end being the chosen Front (the audience), and right and left sides and the back as illustrated. Indication of performers in this area is by means of pins. A white pin represents a female, the point of the pin pointing into the direction she is facing. In 2.3b she is facing front, in 2.3c the right side wall of the room (stage right); and in 2.3d she is facing the back (upstage). A male is represented by a black pin. Examples 2.3e–2.3g show the same facing directions for a man. By using a flat pin (a "tack"), a person, male or female, is represented, 2.3h–2.3j.

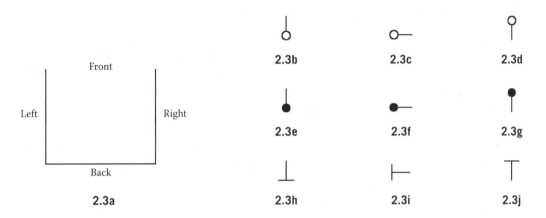

2.3a

2.3b 2.3c 2.3d

2.3e 2.3f 2.3g

2.3h 2.3i 2.3j

Where the pin is placed on the floor plan shows the location of the performer in the room, i.e., the starting position. In 2.3k a person starts in the back right corner of the room. The plan of 2.3l shows a person traveling from the right back corner to the right front corner of the room and then back to the left corner. When it can be clearly represented, more than one path can be shown on a floor plan, as in 2.3l. If the path is complex, more than one floor plan will be needed. Each plan **must start where the previous plan ended**. The plan of 2.3n starts where 2.3m ended, the performer arriving at center stage. In 2.3o, the traveling (the arrow) must start from center stage, the last location of the performer.

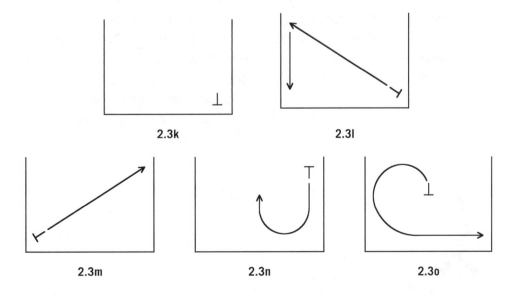

2.3k 2.3l

2.3m 2.3n 2.3o

STRAIGHT PATH

Continuous traveling on a straight path must inevitably end when we come to the edge of the performing area; a turn must take place to face another direction and to be able to go off again in a forward direction. How much of a turn occurs depends on which new direction is chosen. This turn is not important, it happens swiftly and without emphasis. Try traveling on various straight paths with a pause between paths. Use paths that either change direction or continue into the same direction. Such paths may be of short or long duration, may be punctuated by a pause or stillness, or may follow one right after another.

By nature, we are built to walk and run forward, 2.4a, but a performer must meet the demands of greater variation, particularly in dance; thus traveling backward, sideward, and in the directions in between must be experienced. Walking or running backward should be experienced until comfort in doing so is achieved. Looking over a shoulder will enable one to see where one is going. Reaching backward with an arm also helps guard against bumping into someone or a wall. Once different step directions are familiar and comfortable, patterns should be made changing from forward to backward, to side, etc., and combined with changes in length of path and destinations in the room. Fluent changes of step direction as well as of room direction provide interesting and enjoyable patterns. Zigzagging, for example, is the result of a series of short straight paths with quick changes of direction.

The resulting floor design for a series of straight paths might be something like 2.4b, short paths being combined with longer paths. Although it is comparatively simple, the plan of 2.4b can be performed in many different ways if steps of different directions and timing are used. Try this design and try contrasting ways of performing it. First follow the floor design using only forward steps. Then try it always facing the front of the room, changing the step direction as needed to keep traveling on the given path. For the third version, use forward steps on the first part, side on the second, back on the third, side on the fourth, and so on, always traveling on the same design. Example 2.4c is the sign for a straight path. Note how each new path begins where the previous one ended.

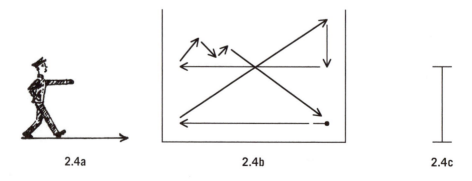

| 2.4a | 2.4b | 2.4c |

DURATION OF PATH

The **length** of a path sign indicates its **duration**, that is, how much time is taken for that path. It **does not show distance** traveled across the floor. Distance is governed by the number and/or the size of the steps taken. More steps usually result in a longer path, fewer steps usually produce a shorter path. Very long steps will obviously cover more ground; very small steps will cover less space.

Experiment with many steps traveling a short distance; these might be small steps on half toe, or with bent knees, or stamping on each step. Then try to achieve a great distance through very few, very long steps which really cover space.

Note the differences between the following: in 2.5a the path symbol is short, the duration is only three counts; the numbers at the side indicate the counts. In 2.5b, the path symbol is much longer, it spans nine counts. In the floor plan of 2.5c, two performers, "A" and "B" are shown to travel different distances toward the front of the room. In 2.5d, A and B each travel for a short duration. This means that A will have to take much larger or many more steps than B to arrive at the indicated destination. In contrast, in 2.5e both A and B have paths lasting for a much longer duration. To reach the same destination, A can take small steps or fewer, larger steps, while B will need very small or very few steps which are slower. Try out these two different versions to experience the difference between distance (space measurement) and duration (time measurement).

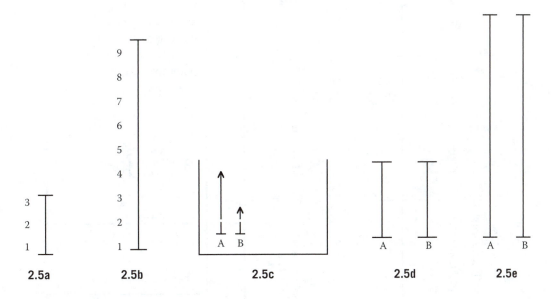

2.5a   2.5b   2.5c   2.5d   2.5e

Reading Study Nos. 6 and 7

STRAIGHT PATHS

Reading Study Nos. 6 and 7 provide a simple symmetrical pattern in which to explore step directions; they start in the center of the room. (1) Perform the studies facing the front of the room all the time. (2) Then explore traveling along the same paths but facing into any room direction you choose. This design of a simple cross is the basic choreographic form of many Asian dance patterns; it is also found in European and in South American folk dances.

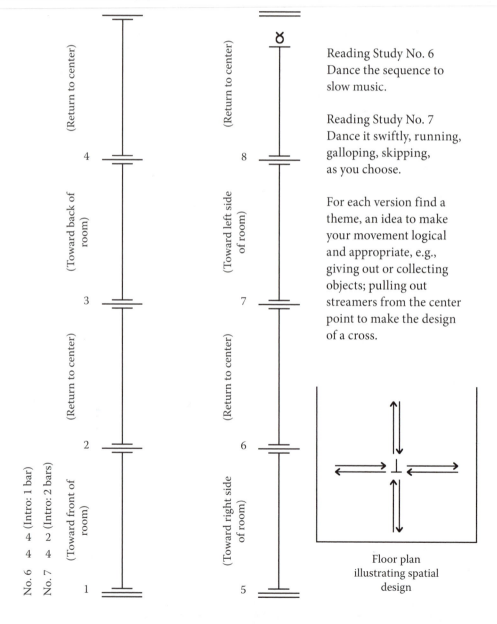

Reading Study No. 6
Dance the sequence to slow music.

Reading Study No. 7
Dance it swiftly, running, galloping, skipping, as you choose.

For each version find a theme, an idea to make your movement logical and appropriate, e.g., giving out or collecting objects; pulling out streamers from the center point to make the design of a cross.

Floor plan illustrating spatial design

READING STUDY NO. 8

DURATION OF PATHS; FLOOR PLANS

In this dance, floor plans are used to provide defined paths in the room. Despite this structure, such "pinning down," there is still much leeway in how this study is to be performed. The main task is to correlate the given segments of the path with the time available. Guided by the floor plans, find a way of performing these straight paths in the timing given. Note use of the stillness sign to add interest to the sequence.

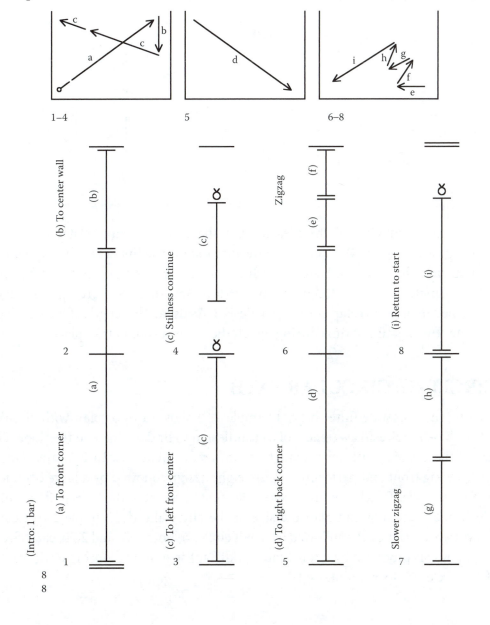

Zigzag Paths

A series of short straight paths may produce zigzag traveling, such as seen in Reading Study No. 7. This pattern, produced by a quick change of front or by changing the direction of the steps taken, is familiar and enjoyable and hence often introduced to children at a fairly early age. The three short straight paths of 2.6a could be interpreted as a to-and-fro pattern, a retracing of the first path, or it could produce a triangle, nothing states that a zigzag is wanted. To express the zigzag idea directly, the sign of 2.6b can be used. This sign represents the concept, it does not show the direction of the steps, the directions faced in the room, nor the number of zigzags, these details are left open.

2.6a   2.6b

This representation of the idea for the shape of the path relates to Design Drawing (see Chapter 14). There the indications show the linear shape in the air to be performed by gestures. Here it is a linear shape on the floor. Although placed within a single straight path sign, it is understood that three or more zigzags will be performed in order to establish a zigzag design. As usual, the length of the path sign indicates the amount of time during which the pattern should take place.

CIRCLING, CIRCULAR PATH

Circling involves a definite shape. Example 2.7a shows a floor plan with circular paths; these require an awareness of a clear design to be described on the floor. The size of the circular pathways stems from different intentions. In 2.7a, the dancer starts facing front and performs a figure eight design followed by a large complete clockwise circle. To achieve this design one must be aware of the focal point around which one is circling and plan the size of the circle ahead. Example 2.7b clearly shows two quarter circles followed by a half circle. In both 2.7a and 2.7b, each circular pathway is produced by a constant, equidistant spatial relationship to the center of the circle, the focal point.

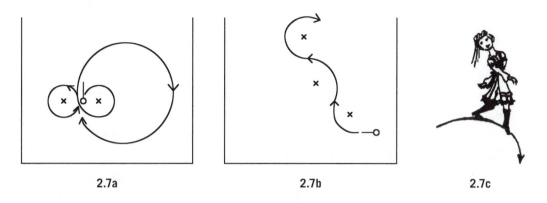

| 2.7a | 2.7b | 2.7c |

NATURE OF CIRCLING

A straight line is spatially economical and is also usually economical in time. Traveling on a straight line usually expresses purpose; there is usually a clear intent, an aim, and a clear destination to be reached. In circling, there is a greater indulgence in the use of space; the time taken may not be important. Circling has the potential of being endless. A physical enjoyment of the sweep of the path as it curves, the constant change of front, may be experienced, each curve felt in the body, 2.7c. Apart from any dramatic motivation, what is the innate physical expression inherent in the circular form? Anyone can mechanically walk a circle. Such movement produces a circle but has no expression as such. What is the basic nature of a circle? How does it get born?

2.8a	2.8b	2.8c
	Top spinning	Off-center spinning
	in balance	producing a spiral

Circling can be experienced as a spatial extension of a turn on the spot, a turn around one's own axis which changes into curving while traveling and from there into a circular path, the axis of turning now lying outside the performer. The larger the circle, the farther away the circular path is from the central axis, the focal point. Think of objects which start pivoting around a center point and then move out into space. One example is the Catherine wheel, the pinwheel firework in which sparks fly out from a central spinning core, 2.8a. Another is a spinning top. When centered it will continue to spin, 2.8b, but if it becomes lopsided it is likely to fly off across the floor, producing a spiral path, as in 2.8c.

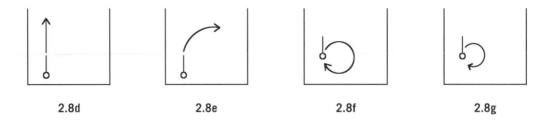

| 2.8d | 2.8e | 2.8f | 2.8g |

While a straight path is spatially restricted—almost as though one is traveling along a narrow passage, circular paths indulge in a greater use of space. A circular path can also be experienced as a magnet, which constantly draws the performer away from the straight line, into a circular arc. The stronger the magnet, the sharper the arc, as illustrated in the above examples. It can also be as though an inner urge, emanating from the torso, deflects the performer away from the intended straight path. A slight twist in the torso can start the center of weight traveling on a curve. Whatever the image, the straight path of 2.8d becomes a partial circle, as in 2.8e, the "magnet" lying to the right of the performer. A greater inner body energy initiating the rotation produces a circle, 2.8f. In 2.8g a "tighter" circle is produced as the feeling of circling comes closer to pure turning on the spot, i.e., a very small circle.

A circle has a center, and the performer should be aware of this focal point. It is around this point that the circular path moves. There is no cutting corners, no "cheating" in performing true circles. It is the fullness of the circular outline which gives enjoyment to performer and observer.

The most common mistake made in starting to walk a circle stems from the performer thinking that s/he starts at the center of the circle. To get onto the circumference, the dancer mistakenly makes quarter turn into the direction of the circling before starting to travel, 2.8h. Note the small dotted arrow in 2.8h. If the performer understands that a true circle should end where it started, then, if s/he has underestimated the time needed to complete the circle, s/he often will use a straight path to return to the starting point, as in 2.8h. The correct path is shown in 2.8i. The concept, which needs to be established, is that one begins, travels, and ends on the circumference of the circle, as if walking around the edge of a circular fountain.

| 2.8h | 2.8i |

Once the concept of one's relationship to the center of the circle is understood, it should be possible to walk perfect circles with any number of steps. If eight steps are taken, it is easy to apportion the number of steps needed for each quarter circle and so produce an even, gradual change of front. But even with a divisible number such as eight or twelve, most performers will describe "balloons" of various shapes by turning too little, too much, or by making uneven spatial adjustments. Some turn too sharply and then end up with several steps straight forward. Many do not realize at first that a perfect circle should end where it started.

Outside aids such as chalking a circle on the floor help to establish the visual image, but more important is to get an inner feel for the circle, an awareness of the shape that your moving center is describing. Once such awareness is developed, circles with five steps, seven steps, thirteen steps, etc., should be tried. As principal of the Philadelphia Dance Academy, Nadia Chilkovsky Nahumck had a large circle painted on the floor of the foyer so that children waiting for class could experiment with traveling on that circle in different ways. Thus, what to them was a game was in fact a valuable teaching aid, and those moments of waiting were put to good use.

Direction of Circling

In circling, as in turning, there is a choice of two directions: counterclockwise (or anticlockwise, to the left), 2.9a, and clockwise (to the right), 2.9b. The abbreviations "CW" for clockwise and "CCW" for counterclockwise will be used from now on for circling. Details on the amount of the circle or arc, the number of circles, and the possibilities of spiraling in or out will be explained in Chapter 3.

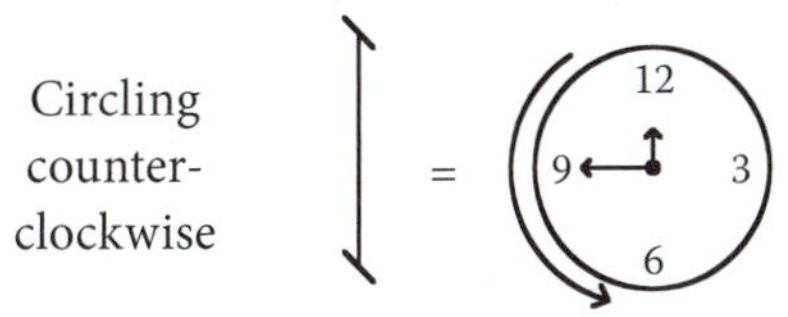

2.9a

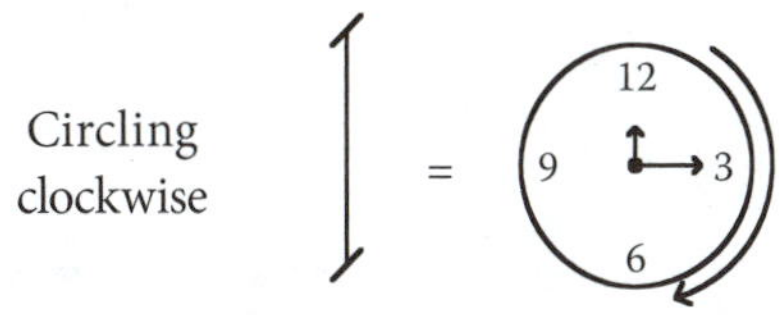

2.9b

If you do not see at once the direction of circling in the circular path sign, let your eye follow the slanting line as you glance up the sign. This points the direction illustrated by the arrows in 2.9c and 2.9d. The CCW and CW signs are combined to produce the indication of 2.9e which expresses circling either way; the choice is left to you.

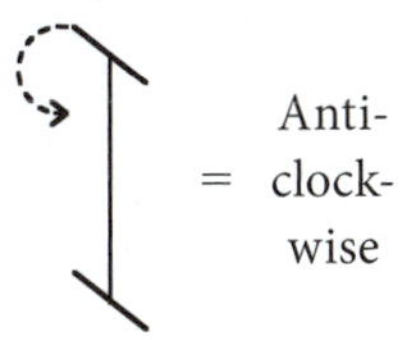

2.9c

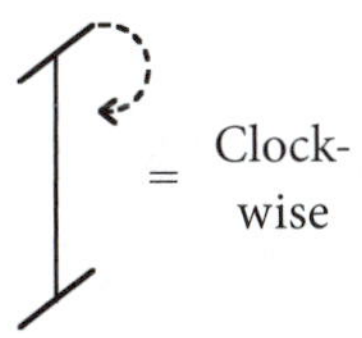

2.9d

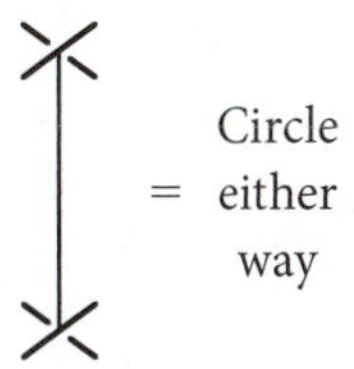

2.9e

Change of Front: As you circle, where you are facing (your front in relation to the room) changes constantly. This is an integral part of circling, 2.9f. When a large circle is performed we are less aware of this change of Front; with a small circle it is more obvious.

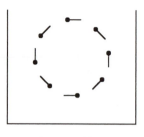

Change of front
2.9f

In Reading Study No. 9, traveling combines straight paths and circling. On a path to a new destination, the performer may have a change of mind and veer off course into another direction. Just as decisiveness in selecting a destination produces a straight path, so other ideas, other inner motives, may cause one to move on circular paths. A circular path might be used to creep up on someone, this aim being hidden until the last moment.

STRAIGHT AND CIRCULAR PATHS

Explore this study first with forward steps. Once you have worked out an overall design for the traveling indications, vary the space pattern by using backward and sideward steps as well. Write in floor plans at the bottom for your version, remembering that each pathway begins where the previous one finished.

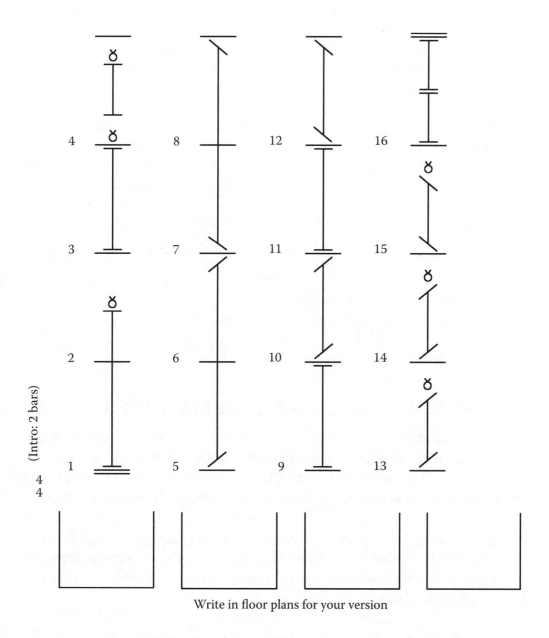

Write in floor plans for your version

CURVING PATH

In curving, the performer consciously indulges freely in space. A sense of flow and a free carriage of the body can give rise to curving paths, as when an elegant hostess sweeps through the room to greet her guests. Similarly, obstacles may be avoided by curving around them. The degree of curve is not important, it should come from the feeling, the momentum, and the expression.

Paths curve without any idea of circling in mind. The curves may vary, often being asymmetrical, but are never seen or experienced as portions of a circle. The performer may irregularly weave in and out between people or objects in the room but no sense of moving around a focal point is present; it is a passing relationship, an approaching and departing. The desire is for a curving progression. Curving allows endless movement without a stop. It is usually accompanied by a sense of curving in the body.

Example 2.10a shows two possible curving paths which weave around four points, one producing shallower curves, the other fuller curves. In 2.10b, the curving varies as you travel around the room weaving in and out around people or objects. Example 2.10c is the sign for curving. (*Note: this sign was formerly used for meandering.*)

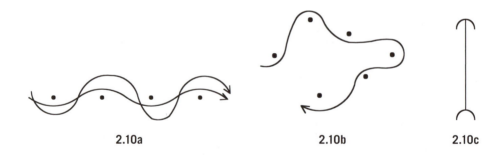

| 2.10a | 2.10b | 2.10c |

RANDOM, FREE-FORM, MEANDERING PATH

A free-form, meandering, or random path is of the moment, it is unplanned, and it is the freest form of pathway. One enjoys the "going" with no thought of a particular path, or of the design the path will make. Such pathways can result from a state of mind, an aimless, indulgent desire to move through space as the moment suggests. Such an unplanned path might stem from a general looking around, perhaps searching for a lost object. A random pathway may be the result of trying to catch a butterfly. Random pathways may be observed when watching children flow out into the playground running around in the space with no particular destination in mind or sense of making paths.

A free-form, meandering pathway is usually randomly curving but may include some unintentional straight or circular traveling. It serves the mood of the wanderer. Example 2.11a shows a possible path for such random, meandering travel; 2.11b is the sign for this form of traveling. Note use of the arrows at top and bottom of this symbol, an arrow indicating motion, the "going" of movement. By the nature of wandering, it takes time to establish a meandering pathway, thus a longer path sign is needed in order for the randomness to be established.

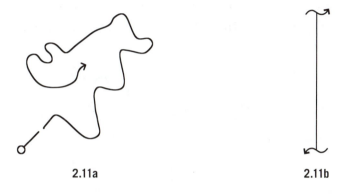

2.11a   2.11b

TRAVELING: ALL FORMS OF PATHWAYS

Reading Practice A combines the different forms of traveling. Because time is needed for meandering, random traveling, the path sign extends from one staff to the next. To show that this is the same path, a caret: < or > is used to indicate "the same," i.e., the same symbol is to continue. The caret is placed both at the top of the third staff and also again at the bottom of the fourth staff, thus linking the two paths signs into one.

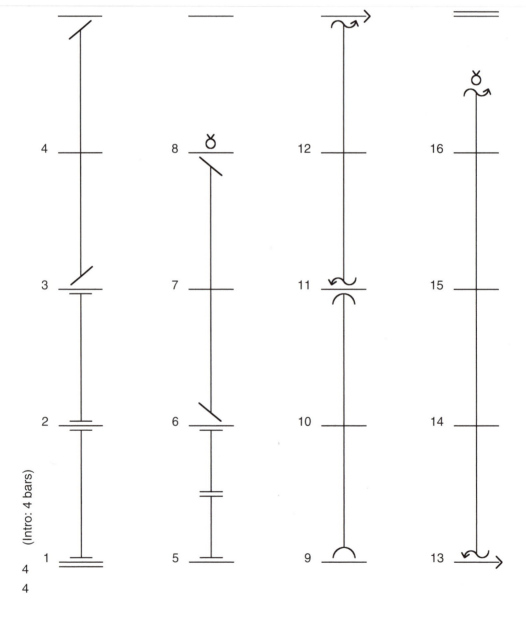

REVIEW FOR CHAPTER TWO

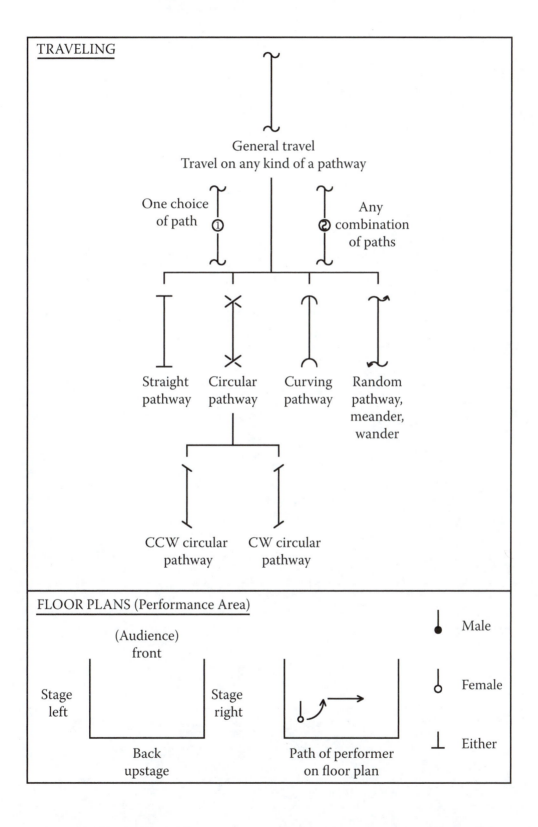

TRAVELING

General travel
Travel on any kind of a pathway

One choice
of path

Any
combination
of paths

Straight
pathway

Circular
pathway

Curving
pathway

Random
pathway,
meander,
wander

CCW circular
pathway

CW circular
pathway

FLOOR PLANS (Performance Area)

(Audience)
front

Stage
left

Stage
right

Back
upstage

Path of performer
on floor plan

Male

Female

Either

CHAPTER THREE
Variations in Traveling

The exploration of traveling has so far been general, now it will be more specific.

THE MAIN DIRECTIONS FOR TRAVELING

From a starting place traveling may occur into the forward, backward, sideward, or the diagonal directions in between. The signs for direction are derived from the rectangle, 3.1a, which represents the central point at a horizontal cross of directions. This symbol is called "place," it is where the performer is located.

The direction signs derived from this rectangle are used for other movements of the body, but in this chapter we explore directions in the context of traveling. When placed within a path sign they indicate the direction the performer travels as judged from the performer's front, i.e., where the performer is facing. This basic shape is modified to "point" pictorially into the appropriate direction, as in 3.1b–3.1e.

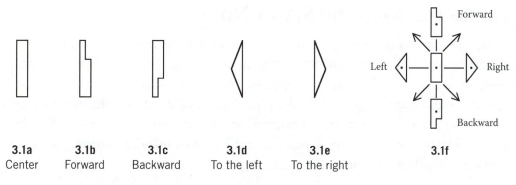

| **3.1a** | **3.1b** | **3.1c** | **3.1d** | **3.1e** | **3.1f** |
| Center | Forward | Backward | To the left | To the right | |

Note how the shape of the symbol points into the desired direction, 3.1f. The diagonal directions which lie between these points will be explored in Chapter 15.

The "any pathway" sign for traveling, 3.1g, allows choice of any direction and of any pathway. Placing the sign for "any direction," 3.1h, inside the path sign, as in 3.1i, makes the statement explicit.

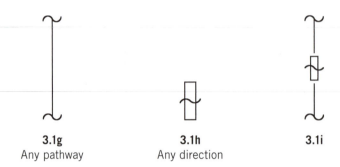

3.1g
Any pathway

3.1h
Any direction

3.1i

DIRECTIONS FOR STRAIGHT PATHS

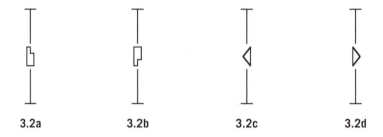

3.2a   **3.2b**   **3.2c**   **3.2d**

Example 3.2a shows a straight path traveling forward; 3.2b is traveling straight back; 3.2c states traveling straight to the left side of the body; 3.2d is traveling straight to the right side. These direction symbols do not state the kind of steps used or even what part of the body is supporting; traveling could be on all fours, as mentioned before.

NOTES FOR READING STUDY NO. 10

While the music for Reading Study No. 10 is in **3/4 meter**, the footwork need not adhere to waltz-like steps, the steps may be many and may "run over" the music beats. It is the traveling that is important. Notice the stillness on count 3 which, interrupting the traveling, adds to the phrasing. In contrast, the phrase of measure 5 to 8 progresses fluently until the rising which marks the end of this part. Similarly the last phrase, 13 to 16, progresses without a break until the lowering at the end provides a final conclusion to the piece.

READING STUDY NO. 10

TRAVELING IN DIFFERENT DIRECTIONS

As degree of circling has not been given yet, follow the floor plans. Note use of arrows on the floor plans for each pathway. Two changes of level while standing are given: rising, going up at the start of measure 8, and lowering, going down, sinking, at the end. Full exploration of directional movements is given in Chapter 5.

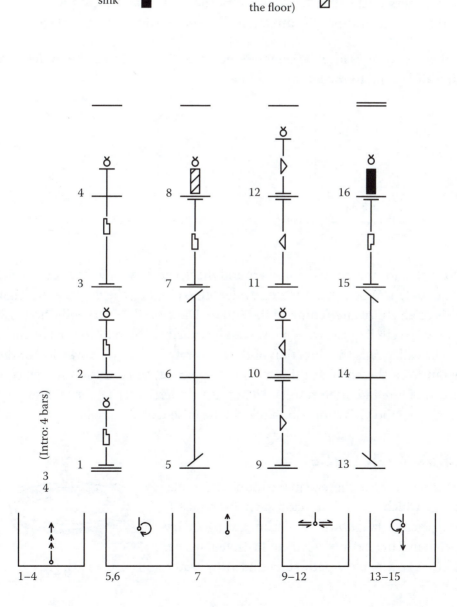

DIRECTIONS FOR CIRCULAR PATHS

When circling is initiated from within the body, circular paths of unpremeditated size and design may result. The movement impetus is free, is of the moment. In contrast, circling can be based on predetermined circular patterns on the floor.

Group Circling

Awareness of a circle, and its center, is more easily achieved when one is dancing in a circular group formation. The other participants provide the size and placement of the circle and there is a strong sense of the center, the fixed focal point to which the performers relate. The relationship to the focal point, facing it, having one's back to it, etc., determines the direction of the steps which will be taken.

When performers face the center of the circle, 3.3a, steps will be **to the right** for circling CCW, and **to the left** for circling CW.

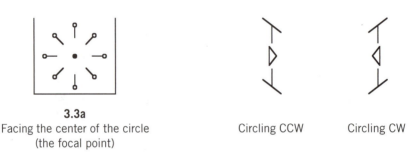

3.3a
Facing the center of the circle
(the focal point)

Circling CCW   Circling CW

Note that for pivoting (turning around the vertical axis) we speak of turning to the right or left. When such turning evolves into circling, the description "right" or "left" is often confusing. Think of the Square Dance call, "Everybody circle right!," and off we go circling CCW. What should be called is, "Step to your right and circle left." The caller calls the direction of the steps rather than the direction of the circling but from these words this fact is not apparent, so confusion in determining direction of circling often results. Hence, the preferred terms for circling are CW for clockwise and CCW for counterclockwise (also called anticlockwise).

Merlin's Magic Circle

When others are not there to make the circle visible, an image which helps to develop such awareness is the magic circle laid down by Merlin, the legendary magician in King Arthur's Court, illustrated in 3.4a. This circle is a narrow path surrounded by water,

3.4a

the opposite of a moat around a castle, and the performer is bound by a spell to travel only on that path, around and around.

As a start, it may be helpful to have a circle chalked on the floor so that its size and placement is clear. Later the performers can express this circle in their movement, keeping exactly to the same circle without it being visibly there.

What are the ways in which you can travel on this path? What variations exist? What are the limitations? In creating a movement sequence on this path, what ingredients are at your disposal? First, there is the direction of circling, CW or CCW. Then there is the possibility of turning to change your relationship to the center of the circle and thus changing the direction of the steps taken. The natural tendency is to take forward steps along the "rim" of the circle, the center of the circle lying to your right, as in 3.4b, which produces CW traveling. Or, keeping the same relationship to the center of the circle, you can circle CCW by traveling backward.

To travel forward and be circling CCW, the center of the circle must lie to your left, 3.4c, and this is true for backward steps circling CW.

If you face out from the center of the circle, that is, with your back to the center, as in 3.4d, you must take sideward steps to the right to circle CW and sideward steps to the left to circle CCW.

Finally, facing the center of the circle, as in 3.4e, traveling must also be with sideward steps—steps to the left to circle CW, steps to the right to circle CCW.

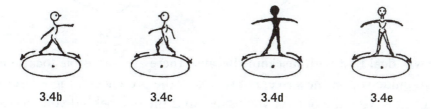

3.4b	**3.4c**	**3.4d**	**3.4e**

By combining the appropriate step direction sign with the appropriate circling sign we can indicate all these possibilities, as illustrated in 3.4fa–3.4i.

When traveling on an established circular pathway, such as Merlin's Circle where the focal point is fixed in space, the appropriate amount of right or left turn is required as a transition for you to travel in the following directions indicated by the path signs and direction of steps.

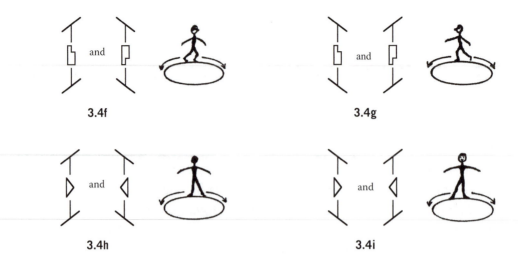

3.4f **3.4g**

3.4h **3.4i**

The Invisible Circles around You

When you are standing in the middle of the room (let us start by facing front) the direction of circling and direction of steps provide eight possible focal point locations, thus, there are eight possible circles you can walk from that spot. In 3.5a, a white pin for a female performer is shown in the center of the eight possible circles surrounding her.

Eight possible circles
that can be performed
from a given point

3.5a

We will deal first with just four. Because there are no visible focal points or circles to guide you in the space, awareness of the presence of these circles—the one in front of you, the ones at your sides, and the one behind you, needs to be strongly established within you. Their center and their size need also to enter the picture. Once this awareness is secure and these invisible circles are part of your imagination, you can enjoy different step patterns and use accompanying arm and body movements to enrich the progression around them. Any accompanying movements should contribute to achieving the path by bearing some relationship to the chosen circle.

In 3.5b the four main circles are shown. For example, circle "a" lies to the right and can be traveled with forward steps for CW circling, or backward steps for CCW circling. For each of these circles the step direction and resulting circling direction is given.

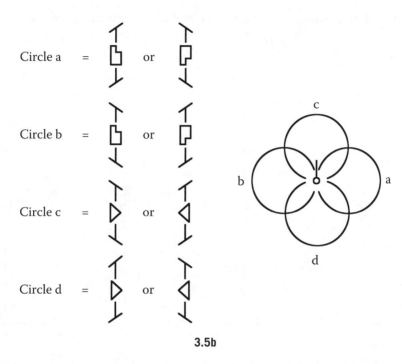

Circle a = ☐ or ☐

Circle b = ☐ or ☐

Circle c = ▷ or ◁

Circle d = ▷ or ◁

3.5b

READING STUDY NO. 11

CIRCLING—RETRACING PATHS

The purpose of this study is to reinforce both the awareness of facing into the focal point (the center of the circle) while circling with sideward steps, and the

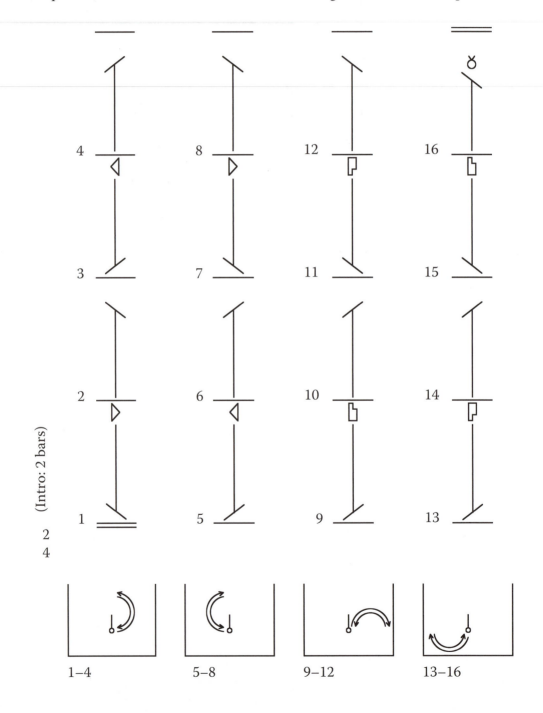

enjoyment of retracing one's path. In the second half of the study, forward and backward steps are taken so that the center of the circle lies first at the dancer's right (measures 9–12), then at his/her left (measures 13–16). These simple half circles can be performed with several different kinds of steps, including gallops, skips, runs, and steps in even or uneven rhythms. As degree of circling is not indicated, the floor plans indicate one possible interpretation.

TRAVELING WITH TURNING INCLUDED

Turning around one's own center, the vertical axis, was introduced briefly in Chapter 2. Turning has the function of changing the direction faced so that one can progress into another direction on a pathway. During the process of traveling there can be the enjoyment of a sudden whip around, a quick full turn which does not impede progress but adds to the enjoyment of being in action, of being "on the go."

Turn (spin, pivot, rotate) to the left

3.6a

Turn (spin, pivot, rotate) to the right

3.6b

An empty turn sign means that the amount of turn is left open to the performer. You may choose a slight degree of turn, or a greater degree, even several turns. The amount of turn may depend on how much time is available.

TURNING INDICATED ON FLOOR PLANS

For Reading Study No. 12, specific floor plans have been provided as suggested interpretations of the movement material. For a specific performance much information still needs to be spelled out—degree of turning, degree of circling, distance covered, and so on. Many of these questions are answered by the floor plans, since to achieve the stated floor design, certain degrees of turning and distances covered must occur.

In Reading Study No. 12, Part D includes a quick turn during the start of the circular path and another about halfway through. Such turns occur on the line of the path, the intention being that the turn is an embellishment, not a change of direction for the path. It is practical, therefore, to make these full turns as they do not affect the line of traveling. Such turns should not, strictly speaking, be shown on the floor plan. However, a tiny loop attached to the path line clearly indicates three factors we need to know: the existence of the turn, the direction of the turn, and where it occurs on the path. This device is used as a convention for practical purposes, as illustrated in 3.7a and 3.7b.

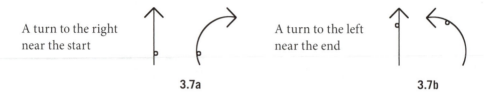

A turn to the right
near the start

A turn to the left
near the end

3.7a   **3.7b**

As you look at Reading Study No. 12, first sense what the material expresses in movement terms, then work out how to organize it in the room. As soon as possible, dance it. Remember you are free to take as many steps as you wish, and may walk, run, gallop, or skip, but it is the traveling that is important. The music accompanying this study is in the form of a fugue, which adds "body" to the piece, giving it added "weight." The manner of performing the study should reflect the tone and structure of the music. Each phrase should be interpreted completely as a movement sequence before the next is tackled. Develop a sense for the evolving sequence so that each change grows kinetically out of the body and is not merely the result of a mental decision.

One possible set of floor plans is given with the study. Examples 3.7c–3.7f give another set, equally possible. There are numerous variations.

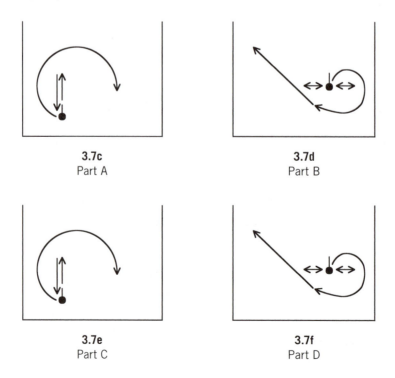

3.7c
Part A

3.7d
Part B

3.7e
Part C

3.7f
Part D

READING STUDY NO. 12

TRAVELING WITH TURNING INCLUDED

Instructions for this study are given in the section "Turning Indicated on Floor Plans." Note the inclusion in measures 29 and 32 of "an action" combined with a slight accent, shown by the white accent sign.

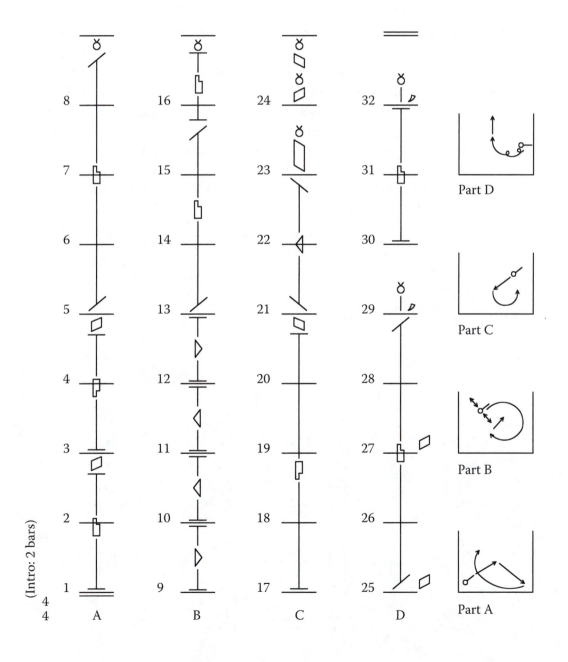

AMOUNT OF TURNING AND CIRCLING

DEGREE OF TURNING

A turning action may be slight, the purpose being to face into another room direction. When you face a new room direction you have a change of Front. Use of the capital "F" denotes this change in orientation, in contrast to "front" (small "f"), which refers to the front of the performer's body.

In the case of "about face," the new Front is implicit in the instruction, a half turn being the means of achieving it. However, one may also be aware of having made a half turn. In a full turn, the action of turning is in itself important. Returning to the previous Front provides a sense of accomplishment. It is interesting to note that when degree of turning is left open there is a natural tendency for performers to use full turns, since returning to the previously established Front (usually the front of the room) provides a satisfying, perhaps reassuring, sense of clarity in orientation. Multiple turns provide an opportunity to indulge in this form of movement; the faster the turning, the more the turning sensation is heightened.

Degree of turn, the amount of change of Front, is shown by placement of a black pin within the turn sign.

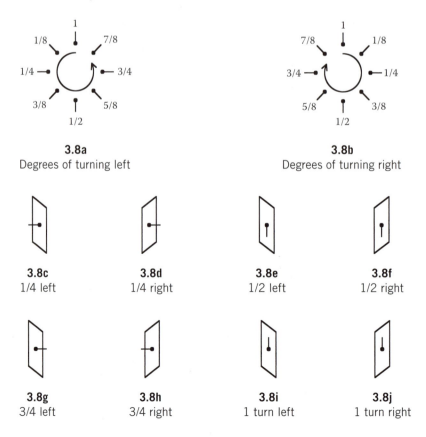

3.8a
Degrees of turning left

3.8b
Degrees of turning right

3.8c
1/4 left

3.8d
1/4 right

3.8e
1/2 left

3.8f
1/2 right

3.8g
3/4 left

3.8h
3/4 right

3.8i
1 turn left

3.8j
1 turn right

Because the numeral 1 is not distinctive enough, the forward pointing black pin, shown in 3.8i, is used instead within the turn sign to indicate one complete turn. For more than one turn, the amounts given within the turn sign are added. Note the use of numbers for two or more turns. The number is usually written first, before the pin that shows an additional fraction of a turn.

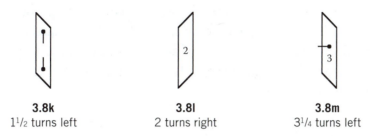

3.8k
$1^1/_2$ turns left

3.8l
2 turns right

3.8m
$3^1/_4$ turns left

DEGREE OF CIRCLING

Degrees of circling are shown with black pins in the same way as for turning. In walking one full circle there is a complete change of Front, as in one full pivot turn. In performing a half circle, you end facing the opposite direction, just as with half a turn, and so on. The black pin is placed in the center of the path sign, the vertical line being broken so that the pin shows clearly and can easily be read.

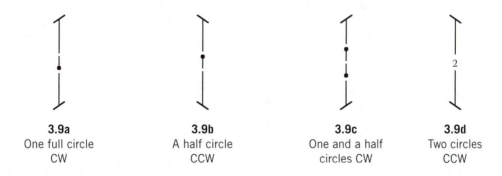

3.9a
One full circle
CW

3.9b
A half circle
CCW

3.9c
One and a half
circles CW

3.9d
Two circles
CCW

The correct path for walking a full circle was described in Chapter 2; it should also be applied to partial circles.

READING PRACTICE B (NO MUSIC)

DEGREE OF TURNING, CIRCLING

On the plans for A and B the wedge symbol: Δ shows where the dancer is facing at the end of a phrase. Such wedges are not usually required in a floor plan, but are used here to provide extra information for the reader. These sequences are designed to be performed with careful awareness of degree of circling, the shape of the circular path, and amount of change of Front. The floor plans illustrate the results if the sequences are correctly performed.

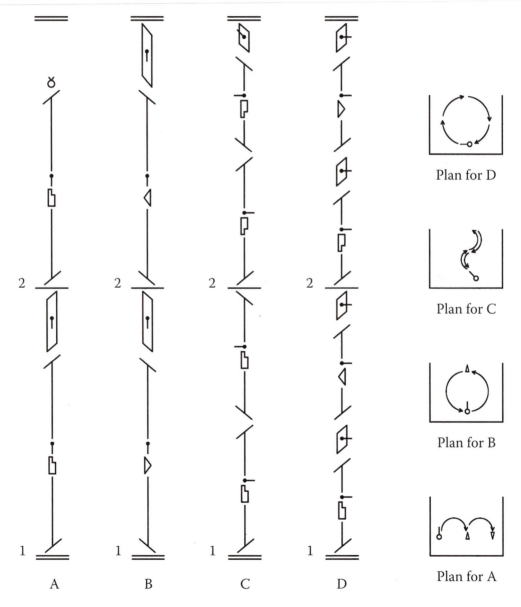

Plan for D

Plan for C

Plan for B

Plan for A

A   B   C   D

TRAVELING WITH CONTINUOUS REVOLVING

Earlier, incidental turning, i.e., a brief spin, a whipping around which does not affect the direction of traveling, was discussed. A different intention and focus is to spread continuous revolving evenly throughout the path. It is comparable to the gradual change of Front which occurs when walking on a circular path. This same gradual change in orientation can occur while traveling on a straight path. Such gradual revolving can also occur on a circular path.

Explore slow, drifting, continuous turning such as might happen when leaves are swirling as they are blown along a path, or the slow graceful revolving performed by a fashion model as she progresses through the room or down a runway, showing off her dress at every angle. Whatever the motivation, the line of the path remains constant but the direction of the steps taken continually changes. For **revolving while traveling**, turning is continuous from the beginning to the end of the pathway. Such revolving while traveling is, in fact, simply turning around oneself while traveling. If performed with fast, multiple turns, the emphasis changes to a turning activity which happens to travel.

To master this combined form, first try turning slowly on the spot, let us say one full turn with 15 steps, making the turning action very smooth and even. Then, with 15 steps, walk a straight path across the floor, observing the line of progression. Now combine these two actions. Whereas all steps were forward when you were not turning, now, to keep placing the feet on the same path as the body turns, each step must be in a slightly different direction judged from the body, i.e., the hips. If you allow yourself to be carried around as though by a soft breeze the steps will take care of themselves, you will not have to think about each one. By the third or fourth practice the desired performance will be there. Try the same path varying the number of steps and the amount of turning. If many turns occur, say one turn for each two steps, then the action has changed to one of spinning while traveling.

For continuous revolving, we need to state the desired path. For example, 3.10a shows a straight path forward. As we can see, 3.10b shows no change of front for the performer. When the turn sign is placed **within** the path sign, turning as well as traveling occurs for the duration of the path sign. **The path is achieved through turning.** Degree of turning is placed within the turn sign as in 3.10c. Example 3.10d illustrates a person gradually making a full turn on this path. Direction for the path is always judged from the starting point, **the first step**.

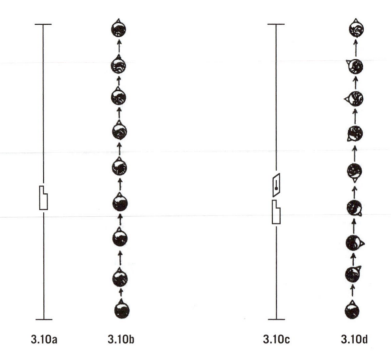

| 3.10a | 3.10b | | 3.10c | 3.10d |

When such traveling with gradual, continuous revolving is indicated on a floor plan, no turning indication (loop) is added to the pathway; the previous device used to indicate separated, quick turns during traveling does not apply because the turning action is spread throughout the path.

Continuous, quick, rhythmically even turning steps on a straight path, called *enchainée* turns in ballet, would be an example of fast, continuous revolving on a pathway (unlike *piqué* turns which involve an uneven degree of turning on each foot). Example 3.10e states that during four counts the performer turns four times while traveling on a straight path to the right. Again, it would be unnecessary to include "loops" on the floor plan as turns are occurring throughout the pathway. The turns have equal importance with the direction and shape of the pathway.

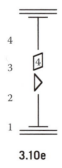

3.10e

REVOLVING WHILE TRAVELING

The 8/8 meter music for Reading Study 13 No. has a drifting, dreamy quality to help the smooth turning action, which must occur during the entire path. Such revolving while traveling is in fact simply turning around oneself while traveling. For Reading Study No. 14, the faster 2/4 meter provides a different mood. Note whether the movement is one of revolving while traveling or an ordinary circular path. Compare measures 5 and 6 with the quick turn during the middle of the last circular pathway in 7 and 8.

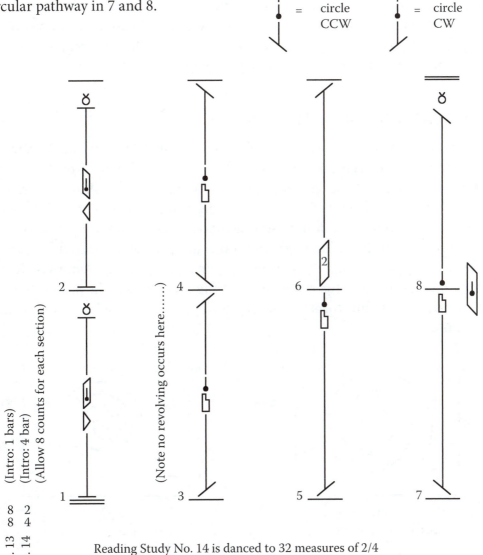

Reading Study No. 14 is danced to 32 measures of 2/4

SPIRAL PATHS

A straight path in a room or on stage must inevitably come to an end as the wall (or a wing) is reached. A change of direction, a turn, must occur for another straight path to be initiated. But a circular path may continue forever with no change of direction needed, no turning to face another direction. Think of the poor donkey attached to a millstone, endlessly tramping the same circular path. When the progression is constantly on the same path, turns and a resulting change in step direction enrich circular traveling.

The monotony of continuing on the same-sized circular path in a solo dance can be avoided through enlarging or diminishing the size of the circle. To enlarge the circle the performer veers away from the center of the circle (the focal point) until the limits of the available space have been reached. To diminish the size of the circle the performer approaches the center of the circle. When this center is reached circling has ceased: it has become turning on the spot.

MOTIVATION FOR SPIRALING

Spiraling inward to the center may result from a gradual desire to end the circular traveling and find a central spot to call "home." It could come from a petering out of movement motivation, hence also of the path. Diminishing energy may produce smaller and smaller circles until one arrives at the center. Conversely, an outward spiral may result from setting off on an exploratory trip in which the adventuresome spirit gradually grows with confidence and the circles widen as more territory is encircled. Group spiraling makes the design more visible and has its own expression; for example, spiraling in increases the spatial tension. Such paths occur in line formations; they occur in the Farandole, an early French folk dance.

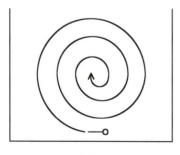

3.11a
Spiraling in to the center

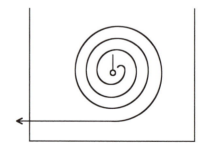

3.11b
Spiraling out and exiting

INDICATION OF SPIRALING

Circling occurs around a center, 3.12a, like the hub or axle of a wheel, 3.12b. This center is the focal point of the circle. As you spiral in, you **approach** this focal point and gradually your distance from the center diminishes. Conversely, as you spiral outward, you **move away** from the center, and the circling becomes larger. Note the shapes in 3.12c–3.12e.

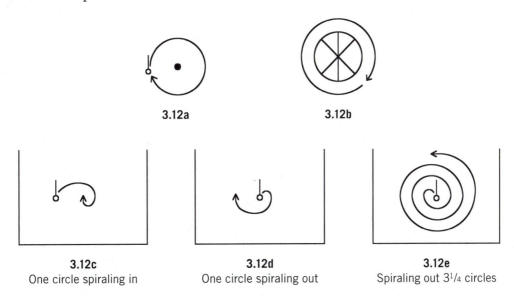

3.12a

3.12b

3.12c
One circle spiraling in

3.12d
One circle spiraling out

3.12e
Spiraling out 3¼ circles

The signs of 3.12f–3.12j are needed within the circular path signs to indicate spiraling.

3.12f
The sign for
focal point

3.12g
The sign for
approaching

3.12h
The sign for
going away

3.12i
Toward the
focal point

3.12j
Away from the
focal point

To provide the open choice in spiraling either in or out, the two signs are combined, as in 3.12k. To open the choice even further, the sign for circling either way, 3.12l, can be used, thus providing the double choice of direction of circling and of

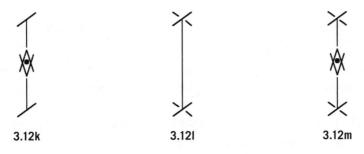

3.12k

3.12l

3.12m

approaching or going away from the focal point (the center) shown in 3.12m. Note that in this case, the greater choice produces the more complex notation statement.

Amount of Circling for Spiral Paths

As can be seen in 3.12c, 3.12d, and 3.12e, a single spiral in or out does not give a strong impression of spiraling; it often feels like a "cheated" circle, one which has become smaller or larger than it should be, ending farther away from the starting point. Thus most spiral paths consist of two or more circlings which are indicated by appropriate numerals. Additional fractions, ¼, ½, etc., are shown with the appropriate black pin.

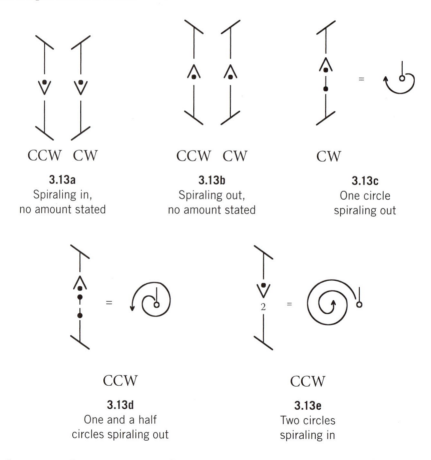

CCW CW	CCW CW	CW
3.13a Spiraling in, no amount stated	**3.13b** Spiraling out, no amount stated	**3.13c** One circle spiraling out

CCW	CCW
3.13d One and a half circles spiraling out	**3.13e** Two circles spiraling in

To determine how many spirals you are making, note each time you return to face the same Front as at the start. When there is a diagram, it is helpful to draw a line at a right angle to your starting position. In 3.13f and 3.13g, the added dotted line visually shows how often you complete one circling.

Spiral paths take time. To achieve a stronger sense of spiraling, complete at least two circles; three are even better.

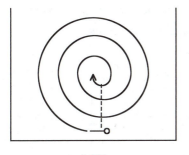

3.13f
Spiraling in to center
3¼ circles

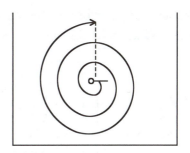

3.13g
Spiraling out with
3 circles

Spiral Paths—Motion or Destination?

No destination has been given so far for the spiral paths explored, they might or might not arrive at the focal point. To specifically indicate arrival at the center, the focal point sign is placed at the end of the path sign and linked to it with a small bow, thus indicating the aim, the destination. Example 3.14a shows two inward spirals arriving at the center, the focal point. In 3.14b, the instruction is to approach your partner (P). In 3.14c, you are to spiral in and arrive at your partner.

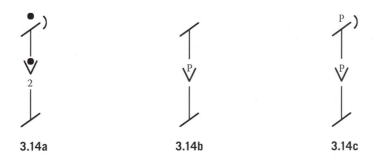

3.14a   **3.14b**   **3.14c**

Reading Study No. 15 may be performed with a drifting feeling, a sense of floating through space on widening and then narrowing circular paths, a progression with a feeling of being pulled on as though by a magnet. Such floating quality should be accompanied by a leading of the center of gravity (weight well forward) so that the steps occur only to transport the body, and not as stepping actions in their own right. In this study, most of the spiraling is done with forward steps; forward being obviously the most comfortable direction, particularly when one is concentrating on the change occurring in the path itself. Later in the study, however, step direction for the paths is left open. The important point is that the performer must plan ahead for the large spiral that ends the study, and this may mean working backward. If the performer does not start this spiral in an appropriate part of the room, there will not be adequate space in which to complete the inward spiral. If this spiral is to be satisfactorily performed (no cheating on shape), choices are limited as to where it may start. Examples 3.14d–3.14g, show four obvious possibilities.

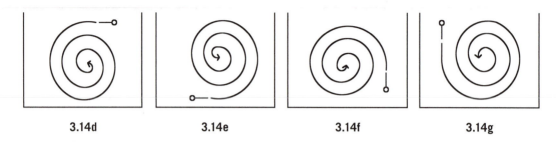

3.14d   3.14e   3.14f   3.14g

READING STUDY NO. 15

SPIRAL PATHS

Note the starting position on the floor plan within this Reading Study. For measures 9–12, choose your degree of circling and direction of path so that you will have room for the large inward spiral that concludes the study.

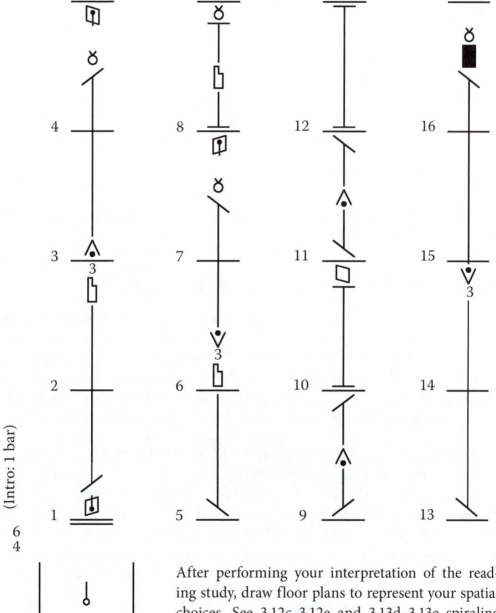

After performing your interpretation of the reading study, draw floor plans to represent your spatial choices. See 3.12c–3.12e and 3.13d–3.13e spiraling floor plan illustrations for guidance.

SEE FLOOR PLAN

A choreographer may not intend a circular path to be performed as a true, symmetrical circle or a spiral to be performed precisely. In these cases, a device is used to tell the reader to look at the accompanying floor plan. This plan illustrates the desired spatial design and location to be reached. A small version of the open rectangle representing a floor plan is placed in the path sign to alert the reader to look at the desired modification.

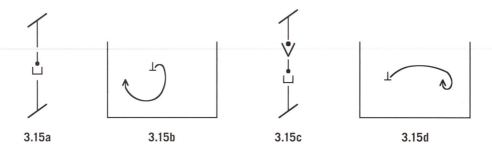

3.15a   3.15b   3.15c   3.15d

In 3.15a, the notation refers the reader to the floor plan because in 3.15b an imperfect circle is performed. In 3.15c, the notation indicates to refer to the floor plan for the performance of the single inward spiral. Example 3.15d reveals that the inward spiral should end curving in tightly.

PHRASING OF MOVEMENT SEQUENCES

It is one thing to read and execute a series of notated movements; it is another to produce a movement sequence which has cohesion, kinetic logic, and expression. When one movement follows another, are they related? Is there a link or is the second action a separate "thought," in no way a development of what went before? Timing can give some indication; a definite break in the movement flow usually means a new start, a new idea. Let us investigate a simple movement sequence to discover the possibilities.

In 3.16a, turning leads into a circular path and then a straight path. Example 3.16b illustrates a possible interpretation of the path traveled. This sequence can be interpreted as turning around the center which enlarges in its use of space to become a circular path. This then becomes spatially more direct, going off on a tangent, so to speak, to produce traveling on a straight path. In itself, this material has a kinetic logic whatever accompanying gestures, dynamics, etc., may be used. It has a sense of space in its development from turning around the central core, the vertical axis.

Each kind of movement has its own kinetic logic. For a movement phrase to have its own logic, there must be a line of development; each new action usually has its "birth" in the preceding one. The germ, the seed, the feeling for beginning a circular path must already be there by the end of the turning action; the seed for traveling on a straight path must already be in the body before the end of the circling. This germinating of a new idea is a small dynamic change which takes place usually in the center of the body, the torso. We do not want to spell out how to achieve these transitions; they take place within, organically, and may not be evident to an observer.

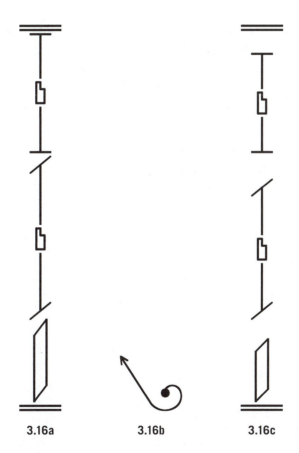

3.16a   3.16b   3.16c

Example 3.16c takes the same material as 3.16a, but the gaps between the actions show enough of a pause to break the thread of the "movement thought," the phrasing. Each action has its own start, each is a new "idea." Each must overcome the moment of inertia which preceded it. Such a kinetic pattern, three separate thoughts, may be just what is wanted. It is important that the difference be clear in movement as well as in the notation, the expression of the movement ideas on paper.

What do we mean by "one movement thought growing out of the previous one"? Let us take a verbal sentence to draw a parallel. "I'll think of you at six o'clock as you leave to go on holiday." This statement carries the message that you care for this person and are aware of what time they are leaving for a trip. This thought progression is missing in the following: "I'll think of you. It will be at six o'clock. You are going on holiday." Movement has a comparable logic in its progression from one movement to another. But one cannot easily put into words just how or why one action grows out of another. A physical, kinetic sense, an understanding of phrasing, needs to be developed.

Complete separation of movement ideas can be intentional in a movement composition; this is particularly true of contemporary choreography. Just as modern music, poetry, and prose may juxtapose unusual, unexpected ideas, sounds, and words to achieve a particular effect, so contemporary choreography may juxtapose unusual, nonsequitur movements for a similar reason. In any study, it is wise to master the traditional forms, to progress from the known to the unknown. Discover fully the simple forms, the usual, logical transitions and make them your own before embarking on more complex possibilities.

REVIEW FOR CHAPTER THREE

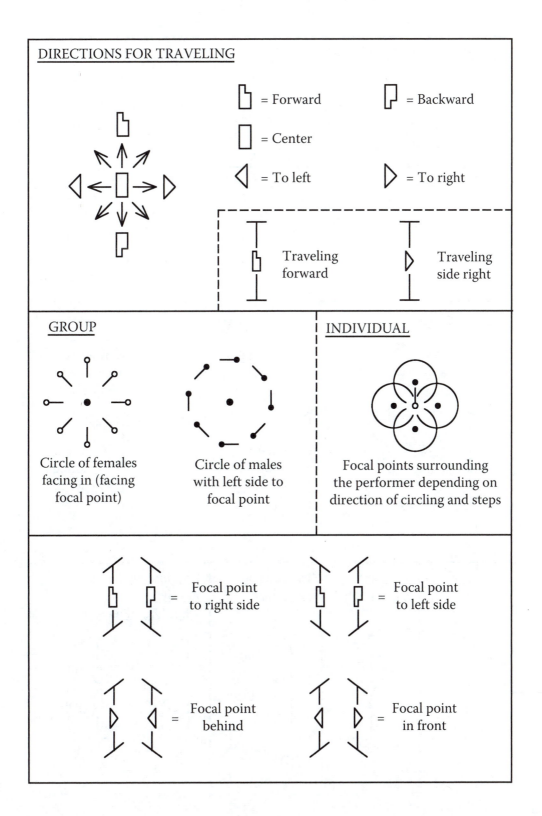

DIRECTIONS FOR TRAVELING

= Forward = Backward

= Center

= To left = To right

Traveling forward Traveling side right

GROUP

Circle of females facing in (facing focal point)

Circle of males with left side to focal point

INDIVIDUAL

Focal points surrounding the performer depending on direction of circling and steps

= Focal point to right side

= Focal point to left side

= Focal point behind

= Focal point in front

REVIEW FOR CHAPTER THREE (CONTINUED)

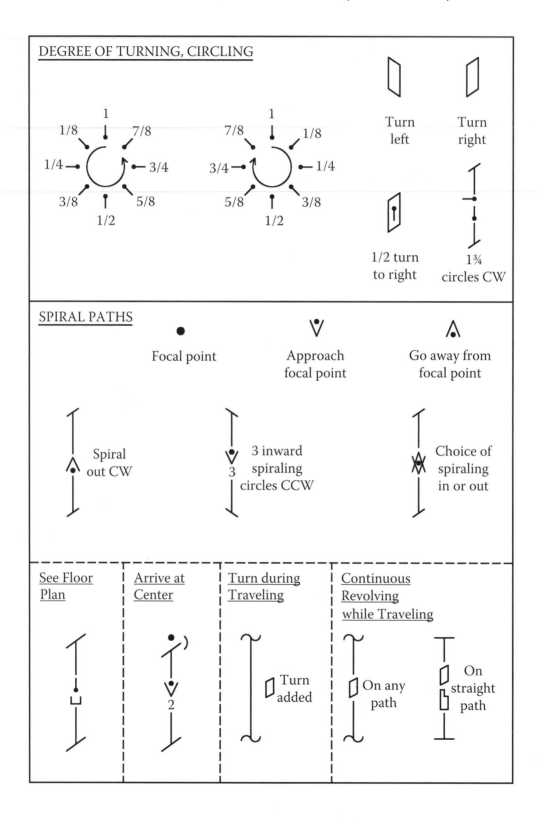

DEGREE OF TURNING, CIRCLING

Turn left

Turn right

1/2 turn to right

1¾ circles CW

SPIRAL PATHS

Focal point

Approach focal point

Go away from focal point

Spiral out CW

3 inward spiraling circles CCW

Choice of spiraling in or out

See Floor Plan

Arrive at Center

Turn during Traveling

Turn added

Continuous Revolving while Traveling

On any path

On straight path

CHAPTER FOUR

Absence of Support: Springing (Elevation); The Five Basic Forms

What is jumping? Why do we spring into the air? We are concerned here with intentional absence of support, neither a momentary absence when someone trips and then falls nor that glorious (though at first strange) total absence of support experienced by astronauts in a weightless state. Think what tumblers and dancers could do with that state. How many somersaults? How many *cabrioles* or *entrechats*? We must, however, come down to earth, as does every spring into the air, and deal with everyday realities.

Nature provides us with many examples of jumping actions. Birds "hop" from twig to twig, frogs "leap" into the air, so do fleas. The Mexican jumping bean may not have been observed by everyone, but jumping fish are familiar, as are grasshoppers.

Children jump around from mere high spirits. They enjoy bouncing like a ball: it is an automatic reflex, a natural way of expending surplus energy. The desire to spring into the air must, therefore, be caused by or coupled with a rise in energy. He who has no energy cannot jump. The reasons for excess energy may vary. It may be joy, it may be anger, rage, or even desperation. In the case of desperation, the performer flings himself in the air, fighting Fate. Let us look at some everyday examples of "springing" actions related to high energy level. An aggressive person will literally (or figuratively) "leap" at a person or at ideas. An activity which is going "by leaps and bounds" indicates progression with extraordinary rapidity—again, high energy level. If someone is told to "hop to it," he or she is expected to move with alacrity. Robbers who "skip" out on their mates use speed and energy. Excessive energy, as in anger, may cause a person to perform stamping jumps on both feet—an expression of extreme frustration.

| **4.1a** | **4.1b** | **4.1c** |
| Anger | Thief on the run | "Stop thief!" |

There may be practical reasons for jumping, such as clearing a big puddle or avoiding a falling brick. However, our concern with this kind of movement is with man's desire to overcome gravity. Rising into the air is an extension of an upward movement, a movement away from gravity. To get higher, we spring into the air, enjoying a moment of freedom, of exhilaration, of flight, an escape from our earthbound lives. This desire to develop the body to surmount and defy the force of gravity, together with the inborn pleasure of jumping and the different forms it can take, leads to tumbling and the stylized exercises featured in gymnastics and acrobatics. In these forms, jumping is combined with revolutions to produce a great variety of aerial "tricks," the range of which is augmented by use of trampolines, high bars, etc. In many forms of gymnastics, skating, and dancing, aerial steps are included to be performed in a very precise way; it is the skill and precision which is admired and for which the performer aims. Here we are concerned not with the final form, but with a basic cause: enjoyment of the doing, rather than concern with just how the movement is done. In other words, we are again concerned with discovering the freedoms of this basic type of movement.

AERIAL STEPS

A word about terminology for this basic form of movement may be helpful here. A general term is needed as well as specific terms for the five basic forms of leaving the ground and returning to it, i.e., one foot to the same foot; one foot to the other; two feet to two; one foot to two; and two feet to one. These will be discussed specifically later on. In the meantime we need to be able to be general, to use terms which do not identify a particular form.

The term "jumping" is widely used to mean any form of springing. To avoid confusion, care must be taken to distinguish between a spring, which may be of any kind, any form, and "a jump," which refers specifically to springing up from two feet and landing on two feet. "Jumping" should mean a series of such jumps. The most appropriate general terms are "springing," a "spring," or a series of "springs." Other appropriate words are "steps of elevation" and "aerial steps." It is important to have a term which does not in itself state any specific form.

Use of Aerial Steps in Dance

What purpose or effect does springing have in dance? Marking the rhythm through springing is common in many kinds of folk dances. The music played may invite a bouncing reaction. The addition of elevation, of steps going into the air, heightens everything beyond the normal in theatrical dance, thus adding greatly to exaggeration and to stylization.

4.2a
Rhythmic springs

4.2b
Aerial tricks

How are aerial steps used by choreographers? They may be for display, mere *tours de force*, or for movement design. There may be dramatic motivation, moments of ecstasy, or despair. Elevation provides highlights, climaxes. The energy of surging emotions is well spent defying gravity, rising above our earthbound existence. Exuberance is well expressed through springing.

4.2c

Spatial Expressiveness

Apart from the enjoyment it imparts of momentarily being suspended in the air, springing may have as its impetus a specific spatial design. Leaving the ground allows both legs to perform gestures at the same time, thus providing opportunity for interrelated actions of leg flexion, extension, spreading, closing, beating, and gesturing in different directions. All these possibilities can be further embellished by including turning.

Much variety can be achieved in performing springing steps by the type of preparation, what the body and limbs do while in the air, and how they react on landing. Twisting, flexing, extending—all can add interest. As long as a good spring is achieved, other contributing actions usually do not overshadow it. Springs are often combined with traveling and with turning; be aware of whether these other actions have equal importance. Attention should therefore be paid to the importance of such accompanying actions, and how much they are being emphasized so as not to overshadow the main action of the spring.

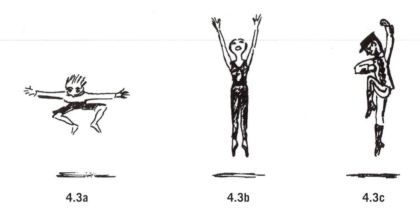

4.3a **4.3b** **4.3c**

Example 4.3a is a spring away from the floor; 4.3b shows springing up to reach toward the ceiling or sky. In a warrior's dance of triumph over an enemy, these two might be combined as in 4.3c. These examples are concerned with vertical space. Example 4.3d expresses freedom in use of lateral space while in the air, while 4.3e shows diving in the forward sagittal direction, an exciting moment for the performer and observer alike.

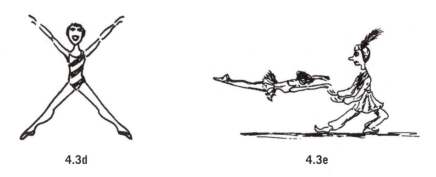

4.3d **4.3e**

USE OF ENERGY IN SPRINGING

While the legs do most of the work in jumping off the feet, concentration should be on lifting the body mass, the center of weight. Some dancers think only of the feet in jumping, and not, as one well-known teacher used to say, of "lifting your bottom"! All parts of the body must coordinate to achieve lifting the center of weight.

Experiment with basic bouncing, rebound springing into the air with no thought of limb placement or body design. The basic sensation of such springing should be discovered and mastered; later the shape and style of movement can be developed without losing the basic dynamic force of jumping. Coordinated lifting gestures of arms and the free leg help to overcome gravity by providing needed momentum. In a jump from two feet, both legs working together have greater strength, so the spring is likely to be higher. Timing and impetus are essential.

Springs which mark the musical beat tend to be performed more or less on the spot; traveling, covering ground rapidly, can be achieved through leaps. In dance, the various forms of springs become stylized to produce different effects; in athletics, style is based on a necessary functional streamlined use of the body.

When we spring, our energy may be directed to vertical travel, jumping as high as possible off the ground, or to propel us horizontally across the floor. The need to travel fast, to cover ground, automatically produces running. Ordinary walking easily merges into running when an increase in energy and speed occur. A slight lift off the ground, a small spring occurs between each step. Running at a slow tempo develops easily into leaps.

INDICATION OF SPRINGING

Though acrobats spring from their hands and Russian folk dancers spring up from their knees and even from sitting, let us consider the ordinary forms based on springing from the feet.

Example 4.4 shows the symbol for any form of springing into the air. It is a three-part sign.

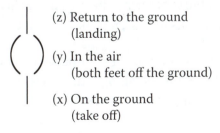

(z) Return to the ground
(landing)

(y) In the air
(both feet off the ground)

(x) On the ground
(take off)

4.4

Each of the movement examples shown in 4.5a–4.5d may be explored and performed in several different ways. If one possibility comes immediately to mind, perhaps a favorite form, then try another, and yet another. Different expressions will result from your choice, particularly if arms, body, and head are allowed to take part, to add coloring to the form chosen for the legs without dominating it and becoming over-important.

We still have not begun to be specific as to which foot steps, what the legs do as you spring into the air, or on which foot you land. As with all these explorations, we go from the general to the specific. Find out the various possibilities, then focus on the specific form of your choice.

SPRINGING COMBINED WITH TRAVELING

Examples 4.5a–4.5d show how springs can be combined with traveling.

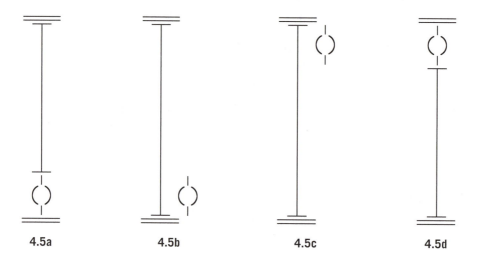

| 4.5a | 4.5b | 4.5c | 4.5d |

A spring can occur before starting to travel, giving the effect of an exclamation before a sentence, 4.5a. A spring can occur during the start of traveling, acting as a burst of energy, an impetus as you begin to travel, 4.5b. In 4.5c, the spring comes during the end of traveling, a burst of energy to stop, a conclusion. If the spring comes after the traveler has finished, as in 4.5d, it is like an afterthought, a new idea.

A spring may occur in the middle of traveling, as in 4.5e. In 4.5f there are three springs. Placement of the sign for springing indicates when that action occurs. Note specific choice here of traveling forward on a straight path. Springing can be applied with other pathways and directions.

Through trying out the different forms of springing, you can discover which lend themselves best to the start of traveling, which to the continuation of traveling, and which to the termination of traveling.

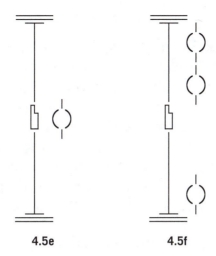

4.5e   4.5f

Although the five basic forms have not yet been specifically explored, it will soon be evident that some forms are more suited than others to traveling. Jumping from and landing on two feet is not the most productive way of traveling—as we know from the sack race. Hopping continuously on one foot tends to tire that leg and cut down on distance traveled. Running and leaping (springing from one foot to the other) is the form chosen most naturally to cover ground. With these thoughts in mind, it may be that there are more preferable interpretations for the springing actions in the above examples than might initially have been expected.

In planning a movement sequence you may wish to state that springing is to be **included**, but just when or how often is to be left open. This idea is expressed by use of a vertical bow, the "inclusion" bow, which has curved ends and a straight center, 4.5g. What is to be included in the main movement is written within the vertical line. Example 4.5h states that at some point springing is to be included as you travel forward, while 4.5 states traveling is achieved through springing.

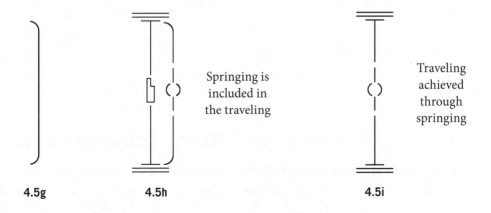

Springing is included in the traveling

Traveling achieved through springing

4.5g   4.5h   4.5i

Size of Spring

When springs occur, what size will they be? How much time will be spent in the air, how much on the ground? Unless distance in traveling is involved, time spent in the air equates with the height of the spring. Differences in height markedly affect function and expression of aerial steps. Springs of short duration in the air may be little bounces of excitement or a gentle marking of the beat or rhythm. Small springs from foot to foot occur in running, an example being jogging. In contrast, a high spring is needed to grasp an overhead object which is out of normal reach, or to jump over an object without touching it such as when leaping over a hurdle. Such jumps obviously spend more time in the air and are of longer duration.

When performed to an even beat, a series of springs can keep time and yet vary considerably in height. Lower springs will absorb the extra time by remaining on the ground, cushioning the landing. A higher series of springs will use a rebound pattern, the landing being an immediate take-off, as though from hot rocks. Between the two extremes of low and high springs is the comfortable resilient spring in which the same amount of time is spent in the air as on the ground.

Because the sign for a spring includes an indication for being on the ground as well as an indication for being in the air, it is possible to show the proportion of time spent on the ground and in the air. Thus each portion and the overall size of the spring, larger or smaller, can be indicated.

Example 4.6a shows a brief take-off and landing with a longer time in the air, while 4.6b shows the reverse: more time spent on the ground before and after the spring itself which has only a short time in the air. Example 4.6c illustrates an ordinary "healthy" size of spring, not especially high nor earthbound.

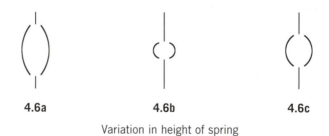

| 4.6a | 4.6b | 4.6c |

Variation in height of spring

Series of Independent and Rebounding Springs

In a sequence, one spring may follow immediately after another so that the landing from one spring is the take-off for the next, a rebound pattern. Or a new take-off, such as a closing of the feet, a step in between or the bending of the legs as in a *plié*, may occur for each spring. A series of these may follow without a break. Example 4.7a shows two complete **sequential springs**, a take-off and a landing followed by a new take-off and landing. Example 4.7b shows a series of **rebound springs** in which, like a bouncing ball, each landing is the take-off for the next spring. It is possible to have a stillness after landing and to spring up again without a new preparation; this is shown in 4.7c. Many sequences start with a spring. If the first spring is to land on count 1 in the music, the moment in the air must happen before count 1. This preparation is called the **up-beat** (i.e., before the beat). Example 4.7d shows such a spring; the landing takes place on count 1, after the first bar line. Note placement of the double bar line indicating start of action.

Try each of these examples varying use of one or two feet for take-off and landing; then experiment with combining these with traveling.

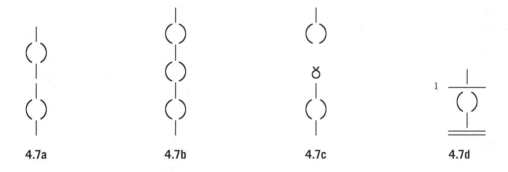

4.7a   4.7b   4.7c   4.7d

READING STUDY No. 16

AERIAL STEPS—SIZE OF SPRING

This study features size of spring: the more time spent in the air, the higher or further the spring, as in the large spring in measures 5 and 6; the less time in the air, the lower the spring or less distance traveled. Also notice which springs are separate and which are rebounding; which springs are performed on the spot and which travel. Counts are given to indicate clearly the beat on which the take-off and landing supports occur. In measure 9–12 "dancer's counts" are given for the two-measure phrase.

READING STUDY NO. 17

AERIAL STEPS WITH TRAVELING

In this study an inward spiraling path and later an outward spiraling path have been given. Note how these spirals are clearly represented on the floor plans. Follow the floor plans as you have done in previous studies.

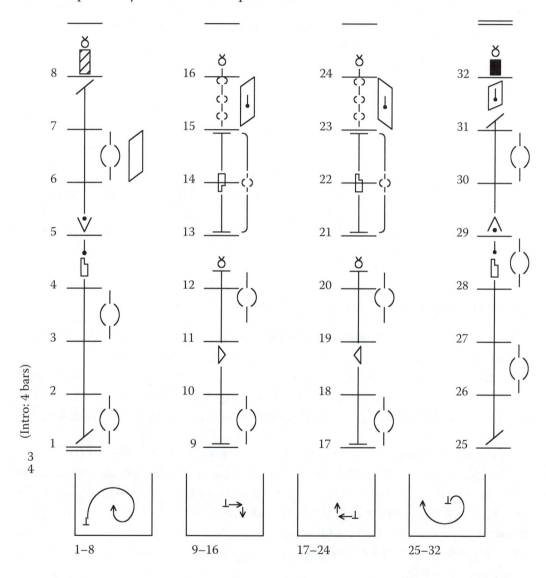

Note regarding placement of information: the main movement activity is centered on the staff. Where two movements are equally important they should share center. See Appendix A for explanation of symbol arrangement.

AERIAL STEPS: THE FIVE BASIC FORMS

Despite the seemingly enormous variety of springing possibilities seen in the many different dance cultures around the world, there are in fact only five basic possibilities for leaving the ground and returning to it using two legs. In ballet, the forms are given particular names; we use these here for explanation. When using notation, no balletic names are needed. These are the five forms.

	Ordinary Name	Balletic Name
1. From two feet to two feet	Jump	*Soubresaut*
2. From one foot to the same	Hop	*Temps levé* *
3. From one foot to the other	Leap	*Jeté*
4. From one foot to two feet	(joining spring)	*Assemblé*
5. From two feet to one foot	(separating spring)	*Sissonne*

* in most schools of ballet

Many people expect skips and gallops to be included in the five basic forms; they are, in fact, combined forms, a step being added to a hop or a leap. A skip is "step-hop, step-hop," or a "hop-step, hop-step" (depending on where the pattern is started), and a gallop is "step-leap, step-leap."

Terminology: Everyday Names

Have we something to learn from the words used in everyday language? Dictionaries use the words "jump," "leap," "hop," "spring," and "bound" interchangeably. It is generally agreed that the word hop refers to a spring from one foot to the same, and a leap is sometimes recognized as being from one foot to the other. The use of the terms in everyday speech is usually different from the classifications given here.

Because there are no ordinary names for Nos. 4 and 5 in the list of five forms, the balletic terms are frequently used. It must be stressed, though, that reference is made only to the basic form of the balletic step and not to the specific variations in use of leg gestures familiar in ballet technique. *Sissonne* and *assemblé* forms appear in national dances and also in modern and jazz dance, but as in those styles they can look very different, they are often not recognized as being *sissonnes* and *assemblés* in the balletic sense.

When looking for an everyday term for *assemblé,* a group of young children suggested calling it a **"lump,"** as it is a mixture of a leap and a jump, going from one foot and ending on two, 4.8a. For *sissonne* they proposed calling it a **"jeap"** as it starts on two feet, like a jump, but ends on one, as in a leap, 4.8b

4.8a
A "LUMP"
closing spring

4.8b
A "JEAP"
opening spring

INDICATION OF THE FIVE BASIC FORMS

By specifying the take-off and landing portions of the spring symbol, we can state which of the five basic forms is being used.

Jump Form (Two Feet to Two)

Example 4.9a shows the general sign for a spring, while 4.9b indicates that it is a take-off from two feet, landing on two feet. These jumps need not be with feet together, various positions of the feet can be used. Notice that the support lines of take-off and landing are connected to the curved air "bows."

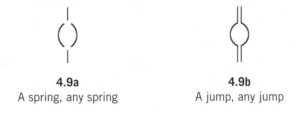

4.9a
A spring, any spring

4.9b
A jump, any jump

Hop Form (One Foot to the Same)

To show a hop on either foot the sign for "either side," 4.11a, is indicated. This sign is composed of a short vertical line (representing the vertical line in the body dividing right and left) and the horizontal ad lib sign meaning "any"; thus "any side." By placing this sign on the take-off we can state the choice of using either foot. Example 4.11b shows a hop beginning on either foot. If the sign were placed on the left foot symbol it would also indicate "either" side. Example 4.11c shows a hop on the left foot while 4.11d states a hop on the right foot. Attachment of one or other of the curved bows to the support indication shows visually whether take-off or landing is on the right foot, the left, or both feet.

4.11a	4.11b	4.11c	4.11d
"Either side"	Hop on either foot	Hop on left foot	Hop on right foot

Leap Form (One Foot to the Other)

A leap that begins on either foot, landing on the opposite foot is shown by 4.12a. In 4.12b, a leap occurs from the left foot to the right, while in 4.12c a leap from right foot to the left is given.

4.12a	4.12b	4.12c
Leap on either side	Leap left foot to right	Leap right foot to left

Skip, Gallop

A familiar combined form of springs is the "step-hop, step-hop" pattern of 4.13a, the new support before each hop being a step. This is the basis of a skip which may start as above or with a hop coming first (hop-step, hop-step). However, to be a true skip and not just a step-hop, an uneven rhythm must be used; this is presented more fully in Chapter 22. Example 4.13b is the basis of a gallop, which also needs an uneven rhythm to be a true gallop.

4.13a	4.13b
Step-hop, step-hop	Step-leap, step-leap

Assemblé Form (One Foot to Two)

Example 4.14a shows an *assemblé* taking off from one foot (which foot is used for the take-off is not specified) and landing on both. Note that the take-off support line is not connected to the air "bows," in 4.14a. For 4.14b, the "either foot" is spelled out more directly by adding a small ad lib sign over the take-off. In 4.14c, the take-off is from the left foot. In 4.14d, the take-off is from the right foot.

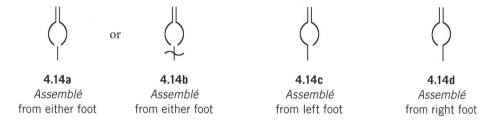

4.14a	4.14b	4.14c	4.14d
Assemblé from either foot	*Assemblé* from either foot	*Assemblé* from left foot	*Assemblé* from right foot

Sissonne Form (Two Feet to One)

Example 4.15a states a *sissonne* from two feet to one with no indication of landing on right or left foot. Again, notice the support line is not connected to the air "bows" for ease of reading, 4.15a. This open choice is spelled out more directly in 4.15b. Example 4.15c states a *sissonne* landing onto the left foot, while 4.15d shows a *sissonne* landing onto the right foot.

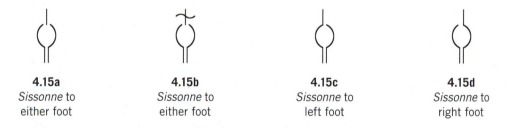

4.15a	4.15b	4.15c	4.15d
Sissonne to either foot	*Sissonne* to either foot	*Sissonne* to left foot	*Sissonne* to right foot

READING STUDY NO. 18

FIVE FORMS OF SPRINGING

BALLETIC VARIATIONS OF THE FIVE BASIC FORMS

Every dance style has its own vocabulary of springs. The following survey is presented here for any readers who may not be familiar with allegro steps in the ballet vocabulary, each of which is a variation of one of the five basic forms. Ballet students who perform these steps often have not actually considered to which basic form each belongs. Rapid leg work such as beats, *ronds de jambe* (leg circles), etc., featured while in the air can almost disguise the basic form. It is important to realize that, even if a particular aerial step may be preceded by a preparation with both feet on the ground, the actual take-off, the spring itself, may be from one foot only. Similarly a spring may end on one foot, the other closing so rapidly that the performer is given the impression that landing on two feet has occurred, which, of course, it did not. It is the moment of take-off and the moment of landing that determine the basic form. For instance, a *sissonne fermé* in which the legs close immediately after the landing is thought to be a jump from two feet to two feet. The step does indeed leave the floor from two feet but the landing is on one foot. Because the closing follows so swiftly the actual landing seems unimportant and hence is unnoticed. In the drawings in 14.16a–14.20e, preparations and conclusions are not indicated, only the actual take-off and landing for each form.

ANALYSIS OF FAMILIAR FORMS IN BALLET

Whether or not classical ballet is the style of movement with which you are concerned, much can be learned by taking a fresh look at the forms of aerial steps used in ballet and other movement forms, to see just what they contain. "Rediscovering" a familiar form can be enlightening and enriching. For example, consider the leg work of a *pas de chat*. What is this movement all about? First of all it is a spring, a spring from one foot to the other. Must it travel? Yes, it travels sideward and possibly slightly forward. Is there any particular body shape needed? Yes, a lateral shape for the legs; therefore the legs must be turned out. Apart from pushing off the ground and cushioning the landing, what must the legs do? Each must flex, the foot pulling in toward the hip to a greater or lesser degree, depending on whether it is a large or small *pas de chat*. Should the legs contract simultaneously? Not in the standard performance. The take-off is from one foot, the free leg flexes, then the other leg flexes—an overlapping action. As a *pas de chat* usually concludes with both feet on the ground, each leg must prepare to approach the floor, the first one to land, the second one to close. The image of springing sideward over a barrel is sometimes used to produce good leg work. In a spectacular *pas de chat*, the leg gestures are timed so that both legs are fully flexed at the same time and remain still for a moment to provide the impression of the body being suspended in the air. In terms of "relationship," a *pas de chat* might have the intention of rising toward the ceiling, in which case arms and head would probably be up. In a Russian *pas de chat* the second leg is usually less bent and is flung backward, the whole movement being more elongated. Much variation can occur in use of arms, head, and shoulders, but this is not our concern here. The purpose of this investigation is to explore the basic material on which a particular finished form is built.

Hop Form

Temps levé

4.16a   4.16b

(On the spot or traveling, the free leg in any position)

Ballonné   *Rond de jambe sauté*

4.16c   4.16d

Cabriole

4.16e   4.16f

(All body directions, with one or more beats)

Fouetté sauté   *Rivoltade*

4.16g   4.16h

Leap Form

Coupé with a spring

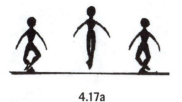

4.17a

Glissade

4.17b
(With slight rising off the ground)

Jeté

4.17c

4.17d

(All forms, on the spot, traveling, with beats, turns)

Pas de chat

4.17e
(All forms including *gargouillade*)

Ballotté

4.17f

Grand pas de basque

4.17g

Temps de flèche

4.17h

Saut de basque

4.17i

Brisé volé

4.17j

Assemblé Form

Assemblé

Brisé

4.18a

4.18b

(In all directions with beats, traveling and turning)

Jump Form

Soubresaut

Changement

4.19a

(Travel, no change of 5th position)

4.19b

(Change from 5th to 5th)

Entrechat

Echappé sauté

4.19c

(All those with even numbers, 4, 6, 8)

4.19d

(Into 2nd or 4th and return)

Saut de l'ange

(Also called *temps de l'ange* or *pas de l'ange* when done with bent legs)

4.19e

Sissonne Form

Temps levé

Entrechat trois

4.20a

(From two feet to one, also turning)

4.20b

(Also uneven numbers, 5, 7, etc.)

Sissonne

Pas de poisson

4.20c
(Also ending closing [*sissonne fermé*];
all directions, with beats, turning)

4.20d

Temps de cuisse

(A *sissonne* with a swift
opening and closing of the
leg before the spring)

4.20e

SPRINGING COMBINED WITH DIRECTIONS

Directional indications may be combined with a spring. We can indicate direction for the take-off support, for the landing support, and also for the legs while in the air. Appropriate placement of the direction sign indicates which leg is being specified. Note the examples given in 4.21a–4.21e.

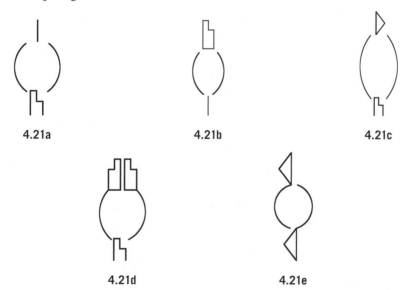

4.21a **4.21b** **4.21c**

4.21d **4.21e**

If a direction symbol replaces the action stroke at the start of the symbol for a spring, it states the direction of that support, usually a step. In 4.21a, this take-off step is forward. As yet no indication is given as to whether it is a step on the right or left foot. Example 4.21b states landing forward; again, no statement is made as to whether it is on one or two feet. In 4.21c, the preparatory support (step) is forward but the landing is to the side. This movement may be performed taking off from either foot and landing on one or both. Example 4.21d shows taking off from a forward step on the right foot and landing forward on both feet. In 4.21e, the sideward left step on the right foot leads into a leap onto the left foot in the same direction.

In the sign for a spring the right curve represents the right leg in the air, the left curve, the left leg. If a direction symbol is inserted in one of the curved vertical lines, it indicates a directional action for that leg while in the air.Example 4.21f shows the right leg gesturing forward during the spring; 4.21g states that both legs open sideward away from each other while in the air.

4.21f   4.21g

The addition of directional indications to springs leads into specific statements which begin to approach a full description of what is taking place. More information on this is given in Appendix B.

READING STUDY NO. 19

FIVE FORMS OF SPRINGING WITH DIRECTIONS

This study combines direction for the take-off and landing supports, as well as directions for leg gestures while in the air. It also features different sizes of springs and accompanying circular paths and turns.

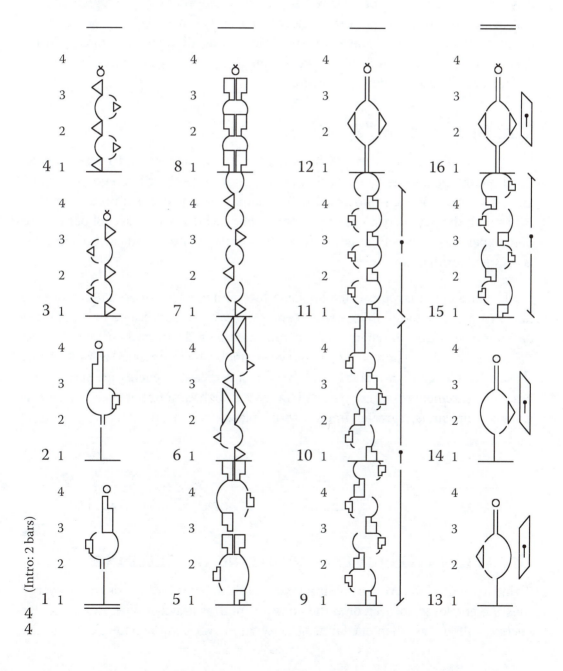

DYNAMICS

Dynamics deals with the ebb and flow of energy in the body. In Chapter 1, accents were introduced to show a momentary rise in energy which immediately disappear. Two other dynamic aspects are being introduced here which involve a rise in the use of energy and also a lowering of energy. For ordinary events in daily life we use the amount of energy needed for a particular task. The energy level needed for standing is less than that required for running; this is taken for granted. Extraordinary events drive us to unusual reactions where body motion and intensity rise high above, or sink below, the norm. For theatrical effect such changes in energy level occur intentionally. How are these changes in energy level judged? Indicated? Energy levels vary with individuals, therefore consideration must be given to what is "standard," or "normal" for each individual person.

The Concept of "Par"

"Par" is that energy level at which the particular movement undertaken can be functionally and efficiently executed. Par is considered the base reference, individually established for each movement task. The par energy level required for sitting is less than the par energy level for jumping. For each activity a level of par can be both experienced and observed. When no dynamic quality is indicated a par level is assumed for that movement.

The idea of par is represented on paper by an imaginary horizontal line, shown here in 4.22a as a dotted line. A rise in energy above par is indicated by an upward curving bow; a drop in energy level is indicated by a downward curving bow, as illustrated in 4.22b. The state of par can be symbolically represented as in 4.22c. In this analysis, degrees of increase and degrees of decrease in energy are relative, no exact measurements are undertaken. However, a slight amount of energy is shown using a white circle, a greater amount with a black circle, as in 4.22d.

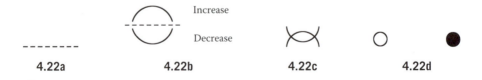

4.22a   4.22b   4.22c   4.22d

Relation to Gravity—fighting or Yielding

As mentioned before, even in the simple state of sitting or standing a degree of energy must be employed to overcome the constant pull of gravity. When all muscular energy is absent, as when one faints, gravity takes over and the body slumps to the ground. As observed before, relaxation of muscular tension when we are tired, for example, allows gravity to take over and we droop. This is so familiar that we do not think about it. But to relax muscles intentionally, to yield to gravity for practical, physical, or expressive purposes, is another matter. We will look at this in detail in a moment.

Fighting Gravity

We consciously increase our energy to fight gravity, to achieve uplift, to feel light, almost weightless. A female dancer uses physical uplift to help her partner during a lift. The upward curving bow of 4.23a indicates an increase in energy and the white circle a slight amount, thus expressing **uplift**, 4.23b. The greater degree of increase in energy shown in 4.23b states a greater amount in fighting gravity, as might occur in a dancer's or athlete's energetic jump or when needing strong uplift. Notice that the amount is placed in the middle of the upward curving bow; in this placement it relates to the vertical line of gravity centered in the person, 4.23b and 4.23c. (See Chapter 10 for information about line of gravity.)

| 4.23a | 4.23b | 4.23c |
| Line of gravity | Uplift | Strong uplift |

Yielding to Gravity

In consciously giving in to gravity we sense the weight of the body, of the limbs and torso. We experience the quality of weightedness. The quality of moving with weight, with an awareness of the weight of the limb, of the head perhaps, may be appropriate for the sequence being performed. In 4.24a, the downward bow states a decrease in energy and the centrally placed white circle indicates a slight amount in relation to gravity, the degree needed to provide a sense of weight to the gestures or steps taking place. Is it the broad, heavy stole worn over the arms that gives the Roman senator weight to his arm gestures? Certainly such added weight affects the expression of the gestures, an expression which we can emulate through muscular change, thus experiencing the weight of the arms. The greater degree, 4.24b, produces heaviness, awareness of the body mass and how this awareness affects movement and adds practical as well as expressive "power." North Burmese dancers use their body weight when chugging forward, feet together, thus digging trenches in the soil with their bare feet. The wrestler's lowering of his center of gravity and connectedness with his weight is an advantage in achieving the desired results. Here, of course, strength is usually combined with heaviness.

4.24a	4.24b
Weighty, weighted	Heavy

Duration

A dynamic quality may occur briefly, may gradually increase or decrease, or may be sustained during more than one movement. In 4.25a, the heavy quality occurs at the start of the movement; in 4.25b it occurs in the middle of the action, and in 4.25c it occurs just at the end.

4.25a	4.25b	4.25c	4.25d	4.25e

Increase toward achieving a quality is shown alongside the movement indication through use of the increase sign. In 4.25d, the quality of uplift gradually increases. In 4.25e, the reverse occurs, the strong uplift quality gradually disappears.

Maintaining a quality is shown by placing the appropriate sign within an angular vertical addition bracket placed alongside the movement indication. In 4.25f, the heavy quality lasts for the duration of the movement. In 4.25g, only the second half of the action has this quality. Example 4.25h illustrates a series of springs all to be performed with uplift; in contrast, 4.25i indicates a heavy step-hop pattern.

The performer should aim at maintaining the stated quality as long as indicated. However, over several movements, there might be a physical need to let up for a moment, but the aim is to maintain the stated quality.

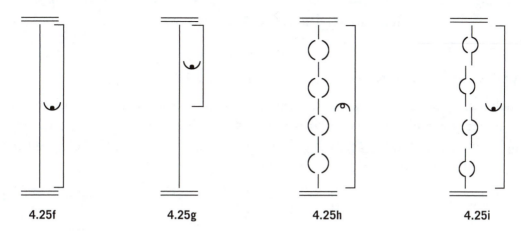

4.25f   4.25g   4.25h   4.25i

Reading Practice C (no music)

DYNAMICS: RELATION TO GRAVITY

In this study there is a contrast between giving in to the pull of gravity, i.e., experiencing weightedness and heaviness, and resisting the pull of gravity, i.e., experiencing uplift and buoyancy. For the first eight measures the 3/4 meter could be a Ländler, a peasant dance from the Tyrol in Austria.

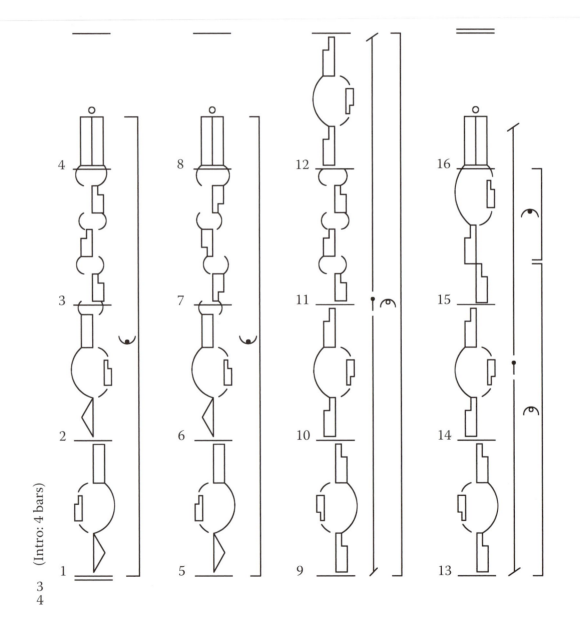

REVIEW FOR CHAPTER FOUR

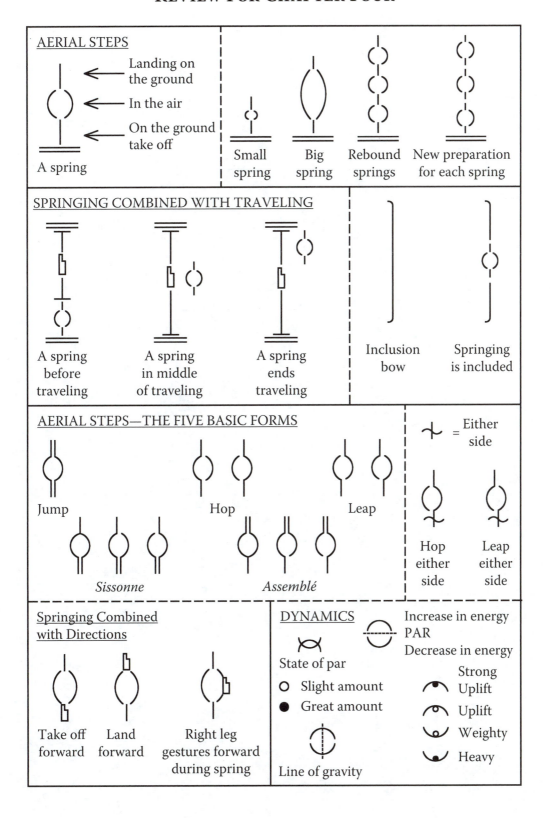

CHAPTER FIVE

Direction—Definition of Space

DIRECTION

Direction (spatial aspect) is the largest category of movement exploration because there are so many ways in which we can relate to directions around us. While most directional aspects have long been in use in dance teaching and choreography, they may not have been "formally introduced" with clear, definitive terminology. Exploration of this topic means discovery, or rediscovery; in the process we may find that we must rethink, reevaluate, and clear away some woolly terminology if we are to be universally understood.

The cardinal directions of forward, backward, side right, and side left have already been introduced briefly to provide specific statements in relation to traveling. Though we grow up knowing the main directions, including up and down, for our purposes here we need to take a fresh look at the whole subject of direction, of the space around us. There is not just one way of looking at spatial directions, not just one way of experiencing them or of referring to them. Space is defined for us by the build of our bodies, by the buildings in which we live, and by the earth and the sky, the universe that we inhabit.

OUR RELATION TO SPACE

By nature we do not like to exist in a void. The astronauts illustrated this in their need for a "floor," "ceiling," and "walls" to relate to in their orbiting space. When performing in a field, a group is perfectly happy if it is dancing in a circle and the dancers can relate direction to that circle. But dancing alone, performers will usually choose a landmark, perhaps a tree or hill, as the point to which to relate. As a rule we move in the

5.1a

defined space of a room or a stage in which there is an established set of directions, 5.1a. For theatre in the round, reference points are established for orientation.

5.1b

In life, a baby becomes aware first of its own personal space, directions based on its own body—the fact that it has a front, a back, right and left sides, head and feet, even though it cannot identify them at that stage. Much later it begins to relate to the room around it.

In daily life, as well as in sports, gymnastics, and dance, we orient ourselves according to our personal directions, to gravity, to the room, and to focal points such as other people and objects. Each of these possibilities will be explored and clearly defined through appropriate terminology and signs.

Our exploration will focus first on familiar directional statements, but will also investigate a broader exploration of directions and levels, such as the freer possibilities of moving in directional areas around the body in terms of the body-as-a-whole, as well as gestural actions.

DIRECTIONS—VARIETY IN EVERYDAY LIFE

Let us consider what concepts concerning direction exist in daily life and how we relate to them.

East, west, north, and south are familiar relative directions. But note that a location that is north to some people is south to others. The idea of being "east of the sun, west of the moon" is poetic. "Go west, young man!" has an open challenge. It speaks of freedom, the open

5.2a

road, and the west stretching out, endlessly, as does the imagination. In movement, many gestures and paths of the body-as-a-whole have such a feeling toward space. A general, free sense of moving in space may be personally satisfying, but for our daily living, the establishment of locations is necessary. On earth a fixed point is defined through specific degrees of longitude and latitude. One may "head south" when driving and may take any road one fancies, but at some point, from practical necessity, one must find the destinational point of a town or village and orient oneself from there. Thus for traveling, east, west, etc., are general terms, relative to where one starts. A destination may, of course, subsequently be added.

Some cities are laid out with specific division into N, S, E, and W, the dividing lines emanating from a designated point. In New York City, Fifth Avenue divides East and West. In that city there is no "North" or "South;" the general terms "uptown" and "downtown" are used, but with changing results. What is still marked as "The Uptown Dispensary" is now far downtown. These terms are merely relative.

In the theatre "upstage" and "downstage" are also relative. One performer may be upstage of another and downstage of a third, as in 5.2b. Two dancers may both move downstage while one remains upstage in relation to the other. The terms "upstage" and "downstage" came from the raking (slanting) of stages toward the audience, designed to make performers located at the back of the stage more visible to the audience. Some European stages are still raked and dancers have to adjust to a different physical balance.

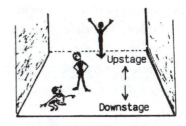

5.2b

Upstage and downstage lead us to "up" and "down," the inescapable (on earth) pull of gravity. No doubt this needs no explanation, up being toward the sky or ceiling, down toward the ground or floor. Many objects, however, have an "up" and "down," as the expression "up-side-down" makes clear. This applies also to humans. Consider the child's delight when first seeing a man upside down, 5.2c.

5.2c

5.2d

5.2e

5.2f

Up and down lead us to "front" and "back." Many objects such as houses and many types of furniture have a front and a back. Boats, cars, and planes, indeed most (moving) objects are built with a definite front and back and hence a right and left side. On a boat the front is the bow (prow), the back is the stern, with starboard the right side and port the left. Boats and cars are designed to move forward, with backward motion used when necessary. Few objects, as indeed few creatures, move sideways. Certain crabs are an exception, as is the sidewinder snake for which sideward and slightly forward is its natural direction of progression, 5.2g. Unnatural, but splendid, are the Lippizaner horses trained to walk sideways as a special gait in *dressage*, a skill required for the horse ballets of centuries ago which is still practiced and admired today.

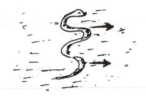

5.2g

Each person's own front, back, right, and left sides may relate in different ways to the front, back, etc., of objects. An everyday situation may have its counterpart on stage in dance movements. The house we live in has a front and a back, etc. One may enter the front door walking sideways because of holding an awkward package, or even walk backwards if helping an infirm person through the door. The direction we are facing and the direction of our steps in relation to an object or person may encompass a wide range of possible combinations. In dance, movements are performed for other than practical reasons, but the basic facts of direction remain.

Consider the comedian sitting on a horse facing backward in 5.2h while the horse trots forward down a one-way street, going in the wrong direction. The clown here is being carried backward but is facing forward in relation to the street direction.

5.2h

5.2i

The words "right" and "left" provide a slight problem since they refer both to the right and left sides of the body and also to the right and left side directions in space. The right foot may step to the left side of the center line of the body and the left arm may move across to the right side of the body as in 5.2i. Thus we must be clear as to whether the words "right" and "left" refer to a direction or to one or other side of the body.

These are some references to direction met in daily living. Many similar usages arise in all kinds of movement studies. Directional descriptions may refer to destinations, that is, arrival at points or situations in space, or they may refer to motion, the "going" of movement. We have already discussed the turning directions, right and left, and the directions for circling, clockwise and counterclockwise; these are relative directions in the same sense that "east" and "west" are. Circling is also relative; no specific path can be undertaken until the direction of traveling is known as well as the degree of circling.

DIMENSIONAL DIRECTIONS
ANY DIRECTION

Before analyzing specific directions and how we relate to them and what they in themselves express, let us consider the first, broadest statement regarding direction, i.e., any direction. This is indicated by a rectangle, the basic shape for direction, combined with the horizontal ad lib. sign, 5.3a, i.e., "any," thus expressing "any direction," 5.3b.

5.3a   **5.3b**
Any direction

The indication of 5.3b means total spatial freedom, i.e., movement in any direction at any level. Later we will explore any level for a specific direction, and also any direction in a stated level.

THE DIMENSIONAL CROSS OF AXES

First we investigate the familiar directions, later we will explore how open statements regarding direction can be made as well as choices for a fuller experience in directional awareness.

We live in a three-dimensional world, and are ourselves built in three dimensions. These dimensions—the vertical (up and down), lateral (side to side), and sagittal (forward and backward)—meet at a center point, and each axis extends in two directions: up-down, right-left, and forward-backward, 5.4a. This is known as the dimensional cross.

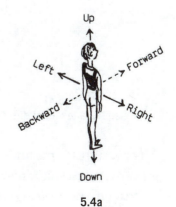

5.4a

The vertical line is represented by a rectangle, 5.4b. Example 5.4c is the center point where the three axes cross, this is also known as "place middle" for the body-as-a-whole. For the body-as-a-whole, in Motif Description, place middle also provides a centered, neutral situation or position for the body.

The signs for the six dimensional directions are as follows: 5.4b shows the basic symbol; 5.4d shows "up" or "high level" (filled with slanting stripes); 5.4e represents "down" or "low level" (indicated as a black symbol). "Horizontal" or "middle level" directions are shown with a dot, as in 5.4c.

5.4b   **5.4c**   **5.4d**   **5.4e**

As explained earlier, the forward, backward, and sideward signs are indicated by modifying the basic shape of 5.4b. Thus the signs become indicators pointing to the appropriate direction, as in 5.4f. In this example, middle level, the horizontal directions, is shown by the addition of a dot.

The illustration of 5.4g shows the dimensional directions appropriately placed around the figure.

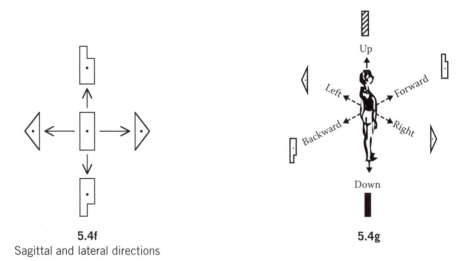

5.4f
Sagittal and lateral directions

5.4g

For gestures of the limbs, middle horizontal movements are parallel with the floor (or nearly so). Gestures may be circular or may flex and extend toward or away from the torso on a horizontal plane.

NOTES ON READING PRACTICE D:
DIMENSIONAL STUDIES

As a first exploration of direction, we will be concerned with expressing the axial directions. No music is provided for these sequences; a gong and/or drum would be suitable. Allow leeway regarding how directions are being interpreted; be concerned only that the movement be clear and truthful. Allow the body to participate in the directional movements to express fully the directional ideas, leaving isolated actions for later exploration.

To add interest to these studies, the accent signs have been included.

◁   or   ▷

A slight accent

A slight accent can happen at any point during a sustained movement—at the start, in the middle, or at the end, as explained in Chapter 1.

Identify what is consistent in the structure of A. Notice in what way the last measure of B varies from the rest of the study. Note the double-sided directions in B. Describe any ideas or associations you derive from C.

READING PRACTICE D (NO MUSIC)

DIMENSIONAL STUDIES

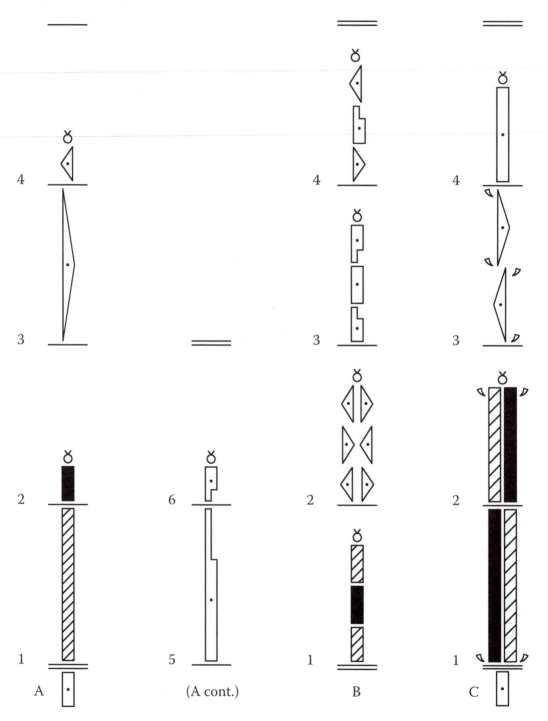

THE DIMENSIONAL PLANES

By combining two of the dimensional axes, four directional points will produce circular planes that dissect the body. The combined lateral (right and left directions) and vertical (up and down directions) produce the **lateral plane**, illustrated in 5.5a and represented by the symbol of 5.5b. The vertical dimension combined with the sagittal dimension (forward and backward directions) produce the **sagittal plane**, illustrated in 5.5c, and represented by the symbol in 5.5d. The sagittal and lateral dimensions combined produce the **horizontal plane** illustrated in 5.5e, and represented by 5.5f. Smaller planes, parallel to these main planes, are located at each joint of the body.

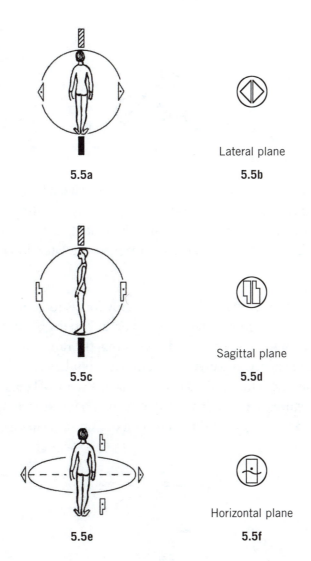

5.5a

Lateral plane

5.5b

5.5c

Sagittal plane

5.5d

5.5e

Horizontal plane

5.5f

Note: In Laban's Space Harmony these planes are rectangular in order to produce the icosahedron form surrounding the body. However, the natural structure of the body is such that all movement is basically circular; thus the planes of movement are also circular.

The sagittal plane divides the body into right and left sides. This plane, 5.5g, is sometimes called the "wheel plane." Riding a bicycle demonstrates the appropriateness of that name; the wheels move on the sagittal plane when traveling forward or backward, 5.5h. Movements can occur at all levels in this plane, but once straight up or down is reached, the body or the limb no longer expresses a sagittal direction; all sense of forward or backward is lost.

5.5g   5.5h   5.5i

The lateral plane divides the body into the front and back halves, 5.5i. This plane is sometimes called the "door plane" as though one were standing in a doorway, or the "wall plane" as with your back to a wall. Movements can occur at all levels in this plane, but once straight up or down is reached the lateral plane is no longer being expressed.

The lateral symmetry of the body makes it easy for us to gesture with arms and legs into the open side directions; the crossed side directions are not as comfortable and require practice. In the case of one-sided crossing, the range can be augmented by including some degree of accompanying turn in the shoulders or hips; however, other parts of the body must hold the original front so that the sense of lateral direction is not lost. Try crossing gestures to experience at what point too much accompanying turn of the body will diminish or eradicate the expression of a crossed lateral gesture.

5.5j

The horizontal plane illustrated in 5.5j, divides the body into upper and lower halves. This plane is sometimes called the "table plane." Movements in this plane involve sagittal and lateral directions in the horizontal level. Parallel horizontal planes exist for the arms at shoulder level, and for the legs at hip level.

MOVEMENT IN THE PLANES

The three planes, derived from the dimensional directions, can be the focus of movement. Concentration can be on keeping within the plane in a two-dimensional manner, as though captured within a flat disk, or as though the movements are brushing or polishing a disk. Through flexion and rotation, particularly for the arms, a range of interesting patterns can be achieved. The limitation of staying within a plane can evoke invention. When we are vertically oriented, as in standing, expressive gestures limited to the horizontal plane may not be as easily physicalized as gestures on the lateral and sagittal planes. Chosen movements in the horizontal plane should strive to be more or less horizontal, parallel to the floor, but with a little leeway being allowed.

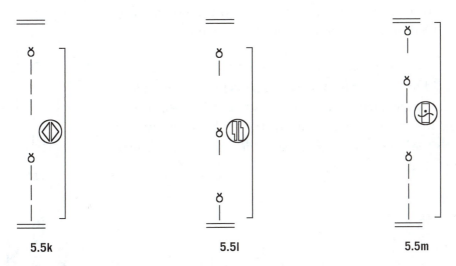

| 5.5k | 5.5l | 5.5m |

An action, or a series of actions are shown to be within a plane by placing the indication for the plane within an angular vertical addition bracket at the side of the action symbol(s). 5.5k, 5.5l, and 5.5m show a series of actions of different durations that occur within the lateral plane in 5.5k, in the sagittal plane in 5.5l, and in the horizontal plane in 5.5m.

THE 27 MAIN DIRECTIONS

The directions forward, backward, right side, and left side have been introduced, but not yet the four diagonal directions lying between them.

THE DIAGONAL DIRECTIONS

Between the sagittal (forward and back) and the lateral (side to side) dimensions lie the four diagonal directions, 5.6a. The slanting line coming to a point visually indicates the directions in question.

By adding the four diagonals of 5.6a, we have the circle of directions of 5.6f, all emanating from the center point.

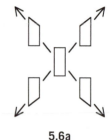

5.6a
The four diagonal directions

| **5.6b** | **5.6c** | **5.6d** | **5.6e** |
| Left-front diagonal | Right-front diagonal | Left-back diagonal | Right-back diagonal |

To this circle of directions we now add levels. Each of these directions may be at low, middle, or high level.

Examples 5.6g, 5.6h, and 5.6i show the range for high level, middle level, and low level. The center point, "place middle," is included as a direction since it is, specifically, a point to which the extremity of the limb can move, for example the hand moving to the shoulder which is the center point of direction for the arm.

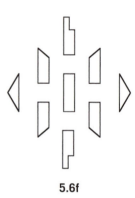

5.6f

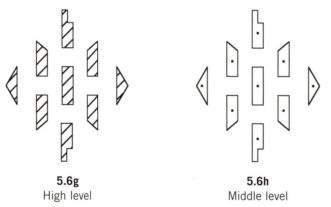

| **5.6g** | **5.6h** | **5.6i** |
| High level | Middle level | Low level |

The 27 main directions

These cardinal directions are those featured in most styles of structured movement. However, many styles of dance take intermediate points as their norm;

for example in classical ballet the arms are not held in a true horizontal line in the sideward and forward directions, but somewhat lower. In Spanish dance, the arms overhead are held slightly behind the head. Many other examples of such minor directional variation can be cited. For our purposes here no such specificity is needed.

PERCEIVING POINTS IN SPACE

In dealing with space, there are infinite points toward which we can move, or through which we can pass. Such richness may seem overwhelming. However, the human eye is limited in discerning minute differences in spatial location. Performing subtle differences in arriving at a directional placement is physically difficult. Other than very small vibrating movements, i.e., slight displacements from an established point, it has been found that a 15° difference in arrival at a destinational point is the smallest degree with which we need be concerned. For movement exploration in this book, only two distinctions are being considered for specific directions: major changes of 45° and, later, displacements that are minor.

DIRECTION AND LEVEL FOR GESTURES

Direction and level for a gesture of a limb is judged by the spatial line from the base of the limb, the point of attachment, to the extremity. For an arm, the base is the shoulder, the extremity is the hand, thus the center point of direction, place middle, lies at the shoulder. In 5.7a and 5.7b, the arm (the limb) is shown in two possible place middle placements. For the leg, the base is the hip; the extremity is the foot. For the whole torso, the base is the hip joint; the extremity is the shoulder line. In 5.7c, the line of the arm is side high from the point of attachment, the shoulder. The line of the leg is forward low from the point of attachment, the hip, as shown in 5.7d. The line of the torso is forward high of the point of attachment, the hips, in the illustration of 5.7e. This analysis can be applied to the following exploration of traveling with gestures.

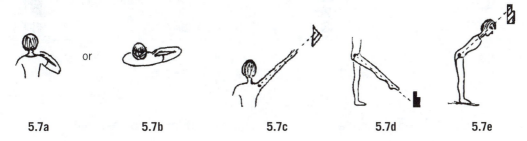

| 5.7a | 5.7b | 5.7c | 5.7d | 5.7e |

COMBINING DIRECTIONAL ACTIONS WITH TRAVELING

Traveling may be accompanied by directional actions. In this case, the two indications are placed side by side, as both actions are equally important. Try out the variations of directional gestures combined with traveling shown in 5.8a, 5.8b, and 5.8c.

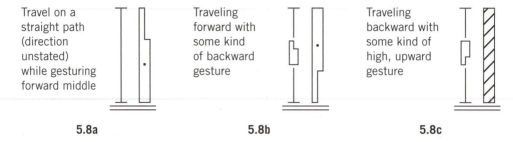

Travel on a straight path (direction unstated) while gesturing forward middle

5.8a

Traveling forward with some kind of backward gesture

5.8b

Traveling backward with some kind of high, upward gesture

5.8c

Placement of gesture statements on the right or left of the traveling sign might appear to suggest use of the right or left side of the body. This is not so, the directional symbol could be interpreted as the right, left, or both sides of the body; the use of right and left body sides is given in Chapter 14. Examples 5.8d, 5.8e, and 5.8f are examples of gestures with circular paths.

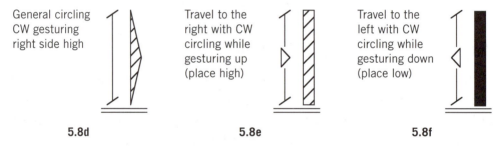

General circling CW gesturing right side high

5.8d

Travel to the right with CW circling while gesturing up (place high)

5.8e

Travel to the left with CW circling while gesturing down (place low)

5.8f

A lowering or rising (a vertical change) of the body-as-a-whole is also written outside the path sign. For a specific statement, the sign for body-as-a-whole is used, 5.8g.

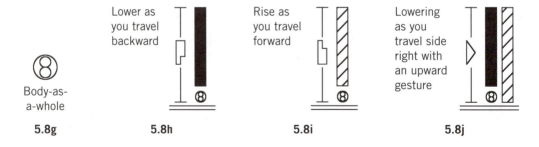

Body-as-a-whole

5.8g

Lower as you travel backward

5.8h

Rise as you travel forward

5.8i

Lowering as you travel side right with an upward gesture

5.8j

Note that direction of travel is shown with a blank direction symbol.

Statement of level outside the path sign, as in 5.8h, affects the level of steps. If indication of level as well as direction is given **within the path sign**, this refers to the **path itself**, uphill or downhill travel.

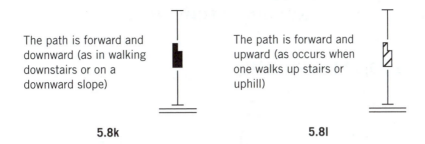

The path is forward and downward (as in walking downstairs or on a downward slope)

The path is forward and upward (as occurs when one walks up stairs or uphill)

5.8k   5.8l

These examples are only a few of many possible combinations involving traveling, directional gestures, and changes in level of the body-as-a-whole.

Notes on Reading Study No. 20

DIRECTIONAL GESTURES

This simple study may be performed with many variations, yet the basic instructions will have been followed.

Some questions will come up regarding how much freedom in interpretation is allowed. Is a step backward permitted to accompany the backward action in measure 6? Would such a step be considered traveling? Yes, if the step is large and there is a full transference of weight. There should be no significant moving away from the original spot; however, a shift of weight may occur to augment the directional movement.

The result of movement into a direction is retained during the stillness. Generally, a new movement produces automatic cancellation of the result of a previous movement and of course, of stillness. Note use of the hold sign: o in measure 4 to indicate retention of the side high gestures during the pathway. This retention will be automatically cancelled by the new gestures in measure 5. In measure 7, the side low gesture during the circling may remain, but need not.

Since the feet will be involved in traveling, accompanying directional actions will likely be performed mainly by the arms and trunk, as the performer chooses. Explore several different ways to perform these accompanying gestures.

The repeat sign ÷ is given next to the upbeat to measure 1 and again at the end of count 3 of measure 8; this indicates that this study is to be performed twice. The measure numbers in parentheses are for the second time through. When the study is repeated, the movement need not be an identical repeat of that previously chosen; variation in interpretation of the same instructions is allowed. The 5/8 meter may be unfamiliar, but the music composed for this study will lead you into the correct time patterns.

READING STUDY NO. 20

DIRECTIONAL GESTURES

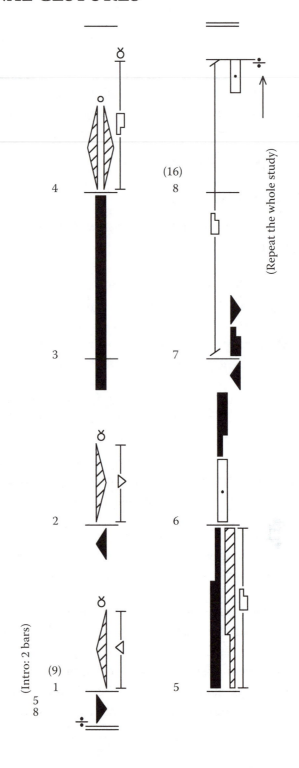

Notes on Reading Study No. 21

DIRECTIONS WITH TRAVELING AND SPRINGING

Reading Study No. 21 combines traveling, directions, and springing. Because of the low level preparation for the first spring, and the fact that the spring spends count 2 in the air, it is likely that both arms will shoot up as well as the body, but other possibilities exist. Gestures accompanying springs need not be full limb gestures. For example, with elbows dropped, both lower arms and hands could be extended up, either symmetrically or with one arm higher than the other.

Although jumping from two feet to two feet is comfortable for a big spring, the take-off or landing could use only one leg, the knee of the other leg lifting up high near the chest to express the upward gesture. In measure 5, only the knees could be going sideward while in the air, rather than both whole legs.

Note the use of Front signs to indicate where the performer is facing.

凸   means face Front, the audience or front of the room

中   means face the back of the room (stage)

The Front sign is given for the starting position and whenever a change in the performer's front occurs. Placed after a turn, or at the completion of a circular pathway, it confirms the new direction faced. Notice the change of Front in measure 8 and a return to Front in measure 10.

DIRECTIONS WITH TRAVELING AND SPRINGING

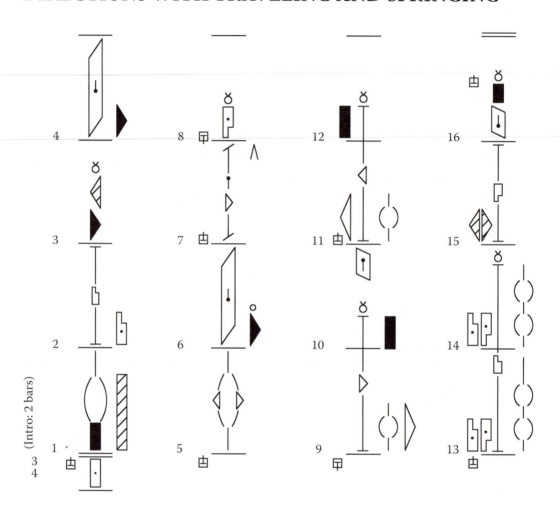

INTERPRETATION OF PLACE (CENTER)

At the center of all directions is "place middle," 5.9a. For a gesture of an arm or leg, place middle occurs when the extremity is near the base, as illustrated in 5.7a. For the body-as-a-whole, in Motif Description, it also provides a centered, neutral situation or position for the body. Used as a starting position, 5.9a, it means a simple standing position, feet more or less together, arms hanging down, 5.9b; this is taken to be a neutral position. Often when one is standing, waiting, the arms are held casually bent, the elbows near the waist, the hands near the chest, 5.9c. In this position there must be no tension in the arms, as tension immediately produces a set position giving the impression that this particular arm placement is of importance. Tension in a limb draws the viewer's eye to that part; a drop in energy, a relaxation of the muscles, allows a limb or the torso to have a passive, neutral expression. If the place middle indication of 5.9a occurs after a low level support, it is understood to mean a return to normal standing on the feet.

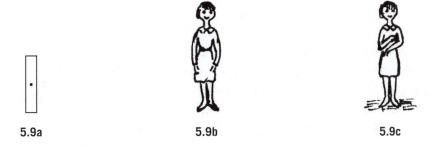

5.9a   5.9b   5.9c

INTERPRETATION, EXPRESSION OF DIRECTIONAL ACTIONS

Now that fundamental information for directional actions has been presented, a depth of interpretation will be given for additional exploration. Let us first investigate a range of choices for expression of directional indications.

How should a forward horizontal directional instruction be interpreted? If one is concerned with, let us say, the right arm, how many different kinds of gestures into the direction of 5.10a are there? Is there a range of expression in this direction?

5.10a

As the body is built to walk forward, the face is normally to this direction and so is the chest: in short, it is the whole front of the body that we present to those

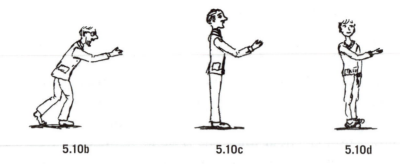

5.10b   5.10c   5.10d

we trust. Forward is the direction of communication. Example 5.10b shows a man moving toward someone; the forward arm gesture is accompanied by a forward inclination of the torso, a postural change that is in harmony with the gesture. In 5.10c, there is no postural forwardness, only an isolated arm gesture. We see at once that this position produces a much weaker forward expression. In 5.10d, a reverse postural action has accompanied the forward gesture. The turning away of the chest and head produces an expression of distrust, of unwillingness, of fear, some form of a negative, a withdrawal of feeling.

The intensity of the expressiveness of any directional movement need not lie in the degree of spatial extension. A minor movement can be more expressive of a partic- ular direction than the actual physical achievement of that direction by a limb. Example 5.10e shows a small but expressive postural leaning forward, while 5.10f shows a person taken aback.

5.10e   5.10f

How might the side middle symbol of 5.10g be interpreted? A stretched arm extended sideward, as in 5.10h, may give more the impression of a railway signal, 5.10i, rather than an expressive arm gesture. In contrast, a slight leaning or shift- ing of the body may convey a much stronger directional message. Compare 5.10h with 5.10j. Much rests on the manner in which the action is performed, the stress, emphasis, etc., which is easily observed in the movement but cannot be shown so readily in illustrations on paper.

A vertically upward movement, represented by 5.10k, will be explored next. Looking up, particularly when accompanied by a lift in the chest and a slight upward gesture of one hand as in 5.10l, can express "up" more strongly than a mechanically performed rise onto the toes with arms extended overhead shown in 5.10m.

Gestures upward or downward, i.e., above or below the horizontal plane, are usually familiar in meaning. Upward movements express great joy, hope, longing,

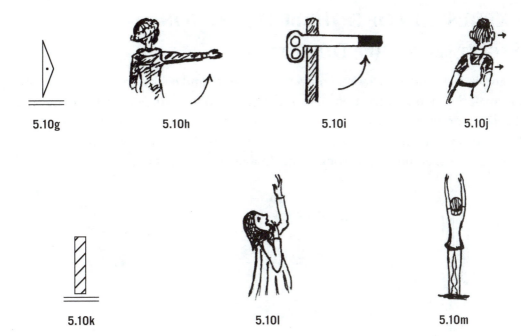

5.10g   5.10h   5.10i   5.10j

5.10k   5.10l   5.10m

lofty thoughts, prayer to a higher being. Upward pull in the body gives self-assurance, self-assertion. It is the direction against gravity, against Fate, whereas downward motion, giving in to gravity, expresses giving in to Fate, giving up, dejection, despair. These affinities are well known; and awareness of them as clear possibilities for expressive use in performance or for choreography is advantageous.

For sagittal gestures, use of one side of the body can extend the spatial range. The upper body may turn, i.e., be included if one arm is being used, or the hips may turn when one leg is active. The original front direction is maintained by the rest of the body. In 5.10n, as the arm reaches backward, the upper body is included. Inclusion of the hip provides longer extension of the leg, illustrated in 5.10o.

5.10n   5.10o

Exploration is needed to find out how much variation in expressing each direction is possible, and how certain gestures, accompanied by the focus of the face, weaken or strengthen the expression of the direction. All of these examples have included expression of a single direction, now we will explore double directions.

EXPRESSION OF DOUBLE DIRECTIONS
SAGITTAL DOUBLE DIRECTIONS

Example 5.11a states horizontal movement forward and backward at the same time, an equal pull in both directions. An *arabesque* used in skating as well as in dancing is a familiar example, 5.11b. Even if both arms as well as the free leg are gesturing backward, the forward extension of the torso and the face looking forward can provide sufficient emphasis to produce the double directional pull, 5.11c.

| 5.11a | 5.11b | 5.11c |

LATERAL DOUBLE DIRECTIONS
Open Lateral Directions

The laterally symmetrical build of the body makes balanced sideward movements more comfortable and easier to perform than movements in sagittal directions. This is particularly true of the open sideward directions. Examples 5.12a–5.12f illustrate the expressiveness of these seemingly simple positions. Note the change in expression when the feet are also opened sideward and also the differences resulting from the level of the arms. Some common interpretations are given in 5.12a–5.12f.

5.12a
Simplicity, modesty: "Here I am." or "At your service."

5.12b
"Welcome!" or "There it is!"

5.12c
"Marvelous news!" or perhaps "Please! Please be quiet!"

The open stance expresses confidence, stability, and the establishment of self. A different use of the head and of palm facing could change the meaning of each stance illustrated in 5.12d–5.12f.

5.12d
"This is what I am,
I have nothing to hide."

5.12e
Presentation, self
assertion or in command:
"I'm ready for anything!"

5.12f
"Success!" "We are
the victors!"

Oppositional Lateral Directions

A lateral oppositional pull can occur with a torso tilt, as in 5.12g in which the free leg extends in opposition to the torso and arm. Such a position is comparable to the sagittal *arabesque* in that the arms may extend in the same or opposite direction as the leg. Example 5.12h is a similar position but the change from supporting on the leg (a vertical support) to lying on the ground affects the overall statement.

5.12g

5.12h

Crossed Lateral Double Directions

Gestures that cross the body allow for more stylization since they are uncommon in everyday life; usually the preference is to turn toward the object or person and use forward gestures.

The crossed lateral double directions, 5.12i, contrast strongly with the open double directions. The legs and arms cross the center line of the body, thus expressing concealment, self-protection, a shutting out of the rest of the world, like the miserable clown in 5.12j. This is particularly true when the crossing involves a twist in the torso, a turning away from the viewer, expressing furtiveness, as in 5.12k.

5.12i

5.12j

5.12k

Vertical Dimension, Vertical Column

Gestures can be confined to the vertical dimension, moving up and down, in and around the vertical column that surrounds the torso when the performer is in the upright state. This column can be imagined to extend upward beyond the shoulders. Movements can explore the "inside" of this column in the upward direction, close around the torso and also below, around the legs, 5.13a. For lower exploration with the hands near the ground, the body needs to bend; hence the vertical column is no longer evident to the observer. But the performer can sense it in that the concept of the vertical dimension has not disappeared. As stated earlier, the vertical line is represented by the rectangle 5.13b. A vertical ad lib. sign placed within this sign, 5.13c, states anywhere on the vertical line, any level. Example 5.13d illustrates the idea of this column.

| 5.13a | 5.13b | 5.13c | 5.13d |

Opposing Vertical Directions

Use of oppositional directions can produce strong counter tensions, each direction being given full value. Interesting combinations can occur in simultaneous use of upward and downward actions, 5.13e. Perhaps one arm is extended up, the other down, as in 5.13f. Downward gestures can be counterbalanced by the face looking strongly upward. Such combinations often cause a particular tension; for example, the strongly lifted stance with downward weight in Spanish dance, or the upward "pull" which accompanies a controlled deep knee bend, a *grand plié,* to assist balance and a smooth lowering. Despairing gestures may occur upward while the body sags,

| 5.13e | 5.13f | 5.13g |

giving in to the downward pull of gravity, illustrated in 5.13g. Many stylized actions produce double "pulls" within the body, double tensions that may result from a use of energy directed in relation to gravity.

PATHWAY OF DIRECTIONAL MOVEMENT

Directional points such as forward horizontal, straight up, side high (slanting upward), side low (slanting downward), straight down, etc., are familiar, particularly in relation to gestures of the arms and legs. A common first interpretation of a directional instruction is to place an extended limb into the direction, as though pointing to the destination. Such indication of a direction is indeed strong, although it may not produce the strongest expression of movement into that particular direction. A directional action is most strongly expressed by a gesture when a spoke-like direct path is taken. This is because the destination and the direction of progression (the path) are one and the same movement.

Such an action occurs when the movement originates near the body center and moves out on a straight path. Example 5.14a states use of center (place middle) in preparation for the forward action. This is illustrated in the punching action of the arm, 5.14b. A kicking leg gesture can have more of the body weight behind it if the foot starts near the hip and thrusts out from there, 5.14c.

5.14a   5.14b   5.14c

Many movements may be from a spatially central situation to a spatially peripheral point. Let us take an ordinary example for the arm in which the hand starts close to the shoulder (in place), as in 5.14d. From there the hand travels on a path forward horizontal, 5.14e, and arrives with the arm normally stretched at the forward horizontal destination, 5.14f.

The motion, the direction of progression, is forward horizontal, and so is the final destination, the final placement of the limb.

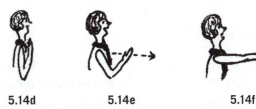

5.14d   5.14e   5.14f

The movement of 5.14d to 5.14f is therefore stronger in expressing forward horizontal than is 5.14g in which the arm moves on an arc toward its destination. Because the arm travels on an arc, the viewer cannot be sure where it will end; only when the limb stops is the destination forward horizontal clear.

5.14g

The curved movement line of 5.14h has a very different expression and function. Starting down, the motion is one of rising as it moves forward. Until it stops, there is no way of knowing the aim, the directional destination. The curved path might be enjoyed for its own sake, the destination being unimportant. In the case of a leg movement such a curved path is functional for a football kick, the curved action lifting the ball into the air, 5.14i. Where this leg gesture will terminate is not known.

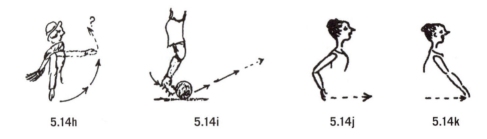

| 5.14h | 5.14i | 5.14j | 5.14k |

Examples 5.14j and 5.14k show a motion, a forward horizontal path for the right arm, the extremity, the hand describing this path. As neither the starting position nor the ending situation is the point forward horizontal, once the motion has ceased, the forward horizontality of the movement has disappeared; it was evident only during the period of motion. This perception of direction, the **direction of progression** will be covered later.

DESTINATION, MOTION

In exploring the physical possibilities for axial directional movements, two categories exist—**Destination** and **Motion**. Details on these are explored fully in Chapter 20; here they are introduced only briefly.

DESTINATION

The expressiveness of directional movement has been discussed. Example 5.14b illustrated arrival of a limb at a stated direction, and 5.14h showed a motion toward the same direction. Not only is the expression different but also the concepts underlying these two movements are different. Used as a destination, the direction symbol of 5.15a should mean arrival at the place high point, illustrated in 5.15b. This destination could also be expressed as an action with the aim of arriving at place high, 5.15c. How one gets there may be quite open, as indicated in 5.15d, "any action" being indicated.

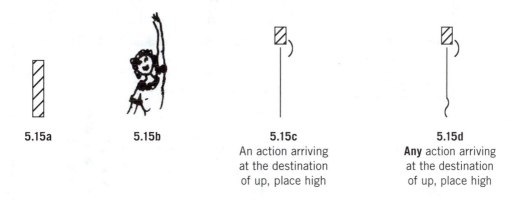

5.15a	5.15b	5.15c	5.15d
		An action arriving at the destination of up, place high	**Any** action arriving at the destination of up, place high

MOTION

The intent of an action may be on going **toward** a directional point and not on the arrival. The elongated "V" sign in 5.16a indicates a motion "toward;" in 5.16b the motion is toward place high, i.e., a vertically upward movement. How far such an upward movement travels is not indicated, often distance may not be important, as illustrated in 5.16c and 5.16d. Movement awareness is on the "going," vs. the goal of reaching a destination featured in the previous examples. The inverted V, 5.16e, is the sign for motion "away." In 5.16f, the movement is away from place high. The result will be a downward movement, but the intent is not related to down, but to leaving, moving away from up.

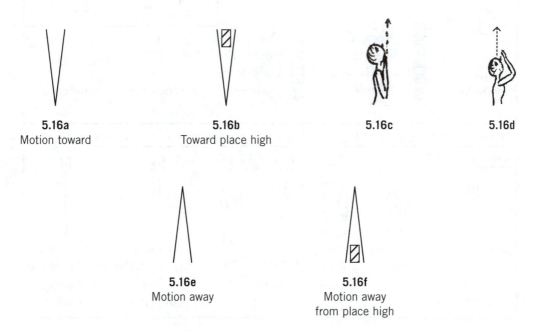

5.16a	5.16b	5.16c	5.16d
Motion toward	Toward place high		

5.16e	5.16f
Motion away	Motion away from place high

REVIEW FOR CHAPTER FIVE

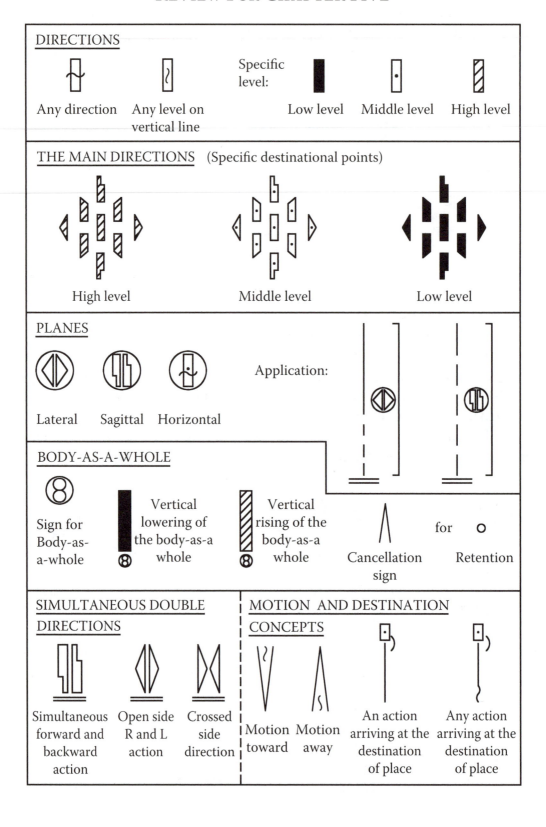

DIRECTIONS

Any direction   Any level on vertical line   Specific level: Low level   Middle level   High level

THE MAIN DIRECTIONS   (Specific destinational points)

High level   Middle level   Low level

PLANES

Lateral   Sagittal   Horizontal   Application:

BODY-AS-A-WHOLE

Sign for Body-as-a-whole

Vertical lowering of the body-as-a whole

Vertical rising of the body-as-a whole

Cancellation sign

for   Retention

SIMULTANEOUS DOUBLE DIRECTIONS

Simultaneous forward and backward action

Open side R and L action

Crossed side direction

MOTION AND DESTINATION CONCEPTS

Motion toward   Motion away

An action arriving at the destination of place

Any action arriving at the destination of place

CHAPTER SIX

Direction—Broader Exploration of Space

From the specific movement investigation of space in relation to the 27 main directions given in Chapter 5, we now open up to investigate broader aspects of direction. The possibilities include being very general, such as allowing freedom in exploring spatial areas and how directions and levels can be given open interpretations. The scope in such openness and the resultant range in movement performance and expression will now be considered.

THE SPHERE WITHIN WHICH WE MOVE—THE KINESPHERE

In the course of exploring traveling in Chapter 5, we explored the **general space** provided by the room. This space is "communal property," so to speak, in that we all share and use it. In moving through the room, called **locomotor movement**, the performer transports his/her own center. When no traveling occurs, movement that takes place on the spot is called **axial movement** because it is around the center, the axis. The space available for such movement is one's own **personal space**. It is the space which our limbs can reach while we remain in one place, a bubble within which we move. This sphere is called the kinesphere.

Within the kinesphere is our "reach" space, the zone within which our arms and legs can move, flexing and extending, our extremities describing large sweeping circles. The torso can also incline, twist, and circle within this sphere. In exploring the space available within the kinesphere, the limbs need to sense the space almost as though it is tangible, like a cloud that can be "felt" as you move through it.

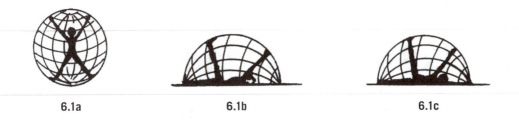

6.1a   6.1b   6.1c

Example 6.1a illustrates this sphere surrounding a performer. When we are lying on the ground, this sphere is cut in half. When lying on your back, 6.1b, only the front half of the kinesphere is available. The reverse is true when you lie on your front. Lying on the right side, 6.1c, makes the left half sphere available for movement, and so on. When we travel, this sphere moves with us. It is our own individual area, our "personal space" that we share only with friends.

Explore the range of movement possible within this sphere, for the arms, legs, and torso, and for combined arm and torso, and leg and torso movements, trying all the possibilities without changing location. Explore "near" space, the area close to your center. In exploring this near space, we are aware of the distance, the nearness, not of the degree of arm, leg, or torso bend used; that is a very different focus. Then explore "far" space, out at the periphery of the kinesphere, the emphasis of the movement is not on the action of extending, the stretching of the limb, but of reaching the fullest expanse of the kinesphere. To explore far space the limbs must extend, and this extension, this reaching out, may involve torso inclusion. Several forms of body inclusion are possible, but none should lead to traveling. Axial movements have their own statement to make.

Experiment with lying on the ground, with changing from standing to lying and to standing again. Imagine the sphere as a great balloon filled with air and you, like the wind blowing leaves before it, moving that air, causing dust particles to rise, to float, to swirl and to whirl. Another image is to think of this space as a volume of water in which you are fully immersed. Drops of color in the water are changed to colored swirls, to spirals, to thin wisps by your movement. Mix the colors from one area with those in another. Every part of the area within the kinesphere can be "felt" as you move through the "water."

MOVEMENT IN THE GENERAL DIRECTIONAL AREAS

Let us now explore gestural movement in the **areas** that lie around the main dimensional directions. A general gesture forward may be anywhere in the area in front of the body. General backward gestures occur behind the body. Similarly sideward area gestures lie at the right and left sides of the body. Example 6.2a is a bird's-eye view of these areas. Also to be explored are the upward, overhead areas (above horizontal) and the downward area (below horizontal), as illustrated in 6.2b.

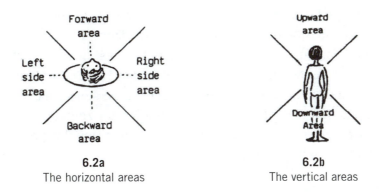

6.2a
The horizontal areas

6.2b
The vertical areas

Gestures in the directional areas are usually easily understood and performed. Curved gestures, arcs, figure eights, etc., are good for making full use of the area to be explored. If downward movements result in a lowering to the floor to sitting, leg gestures can then only be horizontal or move in the high area. In a lying position, this is also true for the arms. As mentioned before, part of the kinesphere is not available. Such a major change in our body situation in relation to our point of support affects the range and expressiveness of directional movement. The greatest range, and therefore the broadest spectrum of possibilities for contrast, occurs when the performer is standing.

Experiment with gestures in these various areas, not aiming for any clear destination, but for an awareness of how such forward area gestures differ in expression from those in the side or backward areas. Explore movement in the upward area and how this is very different from movement in the downward area.

An idea in exploring these areas of direction is to imagine yourself in the dark in a strange room. You tentatively extend your arms, and reach out with your foot to find out what is there. What is at your right? At your left? Behind you? What is above? Is there an obstacle? Is there space in which you can move? Gradually all areas are tested and found to be free.

You can explore these areas of directions using a scarf or ribbon as a visual aid in producing air designs in each area in turn, enjoying, and discovering the full range. Such explorations enrich the understanding and physical experience of how these areas can be used expressively. In composing movement, this kind of investigation can be valuable in opening exploration of every aspect.

EXPLORATION OF MIDDLE LEVEL (HORIZONTAL) AREA—HORIZONTAL PLANE

Horizontal (think of horizon) means, of course, parallel with the floor. Arms move quite comfortably at shoulder level and for most dancers, hip-level leg gestures are comfortable. For our purposes, the horizontal area allows a certain amount of space above and below this true horizontal line as in 6.3a. Straying upward or downward does not detract from the horizontal expression if such change of level is just incidental and not being featured, i.e., a circular horizontal gesture might rise somewhat as it progresses giving it a more three-dimensional expression, without any statement of rising being made.

6.3a   Movement in the horizontal area   **6.3b**

Placement of the torso in a horizontal direction provides a strong statement. Positions and movements used in ice skating are very appropriate: the long extended *arabesque* position, the backward tilt of the torso with the free leg forward, and the sideward horizontal tilt with arms and the free leg also sideward. For dance these positions may be used as transitions, placements to be passed through. Horizontal explorations involving the torso (alone or with accompanying arm gestures) occur more comfortably when bending the supporting leg(s).

A horizontal torso tilt can avoid the expression of a downward movement by the forward focus of the head, as in 6.3b. Horizontal placement of the body may suggest suspension, as in floating on water. Indeed, arm gestures may be reminiscent of those used in the breaststroke.

INTRODUCTION OF AREA SIGN

Example 6.3c, the symbol for "area," is combined with the "any horizontal" (middle level) indication in 6.3d to represent the whole middle level area, which includes all horizontal directions.

6.3c
An area

6.3d
Middle level, horizontal area

Horizontal gestures can occur while kneeling, although here the possible participation of a leg in gesturing is diminished. Kneeling provides great stability in reaching out and exploring backward gestures. From the knees it is an easy transition to sitting and then lying down. Horizontal gestures should first be explored while on the back. "Wait a minute!" you say. "I am on the floor; surely I am **down!**" Spatially, in relation to the vertical line, yes, but physically you are in a horizontal plane. You can move your arms and legs in various horizontal directions, unfolding, or circling them. The legs can perform full circles moving over to the side, beyond your head and around to the other side before returning to where they started. The arms can sweep along the floor and, with the assistance of the torso can make an enormous circle beyond the feet and all the way around. When one lies on his/her side, the sense of direction changes, but not of horizontality. Here there is quite a range of possible horizontal area movements. The range of movement is limited when lying on the front, hence this situation serves best as a transition from lying on one side to the other.

EXPLORATION OF HIGH LEVEL (UPWARD) AREA

The upward area, above horizontal, is most easily explored with the arms; their expression may be augmented by a rise in the body, a lifting of the knee or a high leg extension.

As mentioned before, movements upward may express great longing, joy, ecstasy, perhaps praying, reaching for the unattainable. Up is the direction of pride. Up is away from the fetters of gravity. Heaven is above, not below, and upward gestures may suggest lofty thoughts, communication with higher beings, spiritual ideas. In all directional actions, use of the head, where you are looking, may strongly change the expression. Looking up or looking down while gesturing upward affects the meaning. In 6.4a, the symbol for "area" is combined with the "any upward or high level" indication to represent the whole high level area, as illustrated in 6.4b.

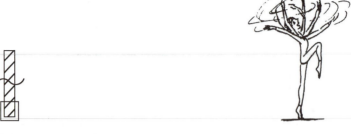

6.4a   Movement in the upward, high level area   **6.4b**

While standing, try the following explorations: an arm rises and gestures upward, the face looks up, and the other arm joins in. What else can be done? Let us assume that most people do not have high leg extensions and so the possibility of incorporating leg gestures in high area movements is limited. Within that upward area, the arms can make circles along the periphery, figure eights, many curved, convoluted "paths," still staying in that area.

Variation can be achieved by moving one arm at a time, then both together, overlapping, etc. If the arms are used in one piece, variation is limited. Allow the arms to bend a little, or a lot. Try sequential movements, a succession in the arm, an unfolding. Allow rotations to occur, these provide a more three-dimensional use of space. The upper body can join in through twisting to augment the range so that the backward-upward area can be more comfortably explored. Leaning the upper body backward can also provide greater scope.

This whole exploration can also be undertaken while kneeling or sitting. It would seem that lowering the body-as-a-whole to the knees would detract from the up-ness of the upward area, but in fact it does not. This is because the area relates to the kinesphere around the person as well as to the level in the vertical line. While on the knees, rising to a high kneel, or a partial rising, can enrich upward gestures. Explore movement with the upper body and arms to find variations in timing and use of emphasis (dynamics).

In contrast to kneeling, sitting frees the possibilities for the legs to contribute to exploration of the upward area of the kinesphere. The torso will have to lean backward or sideward and probably weight taken on a hand to free the leg(s) to gesture upward, as in 6.4c.

6.4c

While lying, arm and leg gestures can easily explore upward movement, as in 6.4d. Upward leg gestures can be augmented by inclusion of pelvis and inverted torso, as in a shoulder stand, 6.4e. Try progressing from lying through sitting, kneeling to standing, and to an upward spring in expressing the upward direction. There are many ways in which such a progression can be achieved.

6.4d   6.4e

Having consciously investigated all these possibilities and the result each produces, check off in your mind how each feels, then drop out of this "state" completely, let the whole body go neutral, perhaps have a good shake, a limp drooping down to the floor to clear your muscular and expressive responses. Now start another upward area exploration, but this time allow the variations to emanate from an inner feeling, an inner desire to move the hands, the arms, to use the head, to expand the chest as they lift upward. In other words, movement will result from the feeling and not from a cerebral instruction. Begin to compose a sequence, a composition that unfolds in an organic way and which is rewarding to perform as well as interesting to see.

Exploration of Low Level (Downward) Area

For movement in the downward area of the kinesphere, below horizontal, leg gestures slanting downward are appropriate as well as low arm gestures augmented by bending the torso, 6.5a. Expressively, downward is the direction of humility, of sorrow, of despair. We lower ourselves as we bow; we hang our heads in shame. It is the direction of earthiness, or relating to the earth in a practical or expressive way. Example 6.5b shows the area box combined with the "any low level" indication to represent the whole low level area.

6.5a   Movement in the downward, low level area   6.5b

For exploration of low area movements, a far greater range can be achieved when standing. The downward-slanting leg gestures can be touching and sliding along the floor. Downward arm gestures, augmented through body inclusions, can involve bending at the hip joints. However, if the torso stays in a horizontal direction, it can detract from the expression of the downward area, even if the face is looking down. A passing "downward" movement of the torso that accompanies and enriches low gestures of the arm(s) need not go below horizontal, but the motion downward is what the observer should see and the dancer feel, **not** a position reached, a destination. Again, timing and dynamics can make the difference here.

Movement in the low area is usually more familiar and more comfortable, thus studies composed within this limitation can vary a great deal. After initial exploration, compose a study concerned with the low area, which grows out of an inner desire to move from within.

When lying, low level gestures are possible if one is supporting on a bench, then arm and leg gestures can be performed below horizontal, as in 6.5c.

6.5c

EXPLORATION OF THE FORWARD AREA

Movement in the forward area includes some width, as illustrated in 6.6a, and all levels, upward and downward, as in 6.6b. In addition, these movements may be near the body or extended out. Movement in a forward area is represented by 6.6c; the open direction symbol, allows any level. However, the addition of the vertical ad lib. sign, as in 6.6d is often preferred as there is then no question that statement of level has been omitted. Movement in the forward area is illustrated in 6.6e.

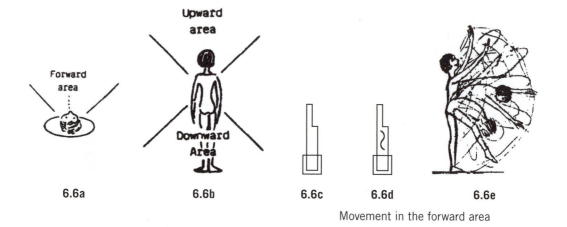

Forward area

Upward area

Downward Area

6.6a   6.6b   6.6c   6.6d   6.6e

Movement in the forward area

As you explore directional areas, notice your movement choice. Is it a one-sided movement? Is it an isolated gesture, of an arm perhaps, or is the arm gesture "supported" by other parts, perhaps augmented by a body inclusion, an inclination of the torso? Does a leg gesture accompany the action, or is it the focal point of the action? In a forward movement, is the weight shifting into that direction? If torso, arms, and a leg move forward, how is balance maintained?

EXPLORATION OF THE BACKWARD AREA

What movement possibilities exist in the backward area? Mobility is much more restricted than for forward actions. Backward arm gestures often require rotation in the shoulder joint, a chest inclusion of some kind or a slight turn in the upper body, as in 6.7a. Any turning action for this purpose is not a change of Front; the rest of the body maintains the previous forward/backward direction. Backward torso tilts may need to be balanced by one leg moving slightly forward. Such a leg action should not be given importance; the emphasis should still be on the backward motion. Examples 6.7b and 6.7c show the symbols for the backward area, in any level.

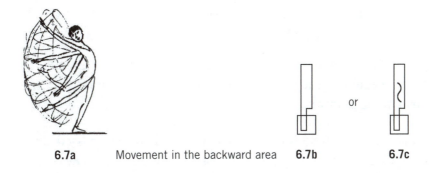

6.7a   Movement in the backward area   **6.7b**   or   **6.7c**

EXPLORATION OF THE SIDEWARD AREAS

The vertical center line divides the body into right and left sides, creating a natural symmetry. Let us first explore use of one side.

In exploring the sideward areas, you should discover the many possibilities for gestures using the open side of the body, the right side for the right arm or leg, the left side for the left. Then explore the closed gestures, those in which the limbs cross the center line of the body. There is a world of difference between use of the open or closed sides, not only in the physical freedom of the open side and in the limitations or restrictions of the closed side, but also in the contrast in expression.

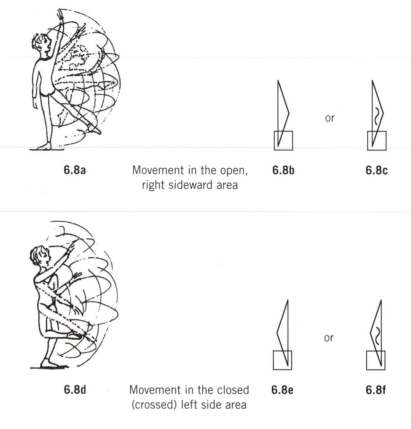

6.8a   Movement in the open,   **6.8b**   **6.8c**
right sideward area

6.8d   Movement in the closed   **6.8e**   **6.8f**
(crossed) left side area

Example 6.8a illustrates gestures into the open sideward area, the right side in this case, represented by the symbol in 6.8b or 6.8c. Torso movement may accompany an arm or leg gesture.

In contrast to 6.8a, 6.8d illustrates use of the closed or crossed side; the right side of the body crossing to the left side area is represented by 6.8e or 6.8f. Though physically not as easy to perform, such actions are very expressive and, because they are less natural, are often used in an exaggerated form in comic and grotesque dances or for unusual body design.

MOVEMENT IN THE AREAS AROUND SPECIFIC DIRECTIONS

As we previously indicated, the symbol for any direction combined with the sign for "an area" is used to show any directional area, as in 6.9a. The whole high level directional area is shown in 6.9b, illustrated in 6.9c and 6.9d. Specifying the place high area in 6.9e narrows the size of the area as shown in 6.9f and 6.9g. This defining of the area is applicable to all 27 main directions, 6.9h–6.9j.

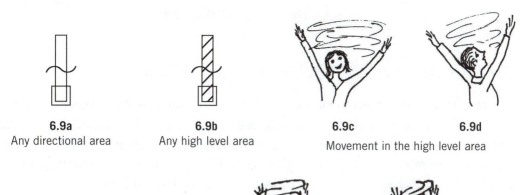

6.9a
Any directional area

6.9b
Any high level area

6.9c

6.9d

Movement in the high level area

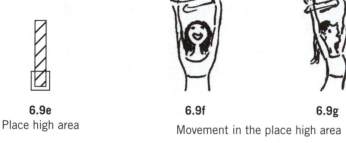

6.9e
Place high area

6.9f

6.9g

Movement in the place high area

THE 27 MAIN DIRECTIONAL AREAS

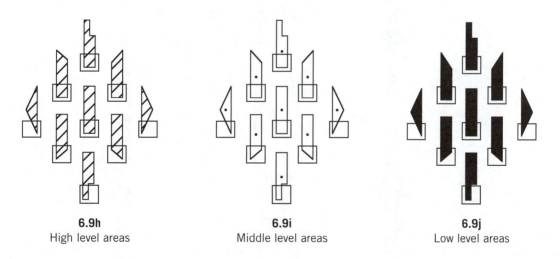

6.9h
High level areas

6.9i
Middle level areas

6.9j
Low level areas

READING STUDY NO. 22

AREAS OF DIRECTION FOR GESTURES

The emphasis in this study is on the freedom of directional areas and on experiencing the difference between moving within a broader general directional area and moving in the more limited area of a specific direction. At the start of this study, a quick upward movement to place high is followed by movement within the general high level area. Movement in the more limited area of place high then follows. Next, movement in any low level is followed by movement in the forward middle area. Find a style of movement that suggests enjoyment of such general spatial usage. In preparation for both measures 5 and 6, a swift movement to place provides a transition into the side middle area. Notice how this is used as a destinational transition

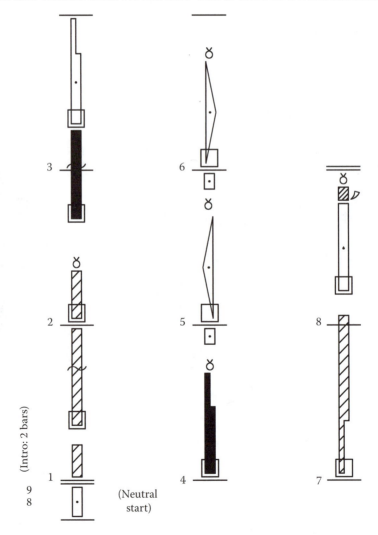

in contrast to moving in the place middle level area in measure 8. The pauses in measures 1 and 8 contrast with the instances of stillness. Note the slight accent which concludes the piece.

OPEN DIRECTION; OPEN LEVEL

FREEDOM IN CHOICE OF DIRECTION FOR STATED LEVEL

Whereas movement within a directional area featured unspecified motion, a movement in a particular level to an unstated direction ends as a destination. It is the choice of directional destination in that level which is open.

In the examples shown in 6.10a, 6.10b, and 6.10c level is stated, but, as indicated by the horizontal ad lib. sign, the direction to be performed is open to choice. Thus the indication of 6.10a, "any high level" may be performed as a forward, diagonal, sideward, backward, or any intermediate high level direction. The same directional choice is true of "any middle level," 6.10b, and "any low level," 6.10c.

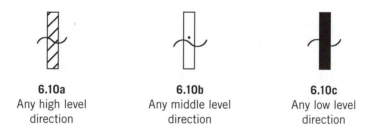

6.10a
Any high level
direction

6.10b
Any middle level
direction

6.10c
Any low level
direction

FREEDOM IN CHOICE OF LEVEL FOR STATED DIRECTION

A blank direction symbol, as in 6.10d gives no statement of level. A reinforced statement is made when the vertical ad lib. sign is placed within the symbol, as in 6.10e. This allows the level performed to be anywhere in the stated direction **between** up (place high) and down (place low). This usage is applicable to all directions, such as any level for right sideward shown in 6.10f or 6.10g.

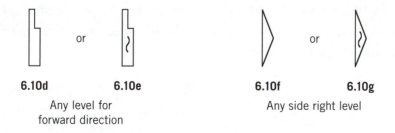

or   or

6.10d   **6.10e**
Any level for
forward direction

6.10f   **6.10g**
Any side right level

FREEDOM IN PERFORMANCE OF OPEN DIRECTIONS

When performing movements into various general directions, use can be made of the full body, torso, and/or limbs. In Language of Dance® a "gesture" refers to an action that does not involve weight bearing. Freedom in performing general directional actions will now be explored.

SAGITTAL GESTURES—FORWARD

The blank direction symbol of 6.11a indicates a movement forward in the sagittal plane with no level stated; 6.11b states the same thing, the vertical ad lib. sign within the symbol emphasizes the freedom in level. As illustrated in 6.11c, the arm gesture could end at any point in the forward sagittal plane. In the illustration of 6.11d, the arms end forward high; in 6.11e they end forward horizontal; while the placement is forward low in 6.11f. When level is indicated, a more specific result is expected. Direction and level for the limbs are judged by the relationship of the extremity to the point of attachment. For the arms, the hand is the extremity and the shoulder is the point of attachment.

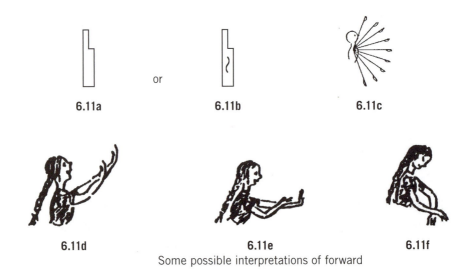

Some possible interpretations of forward

Next, this general sagittal statement is explored in a more general way to discover the possibilities. A directional movement may be an isolated action or, to add expressiveness, body participation may be included. However, no other major movement should occur, unless stated.

Thus the general forward action of 6.11a could be interpreted as in 6.11g–6.11j. In 6.11g, the gestures, posture, and face are all forward, a unity in directional expression. But what of 6.11h? One elbow is backward. Has this detracted from the forward "message," or is it a choreographic embellishment to add style and interest? What about 6.11i compared with 6.11g? Have the arms moving backward weakened the forward expression? In 6.11j the forward leg gesture requires a backward lean to maintain balance. Does this leaning destroy the forward expression? Not if the emphasis of the movement is clearly placed on the forward gestures, the backward leaning being unstressed. Try out various possibilities to discover how far accompanying directional actions can go before the main idea is overpowered and destroyed.

| 6.11g | 6.11h | 6.11i | 6.11j |

Variations on a forward movement

The full possibilities for expression in sagittal movements should be explored. Forward actions range from the natural expressions inherent in approaching someone, to give or take something, or to offering sympathy, etc. The different effects produced by using one arm or both should be experienced, and also different degrees of participation of the torso as a "support" to enhance the arm gesture. Experiment with the torso becoming equally important or even becoming the main movement, the arm gesture thus becoming a lesser accompaniment of the torso movement.

Use of sagittal directions as pure movement design can also be explored—try to find movements which have no "meaning" in the everyday sense, but are expressive through the gestural actions taken and the final destinations reached. All these movement explorations can be enriched by subtle, unobtrusive use of flexion, extension, and rotation or twists of various parts of the body. But none of these added actions should dominate the main directional movement.

SAGITTAL GESTURES—BACKWARD

Arm gestures in the backward direction are more restricted than in other directions because of the body build. Symmetrical backward gestures are particularly limited and finding variations in performance can be a challenge. Backward actions include withdrawing, expressing revulsion, or pulling back to get a better look.

6.12a   6.12b   6.12c   6.12d

6.12e   6.12f

Backward movements with symmetrical arm gestures

By stressing the arms in 6.12c, the movement can express a backward low direction. In moving the torso backward in this example, it may be necessary to balance the weight by a slight forward leg gesture. This gesture must have no importance, i.e., it must be a "neutral" action, without energy. If such a leg gesture were performed with too much energy, the result could be an equal forward-backward movement, a double directional emphasis. If, in this example, the torso lean is stressed and the arm gestures minimized, backward high direction can be expressed. In 6.12d the leg gesture reinforces the backward direction, arms and leg being of equal importance. In 6.12e turning the head to look backward contributes significantly to the backward expression. The head action in 6.12f can add the impression of looking backward, though, in this case, the unity in direction of arms and leg strongly establishes backward horizontal.

LATERAL GESTURES—SIDEWARD

The range of directional movements in the lateral plane can be shown in a similar way. A blank sideward symbol, 6.13a, or the more specific statement of 6.13b, indicate a gesture somewhere in the lateral plane, 6.13c. With no level stated, the gesture could end anywhere sideward between vertically up and down. Examples 6.13d, 6.13e, and 6.13f illustrate possible interpretations. Here both arms are at the same level, they could also arrive sideward in different levels and still fulfill the statement of 6.13a.

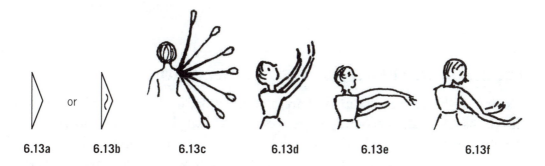

| 6.13a | 6.13b | 6.13c | 6.13d | 6.13e | 6.13f |

PROGRESSION IN DEFINING DIRECTIONS

In Chapter 5 and in this chapter, directions have been looked at in various ways. These ways have ranged from a movement to a specific directional point to unspecified movement in a directional area. We will now provide an overview to show the progression from the most general to most specific.

INCREASING SPECIFICITY FOR AREAS

The broadest statement, the greatest freedom in directional movement is that of any area of any direction, 6.14a. Becoming more specific, an area at any vertical level can be specified, 6.14b. Designating a direction gives the possibility of focusing on any level in that direction; the forward area of 6.14c is illustrated in 6.14e. This same openness of level is applicable to all directional areas. The blank direction symbol states any level, however, addition of the vertical ad lib. sign, as in 6.14d, is often preferred as then there is no question that statement of level has been forgotten.

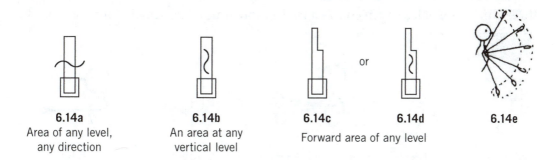

| 6.14a | 6.14b | 6.14c | 6.14d | 6.14e |
| Area of any level, any direction | An area at any vertical level | Forward area of any level | | |

Statement of an area around a specific direction and level, pins down the choice even more as shown in 6.14f and illustrated in 6.14g.

6.14f   6.14g

Forward middle area

INCREASING SPECIFICITY FOR DIRECTIONS

Leaving the broader exploration of areas of direction, focus will now be on stated directions, gradually becoming more specific. As explained earlier, movement to any direction of any level is stated in 6.15a. Any level on the vertical line is indicated in 6.15b. A movement to any forward level is shown in 6.15c; this can also be expressed as 6.15d, attention being drawn to the freedom in level. Example 6.15e illustrates the range of such a movement choice.

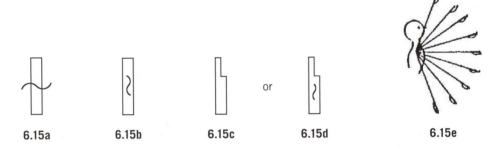

6.15a   6.15b   6.15c   or   6.15d   6.15e

Becoming more specific, 6.15f states a forward horizontal direction. In Motif Notation, the performance of such directions is not expected to be precise. Such leeway in performance could be written as in 6.15g, the vertical ad lib. sign next to the symbol stating more-or-less forward middle, illustrated in 6.15h. For a precise performance of this direction, an asterisk denoting "exact" is placed next to the direction symbol, 6.15i, illustrated in 6.15j. Note that an area provides greater three-dimensional leeway in contrast to the more limited destinational range based on a specific direction.

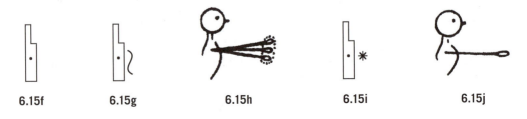

6.15f   6.15g   6.15h   6.15i   6.15j

REVIEW FOR CHAPTER SIX

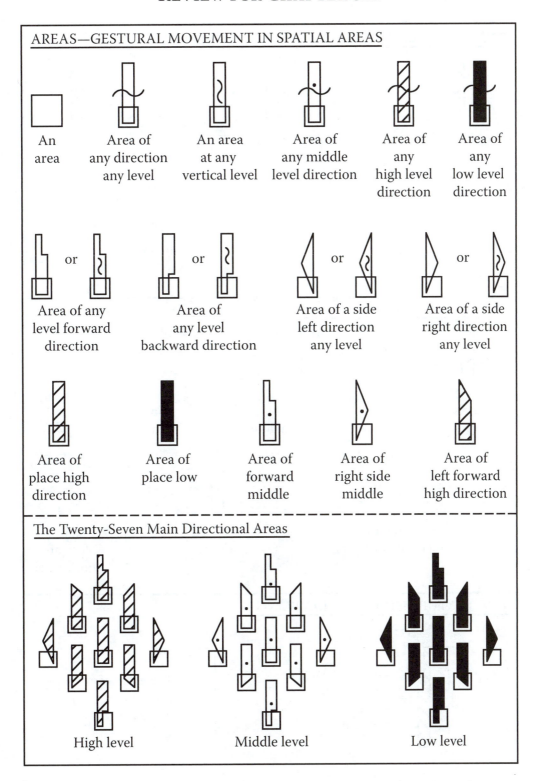

AREAS—GESTURAL MOVEMENT IN SPATIAL AREAS

An area

Area of any direction any level

An area at any vertical level

Area of any middle level direction

Area of any high level direction

Area of any low level direction

Area of any level forward direction *or*

Area of any level backward direction *or*

Area of a side left direction any level *or*

Area of a side right direction any level *or*

Area of place high direction

Area of place low

Area of forward middle

Area of right side middle

Area of left forward high direction

The Twenty-Seven Main Directional Areas

High level

Middle level

Low level

Review (continued)

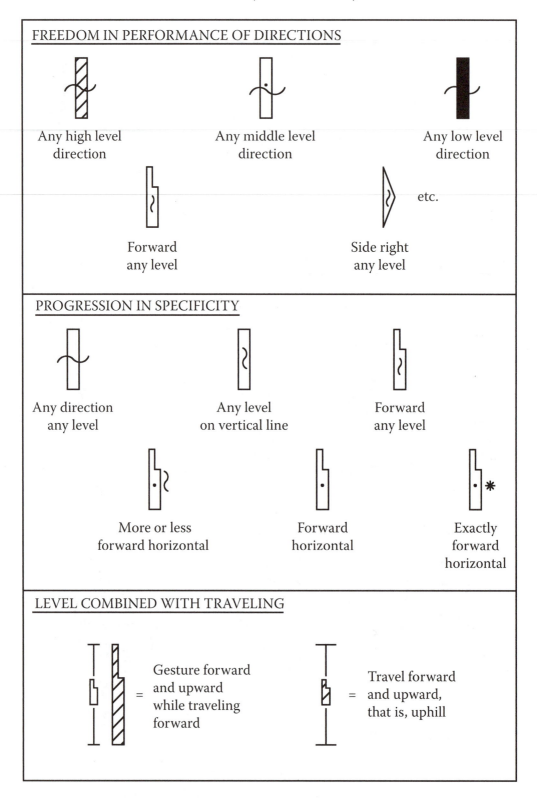

FREEDOM IN PERFORMANCE OF DIRECTIONS

Any high level
direction

Any middle level
direction

Any low level
direction

Forward
any level

Side right
any level

etc.

PROGRESSION IN SPECIFICITY

Any direction
any level

Any level
on vertical line

Forward
any level

More or less
forward horizontal

Forward
horizontal

Exactly
forward
horizontal

LEVEL COMBINED WITH TRAVELING

= Gesture forward
and upward
while traveling
forward

= Travel forward
and upward,
that is, uphill

CHAPTER SEVEN
Flexion; Extension

Perform the simplest action and, though you may have thought of it in other terms, you will doubtless have involved two or three of the "anatomical" prime actions. Because of the nature of the joints in the body and the sets of muscles which move the limb segments, we are able to flex and extend the joints and to rotate (twist) the limbs. These three basic actions—flexion, extension, and rotation—are so much a part of our daily functioning that we have to make a special point of thinking about them and observing when and how they are used in various movement forms.

All our lives we perform actions of flexion and extension without being aware of them because such actions usually occur for other reasons. Many of us curl up when going to sleep at night and enjoy yawning and stretching in the morning. General physical flexion also occurs when one is very cold and the body curls up to keep warm. These and other examples are rather personal actions, not usually performed for an audience. Putting on socks or tying a shoelace also requires doubling up. Reaching into a deep closet or up to a high shelf requires physical extension. Shyness will cause one to close in; joyousness brings expansion. For each of these examples of flexion or extension there is an outside object, purpose, or emotion for which the action is performed. **Flexion** and **Extension** are the "family" names for several specific forms; in this chapter we will focus on the basic forms. Specific forms will be given later in Chapter 17.

Use of space within the kinesphere can range from the most extended gestures, which fully explore the periphery of "reach space," to flexed gestures which occur close to the body, using "near space." Between these extremes lies "medium space."

153

The degree of physical flexion or extension given here are only in terms of a little or much, i.e., slight or marked.

FLEXION

What is the nature of the action of flexing? Flexion incorporates the following movement ideas: drawing in toward the center, becoming smaller, folding up, contracting, bending, closing in, adducting, narrowing, pulling in to a central point, retracting, shrinking, curving, curling up.

Each of these movement ideas evokes a different image—a snail retracting, a cat curling up, a flower folding as it droops, and so on. In most instances the manner of performance is different, and therein lies a whole world of exploration in the differences in expression. The degree of flexion may be partial or full. The action may involve several joints, or only one. The movement idea may be body-oriented (body-centered) or concerned with moving away from something, or with occupying less space. An action of drawing in may be one of hugging oneself with pleasure or drawing in away from some outside person, some danger, perhaps the result of fear.

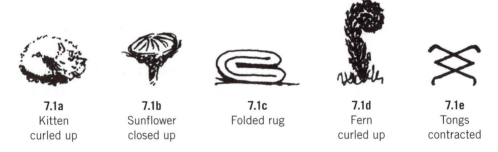

| **7.1a**
Kitten
curled up | **7.1b**
Sunflower
closed up | **7.1c**
Folded rug | **7.1d**
Fern
curled up | **7.1e**
Tongs
contracted |

For the moment, we are concerned with the kind of action, not the specific degree. However, for the general statements needed at this point, two degrees are distinguished—a little (small degree), or much (a greater degree).

The basic sign for the movement of flexion includes the sign for "any" (the ad lib. symbol), 7.1f, thus giving complete freedom as to which form of flexion may be used, 7.1g. By doubling the sign, as in 7.1h, we show a greater degree in the choice of any form of flexion. This greater degree is often used in this book to produce a more emphasized action.

| **7.1f**
Ad lib. | **7.1g**
A little flexion | **7.1h**
Much flexion |

The range for a little flexion is to arrive at a point less than halfway toward your body. Much flexion produces an ending more than halfway toward your body. Examples 7.1i and 7.1j illustrate the range for interpretation of each.

7.1i   **7.1j**

EXTENSION

Extension can take several forms and involve different movement concepts. What ideas, intentions, or aims belong to this category of movement? It may be reaching out, lengthening, stretching, elongating, opening out, separating, broadening, widening, expanding, moving out from the center, becoming larger, or growing. Again, each of these terms evokes a different image and movement quality.

Flexion and extension are partners in that frequently, use of one is followed by the other. We reach out to grasp an object, then bring it in close for inspection. The curled sleeping position is followed by the morning stretch. Breathing in, inflating the lungs, is followed by breathing out, deflating, compressing the lungs. One action may be a preparation for the other. The body enjoys the sensation of closing in or opening out—think of lying in the hot sun on the grass or a beach, curling up in front of a fire in the winter. Countless practical examples can be found.

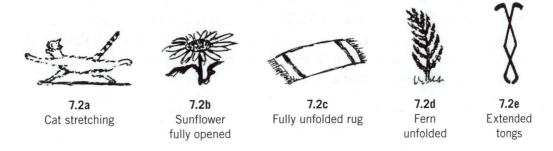

| **7.2a** | **7.2b** | **7.2c** | **7.2d** | **7.2e** |
| Cat stretching | Sunflower fully opened | Fully unfolded rug | Fern unfolded | Extended tongs |

How do these actions relate to dance movement? How are they used artistically? In dance, the two opposite actions are often enjoyed for their own sake. Consider the kind of physical delight evoked by the music of *Afternoon of a Faun*. In the Jerome Robbins version, the boy stretches languidly and then closes in. Many of the subsequent movements in the ballet concentrate on the body actions of extension and flexion, subjective, body-oriented, physically based actions. But let us first be concerned with simple, more naturalistic movements which perfectly express these ideas. Stylization, which can be very subtle, comes later.

The sign for any form of extension is 7.2f, which includes the symbol for "any" to give freedom of choice at this stage. The greater degree, very extended, is shown by 7.2g.

7.2f	**7.2g**
Extended	Very extended

Because our limbs are normally "straight" there is less distance to go in achieving extension. In extending a limb from its normal state when the arm is relaxed, hanging at the side of the body, as in 7.2h, the degree of extension is limited. When the arm is straightened, an extended state is achieved, shown in 7.2i. Very extended, reaching out, involves inclusion of the body, illustrated in 7.2j.

| **7.2h** | **7.2i** | **7.2j** |

A simple, basic movement pattern is illustrated in 7.2k. Here much flexion is followed immediately by great extension, then by stillness. If repeated several times, each performance could be different spatially, different in emphasis, etc. Example 7.2l starts with great extension and the stillness follows much flexion—a very different result. This pattern also has many possible interpretations, even without significant changes in timing.

| **7.2k** | **7.2l** |

EXTENSION: TERMINOLOGY

The word "extension" is used in this chapter and in Chapter 17 with the general meanings of lengthening, stretching, elongating, reaching out, expanding, and spreading. A different meaning is given to "extension" in anatomical terminology; there it is employed to mean the reverse of "flexion." For example, bending the wrist forward (toward the inner, palm side of the wrist) is called "flexion"; what is commonly called bending the wrist backward (toward the outer surface of the wrist) is called "wrist extension" in anatomical studies. Similarly, bending the torso forward is called "flexion," but a backward torso bend is called "extension." This special meaning for the word "extension" can be confusing for students who are studying anatomy and are also encountering other forms of movement analysis such as presented in this book. Consistency and logicality in use of terminology are important. It is interesting to note that in dance and other movement forms a backward torso bend can be performed as a relaxed curve (a flexion) and can also be performed as an extended backward arch in which the actions of elongating and of curving are combined in one movement.

DURATION OF FLEXION, EXTENSION

The actions of flexing and extending may be sudden or sustained. The signs for flexion and extension are not elongated to show extension in time, they remain a fixed size. The vertical line of an action stroke is attached and the length of this line indicates the length of time taken for the flexion or extension. Example 7.3a shows very little time, a swift action. A very short duration line, as in 7.3b, may be added to reinforce the brief length of duration. Example 7.3c shows a slower movement while 7.3d shows a flexion or extension of longer duration. The same applies to the double signs. We state first what the action is to be, then the duration. The vertical line provides only the meaning of length of time, the duration of the stated action; for this reason it is often called the **"duration line."** Observe how the patterns shown in 7.3a–7.3d vary in their use of time.

| 7.3a | 7.3b | 7.3c | 7.3d |

The symbols themselves occupy only a small amount of time but swiftness is not stressed. If a sharp, sudden movement is wanted, an accent, 7.3e, is added. Thus 7.3f shows a sudden, accented extension followed soon by a sudden, accented flexion.

or

Accent
signs

7.3e

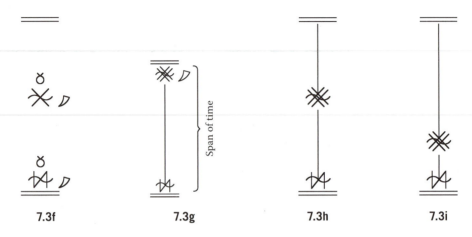

| 7.3f | 7.3g | 7.3h | 7.3i |

Perform each example repeatedly. In 7.3g a slow, sustained extension is followed by a sudden, accented flexion. In 7.3h the duration of the two actions is equal, rather like breathing in and out without a pause in between. Example 7.3i shows a brief extension changing to a prolonged, sustained flexion. In describing these examples, only the basic terminology has been used. The ideas listed under "flexion" and "extension" offer opportunities for many variations. Example 7.3g could be a slow reaching out toward someone, then a sudden retraction, perhaps a response to threatening behavior. Or the idea could be that of a balloon being blown up gradually, only to pop (sudden deflation!). Example 7.3i could be a movement equivalent to throwing a line far out to catch a fish and then slowly drawing it in toward you, perhaps because of resistance met. Find ideas which will give substance to performance of this simple material. Then find enjoyment of the sequences in pure movement, movement for its own sake, no story, no specific dramatic content.

READING PRACTICE E (NO MUSIC)

FLEXION AND EXTENSION WITH DURATION

In this study partners relate to each other in being the opposite or being alike in the timing of their movements and in the choice of flexion or extension. Note organization of information for a duet.

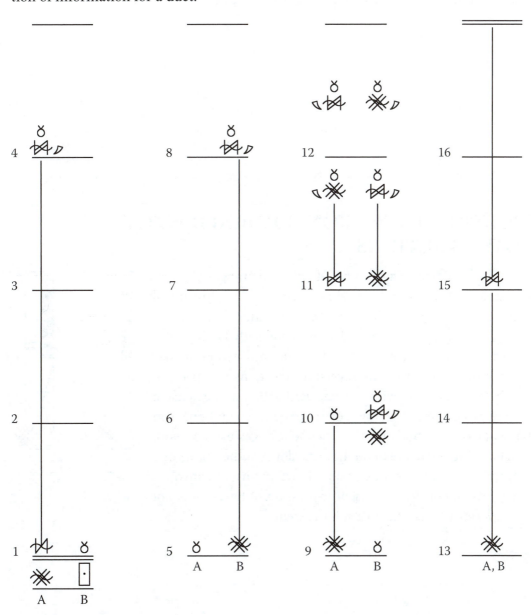

ANY DEGREE OF FLEXION, EXTENSION

So far, two degrees for flexion and extension have been given. The performer may wish to have freedom in choosing the amount. "Any degree" is indicated by placing a short ad lib. sign at the bottom of the symbol. Example 7.4a shows any degree of flexion, while 7.4b states any degree of extension. Timing is indicated as usual; 7.4c indicates a slow movement of any kind of flexing, any degree; 7.4d shows an even slower movement of any kind of extension, any degree.

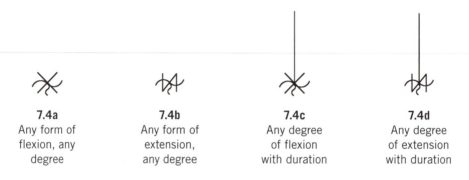

7.4a	7.4b	7.4c	7.4d
Any form of flexion, any degree	Any form of extension, any degree	Any degree of flexion with duration	Any degree of extension with duration

FLEXION, EXTENSION COMBINED WITH OTHER ACTIONS

Flexing and extending can be added to the range of movement already explored—traveling, springing, and directional actions. Example 7.5a shows a side right action with extending followed by a downward movement with flexing. The extension need not be part of the sideward action; it may occur independently. The reverse instructions are given in 7.5b; flexion occurs with the sideward action and extension takes place while lowering. For this, the torso and one arm might close in while the other leg and arm gesture sideward. In lowering you may extend the arms down or the elbows out, or use any spatial arm extension. Lowering usually involves leg flexion, but the movement expression of lowering is not one of flexing since the intent is different.

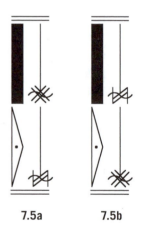

7.5a   7.5b

NOTES FOR READING STUDIES NOS. 23 AND 24

FLEXION, EXTENSION

This study has been provided with two music accompaniments—one slow (track 23 on the accompanying CD) for Reading Study No. 23, one fast (track 24 on the accompanying CD) for Reading Study No. 24. Although the material is the same, the quality of the music suggests very different styles of movement. The faster version will require more practice since there is less time to think and the movement sequences must be translated into memorized muscular patterns of flexion and extension. For the faster version humor may enter the interpretation and the speed may suggest smaller actions and perhaps a greater use of the hands.

Observe the contrast between sudden extensions or sudden flexions and sustained extension and flexion. In measures 9 and 11, the sustained actions include three slight accents. The limb(s) should keep moving despite the accents. The presence of accents with sustained actions, automatically produces certain dynamic patterns. Use of energy is further stimulated by the music.

Rhythmically note the following point: be ready for any swift action which occurs just before a bar line, for example just before measures 6 and 7. Although the music helps significantly in getting this detail right, the manner in which it is performed is important. Such an action is only a preparation for what comes on the strong beat after the bar line. Often, when practicing without music, this preparatory action is given too much importance, its relation to what comes next is not understood. In this study the relationship is fairly obvious, a quick flexion occurs as a preparation for the following extension.

Find an interesting interpretation for this study using the music of Reading Study No. 23, then find a contrasting one using the alternate more jazzy piece of Reading Study No. 24. The slight accents, introduced earlier, are used to highlight the sequence.

Note the use of double-sided directions in measure 10. The retention of the low level (indicated by the hold sign: o) while extending in measure 14, is cancelled by the return to middle level in measure 15.

READING STUDIES NOS. 23 AND 24

FLEXION AND EXTENSION WITH TRAVELING

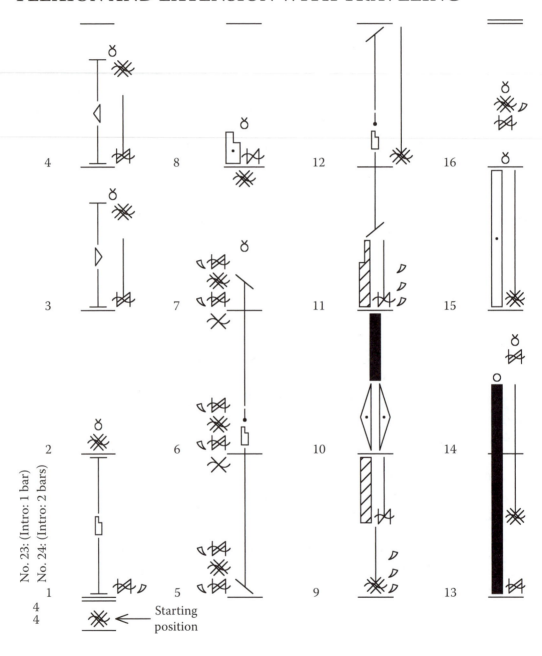

SPRINGING COMBINED WITH FLEXION, EXTENSION

During a spring, flexion or extension of one or both legs can occur. The legs may be extended, spread, or perhaps pulled in, contracted, or a mixture of these possibilities.

Example 7.6a shows a spring during which an accompanying general extension occurs. This action will probably involve the arms and body as well as the legs. The flexion and extension symbol written next to the springing sign infers this action is for the body-as-a-whole, illustrated in 7.6b. In 7.6c flexion accompanies the spring, again a general indication for the body-as-a-whole, illustrated in 7.6d.

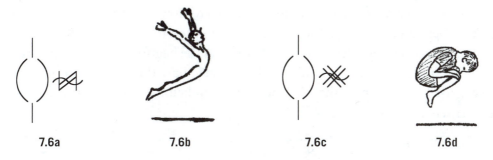

| 7.6a | 7.6b | 7.6c | 7.6d |

By placing the appropriate sign on the actual air line of the spring symbol, we can show what happens to the right or left leg while the body is in the air.

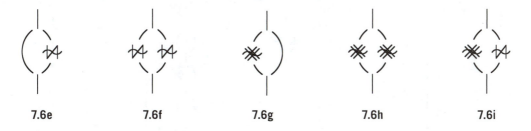

| 7.6e | 7.6f | 7.6g | 7.6h | 7.6i |

Example 7.6e states that the right leg is extended while in the air; in 7.6f both legs are extended. In 7.6g the left leg is flexed, while in 7.6h both legs are flexed. Example 7.6i indicates that the left leg is bent while the right is stretched. When nothing is stated, there is no particular emphasis on leg placement while in the air.

READING STUDY NO. 25

SPRINGS WITH FLEXION AND EXTENSION

The addition of flexion or extension to one or both legs during these aerial steps provides character to the five basic forms. Regarding the music for this piece, the Ländler, a rustic dance of German or Austrian origin, provides immediately a light-hearted, rollicking feeling. Nevertheless, personal energy level in performing the sequence may range from a casual, energy-saving manner to an attack with great gusto.

Choice of form of spring has been left open, however, the leg gestures may suggest hops or jumps. Note the transition from measure 8 to 9: the spring at the end of measure 8 is repeated below the bar line at the beginning of the third staff to facilitate reading. The signs: < and >, called "carets," have the meaning of "the same" and are used here to show that the spring written before measure 9 is the same as that written at the end of measure 8.

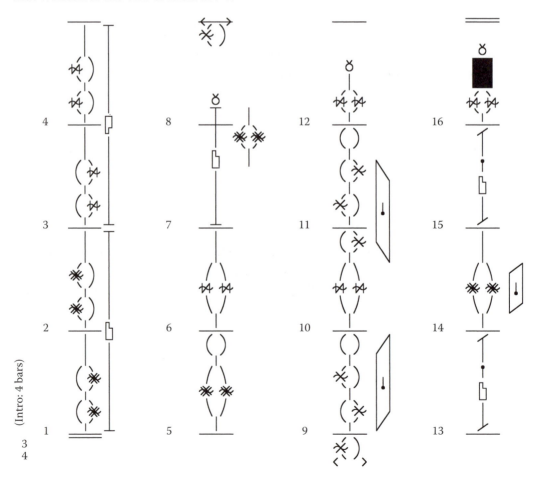

MANNER OF PERFORMANCE

INTENTION: A DIRECTIONAL ACTION OR FLEXION; EXTENSION

When a single limb is extended it is often difficult for the observer to tell whether the action is one of extension or is intended to indicate the particular direction into which the limb happens to extend, a destinational point. The manner of performance, the expression can make the difference clear; however, if two or more limbs extend simultaneously into different directions and involve the torso, the basic message of extension is clearer. For a single limb any suggestion of a direction can be diminished if the limb moves out on a curved path as it extends; spoke-like paths which move out directly from the center are more likely to be seen as directional in intention.

Another directional question arises when a greater degree of contracting, a closing-in movement, also lowers the body near to the floor. Too easily the movement is seen as a lowering. If each movement idea is truthfully executed it should be quite clear when a high degree of flexion is being used and when a spatial movement down is being performed. Several factors can indicate the difference. When lowering occurs the legs usually bend and the body-as-a-whole lowers to the ground, but the torso need not pull together. The neck may relax allowing the head to drop and a slight rounding in the spine provides a harmonious accompaniment to the idea of downness, but these contributing features can be slight. From a standing position the performer can achieve a great degree of flexion for the body-as-a-whole and yet avoid any suggestion of downward motion by closing the free leg in toward the trunk and only slightly flexing the supporting leg. The paths of the limbs as they close in will also suggest or deny any downward movement.

MOTION OR DESTINATION

Until now we have encouraged a general use in experiencing the actions of flexion and extension. But the question soon comes up as to whether a particular **state** (destination) of flexion or extension, a particular degree, should be achieved, or the process, the **motion** of flexing and extending are to be experienced, enjoyed. If a flexion is swift, an arrival point will doubtless be reached; if there is a longer duration, then there is time for the motion itself to be enjoyed as well as, perhaps, a destination to be reached. At this stage these flexion and extension indications may be performed as motion or destination. Further exploration of **destination** and **motion** is given in Chapter 20.

DYNAMICS: FORCE

In Chapter 4 we looked at the concept of "par" in relation to use of energy and the varying degrees of energy employed in relation to gravity. The same degrees of energy apply in relation to how much force or effort is given to a particular movement; the dynamic qualities produced may be gentle, strong, relaxed, or limp (as in "her body went limp").

A slight rise in energy above par may result from awareness, alertness. In a movement, this slightly heightened energy may produce a delicate gesture. If contact is made, a light, gentle touch will result, sometimes called "fine touch." This gentle movement quality is indicated as in 7.7a. The upward curving bow (a rise in energy) is combined with the white circle, which shows a small amount. This circle is always placed at the end of the curved bow. A greater rise in energy will produce a strong movement or position, 7.7b. Strong, forceful gestures are familiar and are often used in work situations where a nail must be hammered, a log sawed through, or an obstinate dog pulled. The task at hand requires strength far beyond the individual's level of par. Without objects against which force is needed, the body can create counter tension using the antagonist muscles, as in a gesture of pressing against an unseen object. Note the difference in the placement of the circles, white or black, compared with the central placement for signs related to the line of gravity, the resisting or use of gravity, given in Chapter 4.

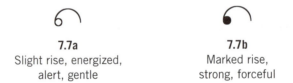

7.7a
Slight rise, energized,
alert, gentle

7.7b
Marked rise,
strong, forceful

Lowering of energy produces relaxation of muscles. These may be relaxed neck muscles, shoulders, torso, hands. Example 7.7c indicates such relaxation. Because the usual par energy is not counteracting the pull of gravity, there will be a drooping, a slight downward movement. A greater, exaggerated degree of letting go of normal muscular tension results in collapse, as in flopping onto a comfortable sofa after a strenuous work-out, or after finishing a physically demanding job. The person lets go of all tension, all energy. Example 7.7d is the indication for this marked drop in energy.

7.7c
Relaxed

7.7d
Flop

Even when the focus is not on relating to or using gravity, it will quietly play its part, this we cannot escape. However, the intention, the awareness behind the movement, may be focussed on the state of the body, not on gravity. These dynamic symbols are added information to indicate the quality of the movement(s) it accompanies, how the movement is to be performed. They can be added to a whole action, part of an action, or they may increase or decrease during the performance of a movement or series of movements.

DURATION OF THE DYNAMIC QUALITY

The force used at the start of 7.8a immediately disappears as the movement continues. In 7.8b, force, strength, appears only at the end of the movement. Example 7.8c shows an action performed with a gentle, fine touch quality. The indication is placed within the vertical square addition bracket and has the duration of the bracket. In 7.8d three actions are to be performed with strength. Only the second action in 7.8e is to be strong, the first could be the preparation for the strong action and the third the recovery. Example 7.8f shows another way of writing 7.8e.

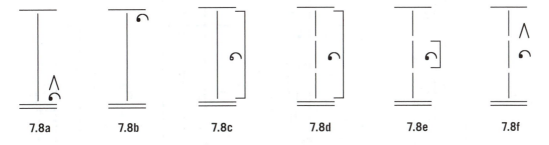

| 7.8a | 7.8b | 7.8c | 7.8d | 7.8e | 7.8f |

Increase and decrease of a particular dynamic is shown by placing the sign within the vertical increase sign (the "toward" sign) or the decrease sign (the "away" sign). In 7.8g, as the performer travels, the energy level is gradually dropping. A sudden drop into a flop occurs at the end of the movement in 7.8h. While performing a sustained movement in 7.8i, strength gradually diminishes. The thought, the feeling, the focus of 7.8g in gradually becoming relaxed, is very different from the concept and the experience of diminishing energy, stated in 7.8i.

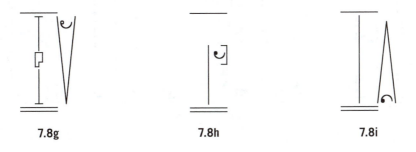

| 7.8g | 7.8h | 7.8i |

Reading Practice F (no music)

DYNAMICS: FORCE

In this study, traveling is accompanied by gestures with different qualities. When traveling on the feet, such gestures will need to be made by the arms, torso, or head, the choice is open. At first, a gesture of sustained strength is followed by diminishing strength. Two simultaneous strong gestures are specified in measure 3. Circling in measures 5–12 is accompanied by gestures that increase then decrease in strength. Four gentle (fine touch) actions follow and then many quick, relaxed gestures, perhaps shaking. The final sustained movements end in a flop.

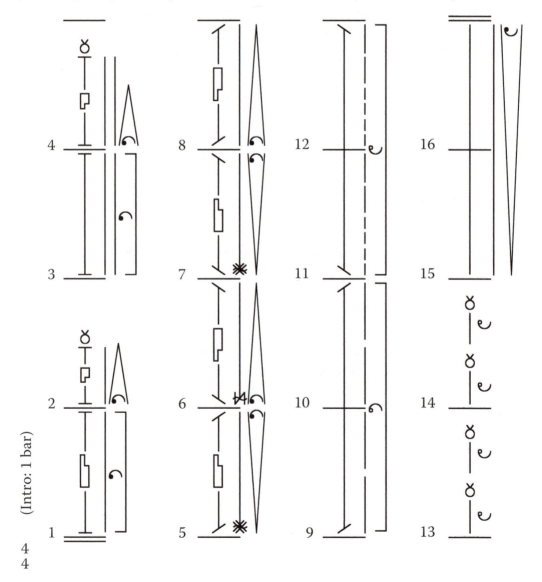

(Intro: 1 bar)

$\frac{4}{4}$

DYNAMICS: EMPHASIZED AND UNEMPHASIZED

The impact of a gesture can be changed according to the emphasis that is placed upon it. Take a gesture extending out, away from the body. Emphasis may be placed on the start of the gesture, in the middle, or at the end; the message it is conveying will be changed accordingly. We are familiar with how emphasis affects speech, the change in meaning when certain words are emphasized rather than others. Attention is drawn to one word (or group of words) rather than another. A slight intensity places prominence on one or other part of the utterance. What factors are used in speech to produce emphasis? Are these same factors used in movement?

The elements are: stress, a slight increase in energy; timing, particularly a slight prolongation; and (for speech) a change of pitch. In place of this, a gesture may include a slight directional deviation, or a passing rotation, for the arm—a small turn of the hand. Exaggeration in use of space may enter the picture, of course, as well as supporting "sympathetic" accompanying movements of the torso, head or, perhaps, of a weight shift.

While these subtle changes can be spelled out in great detail through Labanotation and also through the addition of the Effort-Shape qualities, at this stage we are concerned only with the change in quality and expressiveness of movement that an emphasis brings. For each person, the production of emphasis in movement will vary. Example 7.9a are the signs for emphasis; they are related to the sign for being forceful. Comparable to accent signs, the tail of the emphasis sign points in toward the movement it qualifies, being placed where it is needed. In 7.9b, the right arm gestures diagonally, an emphasis occurring at the start. The emphasis is placed in the middle of the gesture in 7.9c, while in 7.9d the ending is emphasized. It is important to be aware that such emphasis is not to be confused with an accent sign. This is quite a different event. It is true, however, that an emphasis usually includes a slight increase in energy but it need not be sudden, it is more drawn out, at times resulting in a slight slowing down of the movement. In 7.9e, the emphasis sign in the angular vertical addition bracket states that the whole movement is to be stressed.

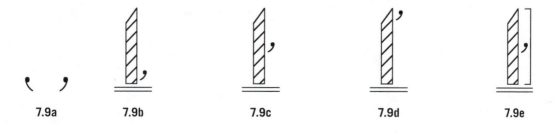

| 7.9a | 7.9b | 7.9c | 7.9d | 7.9e |

Unemphasized is the opposite of emphasized; in speech the voice is quieter, often lowered. In movement it is the energy level that is dropped. Without its normal energy level, a part of the body does not draw the viewer's attention; an unemphasized gesture can become almost inconspicuous. Example 7.9f shows the signs for unemphasized; these signs are related to the signs for weak, relaxed. In 7.9g the left arm is unemphasized, all attention is thus going to the right arm which has emphasis at the end.

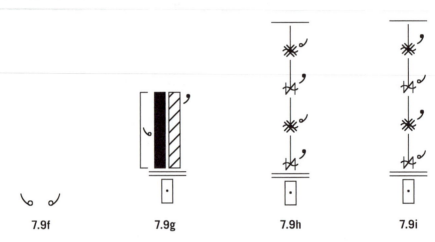

7.9f   7.9g   7.9h   7.9i

Example 7.9h indicates a repeated extension-flexion pattern in which the emphasis is on the extension, the flexion being like a recovery. In 7.9i the emphasis is on the flexion, the extension serving as a preparation for the repeat. Express this by using an arm gesture. This alternating placement of the stress can be compared to repeating "blue sky, blue sky" or "sky blue, sky blue" in which the sky is described or the color blue defined, depending on where the stress is placed.

READING STUDY NO. 26

EMPHASIZED, UNEMPHASIZED DIRECTIONAL ACTIONS

In the following study directional movements are indicated to be performed in a general way or with emphasis or lack of emphasis. Find a range of subtle differences in producing these qualities in the stated direction.

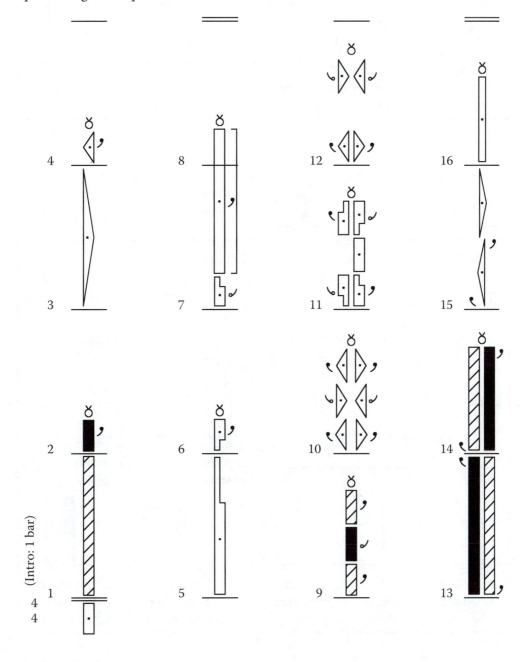

REVIEW FOR CHAPTER SEVEN

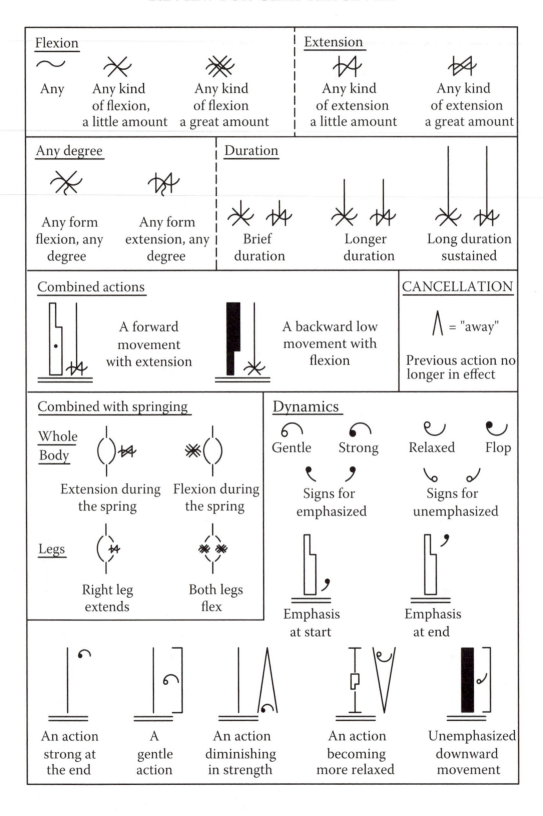

CHAPTER EIGHT

Rotations, Revolutions, Turns

Before investigating this topic, let us check terminology. A rotation? A revolution? Revolution is defined as: a progressive motion of a body around a center or axis, a turn or rotation of the body-as-a-whole. To all intents and purposes the words revolution, rotation, and turn are interchangeable, though for certain movements one term is preferable to another. The synonyms for turning, revolving, are full of descriptive movement—pivoting, swiveling, whirling, rolling, wheeling, etc. Many of these suggest a circular path, in whole or in part. The word "turn," or "turning" is often the general term used for rotations.

Is there something to be learned from our daily use of words such as "turn" and "rotate"? What sort of "movement" do they suggest? For instance we "turn away" from an unpleasant sight. This may be a partial pivot (swivel on the supporting foot), or a turn (twist) in the body. In illness we "turn the corner," a dramatic change has taken place, though no real corner is involved. We "turn the tables," a reversing which suggests a half turn. We "take turns" between people involved in an activity. To "turn over in one's mind" also gives the idea of a circular pattern where there is a return to the same thoughts.

ANY ROTATION, REVOLUTION

Take the term "a rotation." How is this type of movement used by the whole body? If one is lying on the floor, it can be rolling, just as a pencil can roll. It may be spinning if one is on one foot, just as a top can spin. Turning fast is an exhilarating sensation. Prolonged turning can bring on a state of trance as intentionally experienced by the whirling Dervishes. Their counterclockwise turning alternates between slow and fast but they never stop until they fall into a trance-like state. Turning should be experienced at different speeds. Speed of turning affects not only the expression but also the functional use.

Consider the forms familiar in gymnastics, the different forms of rotating, revolving, including cartwheels, somersaults, walkovers (forward cartwheels), etc. The basic forms are often mixed in gymnastics, acrobatics, tumbling, and diving. But these are special skills; let us first deal with the common forms using just the floor. The other forms will be explored in theory, but not covered physically here, as proper training is essential for aerial forms of revolution. We focus on the basic facts applicable to all forms, both for the body-as-a-whole and for occurrences within the body. Certain body areas make use of partial rotations of one form or another. In this chapter we focus on rotation of the body-as-a-whole around the three axes.

Before we become specific, let us enjoy the freedom of any kind of rotation. Example 8.1a is the symbol for "any revolution," "any rotation," any form of turning; the choice of form is left open.

8.1a
Any form of turn, rotation, revolution

Try the following sequence of continuous rotation: while standing, start turning slowly, then keep on revolving while lowering to the floor, turning perhaps on one foot, then down to a knee and onto the hips while swiveling or rolling, and keep turning as you lie down until you begin to rise. While rising, continue to turn constantly.

8.1b

8.1c

8.1d

8.1e

8.1f

Find another way of descending and rising with continuous turning, changing from faster to slower, incorporating flexed and extended body states and using different devices to keep the turning action going, e.g., pushing with a hand or foot. Once on the floor, change the revolving into a somersault and from there into rolling with the limbs closed in. Then try rolling with the limbs extended, the whole body in one line. The basic turning, rotating action can be greatly colored by other actions which accompany it. Each variation provides its own expression and feeling. Discover these and enjoy them.

In a standing situation, turning may be on one foot, on both feet, or a mixture between the two, changing from one foot to the other. A few steps, or many, may occur while turning. For pure rotation one should stay on the spot without traveling. Other contributory actions may occur, such as use of head, torso, or accompanying gestures, as long as none of these becomes dominant and overshadows the main rotary action. The featured movement must still be clearly observable.

What movement facts have we unearthed? Rotation occurs around an axis. When one is standing, turning (pivoting) occurs around the vertical axis, but the same physical activity, performed while one is lying on the floor, becomes logrolling. Continuous rolling in one direction produces traveling.

From the point of view of expression, a minor turning action may have a dramatic origin, for example to face another person, an object, or another room direction. It may occur merely to change the direction of a path; in this case the path and not the turning is important. Or the turning action may occur for its own sake. Spinning, once discovered, is much enjoyed by young children. It becomes an art when a skater climaxes a sequence with a dazzling series of spins. "When in doubt—turn" is the advice given to dancers who suddenly have to improvise in a performance when, for a moment, they have mentally gone blank.

Notes for Reading Study No. 27

ANY ROTATION

This study is intended as an exploration of rotation for the body-as-a-whole. It is so general it could be performed in a number of different ways. To specify that the downward actions are to be for body-as-a-whole and not a gesture, the sign for body-as-a-whole is stated. If an inner feeling for rotating is established, then one rotary action may grow out of the previous one.

Because it starts in a neutral, middle level situation, the first rotation is likely to be on the feet (but need not be). After lowering occurs, some form of rolling on the floor is likely, though swiveling (pivoting) on the knees or hips, or also wheeling could occur. Note use of the hold (retention) sign: O to show that low level is to be maintained until the return to neutral, middle level on the 6th measure. During measure 9 the use of the retention symbol again maintains the low level state until the return to middle, neutral level in measure 15.

Symbol for body-as-a-whole: ⊗

Reading Study No. 27

ANY ROTATION

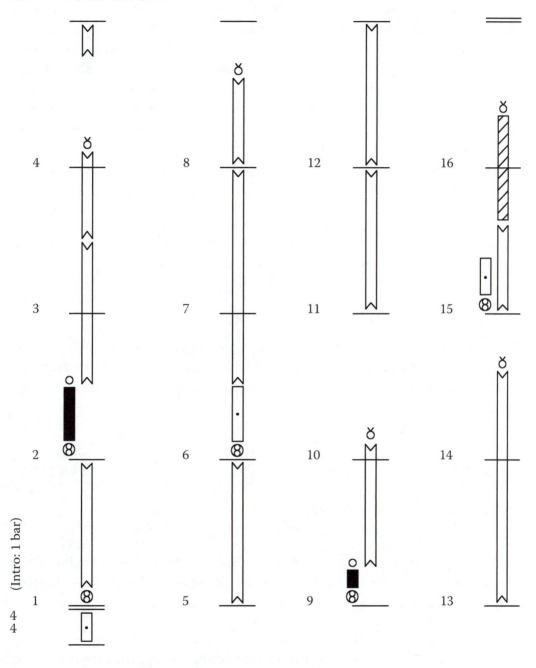

SPECIFIC FORMS OF ROTATION: PIVOT TURNS

All too often turning, pivoting, is thought of as a mechanical action or device, perhaps because so many inanimate objects in life, such as a CD, rotate rigidly. For movement, it is important to realize that the first "notion" of turning, the origin of the motion (as with all movement), takes place in the brain. The thought, the image of the turn, is followed by a reaction in the trunk, the center. Let us consider a turn while standing on one foot. The turn starts in the trunk and **only at the last** moment comes the swivel on the foot. In that sense it is a successive movement. Only when an outside force initiates a turn can the body rotate totally in one piece from the start. The "birth" of a turn occurring in the trunk is more obvious when turning stems from an emotional desire to turn, perhaps to express anger. Dramatic situations allow internal motivation to be evident. In classical ballet elegance dictates that torso preparation be unseen.

As discussed in Chapter 3, the most familiar form of turning is around the vertical axis of the body. The signs for turning to the left, 8.2a, and to the right, 8.2b, restated in the next section, are already familiar.

CHOICE OF RIGHT OR LEFT TURN

When it is desirable to leave the turning direction open, to give a choice, then the composite turn of 8.2c is used*. This sign, in which the right and left turn signs are written one on top of the other, gives the reader the choice of turning either right or left.

| 8.2a | 8.2b | 8.2c | Turn either right or left |
| Left turn | Right turn | Turn either way | |

In 8.2d, as you extend, you may turn either way; then, after the stillness, you may again turn right or left as flexion occurs. Freedom in the choice of direction may occur in an otherwise defined movement sequence.

The simple sequence of 8.2e combines turning, extension, flexion, and stillness. Perform this sequence first lying on the floor using rolling, then try it standing. Find different interpretations for this simple set of instructions. After the stillness,

---

* In Labanotation, the composite turn sign used for **gestures** means rotation in **neither** direction, the limbs should be parallel. In Motif Notation, for the body-as-a-whole, this symbol means to turn either left or right.

the state of extension may remain or may disappear. In Motif Notation, focus is on the next movement, but there is a choice of whether the result of the previous action will be retained or allowed to disappear, i.e., be cancelled. (See Appendix A for Validity Rule.) Try 8.2f standing first, then sitting, then lying on the floor. The degree of turn has not yet been stated. There is, however, a tendency to want to make it a whole turn (an inborn desire to return to a former front), but a 1/4 turn or a 1/2 turn will just as well fulfill the instructions. Try using different amounts, make each turn the same amount or make each turn a different amount. Here you have freedom. The action (a turn) and the timing (swift) have been dictated, but you still have much leeway to do as you wish. Turning with weight on both feet, i.e., swiveling, is limited in degree; the legs become crossed and turning ceases. If, as a preparation, the feet are crossed on the appropriate side, a greater degree of swivel can be achieved—a favorite step in Spanish dance.

8.2d

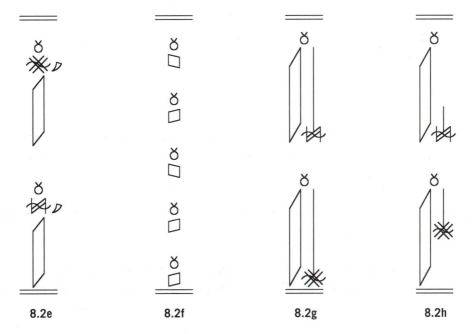

8.2e   8.2f   8.2g   8.2h

The timing of accompanying actions may vary. Example 8.2g illustrates completely simultaneous actions; turning to the right is accompanied by flexion, closing in. After a brief stillness, turning to the right occurs again, but this time accompanied by extension. In 8.2h there is partial overlap; the slow turn is halfway through before flexion starts; extension occurs more rapidly at the start of the second turn, the turn continuing on. It is likely that the extension may be retained though no such retention is stated or required, the performer has the choice to maintain the extension or to let it go away. This set of instructions could be done with one slow turn, or with multiple turns. The short phrases could be performed by a folk dancer, a skater, or a ballet dancer. For the latter two, the extension might take the form of an *arabesque*. Or the whole sequence could be performed lying on the floor—with a very different result. Swiveling on the hips and turning on the knees are also possibilities. The type of support is unstated.

AMOUNT OF PIVOT

The degree of turn (pivot), the amount of change of front, was given in Chapter 3, 3.8a–3.8f. Reading clockwise or counterclockwise, the black pins placed inside the turn sign indicate the amount of turn. Example 8.3a states one full turn to the right; 8.3b shows half a turn to the left and 8.3c shows two and a quarter turns to the right.

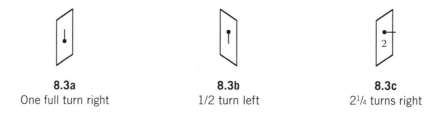

| **8.3a** | **8.3b** | **8.3c** |
| One full turn right | 1/2 turn left | 2¼ turns right |

SOMERSAULTS

Revolutions, rotations in the sagittal plane, i.e., forward or backward somersaults, are familiar to most people from childhood. Like wheels of a car these revolutions have a lateral, side-to-side axis.

Example 8.4a illustrates a wheel revolving while remaining in the same location; it is spinning around itself, but does not travel.

Example 8.4b shows a tumbler performing a similar revolution in the air having sprung up from a trampoline. There has been a vertical rise but no horizontal change of location.

| **8.4a** | **8.4b** |

If a wheel has contact with the ground, as is usually the case when it is a means of transporting a vehicle, 8.4c, then it rolls along the surface and traveling occurs.

The same is true of somersaults on the ground, 8.4d. They become somersault rolls, so you will not end up where you started. A backward somersault will result in traveling backward, 8.4e.

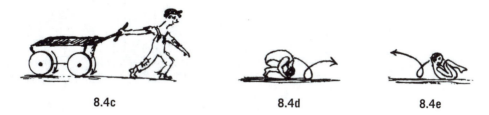

| 8.4c | 8.4d | 8.4e |

The term somersault is commonly used for the form in which the body "tucks in," i.e., is flexed, folded up. But the same form of revolution can occur with the torso and limbs extended. The usual form of this is a forward "walkover," a sagittal "cartwheel" in which each hand and then each foot "walks" into the forward direction, 8.4f–8.4i.

| 8.4f | 8.4g | 8.4h | 8.4i |

INDICATION OF SOMERSAULTING

The choice of somersaulting either forward or backward is shown by the composite sign of 8.5a. A forward somersault (forward roll) is specified by 8.5b, and a backward somersault (backward roll) by 8.5c.

| **8.5a** | **8.5b** | **8.5c** |
| Somersault either way | Somersault forward | Somersault backward |

The signs for somersaulting forward and backward are not only pictorial, they have an interesting origin. A forward somersault is made up of an inward rotation for each side of the body (the right side rotating to the left, and the left side to the right), 8.5d. If two people take your arms, and each twists an arm inward, you will find your body is forced forward into a somersault. If both arms are twisted outward, you will gradually be forced backward, into a backward somersault, 8.5e. Gymnasts working on the rings and retaining the hand grasps find that a forward or backward somersault action will cause the arms to become twisted accordingly.

8.5d   **8.5e**

AMOUNT OF SOMERSAULT

To indicate the amount of rotation for a somersault, numerals are placed within the somersault symbol. Numerals are used because in a somersault there is no change of Front, that is, the performer's orientation in relation to the previously established Front is not changed, as it is with other forms of rotation. Black pins are not used, as they are in pivot turns, because black pins automatically include the degree of change of Front. Examples 8.6a and 8.6b illustrate the use of numbers for amount of rotation in a somersault.

8.6a
Somersault forward
one rotation

8.6b
Somersault backward
$2\frac{1}{4}$ rotations

CARTWHEELS

While in a somersault we have our front or back facing toward the direction of the revolution, in a cartwheel it is the right or left side of the body which is toward the direction of progression. The revolution occurs in the lateral plane around the sagittal axis. Our relationship to the image of a wheel is now different, it is as though we are flat against the wheel, as in 8.7a. The axis of rotation becomes a sagittal axis through the center of the body.

8.7a   **8.7b**

A cartwheel type of rotation can occur without horizontal traveling during a spring in the air as in 8.7b.

Change of Front during a Cartwheel

Cartwheels are very deceptive in that many people do not realize that a full cartwheel also contains a full revolution around the vertical axis of the body. In a full cartwheel there is a return to the original Front. But when half a cartwheel occurs there is a half change of Front. Since, in a perfectly flat cartwheel, the front surface of the performer remains toward the same room direction, it is hard to see that a rotation around the vertical axis has taken place. But when half a cartwheel has been accomplished, the body has also rotated a half turn around its own axis and so the performer will be facing into the opposite direction. Example 8.8a shows a performer starting a cartwheel with the back to the reader; 8.8b shows the completion of half a cartwheel.

8.8a   8.8b   8.8c   8.8d

The performer's front appears still to be away from the reader in 8.8b. But note the different impression made when the head is held up and the back arched, as they usually are in such activities, 8.8c. Because the face and also the hands are toward the reader, you may begin to see that the performer is now facing you. When the legs are dropped to the ground, either toward the reader or away (it makes no difference to the resulting standing position), the performer is then clearly seen to be facing the reader, 8.8d.

It is easier to see what happens if the figure is in profile. Example 8.8e shows the figure up in a straight line, the hands (fingers) pointing forward (F), the nose backward (B). If the figure is seen in the more natural body curve of 8.8f, the forward direction is emphasized. In 8.8g the legs have been lowered over forward (a half forward "somersault") and the performer is about to straighten up, facing F. In 8.8h, 8.8i, and 8.8j the legs are lowered backward (a half backward "somersault") and the performer is again seen to be facing F, 8.8j. Thus in 8.8e the indications F and B are correct, even though at first glance they appear to be wrong.

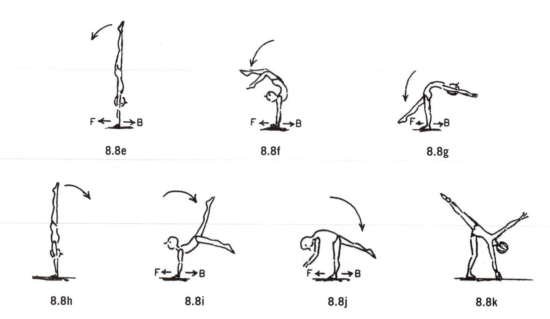

When a cartwheel is performed by a beginner with a flexed body, it is easier to see the full rotation that is made during one cartwheel. The change of front for a half cartwheel takes place only at the moment that the first hand takes weight and the second foot is released. In 8.8k the body may be nearly straight down, but front is still considered to be away from the reader until the moment when all weight is transferred to the hand.

INDICATION OF CARTWHEELING

As we have seen, a cartwheel contains within it a rotation around the vertical axis of the body; thus the sign is based on the turn signs of 8.2a and 8.2b. Arrowheads at the top and bottom of the cartwheel sign indicate the lateral rotation; in 8.9a the cartwheel is to the left. In 8.9b, dotted arrows visually illustrate how the extremities of the sign act as indicators. Similarly, 8.9c states a cartwheel to the right and 8.9d visually indicates the direction.

The sign for cartwheeling either way, 8.9e, contains the composite turn sign for turning either way, but, for practical purposes, only one set of arrowheads is drawn.

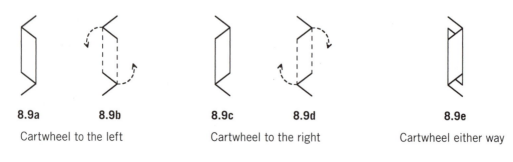

In planning a movement sequence we soon make a decision regarding right or left, but on paper the choice may still be left open.

AMOUNT OF CARTWHEELING

Because of the change of Front in the performance of a cartwheel, the way to indicate amount of a cartwheel is the same as for indicating amount for a pivot turn. Example 8.10a indicates half a cartwheel to the right; 8.10b states a full cartwheel to the left.

8.10a
1/2 cartwheel right

8.10b
One full cartwheel left

CARTWHEELING VS. LOGROLLING

A cartwheeling type of rotation may occur when lying on the floor in a tucked-in position. Spatially, the axis is the same as for a cartwheel, i.e., a sagittal axis, but the sensation is closer to logrolling because it travels along the ground, 8.11a. With limbs extended in line with the body, as in 8.11b, it clearly becomes a logroll, i.e., turning around the longitudinal axis of the body.

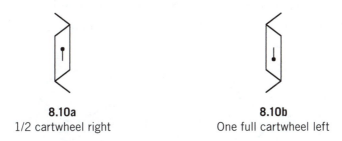

8.11a   **8.11b**

The rotation sign used for a pivot turn around the body's vertical axis while standing, 8.11c, is modified to be logrolling by the addition of the angular support bows, introduced in the next chapter. Placement of this support bow at the start of the rotation symbol and also at the end, as in 8.11d, states that supporting on the floor occurs throughout the turn, i.e., continuous rolling.

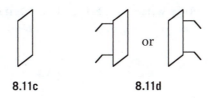

or

8.11c   **8.11d**

HORIZONTAL WHEELING

When lying on the floor on the front, as in 8.12a or on the back, as in 8.12b, the body can rotate as though it is a wheel lying horizontally around a vertical axis.

With the limbs extended and separated, the extremities describe a circular path. When circling clockwise or counterclockwise around a vertical central point while lying it is helpful to have a slippery floor, the wheeling possibly being achieved by the hands and feet "walking" the body around. Or such wheeling may result from outside help, as in 8.12c. In 8.12d the person is lying on her side while two people, one grasping her hands, the other her feet, are wheeling her around. Similar wheeling can happen while on all fours, as in 8.12e. Here again the supports will "walk" the body around, thus producing wheeling on the spot. Wheeling can thus be seen as horizontal circling on the spot; it has a vertical axis as does an ordinary circular path traveled across the floor. The vertical axis can be located at any point in the body, the shoulders, hips, knees, etc., around which the wheeling occurs.

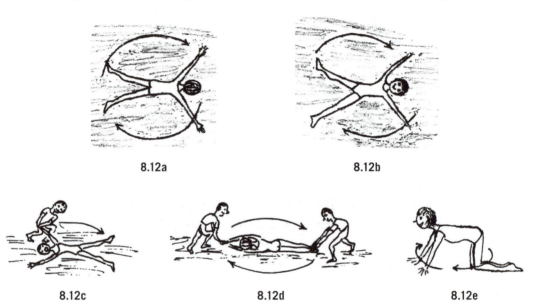

8.12a   8.12b

8.12c   8.12d   8.12e

INDICATION OF HORIZONTAL WHEELING

The circular path signs, shown in 8.13a, are already familiar from exploration of traveling. By adding the sign for a retention on the spot, 8.13b, the circling is changed to be on the spot, i.e., the body wheeling, 8.13c. The open choice of wheeling either way is shown in 8.13d.

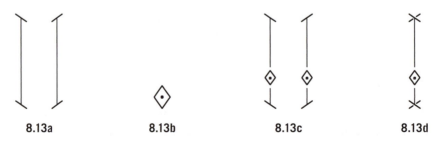

8.13a   8.13b   8.13c   8.13d

AMOUNT OF WHEELING

Because there is a change of Front, black pins are used for amount of wheeling in the same manner as for circling and for pivot turns. Example 8.14a states a 1/4 wheeling to the left, while 8.14b shows 1/2 wheeling to the right. Wheeling to the right a total of 2 1/4 rotations is given in 8.14c.

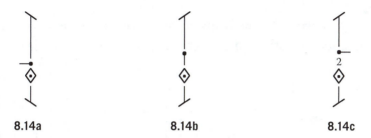

| 8.14a | 8.14b | 8.14c |

TRANSITION FROM PIVOTING TO WHEELING

In a pivot turn in which the limbs are extended horizontally, as in 8.15a, the turn is still clearly seen and experienced as a pivot around a vertical axis, here the right leg. In 8.15b the skater has her limbs and torso horizontal; as she turns, the extremities of the arms and left leg describe a circular path. Note that in 8.15c, even though the supporting leg is bent, the awareness of the vertical axis (illustrated by the dotted line) is still present. In 8.15d even though the rotation is on the knee, the sense of the vertical axis is still there. It is when the whole torso is supporting on the floor or when there is more than one support and the horizontal plane is strongly expressed that the sense of wheeling takes over.

As aerial forms require special training, they will not be investigated here.

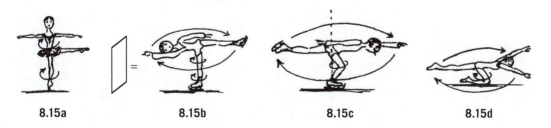

| 8.15a | 8.15b | 8.15c | 8.15d |

ALTERNATE INDICATION FOR HORIZONTAL WHEELING

Because the axis in wheeling is the same as in pivoting, i.e., the vertical axis, the horizontal circling can also be written by adding the statement of axis within the turn sign.

The sign for this axis, 8.16a, is based on the vertical line of gravity thus indicating the vertical axis. When lying, the rotation signs of 8.16b indicate rolling around the body axis; by using 8.16c the vertical axis is specified. In certain contexts this statement for a wheeling action may be more appropriate than the circular path sign. The amount of wheeling is indicated by black pins in the same manner as for circling and for pivot turns.

However, when two different forms of rotation occur at the same time, wheeling shown by the circular path sign is preferred as it stands out clearly from other

Vertical (standard)
cross of directions

8.16a   **8.16b**   **8.16c**

rotation signs. An understanding of the specific forms will help in later exploration of rotations and twists within the body.

The range of variation provided by these rotations enriches movement in many ways. In gymnastics, diving, etc. these revolutions often appear in combined forms.

READING STUDY NO. 28

TURNS, REVOLUTIONS, ROTATIONS

This study may be interpreted in several ways. The inclusion of flexion and extension of the body-as-a-whole suggests the type of revolution which is likely to take place. No specific statement is made yet as to what part of the body is supporting during or between the revolutions. Note that in measures 5 and 9 the rotations could be swiveling or rolling. Also note the separated turning indications in measure 11. The symbol for both arms, shown in measure 6, is given below:

⇑ = both arms

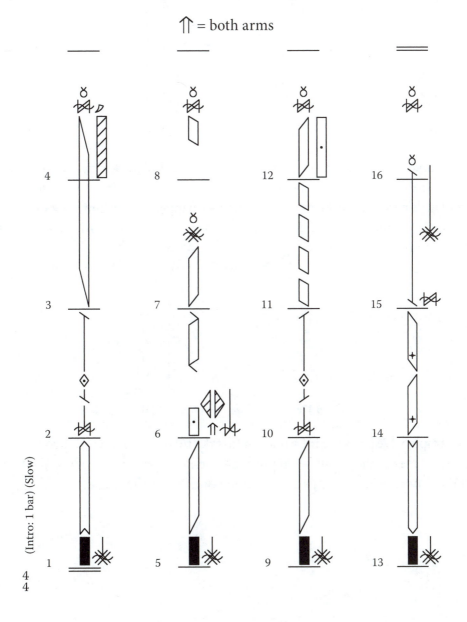

COMBINED TURNING AND SPRINGING

Many variations are possible in combining the actions of turning and springing. The obvious possibility of both happening at the same time is 8.17a. Both are equally important; this is shown by their being placed side by side. The kind of spring is not specified, nor is the amount of turn, but turning to the right is specified.

Let us now look at the main activity, turning, being embellished by the addition of one or more springs. In 8.17b, it is clearly stated that a spring happens at the start of the turn and another at the end.

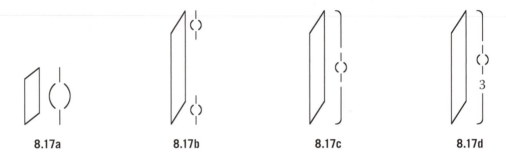

| 8.17a | 8.17b | 8.17c | 8.17d |

Example 8.17c states that springing is to be **included** during the turning; the vertical line of the inclusion bow is broken to insert what is to be included. This statement leaves open how many springs can happen and when they occur. How many springs should occur can be indicated by a number; in 8.17d three springs are to be included.

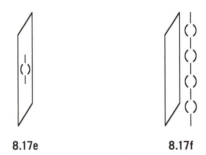

| 8.17e | 8.17f |

Example 8.17e gives the information that the turning is achieved through springing, thus it means there will be no pivoting and no stepping to produce the turning. In 8.17f, four rebound springs are indicated during the turning action.

REVIEW FOR CHAPTER EIGHT

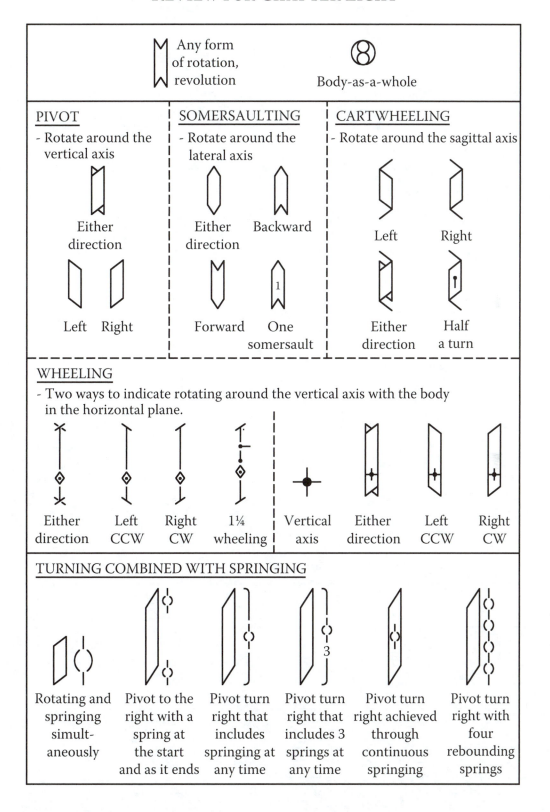

Any form of rotation, revolution

Body-as-a-whole

PIVOT
- Rotate around the vertical axis

Either direction

Left   Right

SOMERSAULTING
- Rotate around the lateral axis

Either direction   Backward

Forward   One somersault

CARTWHEELING
- Rotate around the sagittal axis

Left   Right

Either direction   Half a turn

WHEELING
- Two ways to indicate rotating around the vertical axis with the body in the horizontal plane.

Either direction   Left CCW   Right CW   1¼ wheeling   Vertical axis   Either direction   Left CCW   Right CW

TURNING COMBINED WITH SPRINGING

Rotating and springing simultaneously

Pivot to the right with a spring at the start and as it ends

Pivot turn right that includes springing at any time

Pivot turn right that includes 3 springs at any time

Pivot turn right achieved through continuous springing

Pivot turn right with four rebounding springs

CHAPTER NINE
Supporting; Change of Support

Because of gravity we spend virtually all our lives resting one part or another of our body on the floor or on furniture of some kind. This state is so natural and common that we do not even think about it. Under certain conditions we are aware of how our body is being supported and consciously make a change. When the chair is too hard, we shift our weight to ease one part and take the weight on another. Parts of the body get tired of being weight bearers; aching feet are a commonly shared experience. Lying on the beach, reading, or sunning, we make frequent shifts from sitting, leaning, lying, etc., by rolling over.

Many of the possible modes and changes of support belong in the category of gymnastics or acrobatics, particularly in conjunction with use of different apparatus. For aerialists in a circus, the part supporting is often the armpit, the crook of the knee, even the crook of the ankle. Here we will stick to more everyday, non-specialist examples.

Weight may be supported on only one or on several parts of the body at the same time. A single support may be one foot, one knee (not so easy, the knee cap not having been built as a weight-bearing part), a single hip, the shoulder area (a shoulder stand), the head alone, one hand, and, at one time, a single finger as performed by an acrobat named Mr. Uni.

Double supports can range from two feet, one foot and one knee, foot and hand, foot and shoulder, foot and head, knee and hand, knee and head, and so on. Triple, quadruple, and even five point supports are possible. All these need to be explored to experience not only the moment of achieving such supports but also the transitions between. Many interesting variations can be experienced without great physical skills.

Examples 9.1a–9.1z illustrate a selection of possibilities progressing from a single support to quadruple supports.

NUMBER OF SUPPORTING PARTS

SINGLE SUPPORT

9.1a   9.1b   9.1c   9.1d

9.1e   9.1f   9.1g

DOUBLE SUPPORT

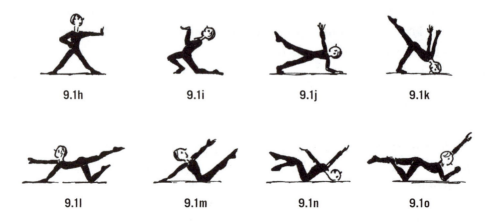

9.1h   9.1i   9.1j   9.1k

9.1l   9.1m   9.1n   9.1o

9.1p   9.1q   9.1r

Triple Support

9.1s   9.1t

9.1u   9.1v   9.1w   9.1x

Quadruple Support

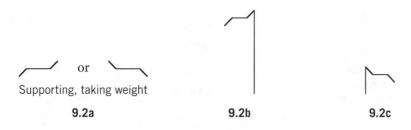

9.1y   9.1z

INDICATION OF SUPPORTING

The angular sign of 9.2a states only the fact of taking weight, of being supported. An action stroke gives a general indication of the movement into a new support, 9.2b. Length of the action stroke shows the duration of this transition; 9.2c shows a quick transition to the new support. Example 9.2b could be interpreted as "rolling" to an adjacent body part, or as a "walking" action from one extremity to another.

or

Supporting, taking weight

9.2a   **9.2b**   **9.2c**

For transference of weight, two very different categories exist:

(1) Transference from one part to an immediately adjacent part as in hip to knee, "rolling" being the term used. (2) Weight transference to a distant part, usually an extremity such as foot to foot, foot to hand, etc. This mode is given the general terms of "walking" or "stepping."

TRANSITION BETWEEN ADJACENT PARTS OF THE BODY—"ROLLING"

We will start by investigating "rolling." A good experience is to move from kneeling to sitting on one hip, the weight transferring along the thigh until it reaches the hip. Then roll over to the other hip and along up to the other knee. Once the torso is on the ground the comfortable, easy way of transferring weight is through rolling, be it logrolling or somersaulting. For a somersault roll the body needs to be curled up. Because the feet are then near the hips, a smooth rolling between hips and feet can take place.

Different forms of rolling may require control and strength depending on the type and speed. In general, rolling is "comfortable" in that no problem of loss of balance, of falling, exists. An interesting roll, the "monkey roll" results from grasping both ankles, feet together, legs turned out, and the back rounded. Rolling can start toward the right side of the body or to the left, transferring to the back and then the opposite side to end sitting up again. Returning to the same front usually takes three such rolls.

Indication of rolling is based on the appropriate revolution sign. Example 9.3a gives the indication for any revolution around the axes of the body. Support signs are added to this indication to show rolling. Example 9.3b shows many changes of support while rotating. This notation is simplified by using one support sign at the beginning and one at the end to express continuous supporting, i.e., that rolling occurs from beginning to end, 9.3c.

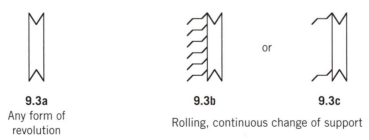

9.3a	9.3b		9.3c
Any form of revolution		or	
	Rolling, continuous change of support		

This indication is further simplified by abbreviating the supporting line, as shown in the logrolling of 9.3d. The supporting signs may be drawn on either side of the symbol as in 9.3e; there is no change in meaning. Example 9.3f shows logrolling in either direction.

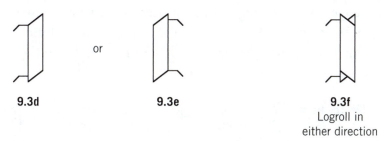

9.3d   or   **9.3e**   **9.3f**
Logroll in
either direction

A somersault either forward or backward rolling on the floor is expressed as 9.3g. 9.3h specifies a forward roll; the performer will automatically curl up as a preparation to accomplish it. A forward somersault in the air is written as 9.3i. This is, of course, only the bare statement with no instructions as to how it is to be achieved.

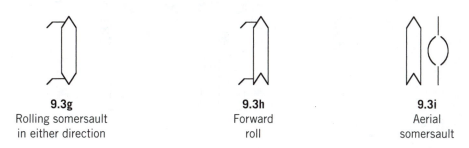

9.3g   **9.3h**   **9.3i**
Rolling somersault   Forward   Aerial
in either direction   roll   somersault

READING STUDY NO. 29

LYING ON DIFFERENT PARTS OF THE TORSO

In this study, changes in supporting on one surface or another are achieved through rolling. Lying on the front, the back, or the side is indicated by stating the surface on which the body is supporting. A small "tick" or line is added to the appropriate side of the torso sign to indicate the surface.

The front surface   The back surface   The right side   The left side   Both feet   Both shoulders

The base line before the starting position of this study visually makes the notation look more self-contained; for that reason it is usually added.

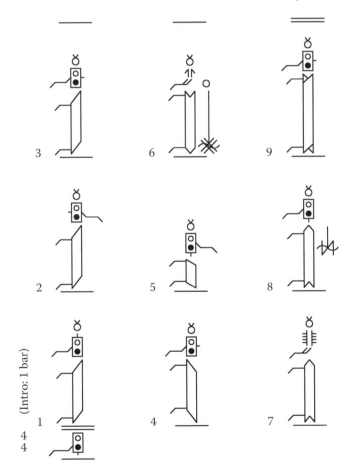

In measure 6, the body draws in and stays that way (holds the flexion) until it extends in measure 8. In measure 9, direction for logrolling is left open.

TRANSITION BETWEEN DISTANT PARTS OF THE BODY—"STEPPING," "WALKING"

As mentioned before, "stepping" and "walking" are the general terms given to transferring the weight from one body "extremity" to another. Walking usually occurs on the feet, but we also "walk" on the knees, or on the hands. In sitting, we can inch forward or backward by "walking" on our hips. Such walking is on "paired parts." Of the less familiar forms, there is transference of weight from a foot to head, from a knee to an elbow, etc., i.e.,"stepping" onto "unpaired parts." In such contexts the hips, knees, elbows, and wrists, act as "extremities" and no rolling occurs.

The basic general indication for transferring weight, 9.4a, is modified to show a "step" of some kind, 9.4b. It is expected that such improvised "stepping" will often take place on the feet, but other possibilities should also be tried. In 9.4c, a turn to the left is accompanied by three "steps." Try this first with foot supports; then find a variation using knees or unpaired body parts. The instructions of 9.4d, a sideward low action with two transferences of weight, suggest use of knee and hand. Sharing of weight is allowed as long as weight is really taken, i.e., not just a lean to maintain balance.

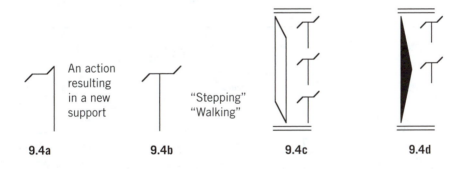

An action resulting in a new support

"Stepping" "Walking"

9.4a   9.4b   9.4c   9.4d

A direction sign and the supporting sign can be combined to show the direction of a new support. Example 9.4e states that the forward action results in a new support, i.e., a forward "step" of some kind. In 9.4f the low backward action results in a new "step," perhaps on a hand or knee (extremity of the thigh). Example 9.4g indicates transference of weight in place, i.e., not into any direction, therefore on the spot. Gradually indications for movement possibilities are combined to spell out more specifically the instructions for a desired sequence.

9.4e   9.4f   9.4g

SIGNS FOR THE MAIN PARTS OF THE BODY

The next stage is to specify which part of the body is taking weight. The appropriate part of the body sign is combined with the support indication. Example 9.5a gives the signs for the main parts of the body, the areas and the joints. Indication of "either hand," "either foot," etc., is given in the next section, as are the general, non-specific signs.

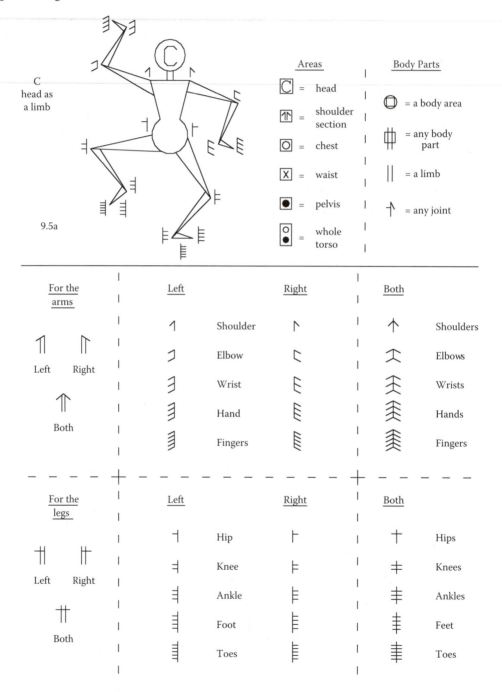

C
head as
a limb

9.5a

Areas

C̄ =	head
⇑Λ =	shoulder section
Ō =	chest
X̄ =	waist
⬤ =	pelvis
o⬤ =	whole torso

Body Parts

⬭	= a body area
⬚	= any body part
‖	= a limb
↑	= any joint

For the arms	Left	Right	Both	
⫞ ⫟	⌐ Shoulder ⌐	⌐	⋀	Shoulders
Left Right	Elbow			Elbows
⫟	Wrist			Wrists
Both	Hand			Hands
	Fingers			Fingers

For the legs	Left	Right	Both	
╫ ╫	Hip		╪	Hips
Left Right	Knee			Knees
╫	Ankle			Ankles
Both	Foot			Feet
	Toes			Toes

SIGNS FOR BOTH BODY PARTS

Use of both hands or both feet, etc., is indicated either by writing both left and right signs, 9.6a and 9.6c, or by combining them into one sign, 9.6b and 9.6d. Examples 9.6e and 9.6f indicate both knees; 9.6g and 9.6h mean both hips; 9.6i and 9.6j show both shoulders.

9.6a	9.6b	9.6c	9.6d	9.6e	9.6f	9.6g	9.6h	9.6i	9.6j
Both hands		Both feet		Both knees		Both hips		Both shoulders	

The conjoined sign for both shoulders must be drawn as 9.6k to avoid looking like an arrow, 9.6l. In drawing the hips signs; the short horizontal tick must be above center, to differentiate between a single hip sign, 9.6m, and the horizontal sideward pin (tack), 9.6n. The sign for both hips is 9.6o or as written in 9.6p.

9.6k	9.6l	9.6m	9.6n	9.6o	9.6p

Note the modification of the single support sign bow to show supporting on two parts at the same time, 9.6q. Example 9.6r indicates three supports at the same time. When kneeling is indicated, the lower legs usually rest on the floor to assist balance. In an upright kneel the lower legs do not support the main body weight.

9.6q	9.6r
Both feet support	Both knees and one hand support

SIGNS FOR: "EITHER SIDE;" "EITHER OR BOTH"

When choice should be left open as to which hand, foot, etc., to use, the "either side" sign, 9.7a, is added to the double part of the body sign. The "either side" sign is composed of a short vertical line (representing the vertical line in the body dividing right and left) and the horizontal ad lib. sign meaning "any"; thus "any side." The either side sign is placed before the double part of the body sign.

9.7a	9.7b	9.7c	9.7d	9.7e	9.7f	
Sign for either	Either hand	Either foot	Either elbow	Either knee	Either hip	etc.

The instruction "either or both" may be needed. For this, a small vertical ad lib. sign in a circle states "any number," 9.7g. When applied to two body parts, it gives the choice of one or both. Examples 9.7h and 9.7i illustrate this usage.

9.7g	9.7h	9.7i
Any number	Either or both hands	Either or both feet

In use of body parts, a general statement may be needed before becoming specific. Example 9.7j is the sign for "any joint"; it is a composite of a shoulder and a hip sign. 9.7k is the sign for an area in the body. It is composed of the square box sign for an area, 9.7l, placed inside a circle, the circle, 9.7m, representing aspects of the body. The sign of 9.7n represents "a limb," i.e., any limb. By combining the two signs of 9.7k and 9.7n we indicate "any body part," 9.7o. Note that this sign is usually simplified to 9.7p.

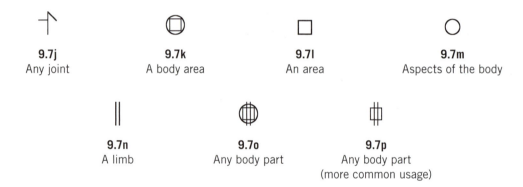

9.7j	9.7k	9.7l	9.7m
Any joint	A body area	An area	Aspects of the body

9.7n	9.7o	9.7p
A limb	Any body part	Any body part (more common usage)

SPECIFIC NUMBER OF LIMBS, BODY PARTS

As noted above, any number of body parts can be shown by the vertical ad lib. sign within a circle, 9.7g. Therefore 9.8a indicates any number of body parts. A specific number is stated by using the appropriate number. Example 9.8b states use of two limbs; in 9.8c three body parts are to be involved in supporting.

9.8a	9.8b	9.8c
Any body part(s)	Two limbs	Three body parts

PART SUPPORTED; PART TAKING WEIGHT

There is logic in having the weight-bearing sign slant downward. At the top end of the sign is written the part being supported (knee, hand, etc.), at the bottom end is written what is supporting, 9.9a and 9.9b. When nothing in particular is shown, the supporting part is understood to be the floor. Example 9.9c shows kneeling on a chair (note the drawing of a chair); 9.9d shows sitting on a chair.

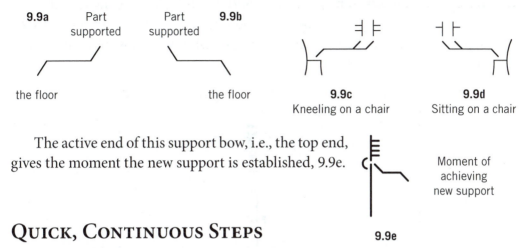

The active end of this support bow, i.e., the top end, gives the moment the new support is established, 9.9e.

Moment of achieving new support

9.9e

QUICK, CONTINUOUS STEPS

"Steps" may be repeated continuously, sometimes in relation to the structure of the accompanying music, but often in an ad lib. timing. For general timing, a simple indication can be given for such continuation of quick "stepping" by using the vertical wavy line of 9.10a. This sign is related to the ad lib. sign and means "continue freely the movement previously indicated." In 9.10b, very fast "steps" of some kind are shown; in 9.10c, the steps are slower as indicated by the more elongated wavy line. Example 9.10d shows rapid walking on the knees.

These indications can be combined with other actions, as for example, in 9.10e. Here the continuous rapid steps include some turning to right or left. These are probably "paired" steps, that is, on both feet or both knees. In 9.10f, walking on the knees is shown to travel to the left. The faster the movement, the smaller the waves in the line become until it represents a rapid vibrating movement comparable to a vibrato or a tremolo in singing.

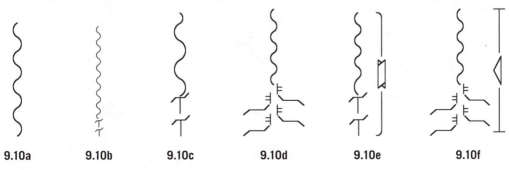

READING PRACTICE G (NO MUSIC)

SUPPORTING ON DIFFERENT PARTS OF THE BODY—"STEPPING," ROLLING

This study in changes of support compares "stepping" ("unpaired" and "paired") with rolling. It progresses from a step, a support on a foot, to kneeling on one knee, to sitting on one hip, weight on one knee and one hand, etc. Transitions between these supports are up to the performer; many variations are possible. Note use of sign for "either side."

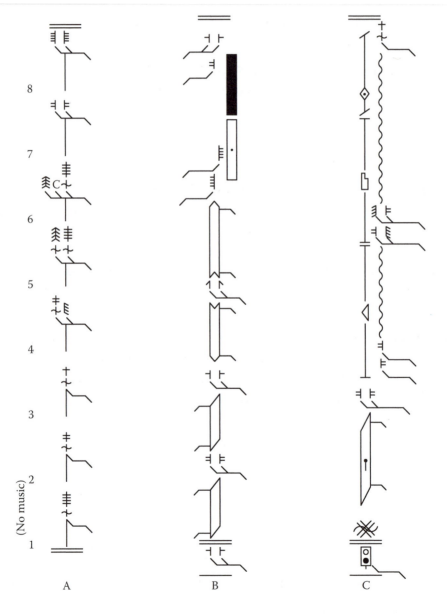

A B C

CHANGE OF SUPPORT ON THE FEET— WALKING, "STEPPING"

PERFORMANCE OF A SINGLE STEP

Transferring the weight from foot to foot, walking, is such a familiar action that we are often unaware of the process. Do we really know what is happening and can we therefore modify performance of steps as needed in a movement sequence? How actually is a simple step, a single transference of weight, achieved?

Where does a single step start? Where does it end? Except for steps in place (on the spot) the working leg has to move out in the direction into which the step is to be taken. Let us say that this will be a forward step.

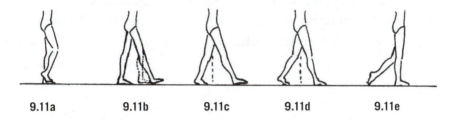

| 9.11a | 9.11b | 9.11c | 9.11d | 9.11e |

Example 9.11a shows the right leg free and ready to take a step. In 9.11b, it has moved forward and is touching the ground; at the same time the weight has shifted slightly forward. But this leg gesture (touching the ground but free of weight) need not lead into a step. Many such gestures occur without a step following. In 9.11c, it is clear that a step will take place because the weight has been shifted forward beyond the toes of the supporting left foot. This is a normal preparation for the transference of weight to the right foot. As the weight is transferred forward there is a moment of double support, as in 9.11d. In a forward step, the back heel usually comes off the floor at this moment. The weight then moves completely onto the new support, 9.11e, and the left leg, released of weight, is free to leave the ground and to begin the preparation, the gesture, that leads into the next step. **A full step, a total transference of weight,** has not been completed until all the weight is on the new support. Moving into an open position on two feet, as in 9.11d, is only a half step.

Try a series of slow steps and sense the weight continuously moving. What happened? Did you pause before starting the next step? Did you perform a favorite variation of a step, rather than keeping it completely simple? Was an ornamental preparatory leg gesture included, an unnecessary flourish? Was importance given to the leg being released, bringing it conspicuously into place beside the other leg? Or did the leg gestures occur only to make the steps possible, that is, having no importance in themselves? This last is the correct performance of the basic action of walking.

The expression of walking can vary enormously according to how the body is held, how the legs flex, extend, their state of rotation, how the feet are placed on the floor, their use in transferring and releasing weight. Even in a simple walk a keen eye will spot significant variations in performances by different people.

INDICATION OF WALKING, STEPPING

The full Motif Description for walking, stepping on the right foot then the left, can be written as 9.12a. This notation states an action ending with weight on the right foot, then the same for the left foot. The sign for a stepping action on any distal part is 9.12b or 9.12c. Because walking on the feet is such a common action, a special abbreviation is used: 9.12d shows the general indication for supporting on the feet. A step on the left foot is 9.12e while stepping on the right foot is 9.12f. Example 9.12g shows stepping on both feet, as after sitting or landing from a spring. Example 9.12h shows a step on either foot. Example 9.12i gives the choice of taking weight on either or both feet.

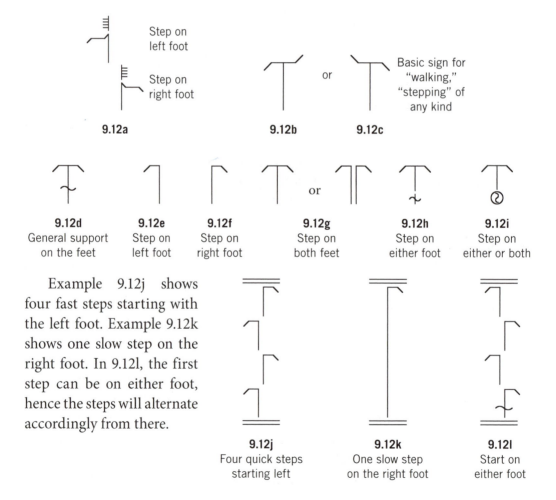

Example 9.12j shows four fast steps starting with the left foot. Example 9.12k shows one slow step on the right foot. In 9.12l, the first step can be on either foot, hence the steps will alternate accordingly from there.

DIRECTION AND LEVEL FOR STEPPING WITH THE FEET

We combine these indications with direction symbols to state the direction in which the steps occur. Example 9.13a states a forward step on either foot. A left sideward step with the left foot is represented in Example 9.13b. In 9.13c, a backward step with the right foot is given.

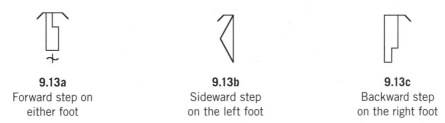

9.13a
Forward step on
either foot

9.13b
Sideward step
on the left foot

9.13c
Backward step
on the right foot

Normal standing on both feet in place is indicated with the middle level support, 9.13d. Standing with the knees bent (*demi-plié*) is shown with the low level place symbol, 9.13e. Standing on half-toe (*relevé*) is written with a high level place symbol in 9.13f.

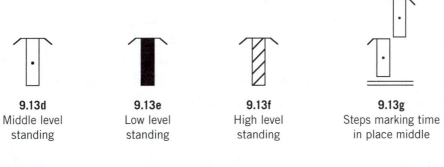

9.13d
Middle level
standing

9.13e
Low level
standing

9.13f
High level
standing

9.13g
Steps marking time
in place middle

The length of the action stroke, or direction symbol, indicates the duration of the transference of weight. Example 9.13h shows a slow sideward low step. In 9.13i, two forward steps in middle level at a moderate tempo take place. Quicker backward steps are shown in 9.13j. Steps becoming increasingly slower are shown in 9.13k, first two high level steps shown right and left, followed by feet together with bent knees and then a slower step backward on either foot. The indication for "either" is included in the timing of the backward step.

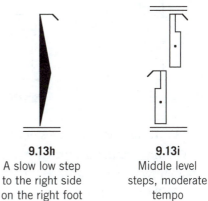

9.13h
A slow low step
to the right side
on the right foot

9.13i
Middle level
steps, moderate
tempo

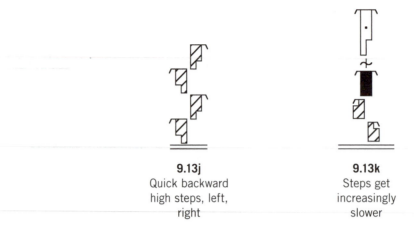

9.13j
Quick backward
high steps, left,
right

9.13k
Steps get
increasingly
slower

Traveling, Turning by Means of Transference of Weight

Rolling, "stepping," or walking actions may occur for several reasons, the most obvious one being to travel. Let us see how, for this traveling, variations are indicated. Example 9.14a is the basic sign for traveling on a straight path. To cover ground when supporting on the feet, walking or running will most likely take place, but the path sign itself does not stipulate this. If rolling is wanted, this can be stated as in 9.14b, the sign for any kind of rolling being placed within the path sign and thereby stating this is the mode through which traveling is achieved. Similarly, if need be, any "stepping," i.e., use of various distal parts of the body, can be shown, as in 9.14c. The notation of 9.14d specifies traveling on the feet.

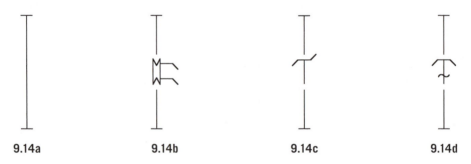

9.14a   **9.14b**   **9.14c**   **9.14d**

    "Walking" on the knees, 9.14e, or on the hands, 9.14f, can be stated as the means by which traveling occurs by placing the indication in the path sign, 9.14g and 9.14h. 9.14g shows traveling on the knees; in 9.14h traveling by walking on the hands is shown. The number of steps or whether one starts on the right or left is not stated. Note use of the caret: < or > in 9.14e and 9.14f to indicate reference is still to the same part of the body.

| 9.14e | 9.14f | 9.14g | 9.14h |

When concentration in stepping is on the transference of weight, the action is usually slower, as previously shown in 9.12k.

Example 9.14i indicates turning which is accomplished through steps on the feet. Example 9.14j states that the turn includes steps; when and how many is left open. The vertical inclusion bow, 9.14k was given earlier. Example 9.14l states at what point two steps occur during the turn, a step on the right foot, and later a step on the left, both quite quick transferences of weight. In 9.14m, the same two steps occur, but each is a slow transference with no break between.

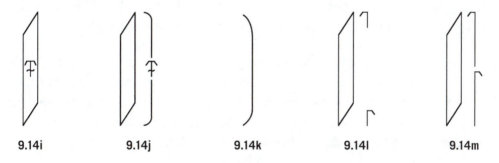

| 9.14i | 9.14j | 9.14k | 9.14l | 9.14m |

Statement of a form of action within a turn sign or a path sign indicates how the main movement is achieved. Comparable to 9.14i, 9.14n shows traveling by means of springing; this could be running, hopping, jumping, etc. Turning through springing is shown in 9.14o. This contrasts with 9.14p which shows that springing is to be included. In 9.14q, only one spring is to occur near the beginning of the turn.

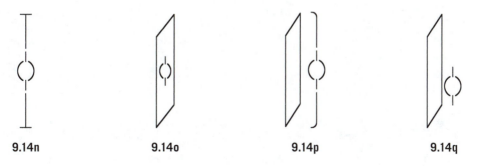

| 9.14n | 9.14o | 9.14p | 9.14q |

NOTES ON READING STUDY NO. 30

CHANGE OF SUPPORT

This study starts lying down; whether lying is on the front, back, etc., is not designated. The logrolling which follows is of any amount, but leads without a break into an action resulting in sitting. The progression then leads into kneeling, then standing. Lowering backward onto the hips is followed by rolling backward onto the shoulders. This soon leads into traveling. In measures 9 and 10, the manner in which traveling is achieved is indicated within the path sign.

Note the drawing of the forward and backward symbols in measure 11. There is no change in meaning if the indicator for the direction is written on the right or on the left side of the symbol; for visual reasons it is drawn on the side that makes it easier to read. At this stage we are not yet specifying movements of the right or left sides of the body, therefore direction symbols can be interpreted as either or both. Because at the start of measure 11, weight is on the right hand and knee, the directional gestures will need to be performed by the left side of the body.

As mentioned in Chapter 5 for Reading Study No. 20, when repeats occur in Motif scores the question arises as to whether identical movement should be performed on the repeat or whether the same material, the same instructions, can be interpreted differently. Nothing yet stipulates either interpretation; therefore it is up to the performer to enjoy the freedom in translating the instructions into movement.

Reading Study No. 30

CHANGE OF SUPPORT

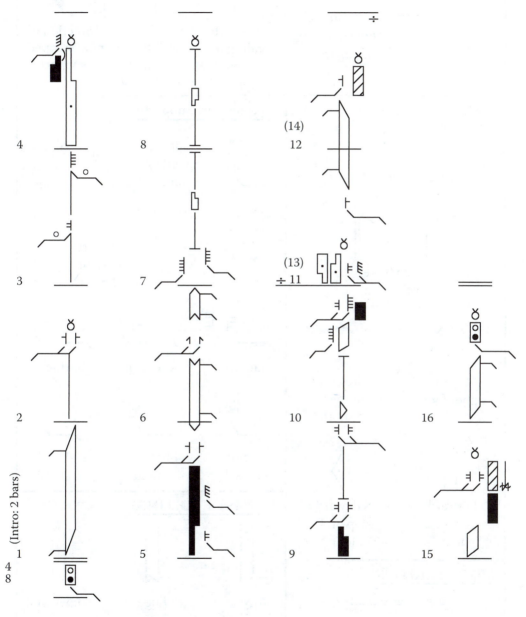

$\overset{\cdot}{\div}$ = repeat (measures 11 and 12 are repeated)

= hold the support (measure 3), cancelled by sitting in measure 5

REVIEW FOR CHAPTER NINE

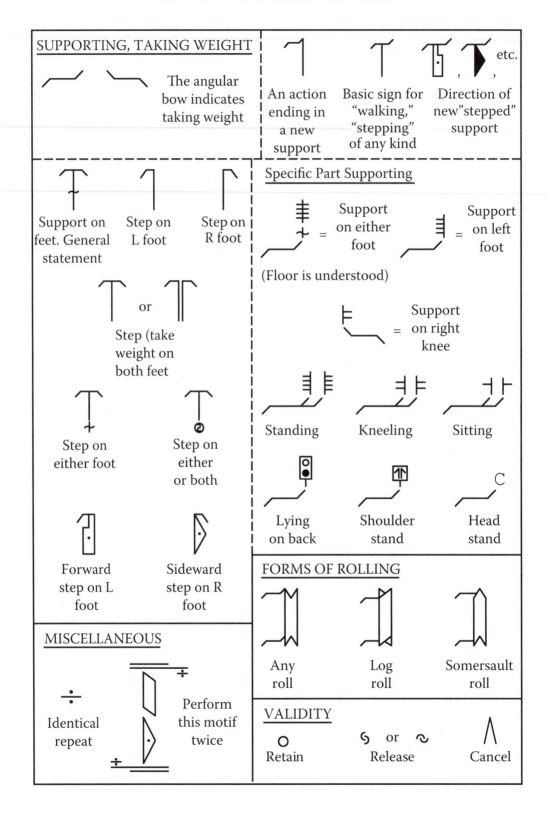

SUPPORTING, TAKING WEIGHT

The angular bow indicates taking weight

An action ending in a new support

Basic sign for "walking," "stepping" of any kind

Direction of new "stepped" support

etc.

Support on feet. General statement

Step on L foot

Step on R foot

Specific Part Supporting

= Support on either foot

= Support on left foot

(Floor is understood)

or

Step (take weight on both feet

= Support on right knee

Step on either foot

Step on either or both

Standing

Kneeling

Sitting

Forward step on L foot

Sideward step on R foot

Lying on back

Shoulder stand

Head stand

MISCELLANEOUS

FORMS OF ROLLING

Any roll

Log roll

Somersault roll

Identical repeat

Perform this motif twice

VALIDITY

Retain

Release

Cancel

Review for Chapter Nine (continued)

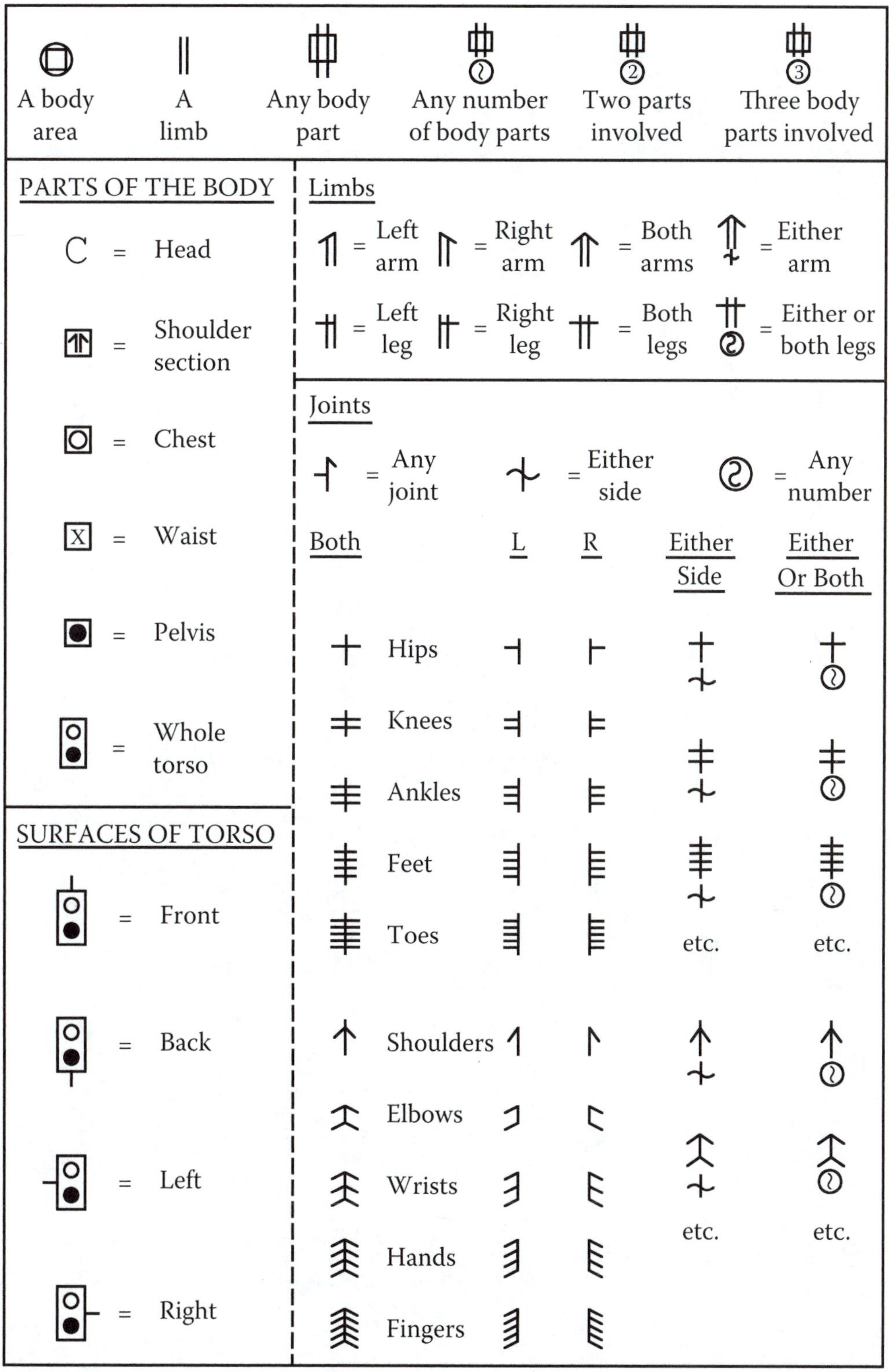

A body area
A limb
Any body part
Any number of body parts
Two parts involved
Three body parts involved
PARTS OF THE BODY
= Head
= Shoulder section
= Chest
= Waist
= Pelvis
= Whole torso
SURFACES OF TORSO
= Front
= Back
= Left
= Right
Limbs
= Left arm
= Right arm
= Both arms
= Either arm
= Left leg
= Right leg
= Both legs
= Either or both legs
Joints
= Any joint
= Either side
= Any number
Both
L
R
Either Side
Either Or Both
Hips
Knees
Ankles
Feet
Toes
etc.
etc.
Shoulders
Elbows
Wrists
Hands
Fingers
etc.
etc.

CHAPTER TEN
Balance, Loss of Balance

Maintaining equilibrium is not an activity that normally occupies our attention. In early childhood, we learned to balance on two feet and in everyday life we function in balance. Only under special circumstances do we find ourselves concerned with balance. An uneven surface or a narrow plank over a brook may cause us to be consciously, actively aware of balance. Otherwise it is only little accidents which cause us to trip that bring home to us what a small surface the foot provides as a base for the weight of the body. It is in the performing arts of gymnastics, acrobatics, dance, and skating that active awareness centers on equilibrium. We marvel at the ballerina who can balance on the tip of her pointe shoe, 10.1a, or the tightrope walker who performs fancy steps and even acrobatic tricks on a swaying wire, 10.1b.

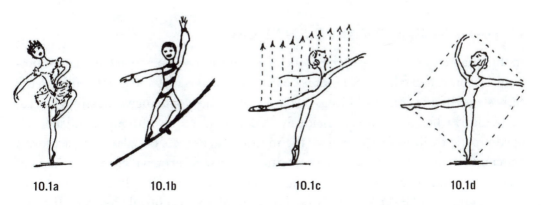

10.1a   10.1b   10.1c   10.1d

A SENSE OF BALANCE

For some performers balance is an inherited gift; others must work hard to achieve it. Indeed, the more we strive the less success may result, for it is a sensation and coordination in the body to be mastered through the right kinetic feeling rather than by concentration on the mechanics. Just as an object needs to be rigid to balance on a small surface, so there needs to be adequate tension, tautness, in the body. This is achieved through upward and downward energy, extension through the spine, an inner uplift. In balancing on half-toe, the performer's concentration should not be on the foot itself, but on the upward flow of energy. The image should be that of the top of the head lifting toward the ceiling, carrying with it the weight of the body. Invisible strings attached to imaginary balloons lift each inner muscle fiber, 10.1c; the performer does not "do the work." If the limbs are extended, the sense of reaching out in space can assist balance. In a held position the lines in space linking the limb extremities can act as "electrical connectors" creating spatial tension between the points of this imaginary shape suspended in the air, 10.1d. If there is movement of the limbs, such movement can also extend energy out into space as well as a produce firm pressure against the floor, thus creating spatial tension. Concentration on projecting out into space, in contrast to concern with muscles in the body, has helped many performers to achieve serene and enjoyable periods of balance. The word "poise" relates to an inner sense of balance. Many body designs (positions) which are to be suspended in stillness require poise, that is, equilibrium both in the physical sense and as an inner feeling and awareness. Balance requires concentration, but too often this produces an introverted, bound flow state, whereas energy should be flowing outward as though the air around takes care of balance. Sensation alone will not solve all balance problems; we need to know a few facts, and also how balance can be used practically as well as expressively.

In Balance; Weight Centered

In this chapter, we investigate the scope of equilibrium from active balance to complete, uncontrolled falling. Balance is not a new idea, it is met and practiced from the early stages of movement training. But active awareness of being vertically centered, particularly when one is not consciously "balancing," requires thought and a developed kinetic realization. To explore the mechanical aspects of balance, to achieve a better understanding of it, we must first find the correct vertical placement of weight, the line of balance in the body, starting with ordinary standing. In the correct centered alignment, the vertical line of balance should pass centrally between the two ears down to just in front of the anklebone, 10.2a. How does it feel to have the line of balance, the plumb line, the vertical line of gravity, centrally placed? The answer comes through personal experience in mastering control and in anatomical understanding. For stillness, even on two feet, awareness of balance is important.

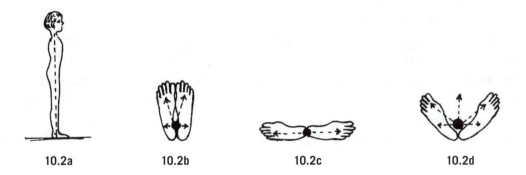

10.2a   10.2b   10.2c   10.2d

Standing with the feet together, experience shifting the weight in different directions over the area provided by the soles of the feet until you have found the true point of balance. Experiment with how far the weight can be shifted when the feet are together, parallel, as in 10.2b; when fully turned out, 10.2c; or when comfortably turned out, as in 10.2d. The triangular-shaped base provided by the two feet in 10.2d is the most stable of the three positions. The more the Center of Weight approaches the edge of the supporting base, the less stable the position. Very little lateral shift is possible with parallel feet, and, clearly, very little sagittal shift for a completely turned out position of the feet, as in 10.2c.

IMAGES TO AID EQUILIBRIUM

Balance that is maintained fleetingly or for more extended periods in dance has an expressive impact. Maintaining balance may be either in stillness or in movement, as in multiple turns or in slow changes of level, as in a controlled full leg bend, a deep knee bend (a *grand plié*), also in a sustained transference of weight which includes level change. For each such action finding an appropriate image can greatly help in achieving the desired result.

10.3a   10.3b   10.3c   10.3d

From a centered position, perform a slow full leg bend (a *grand plié*), 10.3a, 10.3b, and 10.3c. Experience this lowering of the center of gravity as though it were a bead sliding smoothly down a vertical wire, 10.3d. The same image is used on the upward movement—the smooth sliding up the center vertical line until normal standing is reached. Through this image the whole action of lowering and rising concentrates not on the muscular action in the legs, the flexion of the joints, but on the controlled and fluent movement of the center. Apart from the technical advantage which this image gives, it concentrates on the sense of being centered, of being coordinated, of being "in tune." The resulting serenity is very expressive. Such concentration on balance may be for choreographic reasons to express awareness of what one is doing or to provide an integrated control while other expressive gestures take place.

Every moment in the process of transferring weight from one foot to another may be filled with concern for balance. The body stance, the manner in which the arms, head, chest, etc., are held, will be very different from an absent-minded version of walking. A very slow transference of weight from one foot to another into a direction is a good setting for experiencing controlled balance while progressing, particularly if rising and lowering occurs within one step.

INDICATION OF CENTER OF GRAVITY, ACTIVE BALANCE

Every object has its center of balance. In the case of bodies with movable parts the location of the Center of Gravity (C of G) changes according to the configuration of the body, the placement of the parts. Thus we see that the C of G is a movable point, and not a fixed point within the body. In normal, centered standing, for most people it is located near the upper rim of the pelvis. For our purposes we do not need to be exact. Example 10.4a is the sign for the C of G. When in balance, the C of G is on the vertical line, the up/down dimension, 10.4b. Balance occurs when the C of G is above, at, or below the point of support. Here we are concerned mainly with balance above the point of support, the support usually being the floor, though it may be an object or a partner.

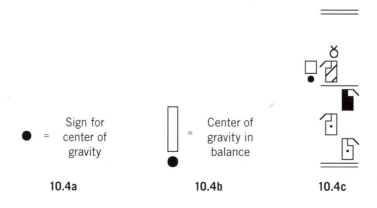

Sign for = center of gravity

Center of = gravity in balance

10.4a   10.4b   10.4c

In ordinary standing, balance is obviously present. When then, is it important to refer to it, to focus attention on it? When does balance need to be stated? Note the following sequence. Find the point of balance at the end of the movement sequence of 10.4c. Three quick forward steps lead into a quick, high step which is then held, suspended in balance. While suspending, the free leg may be in one of several positions. Choose one, for balance is more easily mastered when the free limb has a definite placement. Centering of the C of G has been stated to stress that this awareness is important. An indication for balance is needed when such active awareness is required, be it at the start, during a transition, or at the end of a sequence.

Note that the term Center of Weight is now often used instead of Center of Gravity. For our purposes, these terms are interchangeable.

The indication of the C of G on the vertical line has two functions. As we shall soon see, when falling occurs, the vertical line indication shows the moment balance is regained. When an in-balance state is understood, the C of G indication calls for specific awareness of center. How long is that awareness to last? In 10.4e, there is awareness of balance on the rising but it has not been stated to be retained on the traveling forward or on the forward action; it is, however, again present during the half turn. In 10.4f, the awareness of center is there at the start and is to be maintained (as indicated by the retention sign: o) until the end of the turn where the general cancellation sign of 10.4d states the retained awareness of balance ceases to be in effect, i.e., it goes away. A balance can also be cancelled by a *tombé* or by a true fall.

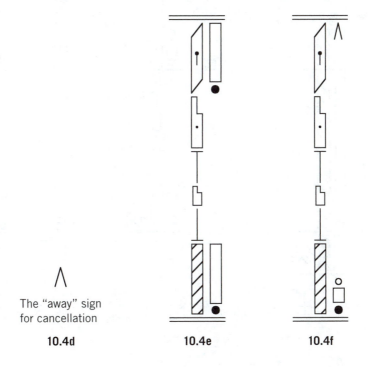

The "away" sign
for cancellation

10.4d

10.4e

10.4f

READING STUDY NO. 31

BALANCE

Concentration here is on the vertical line of balance. The first action in this study is a slow rising of the body-as-a-whole with an awareness of balance. In contrast, lowering combined with flexion in measure 3 is not concerned with balance, but just with the two stated activities. Note that the retention sign: O gives specific instruction to maintain a state. The "away" sign cancels a retained state (indication).

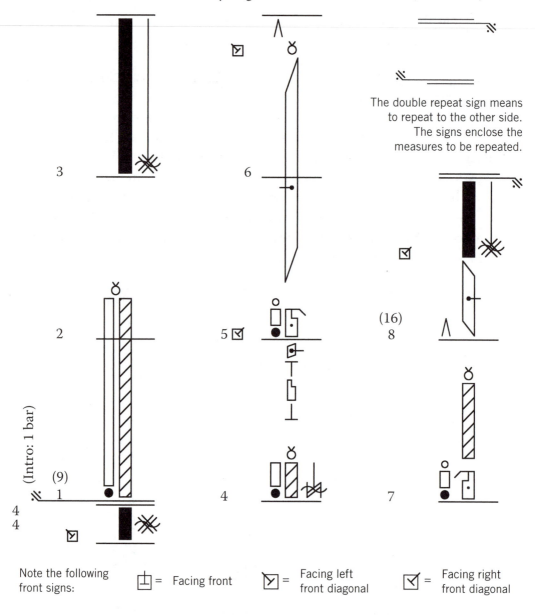

The double repeat sign means to repeat to the other side. The signs enclose the measures to be repeated.

Note the following front signs: ⊥ = Facing front   ⟨⟩ = Facing left front diagonal   ⟨⟩ = Facing right front diagonal

SHIFT OF WEIGHT

Next in the progression from active balance to falling is shifting the C of G within the area of the supporting base, balance still being maintained.

AUTOMATIC SHIFT OF WEIGHT

When carrying a heavy object, such as a suitcase, the C of G of the body automatically shifts to the opposite side to maintain balance. Even with a change in the location of an arm or leg a slight adjustment is made. When arms are raised, a leg lifted forward or backward, or when the position of the head or the torso changes, as in a tilt, there is automatically a shift in the center of balance in the body. We have all seen an untrained person raising a leg forward and have observed the slight backward lean of the torso which occurs naturally to counterbalance the weight of the lifted leg, 10.5a. The trained performer has developed the muscular control to hold the weight of a raised leg while keeping the rest of the body apparently motionless, 10.5b.

| 10.5a | 10.5b | 10.5c | 10.5d |

A familiar example of weight adjustment occurs when tilting the whole torso forward; there is an automatic shift backward of the pelvis, 10.5c. This backward shift need not be exaggerated, taking the weight back onto the heels, as in 10.5d. The trained performer can minimize any displacement of the hips but total absence of displacement is impossible for most people. This is illustrated in the parlor game of standing heels flat up against a wall and trying to pick up an object on the floor placed near the feet, 10.5e. Because the C of G cannot shift backward to compensate the weight of the torso, the person falls forward, 10.5f.

The circus clown can lean at a preposterous angle because his long weighted rigid shoes provide a longer base, 10.5g.

| 10.5e | 10.5f | 10.5g |

INDICATION OF SPECIFIC SHIFT OF WEIGHT

Minor spatial displacements of the C of G within the base of support are shown with pins, the point of the pin indicating the direction. As 10.6a incorporates the ad lib. "any" sign, it states a shift in any direction. Small horizontal displacements are indicated by flat pins ("tacks"). Examples 10.6b–10.6f show how a shift is indicated in the four main directions and also the return to center. In 10.6g, a phrase of shifting to and fro of the C of G is given; here carets state continued use of the center of weight. Slower shifts are shown by following the pin with a duration line, which is tied to the pin with a small vertical bow to state that it is not a separate movement, 10.6h. A series of shifts producing a smooth movement phrase can be shown by enclosing them within a vertical phrasing bow, as in the circular pattern of 10.6i.

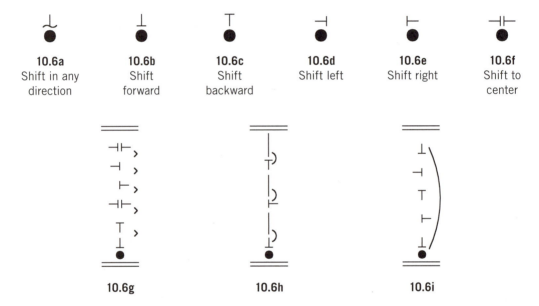

10.6a	10.6b	10.6c	10.6d	10.6e	10.6f
Shift in any direction	Shift forward	Shift backward	Shift left	Shift right	Shift to center

10.6g   10.6h   10.6i

A shifted placement of the C of G affects the expression of a simple walk. Try walking forward with the weight shifted forward, as in 10.6j. This forward shift at the start of traveling may or may not disappear, it is an open statement. In the subsequent examples, retention of weight shift is indicated. Example 10.6k shows the same walk but with the weight always back on the heels. Be sure that it is a displacement of the center of weight and not a slight tilt of the torso or a pelvic displacement, as these are quite different movement ideas. Example 10.6l shows walking backward with the weight forward, while in 10.6m the weight returns to center halfway through traveling forward.

Shifting can also accompany directional gestures. In 10.6n, a retained backward shift of the C of G accompanies a general forward action. Then a general return to center and centering of the C of G both occur. The action stroke, linked to the shift

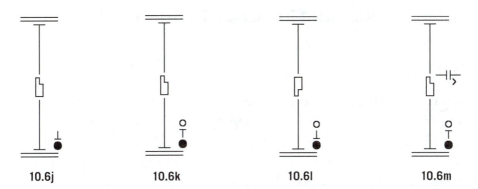

| 10.6j | 10.6k | 10.6l | 10.6m |

with the small vertical bow, shows the duration of this return to center for the C of G. This is followed by a general backward action during which the forward C of G shift is finally cancelled. Level for the main forward and backward actions has been left open to choice.

In 10.6o, sustained forward and backward shifts lead into traveling forward, the forward weight shift being retained. As traveling finishes the weight is again centered. Use of carets avoids repetition of the C of G sign.

Despite such shifts of weight, the performer is still in balance, i.e., not falling, as the center of gravity is still within the base of support. True centered balance, that is, the C of G in perfect alignment over the base of support, can be expressed when need be by the indication of 10.6p. Center of gravity shifts may be small movements, but they may have a marked effect on the expression of other actions or they may contribute to achieving a body placement which aids technique.

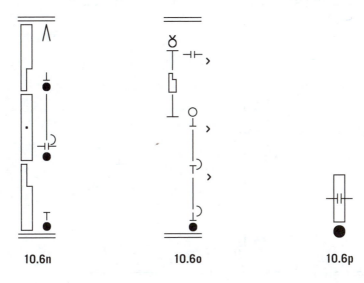

| 10.6n | 10.6o | 10.6p |

READING PRACTICE H (NO MUSIC)

SHIFTING

This study in sustained shifts of weight should be performed with a comfortable turn out of the feet, thus allowing an appropriate base. Enjoy the sustainment of these small movements. Be sure the whole body weight shifts and that it does not become a pelvic movement. Note the use of the phrasing bow in measures 5 and 6 to indicate smooth performance, also use of the caret, < or >, meaning "the same," to obviate having to repeat the C of G sign each time.

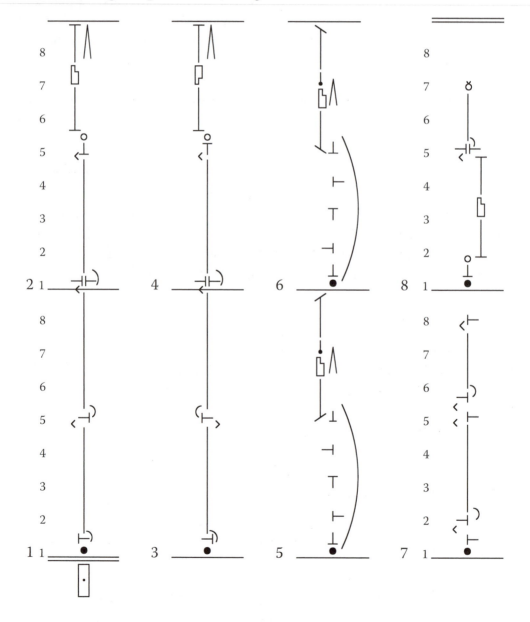

SLIGHT LOSS OF BALANCE; *TOMBÉ*

Though the center of gravity moves when the body weight is shifted, balance is still maintained. The C of G is still under control and within the base of support. When is balance lost? One has only to think of the Leaning Tower of Pisa, 10.7a. At what point, if the leaning increases, will the tower fall? When the line of the center of gravity in the building falls outside the base of support. The larger the base of an object, the greater the distance weight can shift in different directions without loss of balance.

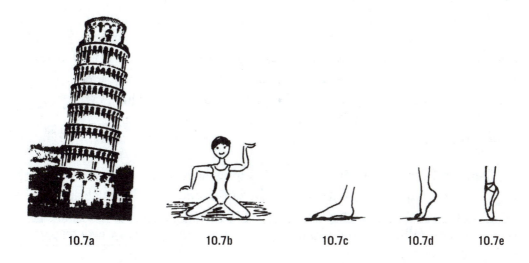

10.7a   10.7b   10.7c   10.7d   10.7e

In 10.7b, the dancer is kneeling with knees apart. Between the feet and knees is a large triangular area of support. This allows a generous range of displacement of the C of G. It is possible to lean in every direction without loss of balance. But on a single foot, 10.7c, awareness must be given to balance, and even more so on half-toe, 10.7d, where the base is so small only a slight shift of weight may produce falling. On full *pointe* (tip of toes), as in 10.7e, balance is even more precarious.

Once the C of G has shifted beyond the outer margin of the supporting base, falling occurs. This falling may be slight and easily controlled, or it may be marked, or even hopelessly out of control. Complete loss of balance will be investigated fully following exploration of slight loss of balance.

As we have seen, in the process of walking, the C of G moves a little ahead of the previous support into the next step. The transition is smooth and there is no sense of falling since the foot for the new support is there, ready to take the weight. If the foot is not there, then falling will take place. The same is true of running; after a moment of weightlessness in the air, the foot contacts the ground and, when no further traveling follows, the C of G becomes centered on the new support. If the running continues, the weight passes across the length of the foot as preparation for the take-off into the next running step. In walking and running, there is no awareness of falling as such, therefore, as a rule, no statement regarding the C of G need be made.

SLIGHT FALLING: CENTER OF GRAVITY IN MOTION—*TOMBÉ*

The first stage of falling occurs when the C of G leads into the direction of the new step. This C of G in motion, a pleasant experience when anticipated, is called *tombé* in ballet terminology. In a rise on two feet, allow the weight to leave center, carrying you into the direction of your next step. The result will be an over curve into a cushioned support, 10.8a. The greater the amount the C of G is in motion, the longer the step needed to catch the weight.

10.8a

The term "Center of Gravity leading" is often applicable for *tombé*, this slight loss of balance. Explore steps in different directions and levels in which such intentional slight loss of balance occurs. Discover at what point a sense of total loss of balance, of true falling, might take over.

INDICATION OF CENTER OF GRAVITY IN MOTION—*TOMBÉ*

Center of gravity leading is indicated by the sign for C of G being placed within a vertical bow, 10.9a. The length of the bow shows the length of time during which the C of G is in motion. This duration can be brief, a preparation for a single

10.9a
Center of gravity in motion (leading)

step, or it may continue over a sequence of steps in the same direction. This is a "passing state" bow in that the movement it indicates—C of G in motion in this case—is over, completed, after the end of the bow. (See Chapter 13 for Part Leading.)

In 10.9b, there is a slight falling (leading of the C of G) into the path forward. This traveling may be a run since loss of balance, even slight, produces the momentum needed to travel swiftly. On the other hand, such slight falling could lead into a walk or leisurely gallop or skip; the manner of traveling is not stated. In 10.9c, a movement up is followed by a *tombé* into a low backward "step." Example 10.9d states specifically that the C of G leads into a sideward step on the right foot. In 10.9e, the end of a turn to the right is linked with a step to the left by a slight falling. The direction of the C of G leading is always the direction of the step or path that follows. Note that this leading bow overlaps slightly the step or path which follows. 10.9f shows the C of G leading throughout the traveling.

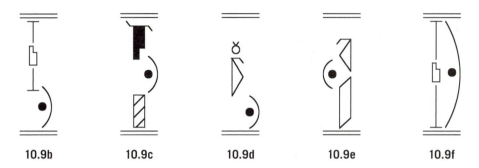

| 10.9b | 10.9c | 10.9d | 10.9e | 10.9f |

OFF-BALANCE TURNS

Multiple turns, such as *pirouettes*, require centered balance. However in certain dance styles, loss of balance can temporarily occur at the beginning of a turn, in the middle, or at the end. The weight is briefly off center resulting in a labile turn, in contrast to a stable, centered turn. A swinging motion may be the impetus for the momentary off-center balance in a turn. Or a sudden swoop may occur during a stable turn, the lean of the torso taking the weight off center. Example 10.10a illustrates a labile turn, 10.10b being the indication of temporary loss of balance at the start of a turn. It is assumed that balance is regained and the turn continues centered.

10.10a   10.10b

FRONT SIGNS

To provide a more definite statement concerning paths traveled and directions faced, it is important to know your orientation in the room. This aspect of spatial orientation is investigated in detail in Chapter 15; for now we introduce the main signs. Once the Front of the room or of the performing area has been determined, the "compass" of the Constant Directions is set. The performer is at the center of these directions. In 10.11a the letter P represents the performer.

10.11a
The Front Signs

The appropriate Front sign is placed at the left of the movement notation at the start of the score. When a new Front is established, such as after turning or after a curved pathway, the sign for this new Front is stated and this Front is maintained until another needs to be indicated. Note that to distinguish such orientation to the room or stage from the physical front of the body, a capital "F" is used. For minor changes of Front, the slight transitional turn which produces the new Front, is usually not important and so, for a general Motif Description, this unemphasized turn is not written. The eight Front signs are named in 10.11b.

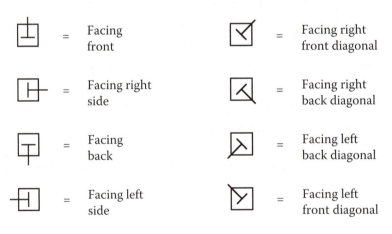

10.11b

READING STUDY NO. 32

CENTER OF GRAVITY IN MOTION—*TOMBÉ*

In this study, the speed of the *tombé* movement varies, some being "pulled out" rather than rushed into. A swaying quality in the body will help the falling movement, particularly for the curved path of measure 21 and the lilting to and fro of measures 25–28. Once the footwork has been memorized, minor arm and body movements can accompany it. Active balance is stated in measures 4, 12, and 29. Note slight changes in facing direction shown by the Front signs.

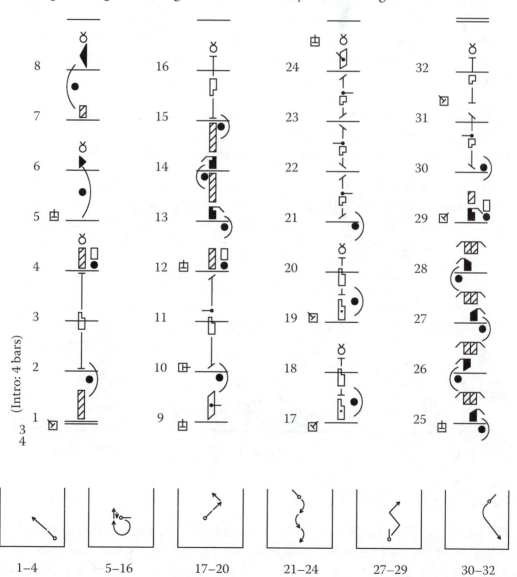

FALLING: FULL LOSS OF BALANCE

Complete loss of balance is an experience that few people enjoy. But, to state it more accurately, it is not the loss of balance which is distressing but the subsequent contact with the floor or other hard, injurious object. A true fall occurs when the C of G is no longer on the vertical line above the supporting base; it has moved far beyond, as in 10.12a. Without a new support quickly taking place under the moving C of G, the person will go crashing to the floor. The new support is usually a foot, the result of a deep lunge, as in 10.12b where the right foot has darted forward to catch the weight and terminate the state of falling. We have all seen a person badly lose balance, 10.12c, and despite attempts to regain it, end up "strewn" on the floor, 10.12d. Falling in one piece, "flat as a board" on one's face, 10.12e, is an extreme version which requires some nerve, as does the same kind of fall sideward or backward. In these falls the path of the C of G is an arc peripheral to the previous point of support.

In dance one must be able to produce such an action intentionally when the choreography demands it. We must learn to control falling (if one can put it that way) and have it as a servant at our command to be used when needed.

10.12a   10.12b

10.12c   10.12d   10.12e

INDICATION OF FALLING

The basic indication for being "off the vertical line," i.e., **not in balance**, therefore falling, is 10.13a. Falling is indicated by specifying the appropriate direction symbol into which the C of G moves, as in 10.13b–10.13d. A main direction symbol automatically shows that the C of G is no longer on the vertical line, i.e., in balance, therefore the slash for "not" is not needed for a specific direction symbol. The level in lowering toward the floor is not needed for the general description we are using here; thus the direction symbol is left blank.

A rare event is a fall in place. Such a fall occurs when your feet slide out from under you, or is achieved by lifting the weight and moving the legs away so that the body falls straight down. To indicate this, the basic sign for falling, 10.13a, is shown to be at middle level, middle level being the floor, 10.13e. For this the slash is needed to indicate the idea of falling.

10.13a	**10.13b**	**10.13c**	**10.13d**	**10.13e**
True fall, total loss of balance	True fall forward	True fall sideward right	True fall backward	A fall in place

DURATION FOR LOSS OF BALANCE

The length of the falling symbol indicates the amount of time it takes **to achieve loss of balance.** Once the C of G moves beyond the base support, falling takes place. The duration of falling is usually brief, unless prolonged by traveling, which will be seen later.

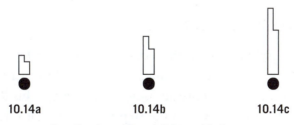

10.14a	**10.14b**	**10.14c**

Duration to **achieve** full loss of balance

FALLING WITH TRAVELING

When falling precedes traveling the direction of falling and of travel must be the same. This is because traveling is a path for the body-as-a-whole which includes the C of G. It is not possible, for example, to fall sideward while traveling forward. Example 10.15a states falling and traveling to the right; 10.15b indicates falling and traveling backward.

10.15a   10.15b

When falling and traveling occur at the same time, such as in a falling run, the C of G is constantly ahead of the point of support so that no centering of balance can take place. Performing such a run requires nerve; it is like continuous stumbling without the security of regaining balance. Improvise using such runs and observe when falling actually begins and where it ends; balance may be regained before you intended it to do so. Observe how the "brakes" can be applied to halt the falling. When occurring with traveling, timing for loss of balance may be relatively slow or it may be sudden. Similarly, regaining balance may be gradual or sudden. The most sudden, of course, is arriving flat on the floor, or being "caught" by a partner. Once the C of G is off-balance it may be difficult to control it, but contact with another person or a wall can prevent a complete fall.

CANCELLATION OF LOSS OF BALANCE

Termination of falling is indicated by use of: (1) an "away" cancellation sign; (2) a return to balance; (3) a support which allows no further falling, e.g., torso on the floor. First we investigate the familiar termination of falling by a new step.

FALLING ONTO NEW SUPPORT

Loss of balance while supporting on the feet is most comfortably rectified by sudden placement of a foot under the C of G as illustrated in 10.16a and 10.16b, the right foot having darted forward to take the weight under the C of G. This action is written in 10.16c, the "away" cancellation next to the step indicating that the falling state is no longer in effect. If the step is not long enough, as in 10.16d, the foot will not be placed under the C of G and the person will still be falling. A series of such ineffectual steps will produce continuous falling on each step, as represented by 10.16e. Note the retention symbol after the falling indication in 10.16e to state clearly the continuation of falling.

If awareness of balance is important, cancellation of falling is indicated as in 10.16f, the caret referring to "the same" previous indication of the C of G. If no retention symbol is indicated for falling, as in 10.16g, when the falling ceases is left open to the performer.

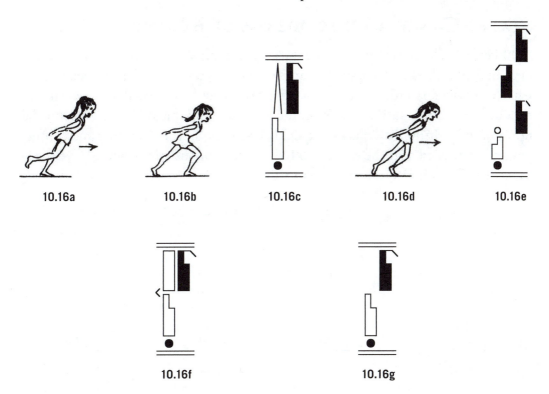

10.16a 10.16b 10.16c 10.16d 10.16e

10.16f 10.16g

Falling may occur into any direction and onto various parts of the body. Example 10.16h illustrates a turn followed by falling backward and ending with an in-balance support on the right foot. In 10.16i, a sideward fall is caught on the right hand and knee, illustrated in 10.16j. Because the body could continue to fall further, i.e., to the hip, the "away cancellation" confirms the cessation of falling. The lowering action of 10.16k is followed by a fall to the right which ends on the right hip. Once weight is on the hips or torso, falling for the body-as-a-whole has ceased. Since the body cannot fall further when supported by the floor, the "away" cancellation is therefore not necessary, but can aid the reading process.

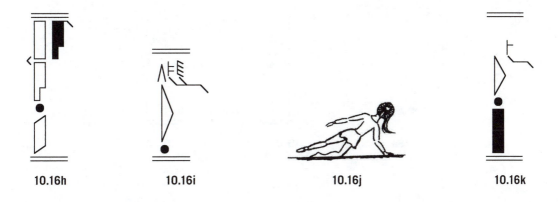

10.16h 10.16i 10.16j 10.16k

STATED CANCELLATION OF LOSS OF BALANCE

In 10.17a, balance is quickly lost at the start of traveling. Whether balance is regained or falling continues is not stated. Example 10.17b states that balance is slowly lost while traveling forward, the "away" cancellation is given at the end to show balance regained. To show continued falling, the retention sign must be added, as in the next examples. In 10.17c, balance is quickly lost at the start of traveling and continues until cancelled near the end. In 10.17d, the continuous falling while traveling is cancelled by a return to centered balance at the end.

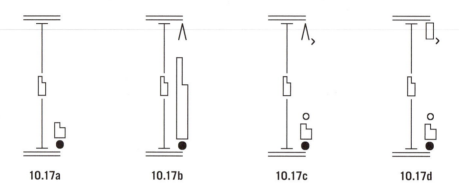

10.17a	10.17b	10.17c	10.17d

MOMENTARY FALLING

Momentary falling requires a falling indication to be written in the curved vertical bow, 10.18a. The duration of the falling is the length of this "passing state" bow. Such falling may be unintentional, as in a trip occurring while traveling, 10.18b. By using the inclusion bow, as in 10.18c, we show that momentary falling is to be included at some point while traveling, just when is up to the performer.

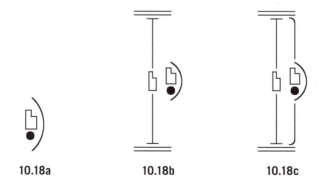

10.18a	10.18b	10.18c

A brief resumé of the three forms of cancellation of falling is given here.

A fall is cancelled by:

1) a new support with an "away" cancellation sign.
2) a return to centered balance if an awareness of center is important.
3) a resulting support on the pelvis or torso. Note that a new support on a foot, knee, or hand, may not completely stop a falling action; if it is intended to do so, the "away" cancellation sign is needed with this ending support.
4) the end of the "passing state" vertical curved bow which indicates the C of G in motion.

NOTES ON READING STUDY NO. 33

In Reading Study No. 33, note use of the caret meaning "the same" to obviate the need to repeat the Center of Gravity pre-sign.

Find images for this study, perhaps wind or waves causing you to lose balance. Note the significant change between the moment when falling occurs and when balance is regained. During this study, the basic pattern of falling and catching the weight on one foot is augmented by falling leading into brief traveling, then into longer traveling, and finally into weight being caught on hand, foot, or knee.

READING STUDY NO. 33

FALLING

Note change in facing direction for measure 9, 11, and 13. In measure 12, momentary falling occurs during backward circling.

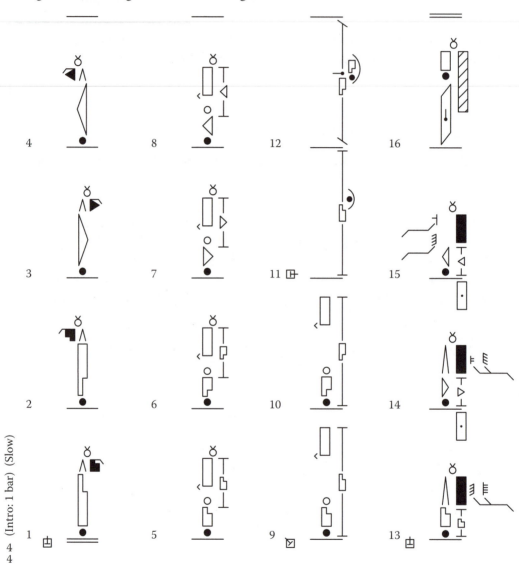

CENTRAL "FALLS"

The term "a fall" or "falling" is given to certain movement sequences met in modern dance and also in other forms of free, flowing movement. In these "falls" no actual loss of balance occurs. They are sequences in which the body, the C of G, lowers on a central line, **always over a point of support**. This occurs through sequential change in supporting part, such as the process of kneeling, sitting, and lying. Because the movement is usually swift, and often performed with abandon, the performer does not realize that at no time is the C of G not over a point of support. Therefore the sequence may also be done in slow motion. When a person falls as a result of fainting, the body relaxes and moves downward sequentially, lowering centrally as the knees weaken and give way, the rest of the body following.

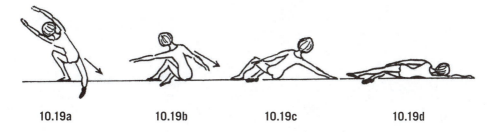

10.19a   10.19b   10.19c   10.19d

Examples 10.19a–10.19d illustrate a typical sideward "dance fall." Note how the body leans into the opposite direction to the "fall," thus helping to preserve balance. Lowering the torso is aided by the hand taking some weight as it slides along the floor. Such "falls" are also performed in a backward or a forward direction through greater use of the hands sliding along the floor. In these central "falls," experienced as "waves breaking on the shore," the line of the lowering of the C of G is more vertical, because it moves in balance over one support after another. To indicate this type of movement, the basic sign for a fall is modified by adding a vertical, downward pointing arrow, to represent the C of G lowering on the vertical line over each support; 10.19e is the general indication for such falls. Examples 10.19f–10.19i show central falls in the main directions. The sequence of 10.19a–10.19d would be written with the basic indication of 10.19i.

| 10.19e | 10.19f | 10.19g | 10.19h | 10.19i |
| Indication for central "fall" | Forward central "fall" | Backward central "fall" | Left central "fall" | Right central "fall" |

In contrast to this relatively simple "fall" is the highly stylized Graham "fall" which, beginning with a contraction and a twist, lowers the body centrally over clearly defined supports. This sequence is learned slowly at first and later speeded up so that the excitement of sudden descent to the floor is present, but at no point is there actual loss of balance. This fall contrasts with, for example, the peripheral Graham fall, a true fall, which commences with one foot sliding out diagonally leading into a forward torso tilt with the weight being caught on the hands. In understanding movement, it is important that we are clear on when a true fall, i.e., a true loss of balance, occurs.

Reading Practice I (no music)

Central "Falls"

Only an outline is given here for the central falls described; use of the arms and torso counter-balance will need to be included to provide a smooth lowering to the floor. Some indication of transition from kneeling to sitting to lying is given. The forward fall is taken more slowly and the recovery is given in outline, a turn leading into the return to middle, normal level.

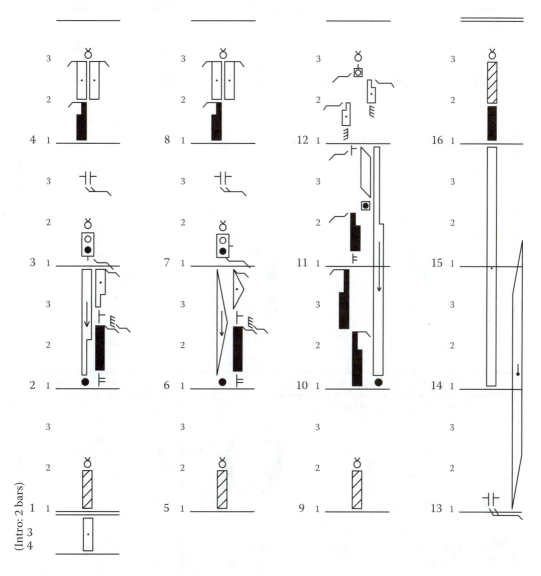

REVIEW FOR CHAPTER TEN

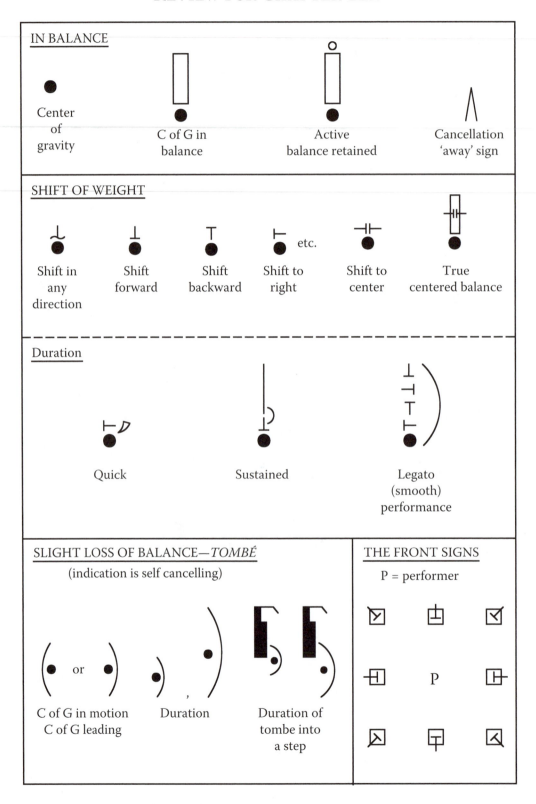

IN BALANCE

Center of gravity

C of G in balance

Active balance retained

Cancellation 'away' sign

SHIFT OF WEIGHT

Shift in any direction

Shift forward

Shift backward

Shift to right   etc.

Shift to center

True centered balance

Duration

Quick

Sustained

Legato (smooth) performance

SLIGHT LOSS OF BALANCE—*TOMBÉ*
(indication is self cancelling)

or

C of G in motion
C of G leading

Duration

Duration of tombe into a step

THE FRONT SIGNS

P = performer

P

REVIEW FOR CHAPTER TEN (CONTINUED)

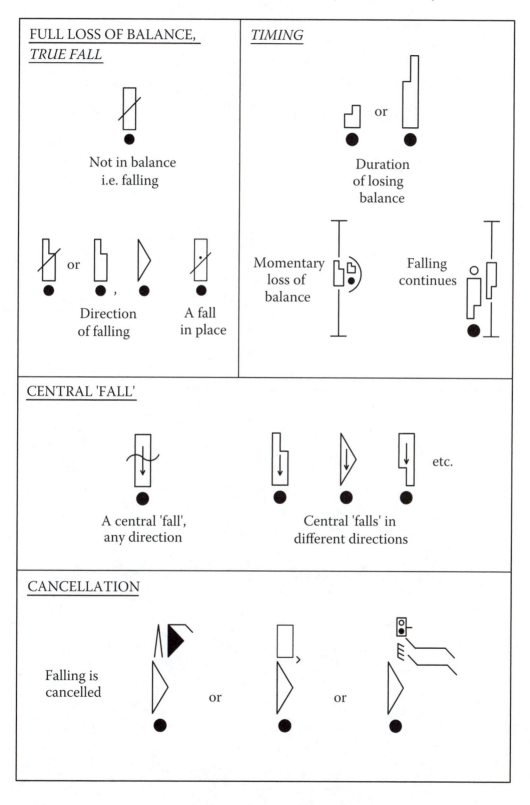

FULL LOSS OF BALANCE, *TRUE FALL*

Not in balance
i.e. falling

or

Direction
of falling

A fall
in place

TIMING

Duration
of losing
balance

Momentary
loss of
balance

Falling
continues

CENTRAL 'FALL'

A central 'fall',
any direction

Central 'falls' in
different directions

etc.

CANCELLATION

Falling is
cancelled

or

or

CHAPTER ELEVEN
Relationships

Relating to the environment begins right after birth. Around us are people, objects, the room. Gradually "the room" extends to be the house, the village, the country, the world. How physically do we relate to all these? The baby is aware of someone there; he sees the person, he reaches out, touches, grasps. A baby's early movements are based on flexing, extending, and rotating in the process of becoming aware, of discovering himself and his surroundings. Before long, actions become functionally directed with a reason, a motivation behind them. The baby becomes increasingly involved with the surrounding people and objects.

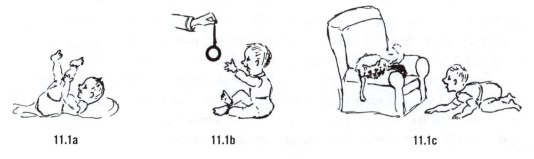

11.1a   11.1b   11.1c

   Progression in becoming aware develops from self, to other people, to moving objects, to stationary objects, to the surroundings. In our exploration of movement, our concern so far has been with basic actions. Now we need to consider both the purpose and the result of such actions. So often the relationship achieved is more important than the movement (the "verb") through which that particular relationship was achieved. Thus relationships in themselves are not actions, they belong to the category of results produced by different kinds of actions.

243

FORMS OF RELATING

The aim of an action may be far more important than the type of movement used to achieve it. To reach out and touch an object we may use extension. If the object is too far, traveling will have to occur. To touch an object on the ground, lowering will need to take place, and so on. The actual movement used to produce contact will depend on placement of the object and the direction and distance in relation to the performer—in front, behind, at the left, near, far, etc. The form of the movement is often of no importance to the mover; he is often quite unaware of what he does to reach his objective. Only the purpose, the aim, the end result matters. For stylized theatrical dance, actions used may be specifically choreographed, importance being given both to the end result and to how it is achieved. Because the aim of an action is so often of prime importance, specific terms and signs have been created to represent the possibilities. The basic sign for any relationship, 11.2a, is a composite of two key signs for relating. It is used when open choice of **any form of relating** needs to be indicated. For our purposes we will focus on the specific forms of relating. The following presentation starts with the slightest degree of relating.

11.2a
Any form of relating

AWARENESS, SENSED RELATING

You are sitting and reading. Suddenly you are aware that someone has entered the room behind you. Before you even turn to look, your body is expressing awareness, usually marked by a very slight heightening of tension in the body, often the head, neck, and shoulders. The attitude is one of "attention." Your concentration has shifted from reading to awareness of another person. Such awareness, for which the fine nerve cells send signals, is like radar; energy impulses can almost be seen to emanate from the performer to the other person. Radar is an apt image, since a comparable inborn sense of awareness exists, more highly developed in some than in others. Consider two people working in a small kitchen. With "radar" tuned in, person A will sense from a slight motion made by B the need to move slightly to one side so that B can reach a needed utensil. If A lacks such developed awareness B must verbally ask A to move over before action can be taken.

How does "awareness" occur in performing? It may be in relation to another person as happens in a play, a dramatic situation. Or there may be an awareness within one's own body as when both hands are aware of one another despite being spatially far apart. A good example is when the arms move in a parallel fashion, and awareness of the one to the other needs to be maintained. This can be seen in the mime action of carrying an invisible box, the hands retaining the same distance apart. This awareness as part of more abstract movement produces a slight intensity, a heightening of performance which adds to the enjoyment both for performer and viewer. In the balletic attitude position, the hand (the extremity) of the arm which is up should relate to the foot of the raised leg, 11.3a, thus completing the arc, the circular line of energy. There is no overt action of the extremities toward each other but a distinct aware- ness, a kinesthetic sense resulting from using kinesthetic imagery. In many dance poses, the relationship of the limbs is not just a matter of spatial placement; the limbs are aware of each other, as dancers are aware of one another on stage (or should be). Such awareness height- ens dance and lifts it above an ordinary everyday event.

11.3a

Awareness is the basic form of relating in that it is the first degree, the least "active" of the many possibilities. In all states of relating it is **the aim**, the idea, we are concerned with here, not the actual movement that occurs to produce the state of relating.

INDICATION OF AWARENESS

The sign for awareness, 11.4a or 11.4b, indicates a relating of an indirect nature, usually at a distance, the performer making no overt action in relation to the source of this awareness, the point of interest. The term "point of interest" refers to a person, object, or part of the room to which the performer relates. Note that in the sign, the "cup" can be drawn facing the opposite direction when this place- ment is more practical for the information needed. Example 11.4c illustrates mutual awareness that can occur between two people, two parts of the body, etc. Signs with dotted lines represent weaker states. Solid lines, seen later, indicate "stronger," active relating.

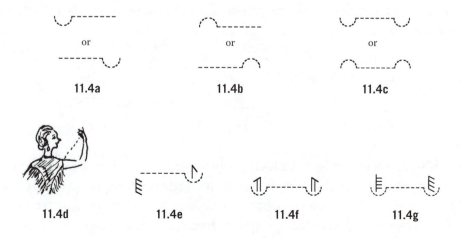

| 11.4a | 11.4b | 11.4c |

| 11.4d | 11.4e | 11.4f | 11.4g |

Example 11.4d illustrates a position in which the right hand relates to the right shoulder; 11.4e is the notation of such relating. Example 11.4f shows mutual relating, awareness, between the right and left arms, and 11.4g indicates awareness between the right hand and the right foot, as illustrated in 11.3a.

ADDRESSING, ACTIVE RELATING

Active relating occurs when a visible movement of some kind is made with the aim of relating to someone or something. The general term **"addressing"** is used to specify this form. Many everyday actions produce addressing. "What was that?" you think as you glance out of the window. "Put it over there," you say, pointing to a desk without looking. "He went that way," you indicate by a backward diagonal tilt of your head.

The most obvious forms of addressing are looking at, gesturing toward, or pointing to the object of interest. Looking may mean directing the whole front of the body to the person or object, or only turning the head, or perhaps only looking with the eyes. The term "addressing" suggests that looking is the main activity; but in fact looking may not be present at all. A gesture toward the point of interest may be made with the arm, the hand, and, in stylized movement, with a foot, knee, hip, elbow, etc. The gesture is such that it clearly expresses addressing. The action which produces or results in addressing may be one of turning, leaning, extending, contracting, shifting, moving toward or away, etc. If looking in the same direction accompanies an addressing action, the addressing has greater impact.

INDICATION OF ADDRESSING

When an overt action is made toward or in relation to a person, object, etc., the sign of 11.5a or 11.5b is used. If there is mutual addressing, i.e., two active parts, the sign is drawn as 11.5c. Note that while the "cup" in the addressing sign usually faces "up," 11.5d, it may face in the opposite direction when this provides better placement for the information.

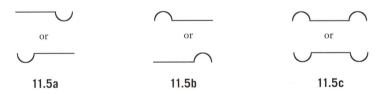

The timing of a movement producing a form of relating is indicated by the length of the action stroke. Relating may occur at the beginning, in the middle, or at the end of a movement. The moment when relating occurs may depend on whether the point of interest is stationary or is moving. Example 11.5d shows an action which ends addressing. In 11.5e addressing is achieved suddenly; in 11.5f a slow action starts with addressing. Note that the addressing bow is attached to the action.

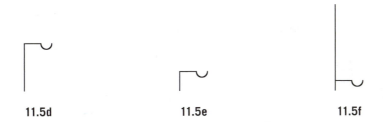

| 11.5d | 11.5e | 11.5f |

PERSON OR OBJECT BEING ADDRESSED

The active part of the addressing sign is the straight line; this is drawn from the staff of the person who is active, the one who is doing the relating. Inside the "cup" is placed the indication of the person or object being addressed.

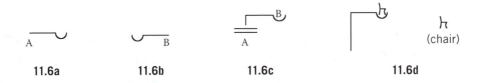

| 11.6a | 11.6b | 11.6c | 11.6d |

In 11.6a person A is active; in 11.6b it is person B. The addressing sign may extend either to the right or left, whichever best fits the organization of the information. In 11.6c, A is addressing B. Example 11.6d shows an action that ends addressing a chair. The object is drawn pictorially or represented by a word.

Example 11.6e indicates that the left hand addresses the right hand. In 11.6f, an action stroke indicates the timing of the left hand movement, the specific action is left open to the performer's choice. Example 11.6g stipulates that it is a sideward gesture for the left hand. In classical mime the gesture for "marry" involves the right index finger pointing to the left ring finger. Fingers are written with a five-stroke sign, as in 11.6h. A dot is added to the appropriate stroke to show the thumb, 11.6i, the little finger, 11.6j, or the index finger, as in 11.6k. Thus 11.6l states the mime gesture for "marry." Here the addressing sign is drawn to the left since it is the right index finger which is active in relation to the left ring finger.

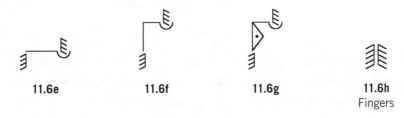

| 11.6e | 11.6f | 11.6g | 11.6h |
| | | | Fingers |

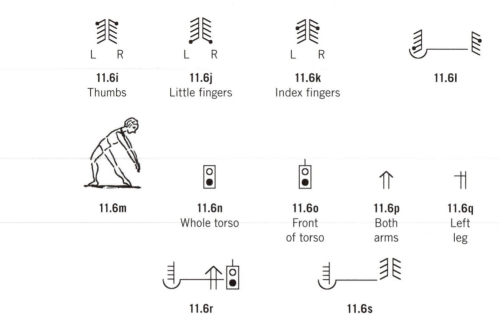

11.6i	11.6j	11.6k	11.6l
Thumbs	Little fingers	Index fingers	

11.6m	11.6n	11.6o	11.6p	11.6q
	Whole torso	Front of torso	Both arms	Left leg

11.6r	11.6s

Example 11.6m shows a familiar movement of the torso inclining over (relating to) the extended leg while the arms relate to the leg by taking a line parallel with it. Example 11.6n is the sign for the torso. By adding a tiny stroke to the front of this sign we indicate the front surface of the torso, 11.6o. Example 11.6p is the sign for both arms while 11.6q indicates the left leg. Example 11.6r is the notation for the idea behind 11.6m. If, in 11.6m, the relating was intended to be for the extremities, that is, the hands addressing the foot, it would have been written as 11.6s.

MUTUAL ADDRESSING

When two people or two parts of the body address one another, the sign with the double "cup" is used.

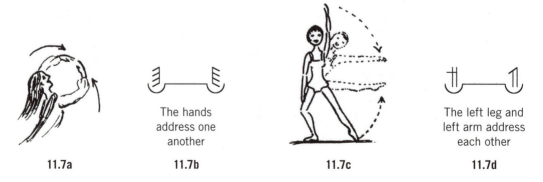

11.7a	11.7b	11.7c	11.7d
	The hands address one another		The left leg and left arm address each other

In 11.7a, as the arms move, the hands relate to each other. This can happen even when they are fairly far apart. In 11.7c, the left arm and left leg address one another, this being the intention of the spatial change in location.

READING STUDY NO. 34

AWARENESS, ADDRESSING

This study explores awareness and addressing in different ways. For this, it may help to have two people, A on your right, B on your left, so that they are visibly there to be addressed. Each may react in some way to the performer's movements, acknowledging the addressing, turning away, and so on. If you are to avoid extending too soon in measures 3 and 4, the gesture which addresses first A and then B will need to be circular in nature. Be aware of the timing of relating as addressing occurs at the start of an action, during, or at the end.

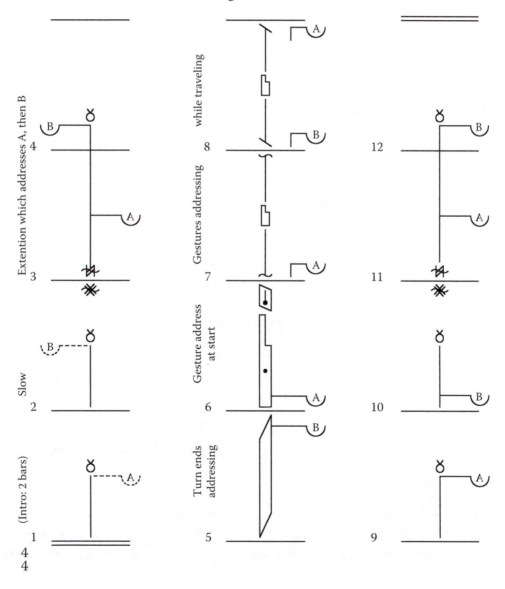

MOTION TOWARD; MOTION AWAY

We continue to progress from the least to the most interactive form of relating. The next stage after addressing is motion "toward." Such action is gestural, axial (i.e., non-locomotor), and may be a gesture of the body or of a limb, that is, a spatial displacement toward the person or object concerned. Such a gesture may be one of inclining the head, of leaning the torso, or a gesture of an arm or hand. It might be a gesture of the leg, for instance if one is angry and wishes to indicate kicking the person or object away. For comedy, a hip, elbow, or heel may be used. We are giving importance to gestures **toward** since they are moving closer to the point of interest, but gestures **away** can also be indicated. The fact that they move away may suggest some degree of negative reaction or relationship such as raising one's hand (in reality the arm) backward to strike a person. However, one may draw back in surprise and pleasure at seeing a loved one, a movement that may be a preparation to move toward that person.

INDICATION OF MOTION TOWARD AND AWAY

Motion **toward** is written by placing the indication of the point of interest (represented here by the ad lib. sign) within an elongated "V" sign, 11.8a. The length of the sign shows duration, 11.8b being a quick gesture of some kind toward your partner (P). Example 11.8c is a much slower gesture toward a chair.

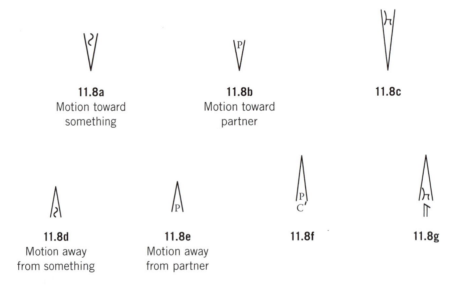

11.8a
Motion toward
something

11.8b
Motion toward
partner

11.8c

11.8d
Motion away
from something

11.8e
Motion away
from partner

11.8f

11.8g

Motion **away** is written by placing the sign for the point of interest (represented here by the ad lib. sign) within an inverted "V" sign, 11.8d. Example 11.8e shows a movement away from your partner; in 11.8f the head makes a motion away from P. In 11.8g the right arm makes a slow gesture away from a chair. With a movement of toward and away, the performer does not travel, does not arrive at the point of interest.

Note that a slim version of the basic sign for "away": ∧ is used alone as a general cancellation when something which was retained is no longer to be in effect, that is, one has "gone away from that state," it has "disappeared," one should "forget about it," no particular state is taking its place.

APPROACHING, PATH TOWARD; RETREATING, PATH AWAY

Approaching, i.e., traveling toward a person, object, or part of the room, may occur for a variety of reasons, and the timing, the mode of approach, and any accompanying gestures may vary considerably, but the main action of progressing closer without arriving, is the same. Approaching may be based on a dramatic motivation, a strong reason for getting nearer, or it may simply occur for a practical reason or for choreographic design as in a folk dance where couples approach one another and then move away. **Retreating**, moving away with traveling, need not express desertion; leaving, backward traveling away, may occur in order to get a better view, as in appreciating a statue or building. A photographer moves away to get a better composition, and so on. Approaching and retreating may occur on a direct path or on a circuitous one; in the latter case the aim, the focal point, may be less obvious or even hidden.

INDICATION OF APPROACHING, PATH TOWARD

Approaching is an action of traveling; therefore the appropriate path sign is used in combination with the indication of what or who is being approached. Example 11.9a states that any path may be used in approaching a person or partner (P), i.e., that the type of path may be varied during the approaching. Example 11.9b indicates an approach to P on a straight path. If approaching is on a circular path, as in 11.9c, the performer may gradually curve in closer to P, approaching through spiraling in, as illustrated in 11.9d, where Y is the performer. In all of these examples, the performer does not arrive at P.

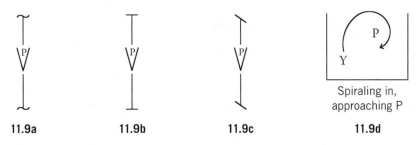

Spiraling in,
approaching P

11.9a   **11.9b**   **11.9c**   **11.9d**

INDICATION OF RETREATING, PATH AWAY

Traveling away, departing from a person, place, or object, is shown by combining the "away" sign with an appropriate path. Example 11.10a states moving away from P on any path; in 11.10b a straight path is indicated, while in 11.10c the performer moves away, on a counterclockwise circular path, thus gradually spiraling outward, away from P, as illustrated in 11.10d.

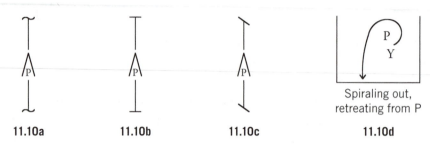

Spiraling out,
retreating from P

| 11.10a | 11.10b | 11.10c | 11.10d |

ARRIVAL, DESTINATION OF PATH

The final stage in approaching a point of interest is **arrival at that point**, that is, reaching the destination, the person, object, or part of the room. Paths to a destination may vary from direct (a bee-line to a selected spot) to indirect (curving or wandering, meandering around as if hiding the ultimate aim). A straight path with a destination may be traveled slowly—representing the idea that fate is calling, it is your destiny. A path may be purely decorative, choreographed, as in a gracious ballroom scene for which direct paths might seem inelegant and so curved paths are used, the lady waltzing in sweeping curves across the floor to arrive at a new partner.

INDICATION OF DESTINATION

The concept of an action with a particular destination, an aim, or an arrival at a particular state, is expressed as 11.11a. At the end of the action stroke is written the aim; here total freedom in choice of an aim is shown by the ad lib. sign, this is connected to the action stroke with a small linking bow to indicate the end result of the action.

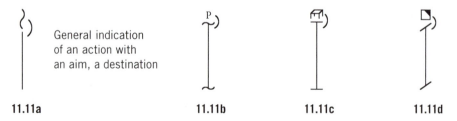

General indication
of an action with
an aim, a destination

| 11.11a | 11.11b | 11.11c | 11.11d |

For a specific statement of the destination of a path, we write the indication for the person, object, or part of the room at the end, and link it to the path sign with the small vertical bow to show that this is the aim. In 11.11b, any path leads to joining, (arriving at) your partner. In 11.11c, a straight path ends at a table, while in 11.11d circling clockwise is destined to conclude in the right front corner of the room or stage. (See 11.12a, 11.12b, and 11.12c for area of the room signs.)

AREAS OF THE ROOM (STAGE)

It is important to be able to state the performer's location in the performing area, usually a room or stage, for which the nine main areas given here are sufficient for our present needs.

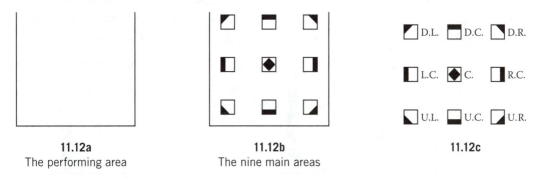

11.12a	11.12b	11.12c
The performing area	The nine main areas	

Example 11.12a illustrates the room or stage; 11.12b shows the nine main divisions. In 11.12c, these are identified as: C = center; DL = downstage left; DR = downstage right; DC = downstage center; UL = upstage left; UR = upstage right; UC = upstage center, and so on. These signs indicate the stage location of the performer and the destination of a path, as indicated in 11.11d.

READING STUDY NO. 35

TOWARD, AWAY; APPROACHING, RETREATING; DESTINATION

PARTNERS RELATING, ENDING APART

Once the sequence of this brief duet has been worked out, the spacing and distances established and the movements coordinated with the music, it is an enjoyable study to perform as it allows for personal interpretation, despite the degree to which actions are specifically stated. In measure 3, A approaches B and also gestures toward him/her. Note that in measure 6, the B in the circular path sign means A circles around B, i.e., B is the focal point of the circling. B also circles around A. At the end of measure 9, B has arrived at A, A is in front of him/her (as stated by the Meeting Line).

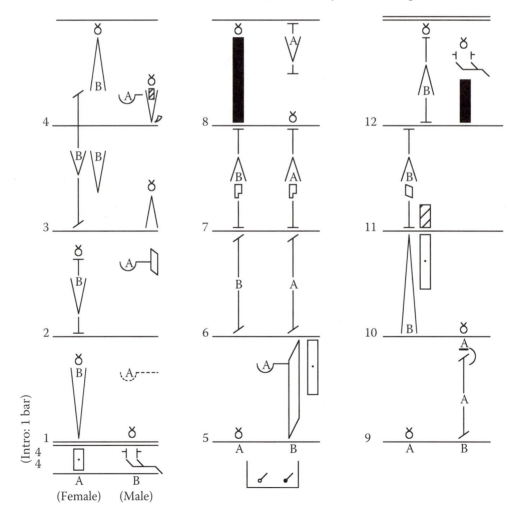

NEARNESS

Proximity to a person or an object may be for a practical need, as in being near an apparatus or object soon to be used, or it may have dramatic significance—think of Tosca with her hand near the knife with which she is soon to stab Scarpia. Choreographically, **nearness** is often used to produce a stylized version of an everyday action, thus removing it one step from reality. A hand near another person's shoulder without actually touching can be more full of meaning than if an actual touch occurred. Palms near each other express a formalized version of prayer. Stopping short of actually touching another person can express hesitation, great tenderness, delicacy of feeling; it can also be restrained anger—"Wait till I get my hands on you!"—a threat not yet carried out.

INDICATION OF NEARNESS

The sign for near, close to, is a dotted horizontal bow, which may be swung upward or downward, 11.13a. This bow connects the indications of the two parts involved.

| 11.13a | 11.13b | 11.13c | 11.13d |

Near, close to

Example 11.13b shows the hands near each other; in 11.13c, A's right hand is near B's left shoulder. The closeness of A's right foot to B's right foot, 11.13d, can be important in ballroom dance and in other partnering sequences. Example 11.13e states the hands are near the opposite shoulders, illustrated in 11.13f.

| 11.13e | 11.13f |

Timing for motions toward or away is shown by the length of the "V" sign; for approaching, retreating, and destination, timing is indicated by the length of the traveling sign. The horizontal bow signs for relating show only the moment when a particular relationship occurs or is achieved. The duration of the action that leads into an addressing, nearness, etc., is shown by the length of the movement (action line) that results in that form of relating. This action may be quite swift or very sustained.

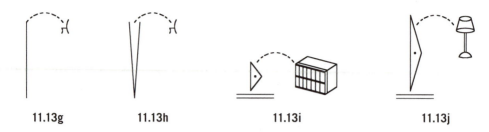

| 11.13g | 11.13h | 11.13i | 11.13j |

Example 11.13g states that the aim of an action is to end near a chair. In 11.13h, an approaching gesture ends near a chair; in the context, this description may be more appropriate. In 11.13i, a quick sideward gesture ends near the corner of a bookcase; in 11.13j a slower, similar gesture ends near a lamp. Note placement of the end of the bow to indicate as closely as possible what part of the object is being related to.

ENCLOSING NEARNESS

A butterfly is on the table; you put your hand over it to hide it without touching it. Your hand closes slightly (becomes curved) as it suspends just above the butterfly. **Enclosing nearness** also occurs when the hand protects a candle flame from blowing out. Such enclosing without touching suggests a special relationship with the object, a protectiveness, a tenderness. It can be a stylized form of enclosing without actual contact.

INDICATION OF ENCLOSING NEARNESS

The dotted bow for near is combined with the "X" for flexion, closing in, to express enclosing without touching, 11.14a.

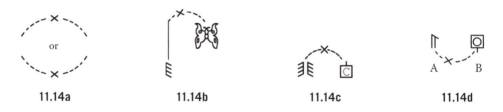

| 11.14a | 11.14b | 11.14c | 11.14d |

Example 11.14b shows the hand around but not touching the butterfly. The "X" is placed closer to the active part. In 11.14c both hands are "enclosing" your face; this is like "burying" your face in your hands without actual contact. Note the sign for face, the front surface of the area of the head. In 11.14d, A's right arm is enclosing B's back, a sympathetic gesture which has not produced an actual hug. The limb, hand, arm, etc., will curve according to the shape of the object. Note the sign for the back surface of the chest.

TOUCH, CONTACT

Whereas nearness may suggest that touching may occur, for actual touching, tactile **contact** takes place. All the examples illustrating nearness can occur with touching. The reason for touching may be practical, functional, decorative, or expressive. The manner in which a **touch** occurs, the use of speed and energy, may range from a careful, delicate contact with a fragile object to the sudden energy of a clap or slap. Repeated contacts, as in tapping, may express rhythmic patterns, as in the Bavarian Schuhplattler dance which features clapping and slapping various parts of the body—thigh, ankle, etc.—in a rhythmic sequence, illustrated in 11.15a. Touching naturally involves the hands, but other body parts also come into play—a foot touching the floor, or a knee, or hip pushing an object away, etc. Contact of the legs often occurs while jumping, for example when the legs beat in a *cabriole*. When two performers are involved, touch is one step closer to being involved with the other person in either a positive or negative way, as in caressing or punching.

11.15a

INDICATION OF TOUCH, CONTACT

The sign for contact, touch, is a horizontal bow, 11.15b. This bow is drawn connecting the parts which touch. It may be swung upward or downward.

or

11.15b

Examples 11.15c–11.15f show some typical examples of contact.

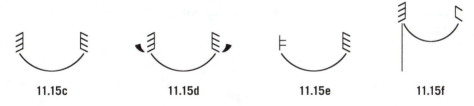

| 11.15c | 11.15d | 11.15e | 11.15f |

Example 11.15c shows contact between both hands. In 11.15d, strong accents have been added to produce sound, i.e., a clap. Accents next to each hand indicate that both hands are active in the strong, quick contact. In 11.15e, the hand touches the knee. In 11.15f, the left hand slowly moves to touch the right elbow. The position with the right hand touching the left elbow and the left hand touching the right elbow is familiar from the Sailor's Hornpipe, notated and illustrated in 11.15g.

11.15g

GRASPING

When a contact is accompanied by enclosing, it produces a grasp. Whereas a touch may be momentary, that is, a passing occurrence, **grasping** (clasping, encircling, enclosing) an object, a part of oneself or another person, denotes a greater degree of involvement because grasping usually has some duration.

The hands are commonly the instrument for grasping, but other parts of the body also serve—as when elbows are linked in a folk dance, a knee grasps a barre, or the arms encircle an object or embrace a person. A leg or both legs may also "embrace" though with less facility. It is important to note that a contact with enclosing **does not include weight-bearing,** this is a further degree of involvement in relating. How a grasp occurs can vary greatly in expression depending on the purpose or reason: grasping a person's arm to provide warm reassurance, or an arresting grip, and so on. Holding a pencil in the mouth may be a form of grasping, as is the action of hugging. Often we "hold," or grasp an object to steady it.

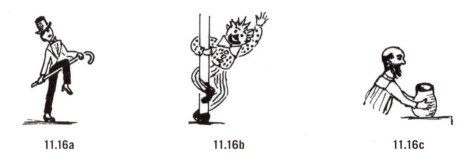

11.16a   11.16b   11.16c

INDICATION OF GRASPING

Enclosing contact, grasping, is written by combining an "X" for flexion with the contact bow, 11.17a.

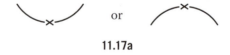

11.17a

In an ordinary hand clasp, one hand grasps the center portion of the other hand, its thumb being inside the thumb of the other hand. In the illustration of 11.17b the left hand grasps the right.

Example 11.17c shows the right hand grasping the left wrist; in 11.17d, B's right hand grasps A's right hand. Note that the "X" is placed closer to the part or person

Usual form of hands grasping each other. Here the left thumb is shown to be on the outside.

11.17b

which is active in the grasping or embracing. Both hands grasp equally in 11.17e, as happens when people shake hands. This is represented by an "X" being placed near to each hand, showing that both are active. Each of these occur in daily life as well as in choreography.

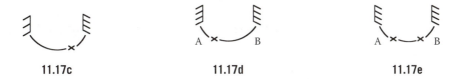

| 11.17c | 11.17d | 11.17e |

Folk dances often employ grasping movements. Linking elbows, as in a square dance, is shown in 11.17f. In this example the "X" is placed in the middle of the bow, leaving open interpretation as to which is active or that both could be mutually active. Example 11.17g states that the left hand grasps the left side of the waist and the right hand grasps the left hand, a position sometimes taken while waiting. Example 11.17h shows B's hands grasping A's waist, a position often used in folk dances when turning.

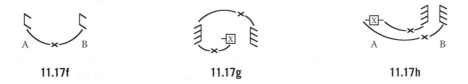

| 11.17f | 11.17g | 11.17h |

Note that the degree to which the hand or limb flexes depends on the size and shape of the object or part of the body being grasped. In each instance, only the single "X" is used to indicate the grasp.

FINGERS GRASPING

Examples given so far in the use of the hand for grasping have often represented the natural action of the thumb closing in opposition to the fingers. Occasionally only the fingers grasp, or it may be only one finger. The signs for the fingers are shown in 11.18a–11.18e.

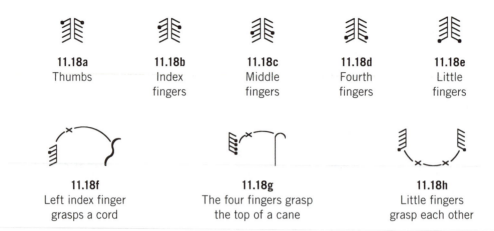

11.18a Thumbs	**11.18b** Index fingers	**11.18c** Middle fingers	**11.18d** Fourth fingers	**11.18e** Little fingers

11.18f Left index finger grasps a cord	**11.18g** The four fingers grasp the top of a cane	**11.18h** Little fingers grasp each other

Examples 11.18f, 11.18g, and 11.18h show some familiar examples of grasping with the fingers.

INTERLACING

A more symmetrical hand grasping occurs when the fingers interlace, 11.19a. **Interlacing**, entwining, penetrating is indicated by a double X. This usage is a convention to show this different kind of enclosing.

11.19a	**11.19b**	Hands clasped with fingers intertwining

Example 11.19a is written as an action of the hand as a whole since the bulk of the hand, the palm, is involved. If, as in 11.19b and 11.19c entwining of the fingers involves only the fingers it is written as such.

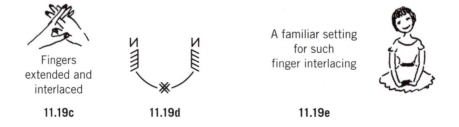

Fingers extended and interlaced **11.19c**	**11.19d**	A familiar setting for such finger interlacing **11.19e**

These are only general indications in exploring a few basic possibilities for such hand relationships. Obviously much more must be stated to produce specific configurations.

SUPPORTING, CARRYING

In general, support is comparable to touching but the contact includes the important fact of taking weight, of **supporting** an object or person, or of the performer being supported. Transference of weight, complete or partial, may be onto an object. Partial transference occurs when leaning against a tree as in 11.20a or when one leg takes weight on a chair shown in 11.20b. In work with a partner or apparatus, many **carrying** variations occur.

11.20a   11.20b

A simple carrying support occurs when the object (or person) rests on a surface of the body, as when a waitress carries a tray, 11.20c, or a jar is carried on the head, 11.20d. It may be a person sitting on someone else's knee, as illustrated in 11.20e, or a person can be supported by an object, such as a large ball, shown in 11.20f. Note that in each of these examples no grasping occurs.

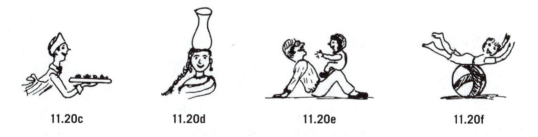

11.20c   11.20d   11.20e   11.20f

INDICATION OF CARRYING SUPPORT

The sign for taking weight is already familiar from our exploration of supporting and change of support in Chapter 9. Now we are concerned not just with supports on the floor, but with supporting an object or a partner.

The angular bows of 11.21a and 11.21b can be used when no doubt exists as to which is carrying and which is being carried, e.g., a feather in the hand.

11.21a   11.21b

The bow of 11.21c or 11.21d shows at the top what is being carried and below the part or object doing the carrying, the supporting. Forms of the bow for supporting can vary according to the placement and the information needed. The bow must, however, always be angular in shape. The forms of 11.21e and 11.21f can also be used when needed.

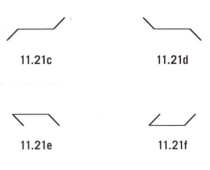

11.21c

11.21d

11.21e

11.21f

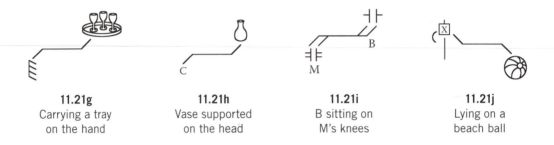

| **11.21g** | **11.21h** | **11.21i** | **11.21j** |
| Carrying a tray on the hand | Vase supported on the head | B sitting on M's knees | Lying on a beach ball |

Examples 11.21g–11.21j show the notation for the carrying aspects of the illustrations of 11.20c–11.20f; 11.21g shows the right hand carrying a tray; in 11.21h a vase is supported on the head; 11.21i shows a baby (B) being carried (hips supporting, sitting) on a man's (M's) knees; and in 11.21j the person moves into lying on the front of the waist on a large beach ball.

GRASPING SUPPORT

Grasping an object may lead to picking it up to carry it; we now bear the weight of the object or person, but now through an enclosing and not just supporting on a body surface. Carrying a partner may involve both arms, one arm, or both hands, depending on the position established and whether the partner is helping or others are contributing to the support. With most objects, carrying includes grasping because it produces a more secure hold. The degree of closing the hand, of folding the arm, etc., depends on the shape of the object. In carrying a stick, the hand may close around it almost into a fist, 11.22a, whereas carrying a large ball will require a more open, but still curved, hand, 11.22b. The part of the body doing the **grasping support** will automatically adjust to the size and shape of the object. In example 11.22c, the elbow grasps as it carries the walking stick.

11.22a   **11.22b**   **11.22c**

INDICATION OF GRASPING SUPPORT (CARRYING-WITH-GRASP)

For grasping support an "X" is added to the carrying bow, 11.23a–11.23f. As with enclosing and grasping contacts, the "X" is placed closer to the indication of the person actively doing the grasping support. Since the "X" indicates the active person, the bows of 11.23a and 11.23b and 11.23e and 11.23f are usually used since they are less space consuming.

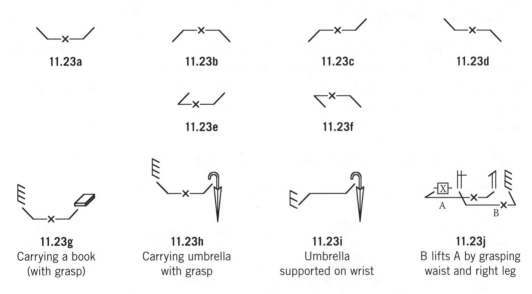

11.23a   **11.23b**   **11.23c**   **11.23d**

11.23e   **11.23f**

11.23g
Carrying a book
(with grasp)

11.23h
Carrying umbrella
with grasp

11.23i
Umbrella
supported on wrist

11.23j
B lifts A by grasping
waist and right leg

Example 11.23g shows the action of carrying (with grasp) a book in the right hand. In 11.23h an umbrella is carried by the handle, but in 11.23i the umbrella is resting on, supported by the wrist, no grasping occurs. Example 11.23j shows a boy carrying a girl, his left arm around her waist, his right hand grasping her right leg. The boy's arms are active in grasping shown by the placement of the "X" in the support bows. This example gives only the basic facts of carrying-with-grasp; details on exact placement of the arm and hand, and what happens before and during the lift all need to be spelled out for a specific performance.

INDICATION OF INTERLACING, PENETRATING

Objects such as a basket made of open wickerwork may be handled with the fingers penetrating the spaces. Use of the double "X" sign with grasping or grasping support bows indicates such penetration, entwining. In 11.24a, both hands carry the wastepaper basket, fingers interlacing the wire structure, while in 11.24b the fingers penetrate the hair.

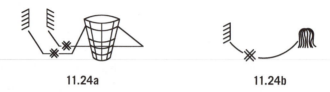

11.24a   11.24b

SUPPORTING; GRASPING SUPPORT WITH A PARTNER

Examples 11.25a–11.28d show some familiar supports which occur when working with a partner. Only the form of supporting, the focus of the activity, is written in the notation. In each case, the feet are also supporting on the floor; this is not given in the notation except for in 11.27d, where A's hands are supporting on the floor.

MUTUAL SUPPORT: LEANING TOWARD

Note the addition of a small stroke to indicate the back of the torso.

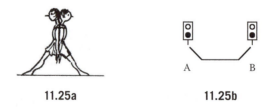

11.25a   11.25b

MUTUAL SUPPORT: LEANING AWAY

Here each person also supports the other, but by grasping.

11.26a   11.26b

PARTNER TAKING PARTIAL WEIGHT

Person A leans toward B who prevents her from falling by a grasping support of her left ankle. In this relationship, grasping need not occur; it could be plain supporting, in which case a supporting bow without an "X" would be used.

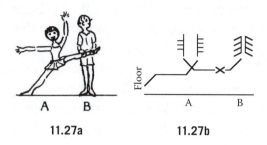

11.27a   **11.27b**

Here is the familiar wheelbarrow position in which the girl's hands are supporting on the floor while the boy is supporting her feet (grasping her ankles); it is written in Motif Description in 11.27d.

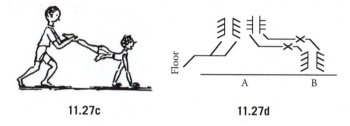

11.27c   **11.27d**

More detail must, of course, be written to get the exact position, the direction faced, angle of the body, etc. Addition of such details leads into Structured Description in movement notation.

PARTNERS RELATING WITH DIFFERENT RELATIONSHIPS

Working with a partner may involve more than one form of relating. Example 11.28a shows B supporting A with his hands on her back. Her left ankle is grasping his left ankle, shown in 11.28b. In 11.28c, A's right foot touches B's left knee, while B's right hand grasps A's left shoulder, 11.28d. Indication for the active part when using a bow without an "X" will be explained in Chapter 12.

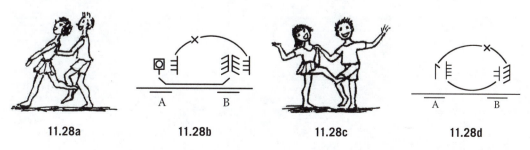

11.28a   **11.28b**   **11.28c**   **11.28d**

Notes on Reading Study No. 36

ADDRESSING, NEARNESS, TOUCHING, GRASPING, SUPPORTING, GRASPING SUPPORT

In this duet for two young people—not too serious, "A" being the girl, "B" the boy, how the partners relate is featured. At the conclusion, they end together. Strict timing is not important; it is the relative timing which is significant, that is, how one person reacts to the other, when both move together and so on. Note the accent and release sign for B in measure 7 which shows that he taps her and then immediately releases. In measure 7 and 9, there is a retention sign above the support bow which indicates that supporting is maintained throughout the action that follows.

-[X]- = sides of waist   ↺ or ↻ = release, let go   ∧ = cancel, move away   [C] = face

Meeting line
— = (the line represents   A̅ = A is behind you   B̲ = B is in front of you
the performer)

READING STUDY NO. 36

ADDRESSING, NEARNESS, TOUCHING, GRASPING, SUPPORTING, GRASPING SUPPORT

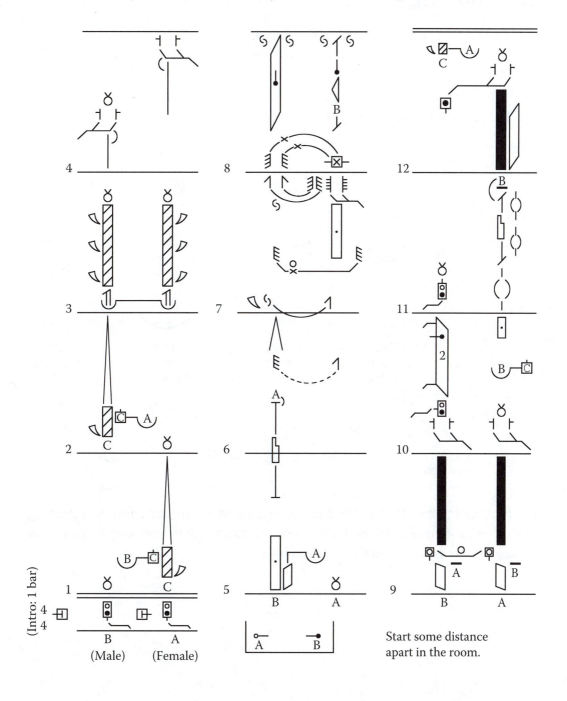

(Intro: 1 bar)

$\frac{4}{4}$

1   B (Male)   A (Female)

5   B   A

9   B   A

Start some distance apart in the room.

PROGRESSION IN RELATING

As stated earlier, there is a progression in the degrees of relating from the least to the most involved. When it is desired to indicate that a form of relating occurs, but it does not matter which form that it is, the general indication for relating can be used as shown in 11.29a.

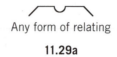

Any form of relating

11.29a

The progression of relating is illustrated in 11.29b–11.29n.

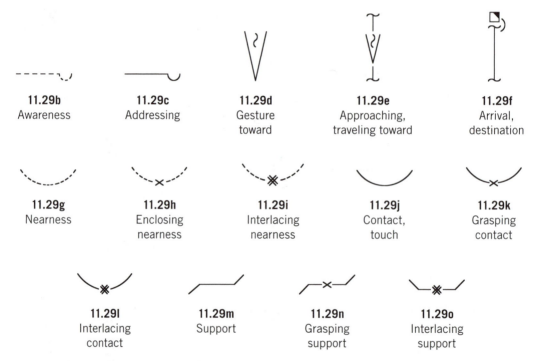

| **11.29b** | **11.29c** | **11.29d** | **11.29e** | **11.29f** |
| Awareness | Addressing | Gesture toward | Approaching, traveling toward | Arrival, destination |

| **11.29g** | **11.29h** | **11.29i** | **11.29j** | **11.29k** |
| Nearness | Enclosing nearness | Interlacing nearness | Contact, touch | Grasping contact |

| **11.29l** | **11.29m** | **11.29n** | **11.29o** |
| Interlacing contact | Support | Grasping support | Interlacing support |

Further information on the analysis and notation for these forms of relating, such as indication of active part, duration and maintaining of passing states, sliding states, etc., are given in Part Two of this book.

READING PRACTICE J (NO MUSIC)

THE STORY OF A BONBON

This little mime sequence is to be explored and performed without music.

- means inside
- BB = Bonbon
- ⌣C = mouth
- extend, stretch
- three-dimensional extension
- three-dimensional flexion
- Sliding contact, brush

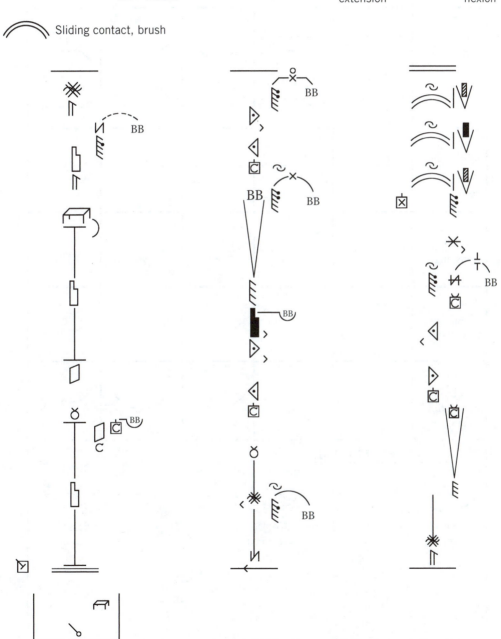

REVIEW FOR CHAPTER ELEVEN

CHART OF RELATING BOWS

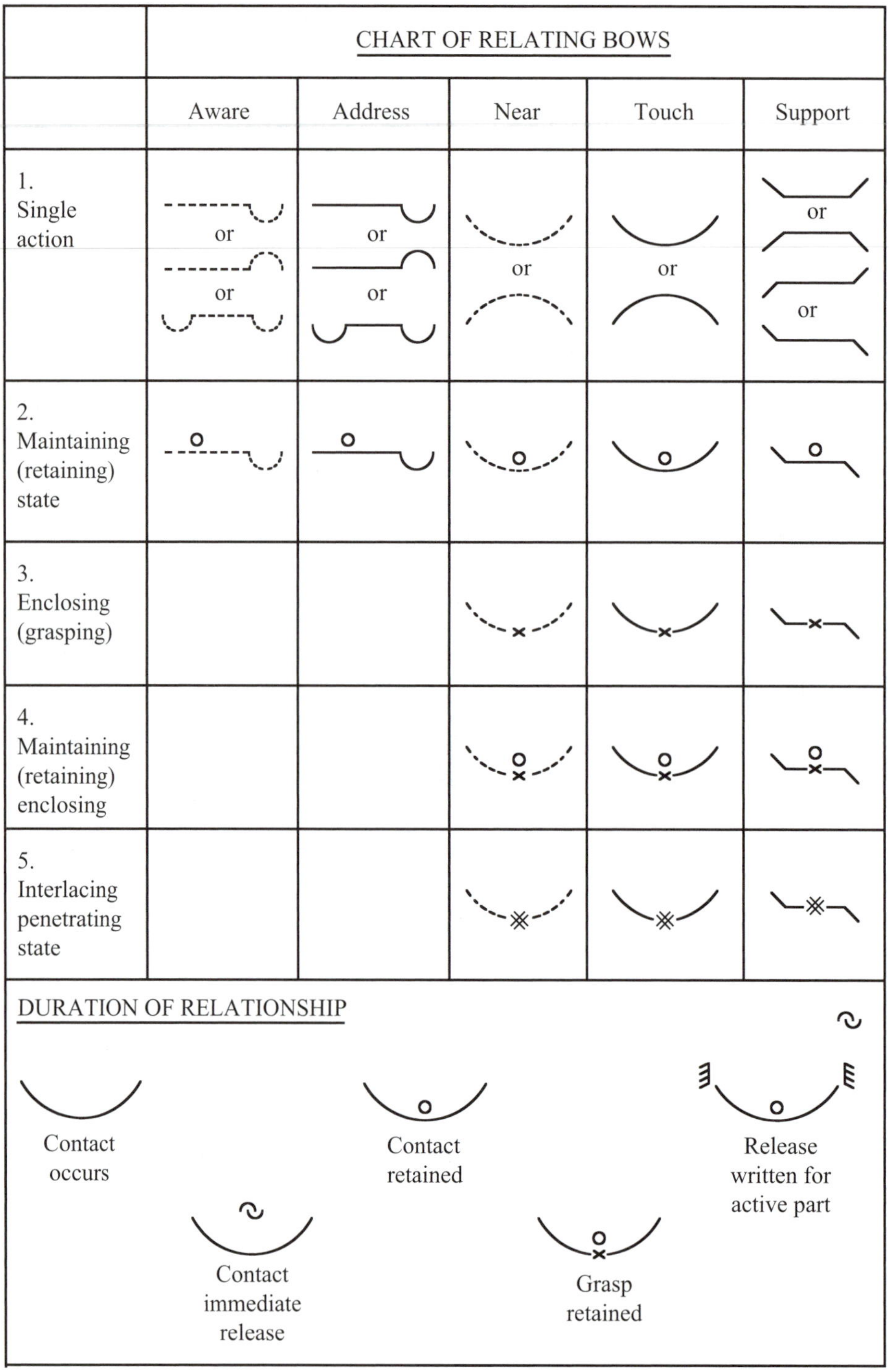

	CHART OF RELATING BOWS				
	Aware	Address	Near	Touch	Support
1. Single action					
2. Maintaining (retaining) state					
3. Enclosing (grasping)					
4. Maintaining (retaining) enclosing					
5. Interlacing penetrating state					

DURATION OF RELATIONSHIP

Contact occurs

Contact retained

Release written for active part

Contact immediate release

Grasp retained

REVIEW FOR CHAPTER ELEVEN (CONTINUED)

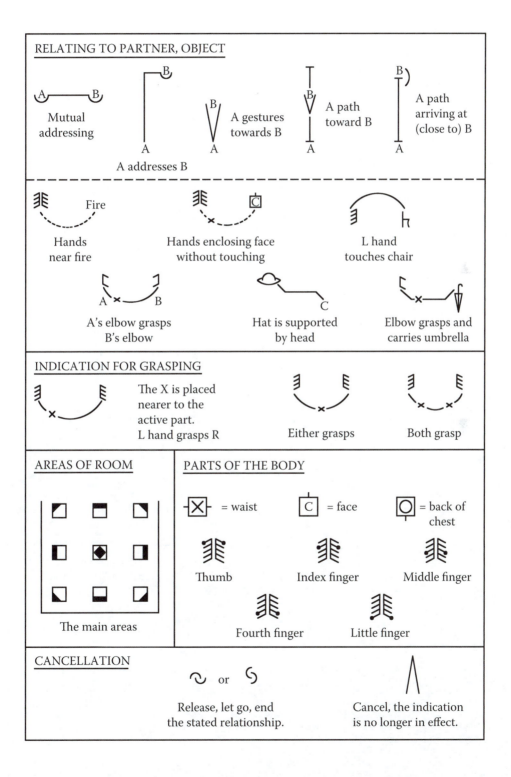

RELATING TO PARTNER, OBJECT

Mutual addressing

A addresses B

A gestures towards B

A path toward B

A path arriving at (close to) B

Hands near fire — Fire

Hands enclosing face without touching

L hand touches chair

A's elbow grasps B's elbow

Hat is supported by head

Elbow grasps and carries umbrella

INDICATION FOR GRASPING

The X is placed nearer to the active part. L hand grasps R

Either grasps

Both grasp

AREAS OF ROOM

The main areas

PARTS OF THE BODY

= waist

= face

= back of chest

Thumb

Index finger

Middle finger

Fourth finger

Little finger

CANCELLATION

or

Release, let go, end the stated relationship.

Cancel, the indication is no longer in effect.

CHAPTER TWELVE

Relationships: Further Development

INDICATION OF ACTIVE PART IN RELATING

In many instances of relating, it is quite clear from the context as to which part is active and which part is passive. When a clear statement needs to be made, the active part is indicated by: (1) thickening the end of the bow for the active part; (2) placement of the accent sign when a clap occurs; or (3) placement of the "X" within the bow when grasping occurs.

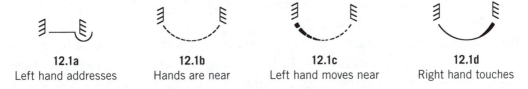

12.1a	12.1b	12.1c	12.1d
Left hand addresses	Hands are near	Left hand moves near	Right hand touches

In addressing, the active part is that from which the straight line extends. The left hand addresses the right in 12.1a. In 12.1b, the simple statement is made that the hands are near each other. The active side is indicated by thickening the appropriate end of the bow, thus in 12.1c, the left hand is active. In 12.1d, the right hand touches the left. The right knee is active in 12.1e, while in 12.1f both knees are active. This device of thickening the active side is applied to nearness, contact, and to a support bow, when needed.

12.1e	12.1f
Right knee touches left	Both knees active in touching

When clapping occurs, placement of the accent sign states which hand is active in making sound.

12.1g	12.1h	12.1i
Right hand claps left	Left hand claps right	Both equally active in clapping

For grasping, placement of the "X" indicates the active part. In 12.1j, the right hand grasps; in 12.1k the "X" in the middle leaves open to choice whether either hand or both hands are active; in 12.1l, both are specified. This use of the "X" to show the active part is also true for the bow indicating enclosing nearness and grasping support (support with grasp).

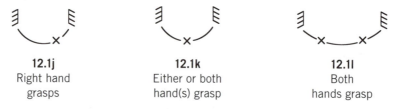

12.1j	12.1k	12.1l
Right hand grasps	Either or both hand(s) grasp	Both hands grasp

A support is indicated by modifying the angular bow to show what part is taking weight and what part is being supported. The end that slants down shows where weight is placed. The end that slants up shows the part or object being supported. In 12.1m and 12.1n, the drawing of the supporting bow indicates the supporting part. When space limitations require use of symmetrical bows, i.e., both ends slanting upward or both slanting downward, the active end (the part supporting) is shown by thickening that end, as used to show active part for nearness and contact bows. In 12.1o, the left side of the bow is thickened to show the hand is the support, although a pencil is not likely to be supporting you! In 12.1p, the right hand carries (grasps) a scarf, shown by the placement of the "X," (it is not the scarf that is grasping the hand).

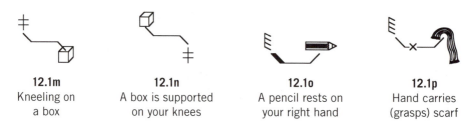

12.1m	12.1n	12.1o	12.1p
Kneeling on a box	A box is supported on your knees	A pencil rests on your right hand	Hand carries (grasps) scarf

TIMING, DURATION OF ACHIEVING A RELATIONSHIP

SPECIFIC MOMENT OF RELATING

A very small unit of time (imagined as a small rectangular box) is understood to exist at the **active end** of the bow to indicate the moment at which the relationship takes place.

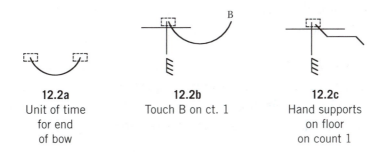

12.2a	12.2b	12.2c
Unit of time for end of bow	Touch B on ct. 1	Hand supports on floor on count 1

TIMING OF ACHIEVING A RELATIONSHIP

The length of the action stroke or of a specific movement symbol indicates the time taken to achieve the relationship. Example 12.3a indicates that A quickly addresses B. In 12.3b, A's movement takes more time and ends addressing B. Relating can occur during an action. In 12.3c, A addresses B halfway through the movement. In 12.3d, addressing occurs at the start of an action, but nothing is specifically stated here concerning how long the addressing lasts; duration is left open. This same application is true for other forms of relating.

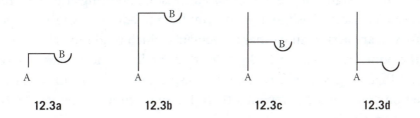

12.3a	12.3b	12.3c	12.3d

DURATION OF A RELATIONSHIP

RETAINING A RELATIONSHIP

In Motif Description the result of an action may or may not be over (automatically cancelled) when something else happens. By itself, an indication of relating does not state whether it should remain or should be cancelled (disappear). For example, in a touch, after contact is established, as in 12.4a, how long does it last? This example gives no indication whether the touch is to release immediately or if it should be held. Example 12.4b states that contact should remain, be maintained, i.e., continued.

12.4a   12.4b

For the generic indications where only the bow is shown, the hold sign is centered, as in 12.4b. The meaning of this hold sign may be "maintain," "retain," "keep," or "hold," whichever suits the context.

In 12.4c, person A addresses partner P at the start of the action and maintains that relationship. In 12.4d, the addressing occurs in the middle of the action and is retained. Example 12.4e states that A addresses B and retains this relationship while circling. The hold sign is placed nearer the active person.

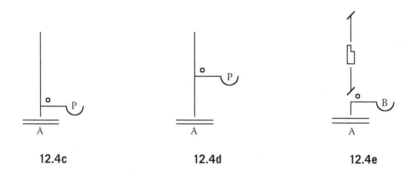

12.4c   12.4d   12.4e

These same timing and retention indications are used for all the relationship signs. In 12.4f, the right thumb continues addressing, pointing at B. This retention may be needed because B is moving and you have to adjust to retain the pointing, or because you are performing other movements which might interfere with maintaining the pointing. Example 12.4g states that the left hand remains close to the head. In 12.4h, the right hand continues to grasp the skirt. While in 12.4i the parrot supported on your shoulder remains there for some time. Placement of the hold sign indicates active part.

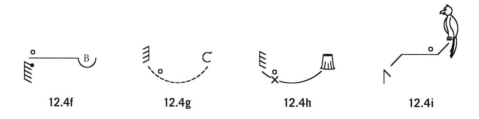

12.4f   12.4g   12.4h   12.4i

CANCELLATION OF RELATING

For each case in which a hold (retention) is used, the reader will look ahead for the release sign to see at what point the retention is cancelled. Note that the term "release," which cancels a held relationship, has no connection with the torso movement called "a release" in the Martha Graham technique. The release sign is derived from a broken hold sign, 12.5a, the two parts being linked to make one sign, as in 12.5b or 12.5c. This sign means let go of the relationship, release the contact. When only the bow is shown, as in 12.5d, the release sign is centered over the bow. Immediate cancellation after a relationship bow indicates a momentary relating; in 12.5e the addressing is very brief.

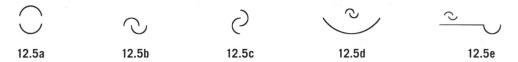

| 12.5a | 12.5b | 12.5c | 12.5d | 12.5e |

For specific statements, the release sign is placed above the active part, i.e., the part that releases and so terminates the relationship. In 12.5f, the left index finger releases immediately after touching the chair, as if testing wet paint. The mutual hand grasping in 12.5g is held until the right hand releases, indicated by the release sign placed above the right hand, the active part.

| 12.5f | 12.5g |

The release (broken hold) cancellation sign is only used to cancel relationships—it is not used in any other context. The movement which produces the release is often a slight reversal of the action that produced the relationship. For example, if a forward movement produces a touch, the release will probably be a slight backward movement.

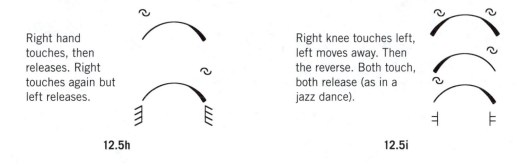

Right hand touches, then releases. Right touches again but left releases.

Right knee touches left, left moves away. Then the reverse. Both touch, both release (as in a jazz dance).

| 12.5h | 12.5i |

A retained relationship can also be cancelled by a new form of relating, as illustrated here. In 12.5j, the retained nearness is cancelled by being changed to a grasp.

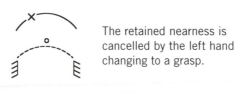

The retained nearness is cancelled by the left hand changing to a grasp.

12.5j

In examples such as s 12.5h, 12.5i, and 12.5j and in the Reading Practice K, we assume that subsequent movement indications are for the same stated body part, that the same pre-sign is still in effect.

READING PRACTICE K (NO MUSIC)

ACTIVE PART, DURATION, RETENTION, CANCELLATION

In this study on timing and duration, allowance must be made for unwritten accommodating movements, for example, the body bending forward to slap the feet in measure 6, count 1, and its expected return to normal on count 2 in measure 6.

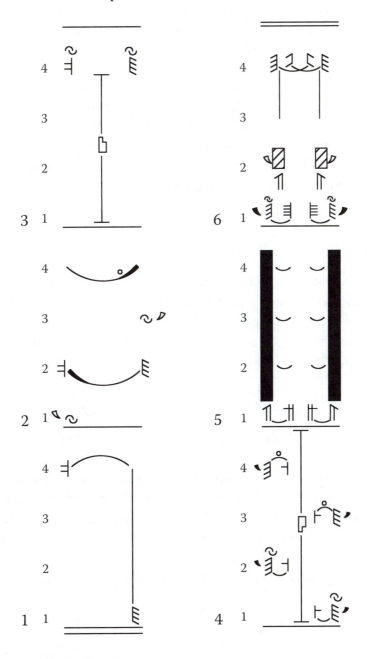

A PASSING (SLIDING) RELATIONSHIP

Movement of a limb that is involved in a relating state may result in a moving, that is, a **"passing"** or **"sliding"** relationship. Such continuation is possible for all relationships expressed through horizontal bows. Note that in the progression of relating, as given in Chapter 11, the actions of toward and away, approaching and retreating, and arrival at a destination do not get modified in the ways being presented here.

Such a moving relationship is familiar when touching occurs, a sliding action being produced. If the touching limb moves and touching is retained, it becomes a sliding, brushing relationship. In this situation, a single contact becomes a moving, sliding contact; this is shown by doubling the relationship bow.

A passing awareness, 12.6a, could occur to a person who is resting quietly but who is alert to people passing around, or to a person passing through a room of strangers, aware of them but not looking at them. Example 12.6b could show glancing at a partner head to toe, or addressing a group of people. Passing nearness is given in 12.6c, with 12.6d being a passing enclosing nearness, as in a stylized caressing of a precious object without touching it.

| 12.6a | 12.6b | 12.6c | 12.6d |

Example 12.6e shows a sliding touch, while 12.6f is a moving grasping contact. Interlacing can also be a moving action, as in 12.6g. The doubled angular support sign, 12.6h, indicates a sliding support, as in skating. A moving grasping support, 12.6i, can occur when the object being grasped is sliding, or the person grasping is sliding, as in sliding down a pole.

| 12.6e | 12.6f | 12.6g | 12.6h | 12.6i |

These possibilities will now be applied to specific examples. Example 12.6j shows person A being aware of the people moving around him/her. Example 12.6k shows glancing across a partner, the sign of 12.6l being the eyes. A passing addressing could also be glancing at a shop window, or could be a gesture as in waving at a group of people. In 12.6m the left hand passes near the head. A sliding contact, touch, could be the palm brushing the table top, as in 12.6n, perhaps as in polishing it.

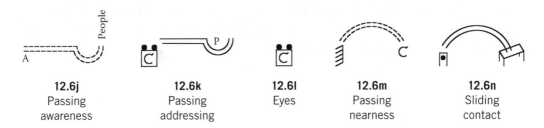

12.6j	12.6k	12.6l	12.6m	12.6n
Passing awareness	Passing addressing	Eyes	Passing nearness	Sliding contact

In 12.6o, the right hand "rubs" (with grasping) the left arm as in pulling a sleeve down. Fingers running through your hair is an example of a sliding interlacing, (penetrating) contact, as shown in 12.6p. A sliding support is represented by 12.6q, in which the hat is sliding off the head. The sliding grasping support of 12.6r shows a wet glass slipping out of the right hand, as it travels downward.

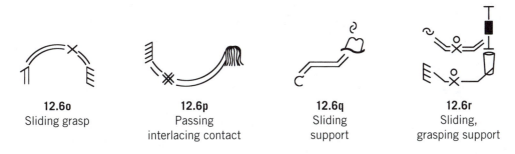

12.6o	12.6p	12.6q	12.6r
Sliding grasp	Passing interlacing contact	Sliding support	Sliding, grasping support

If the above "passing" relationships occur only for a moment, the release sign follows immediately. If the indicated state is to be maintained, this is shown by adding the retention sign. As explained previously, for a static state, such as a touch, a hold sign means "keep," "hold," "remain"; for a passing "sliding" relationship, it means maintain, i.e., "Carry on!," continue with what you are doing. In 12.6s–12.6v, the stated relationship is to continue.

12.6s	12.6t	12.6u	12.6v

For passing relationships to occur, movement is required. A particular movement may continue for some time but the relating may cease sooner. In 12.6w the right arm addresses the crowd throughout the gesture.

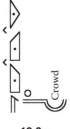

12.6w

The right foot sliding along the left leg, in 12.6x, continues as the right leg contracts. In contrast, 12.6y shows a brief sliding for the hand which is then repeated, as if flicking dust off an object.

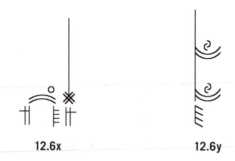

12.6x   12.6y

READING PRACTICE L (NO MUSIC)

PROGRESSION IN RELATING

A good way to explore the whole range of stages in relating is to use a light chair as a prop. There is no music for this study, the numbers alongside refer to sections. Measure 13, 28: dotted vertical line means resultant. —O— = above.

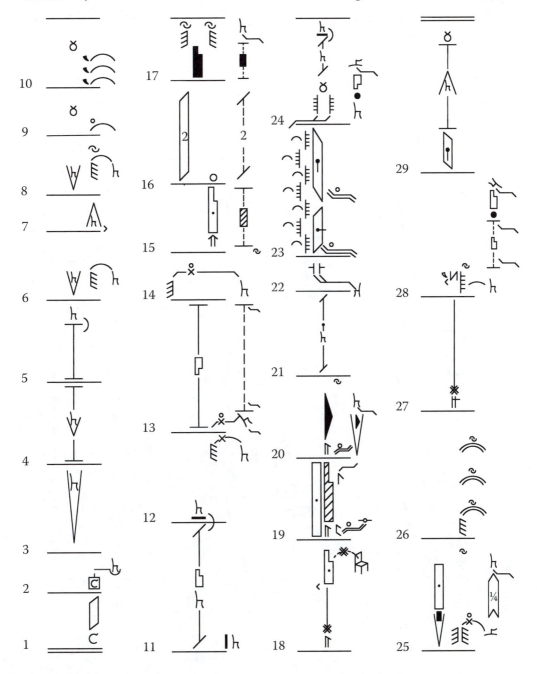

READING STUDY NO. 37

PARTNERS RELATING

A duet for a girl (G) and boy (B) telling a little story.

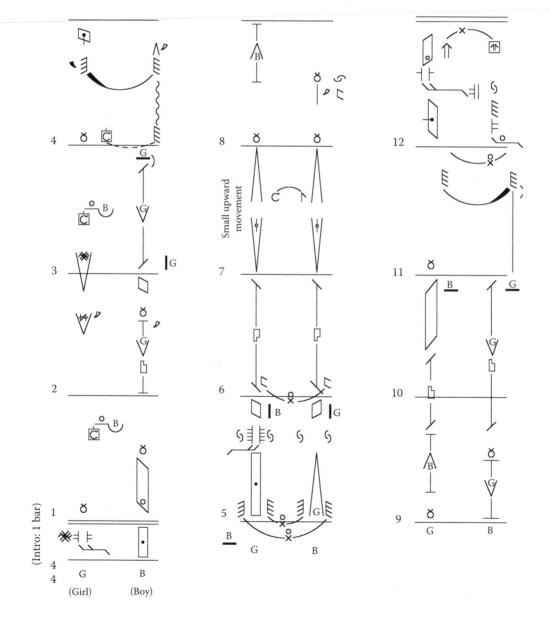

RELATIONSHIPS: ORGANIZATION OF WRITING

When using forms of relating to create movement studies, some guidelines can be helpful to identify the movement components being used and how the motif symbols can best be arranged to produce a "reader-friendly" score. The first step is to identify which elements you will be dealing with.

IDENTIFYING THE COMPONENTS

Identify the form of relating; is it static or moving
Identify what is relating, i.e., person, parts of the body, prop
Identify active part when applicable
Identify actions producing the relating
Determine duration of actions and duration of the state of relating
Determine whether retention or cancellations signs are needed

ORGANIZATION OF INFORMATION IN SCORE WRITING

Reference will be made to the readings in this chapter and to Chapter 11 to illustrate tips for writing a "reader-friendly" score.

1. Once the type of relationship is determined, the appropriate "bow" or other indication is selected. When an object is involved, the part to be contacted is shown as pictorially as possible. In 12.7a, A's foot touches the front leg of the chair; in 12.7b the foot touches the seat. In 12.7c, B's hand grasps the pole at

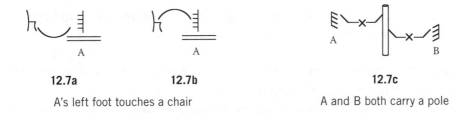

12.7a	12.7b	12.7c
A's left foot touches a chair		A and B both carry a pole

a place lower than A's grasp.

- **Reading Study No. 38: Relating to Objects, Chapter 12**: This study illustrates contact with different parts of an object. In measure 5 the ribbon is grasped at one end, marked "A." At the start of measure 9 the right hand grasps end "B." In measure 11 the center of the ribbon is grasping the person's neck. Note how the hands relate to the cane in measure 12. First the handle of the cane is grasped by the right hand, then the other end is grasped by the left hand. On the springs, the knees hit the center of the cane.

2. Bows ending outside the movement staff with no designated object or person stated, are understood to relate to the floor, 12.7d. For a specific statement the sign for the floor, a "T" (for terra) in a box, can be used, as in 12.7e.

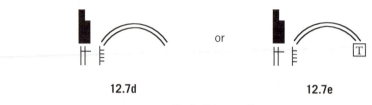

12.7d   **12.7e**

Foot slides on floor

3. Write body parts on the corresponding side of the main actions or staff when possible, i.e., the indication for the right hand on the right side.
   - **Reading Practice J: The Story of a Bonbon,** Chapter 11, staff 2: the index finger of the right hand touching the "BB," is drawn out to the right across from the main action of stretching the arm.

4. Right side body parts can be written on the left and vice versa when such arrangement of information will make reading more clear.
   - **Reading Practice L: Progression in Relating**, Chapter 12, measure 23: Note that the sliding support bows are written on the right side of the main actions of turning while the alternating feet contacts are placed on the opposite side; thus the symbols will not have to compete or overlap. In instances where more than one form of relating occurs at the same time, experiment with different ways of organizing the information to find the best placement of the symbols for ease of reading.

5. Align related information, such as for a body part, in a vertical column in the staff, again for ease of reading
   - **Reading Practice L: Progression in Relating**, Chapter 12, measures 6–10: actions for the right hand are written on the right side of the staff and vertically aligned. Note the indication for the hand to move away from the chair, and in measures 9 and 10, the active release, the hold and the taps of the hand on the chair.

6. When writing a score for two dancers, the relationship bows are likely to connect the two staffs in relating one dancer to the other. Variations in writing placements can be tried to find the most "reader-friendly" arrangement.

- **Reading Study No. 37: Partners Relating**, Chapter 12, measure 4:
  B's right hand (written at the right of his staff) is connected to the sign
  for G's face with the nearness bow. Also in this measure, the contact bow
  shows that G's left hand (written to the left of her staff) is active in slapping
  B's right hand.

- In measure 5: the cancellation signs are aligned above G and B's hands at
  the moment of release. Also in this measure, G and B are grasping hands,
  repeated here as 12.7f; more than one part of the body is relating, thus more
  than one bow needs to be stated. This choice of writing shows the hands
  placed on the corresponding sides of the staff for each dancer and then
  linked. An alternative might be 12.7g, but here it is not clear which hand is
  grasping which. Example 12.7h shows another placement which is clear but
  perhaps not as easy to read as 12.7f. The composite sign for "both" arms can
  be used at the end in measure 12 where G's arms are embracing B's shoulders,
  there is no question here of interpretation.

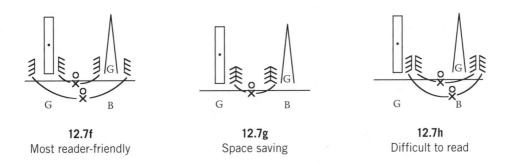

| **12.7f** | **12.7g** | **12.7h** |
| Most reader-friendly | Space saving | Difficult to read |

- In measure 6, because B's right elbow is written on the right of his staff, the
  bow showing linking elbows is drawn across the path indication.

- **Reading Study No. 35: Toward, Away, Destination,** Chapter 11,
  Measures 7 and 8: these provide a good example of organization of
  material. After B taps A on the shoulder, he grasps her hand, taking weight
  to help her rise from sitting. As she stands on her feet, she places her hands
  on his shoulders. His hands then grasp her waist, and, as he turns, she
  walks in a circle around him. Note the B within her path sign showing that
  he is the focal point of her circle. They let go of each other, they turn until
  they are back to back and then, taking weight on the backs of their chests,
  lower to the floor. Note how the notation for the main activity is centered
  in the person's staff.

READING STUDY NO. 38

RELATING TO OBJECTS

On the table are a book, ribbon, cane, and a ball. Note use of ribbon with ends marked "A" and "B." In measure 13, the right arm reaches out to grasp the ball.

RELATIONSHIPS—PROGRESSION IN DEGREE OF RELATING

Row	FORM OF SYMBOL	SLIDING/ PASSING	RETENTION STATIC STATE	MOVING STATE	ACTIVE PART
Interlacing, Penetrating-nearness, contact support					
Grasping Support					
Support					
Grasping Contact					
Contact, Touch					
Enclosing Nearness					
Nearness					
Destination Arrival					
Approaching, Retreating					
Toward, Away					
Addressing					
Awareness					

REVIEW FOR CHAPTER TWELVE

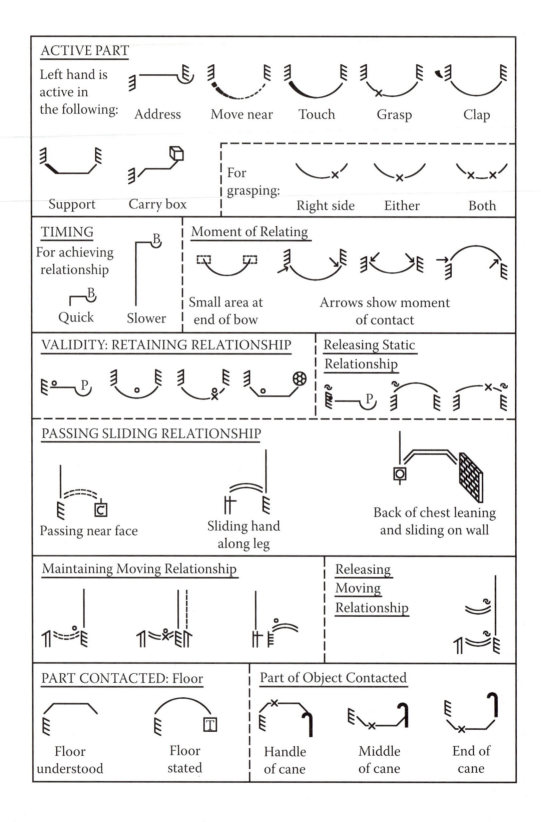

ACTIVE PART

Left hand is active in the following:

Address   Move near   Touch   Grasp   Clap

Support   Carry box

For grasping: Right side   Either   Both

TIMING

For achieving relationship

Quick   Slower

Moment of Relating

Small area at end of bow   Arrows show moment of contact

VALIDITY: RETAINING RELATIONSHIP

Releasing Static Relationship

PASSING SLIDING RELATIONSHIP

Passing near face   Sliding hand along leg   Back of chest leaning and sliding on wall

Maintaining Moving Relationship

Releasing Moving Relationship

PART CONTACTED: Floor

Floor understood   Floor stated

Part of Object Contacted

Handle of cane   Middle of cane   End of cane

CHAPTER THIRTEEN

Body Initiations: Central, Peripheral; Part Leading, Guidance

Initiation of an action, its source in the body, how it flows out as movement—all greatly color the intent, the expression and meaning of a movement. We are dealing here not with an individual basic form of movement but with the manner in which basic actions can be performed. These modifications affect the expression by adding color and interest. Movement may begin with an internal body awareness, producing a heightened energy in a particular part of the body. Such a heightened, focused state is called "point-of-interest." This state may occur in a central part of the body, such as chest, pelvis, hip, or shoulder, or in a peripheral part, such as the hand, foot, or head. A central or peripheral awareness may initiate a part leading movement.

Exploration of part leading provides no technical challenge, but rather one of sensitivity. The more such specific details are added to a basic form, the more a particular style emerges. This style may be highly individual or it may combine details which produce a recognizable cultural type with a known origin and name. Guidances, a related form of part leading, may use a surface or an edge of a limb. In this chapter we will progress through physically central or peripheral movements to part leading and guidances.

CENTRAL AND PERIPHERAL

The idea and application of central and peripheral deal with two separate categories—the spatial aspects or the physical. Movement can be spatially central or peripheral in relation to the performer's kinesphere; or movement can also make use of central or peripheral parts of the body. We will first deal here with the latter.

PHYSICALLY CENTRAL AND PERIPHERAL

Central and peripheral movements were, from the early days, part of Rudolf Laban's theatrical dance expression. The most striking central form was the "impulse," a movement where energy thrust outward from the core (the center) of the torso. Such minor central actions may initiate other movements. Peripheral movements focus on the extremities of the body, the distal parts initiating or leading spatial changes. In general, central movements involve parts of the torso, which could be a shoulder or hip displacing, shifting, or contracting. Peripheral movements feature the head, hands, and feet.

Each limb has central and peripheral parts. For the arm, the shoulder is more central than the elbow. The fingertips are the most peripheral part of the arm; the hand is also peripheral, but less so than the fingertips. In considering the hand itself, the wrist is the central part. When the elbow is sharply bent, it can act as a peripheral part for the arm. These same specifications apply also to the legs, although anatomically the legs are more restricted in their range of movement and articulation.

NOTATION OF PHYSICALLY CENTRAL, PERIPHERAL

For certain notation indications a circle represents body aspects, 13.1a. To indicate central and peripheral, the circle is divided vertically, as in 13.1b. Short horizontal strokes pointing inward indicate central aspects, 13.1c. For peripheral indications, the short strokes point outward, 13.1d. Only one half circle, generally the right half circle, is used to specify these concepts. However, when more suitable, the left half circle is used. These indications can be placed on the left of the staff, although placement on the right is more usual. Examples of each are shown in 13.2d and 13.2e.

13.1a
Aspects of
the body

13.1b

13.1c
Physically
central

13.1d
Physically
peripheral

SPECIFYING A CENTRAL OR PERIPHERAL ACTION

Any action can be designated to be executed by a central or peripheral body part. In 13.2a a sustained action is performed by a central part; in 13.2b it is an action of a peripheral body part. A physically central action followed by a physically peripheral action is shown in 13.2c. In these examples, the physically central and peripheral signs are used as pre-signs, placed like body part signs before the action symbol. These same signs, when placed within an angular addition bracket can modify several actions. A rhythmic pattern of peripheral actions is shown in 13.2d. This could equally be indicated as in 13.2e. In 13.2f, four peripheral actions are to be performed. Note that in each example, the open side of the symbol faces in toward the movement.

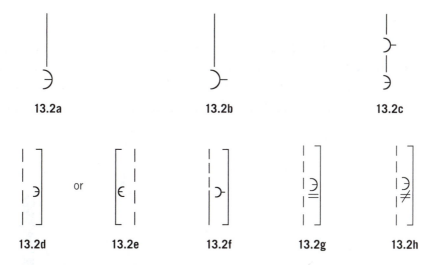

13.2a	13.2b	13.2c

13.2d	13.2e	13.2f	13.2g	13.2h

For 13.2e and 13.2f, the question arises as to whether one body part is to be used or if different parts may be involved. Each option can be stated. The equal sign indicates the same part is used for each action, 13.2g. The unequal sign, 13.2h, states that each action is performed by a different part.

Example 13.2i starts with a single central action followed by stillness, then by a single peripheral action, followed by a stillness. Three actions then occur for the same peripheral part. This information is most clearly written within a vertical addition bracket. The sequence ends with two central actions by different parts.

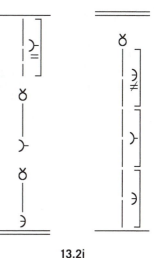

13.2i

PART LEADING

A movement may be initiated or led by a central or peripheral part of the body. From the general statement of central or peripheral, we progress to designating specific body parts. Parts which are at the center of the body, i.e., parts of the trunk, relate to space more in the sense of pressing against it or pushing it aside, as though space were a tangible foam cloud. A movement which is led by a central part may flow out to other parts. Movements for central parts of the body are limited spatially; in contrast, a peripheral part, such as the fingertips, has the whole range of the kinesphere to explore in its role as the part leading.

INDICATION OF PART LEADING

A part of the body that is to lead an action is written inside a curved vertical bow, 13.3a, which is placed adjacent to the main movement it qualifies. In 13.3b a sideward action is led by a central part of the body. A peripheral body part leads the upward movement in 13.3c. Example 13.3d provides reading practice for these possibilities.

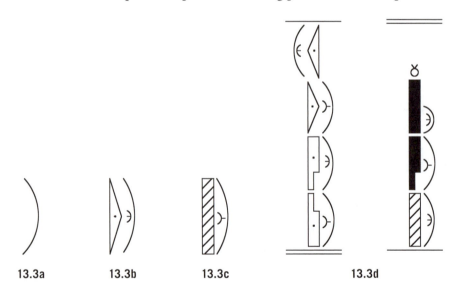

| 13.3a | 13.3b | 13.3c | 13.3d |

READING PRACTICE M (NO MUSIC)

CENTRAL AND PERIPHERAL BODY PARTS LEADING

Placing the part leading bow on the right or the left side of the movement statement may suggest use of right or left side of the body, but this need not necessarily be so (see Chapter 14).

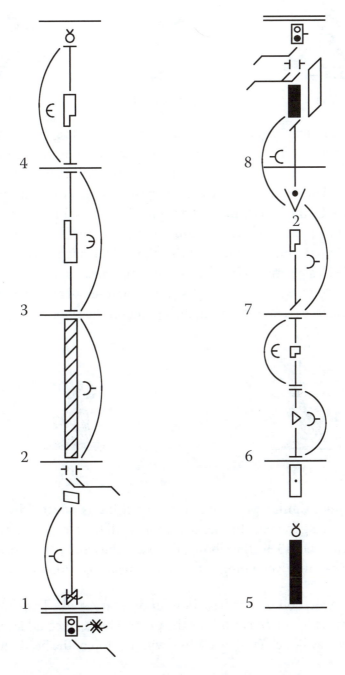

USE OF SPECIFIC BODY PARTS

The kind of movement, its direction and level, may dictate what specific part will be leading. Conversely, the body part leading may influence the level and direction of the main movement and articulation of the body. Let us take the simple action of lowering and rising. Lowering of the body may be led by the knees, as in 13.4a.

13.4a   13.4b   13.4c

Such lowering may produce very little lowering in the rest of the body; the spine could remain vertical, yet a lowering of the whole body has taken place. If, however, lowering is led by the head, 13.4b, the head will bow first, the rest of the body following. The result will be a curved spine, a much more closed conclusion. If lowering is led by the hands, 13.4c, the expression of reaching for the safety of the floor can result. In another interpretation, the spine may be curved but the head may still remain upright. Leading with the hips, which suggests a desire to sit, will produce a folded leg position. Use of the front of the chest in leading downward may suggest compassion toward something on the floor (a small animal perhaps?), while leading with the face stresses focusing on a point on the floor nearby.

13.4d   13.4e

In a somewhat similar way, the manner of rising is affected by which part is leading. By exploring the possibilities of leading with the face, 13.4d, with the top of the head, with a hand, 13.4e, the elbows, the back, the front of the chest, a shoulder, and so on, one can uncover a range of different meanings, moods, and emphases.

A simple exploration can be based on an ordinary walk. Traveling may be led by a hand, perhaps by the finger tips or the palm. The head could lead. Very different expressions may be achieved by leading with the top of the head, the face, or—to be even more specific—the chin. The chest or the hips may initiate traveling. Many people walk leading with the knees. In the stylized balletic walk, each step is led by the foot, the tip of the toes when the leg is straight, by the instep if the leg unfolds.

Observe the different feeling and expression which result when leading with an extremity as opposed to a central part of the body. Smaller surfaces, such as finger-tips or the tip of a foot, seem to penetrate space, to explore, to search. The elbow and knee often act like extremities but are limited in scope, their leading actions being arc-like, that is, following curved lines.

INDICATION OF SPECIFIC PART LEADING

The most general statement for part of body leading is 13.5a, i.e., any body part. Example 13.5b indicates lowering led by the right hand, as might occur in picking up an object. In 13.5c, rising and extending are led first by the elbows, then by the hands, as might happen in a yawning stretch. In 13.5d, the left hand leads an advancing movement and the turn which follows. Note that the left leading is written here on the left side of the action, a reader-friendly placement. One interpretation of this notation could be exploring in the dark, reaching out to feel what might be there.

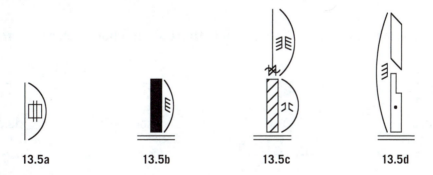

| 13.5a | 13.5b | 13.5c | 13.5d |

SURFACES AND EDGES OF HANDS AND FEET

Generally, indication of the hand allows considerable freedom in exactly how the hand is used; the interpretation chosen will be that most appropriate to the movement it qualifies. Use of particular surfaces and edges of the hand can be most expressive in conjunction with specific actions. The edges of limbs, particularly the edges of the hand and lower arm, cut through the space around. We see such cutting in the karate chop in which a wooden board is sliced with the little finger edge of the hand. Examples 13.6a–13.6g show the signs for the surfaces and edges of the hand and foot.

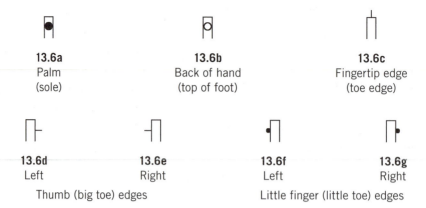

13.6a	**13.6b**	**13.6c**
Palm	Back of hand	Fingertip edge
(sole)	(top of foot)	(toe edge)

13.6d	**13.6e**	**13.6f**	**13.6g**
Left	Right	Left	Right
Thumb (big toe) edges		Little finger (little toe) edges	

The signs of 13.6a–13.6c are placed on the right side of the notation or staff when they refer to the right hand or foot, on the left when they refer to the left hand or foot. Example 13.6d shows the left thumb/toe side, 13.6e the right thumb/toe side. In the same way the little finger signs indicate left, 13.6f, and right, 13.6g. To identify use of hand or foot, the appropriate signs are combined.

13.6h	**13.6i**	**13.6j**	**13.6k**
L and R palm	Sole of left and right foot	Back of left and right hand	Top of left and right foot

These same signs can indicate use of both hands and both feet, as illustrated in 13.6l–13.6o.

13.6l	**13.6m**	**13.6n**	**13.6o**
Both palms	Soles of both feet	Back of both hands	Top of of both feet

To give the choice of either right or left, the sign for either side, 13.6p, is placed before the sign for both palms or both feet as shown in 13.6q–13.6t.

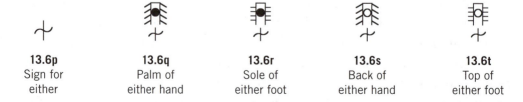

13.6p	**13.6q**	**13.6r**	**13.6s**	**13.6t**
Sign for either	Palm of either hand	Sole of either foot	Back of either hand	Top of either foot

To designate whether a surface or edge indication refers to a hand or foot, the signs are combined as below. The small horizontal stroke always indicates the thumb (big toe) edge, the dot always refers to the little finger (little toe) edge. This applies even when, for practical purposes, these marks need to be placed on the other side of the basic sign. Thus the main indications for right or left hand or foot remain unchanged, illustrated in 13.6u–13.6x. Note that the little finger dot, which usually is placed on the outer side of the sign, 13.6f and 13.6g, in these particular cases needs to appear on the inner side.

13.6u	13.6v	13.6w	13.6x
left hand right hand	left foot right foot	left foot right foot	left foot right foot
thumb edge	big toe edge	little finger edge	little toe edge

SURFACES OF THE PARTS OF THE TORSO

Surfaces of the parts of the torso are indicated by placement of a short stroke on the appropriate side or corner of the basic sign.

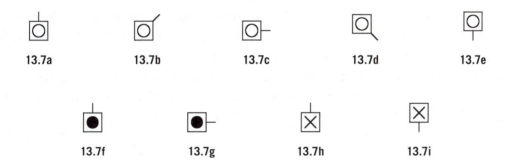

13.7a 13.7b 13.7c 13.7d 13.7e

13.7f 13.7g 13.7h 13.7i

Example 13.7a shows the front of the chest; 13.7b the right front diagonal surface of the chest; 13.7c the right side of the chest, and so on. The same device is applied to the pelvis (13.7f being the front surface, 13.7g the right side), and also to the waist (13.7h being the front of the waist, 13.7i the back of the waist).

TIMING FOR PART LEADING

A leading activity may occur all through a movement or may occur only at the start, or only toward the end. As the curved vertical bow has time significance, such differences are easy to show.

Examples 13.8a–13.8d are based on raising the arm to the side. This simple movement can be performed with many variations. Let us assume that in each version the arm starts down.

In 13.8a, the right arm moves in one piece as a unit with no emphasis or stress on any one part. Example 13.8b states that the movement is led by the shoulder, i.e., raising the arm is initiated by the shoulder. The length of the bow indicates the duration of the part leading from start to finish. At the start of the bow, the part leading comes into action and continues throughout. If the bow and the movement end together, the leading is understood still to be in effect. It will disappear with the next movement. In 13.8b, the shoulder is still displaced at the end. Because in 13.8c, the bow terminates sooner, the leading action also terminates sooner, the shoulder returns to normal. Leading with the elbow, 13.8d, requires some curving of the arm; this curving disappears halfway through the gesture, the arm finishing with its normal carriage.

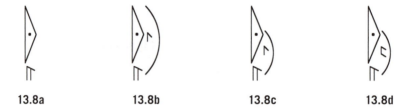

13.8a   13.8b   13.8c   13.8d

Example 13.8e shows the general indication for hand leading, while 13.8f specifies use of the fingertips. To accomplish fingertip leading, a wrist flexion must occur at the start so that the fingertips can be directed into the line of movement. Here the leading action ends before the conclusion of the movement so that the arm finishes in its normal alignment. In 13.8g, fingertip leading occurs only toward the end of the arm gesture.

13.8e   13.8f   13.8g

READING STUDY NO. 39

PART LEADING

In measures 7 and 8, because of the traveling, the part leading will doubtlessly be the palm, not the sole of the foot. Use of the palm here could be specifically stated. In measure 7, placement on the right side of the path suggests use of the right side, but this need not be so.

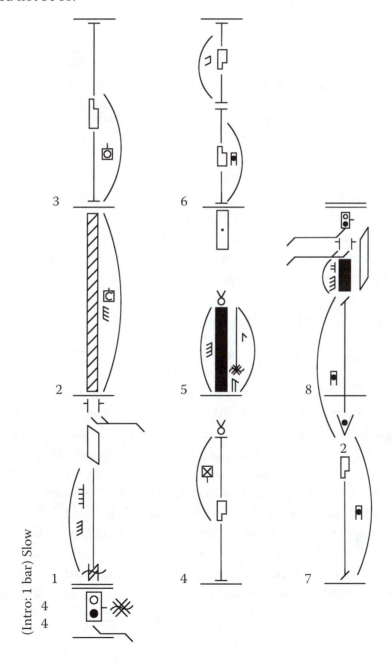

GUIDANCES

Leading usually means that one person goes ahead of the other, as in 13.9a. When a part of the body **leads** it does "go ahead," i.e., a joint "bulges out." When one person **guides** another, 13.9b, a slight pressure is exerted, the kind of guidance the gentleman gives to the lady in ballroom dancing. For guidances of gestures of the limbs, a surface or edge faces the direction of the movement, "guiding" the limb through space. In such guiding there is an awareness of the limb surface passing through the air, often with very slight pressure.

13.9a   13.9b

Guidance involves different surfaces of the limbs. The sign for the inner surface, 13.9c, is the indication for the "dark," inside surface when your arm or leg is fully bent. Example 13.9d is the sign for the "light," outer surface; 13.9e and 13.9f are the thumb or big toe edges of the limb, left and right; 13.9g and 13.9h are the little finger or little toe edges of the limb, left and right. These surfaces and edges apply to the whole of the limb, arm, or leg, judged when it is in a neutral, untwisted state.

13.9c   13.9d   13.9e   13.9f   13.9g   13.9h

Depending on the direction of the movement, a slight, unemphasized inward or outward rotation of the limb usually precedes a specific guidance. An outer surface guidance of the arm to side middle, as in 3.9i, results in the palm facing down. The inner surface guidance of 13.9j requires an outward preparatory rotation of the arm and will conclude with the palm facing up. In 13.9k, the thumb edge brings the thumb immediately into the line of the movement so that the palm faces forward from the start. But this palm facing is incidental; the emphasis is on the thumb edge cutting through the air. Inward rotation is needed to start the little finger guidance of 13.9l. Each of these guidances can have time significance, as illustrated in 13.9m in which the arm returns to its standard alignment at the end of the gesture. Find the different feeling and expression for each of these guidances in this spatial setting, then experiment with each guidance for different directional movements of the arms.

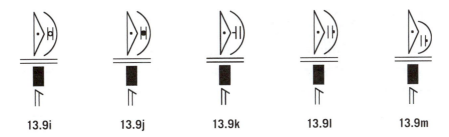

| 13.9i | 13.9j | 13.9k | 13.9l | 13.9m |

Raising the arm forward and ending with the palm facing down, 13.9n, makes a particular statement. Arriving at the same end result through an outer limb surface guidance, 13.9o, has a particular "air" about it. At the start of the movement, the arm unobtrusively turns slightly inward so that the outer surface (the back of the hand and lower arm) leads into the direction of the movement. Though no dynamics are mentioned, there will inevitably be a slight pressure against the air by the guiding surface. The palm ends facing down, as before, but not by intention; this palm facing itself has no importance. As will be explored in Chapter 18, palm facing is very expressive when used intentionally. The important issue in guidances is how the leading surface of the limb is aware of the air as it moves through space.

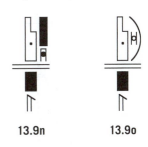

13.9n   13.9o

Because they are narrower, the thumb edge and little finger edge of the hand often serve to "cut" through space. Such cutting may be with the edge of the hand as a whole, or a leading action involving the portion near the wrist; in the latter case the bulk of the hand follows passively, a slight angle (bulging out) being produced at the wrist. Familiar arm patterns should be tried with a variety of different guidances and parts leading so that the different effects and expressions may be observed and experienced.

Though less flexible than the arms, the legs can perform many interesting variations. Investigation can center on a simple leg contraction, as in 13.9p, a full *retiré* in ballet. This movement can be performed by leading with the point of the knee, leading with the top surface of the thigh, with the foot, or with the calf surface of the lower leg. In each case the same final position can be reached, but the emphasis, the placement of that little extra energy, will result in a different expression. Explore other variations in guidance for leg gestures.

13.9p

READING STUDY NO. 40

PART LEADING, GUIDANCES

This is a flowing, swaying study in slow waltz time. Note that the placement of the bow on the right or left side of the movement symbol may suggest use of right or left side of the body.

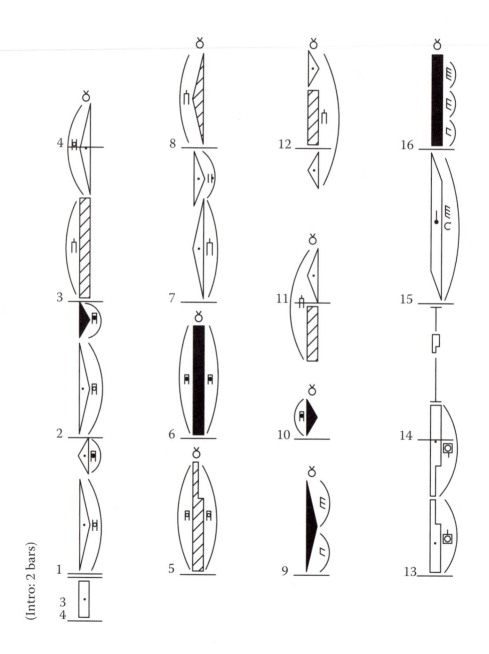

VARIATIONS IN WALKING

In the simple activity of walking, one can observe a great number of variations among people in the street, let alone among trained performers. Let us disregard differences in timing, in size of step, in how the foot is placed on the ground, and be concerned only with part leading, specifically how the leg is brought forward to take the next step. Starting at the top of the leg we see examples of hip leading, 13.10a. Hip initiation can involve a very slight or a marked pelvic rotation, the most exaggerated being when the side of the pelvis initiates each step as in 13.10b. The outer (front) surface of the leg, 13.10c, or the knee, 13.10d, may lead the leg. The foot in general, 13.10e, or the instep, 13.10f, may start the leg swinging forward. In the stylized ballet walk, the tips of the toes lead, 13.10g. Other parts may initiate traveling; such as the pelvis as a whole, which may happen when the chest is sunk and displaced backward. Leading with the chest may express a desire to travel, a feeling of lightness, of determination, or perhaps self-importance.

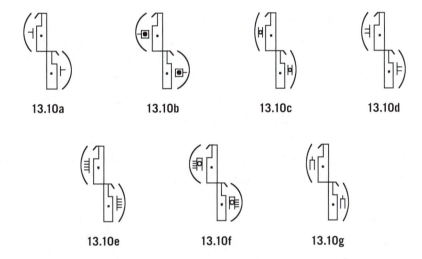

13.10a	13.10b	13.10c	13.10d

13.10e	13.10f	13.10g

A similar exploration can center on a simple skip in which the free leg is raised forward slightly bent. The manner of raising this leg can vary from its being led by the front of the thigh, by the shin, the knee, instep, or, if the leg is turned out, the inner, big toe surface of thigh, lower leg, heel, or foot.

A different rhythmic inner impulse results when a new initiation comes with each step. An initiation of a body part may begin a movement and then disappear as in 13.10h. These are only some of the possibilities which can be indicated through the use of appropriate symbols.

13.10h

LEADING; PASSIVE, RESULTANT

As mentioned earlier, leading may also take place when two or more people are traveling together; one may take the lead and the others follow. In 13.11a, four people, designated as "A," "B," "C," and "D" travel on a straight path. Identification of the leader is tied to the start of the path sign by a short vertical linking bow. In 13.11a, person A is identified as the leader. In 13.11b, person D leads the circular path.

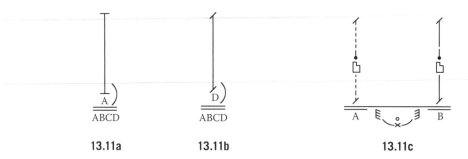

| 13.11a | 13.11b | 13.11c |

Two performers may travel side by side, yet one may be the leader. Example 13.11c shows A and B holding hands as B leads A in a clockwise circle. A is shown to be passive by the path sign being written with a dotted vertical line. Dotted vertical lines mean "resultant," "passive," in contrast to solid vertical lines which mean "active," as in the basic action stroke. In 13.11d, B, who is holding A's hand, is shown to be turning on the spot to the right, while A passively travels on a circular path being led by B. Quite the reverse is stated in 13.11e. Starting with elbows linked, A circles around B causing B to pivot on the spot. Dotted passive lines next to the turn sign indicate the resultant nature of the action.

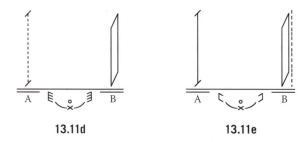

| 13.11d | 13.11e |

Gestures may be resultant. In 13.11f, the arms react passively, centrifugally, swinging outward and upward as a result of the fast turning action; this resultant reaction is shown by the dotted lines. If the destination of the arms needs to be stated and the movement is not an active raising of the arms, a dotted vertical line is placed alongside the direction symbol to indicate the manner of performance for this movement, 13.11g. The arms are guided just enough to arrive at the stated destination but the basic passive nature of the spatial change is still dominant.

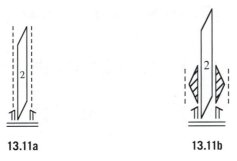

13.11a   13.11b

READING STUDY No. 41

RESULTANT, PASSIVE MOVEMENTS

$\underline{B}$ = B is in front of you |B = B is on your right   A| = A is on your left $\underline{A}$ = A is in front of you

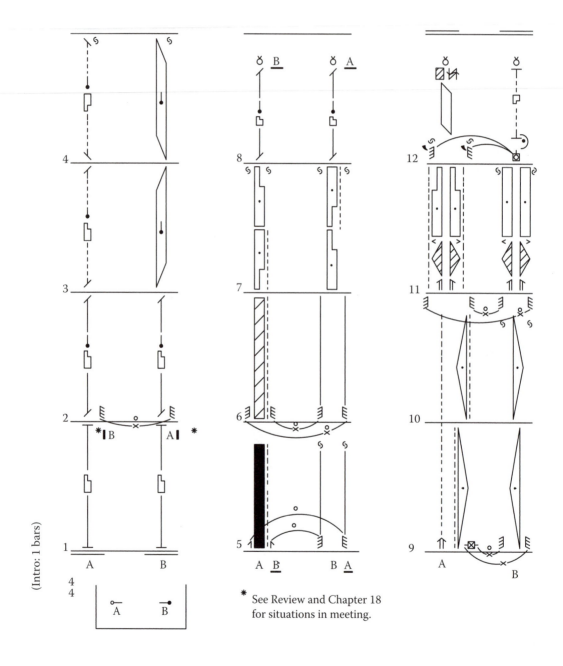

(Intro: 1 bars)

$\frac{4}{4}$

* See Review and Chapter 18 for situations in meeting.

REVIEW FOR CHAPTER THIRTEEN

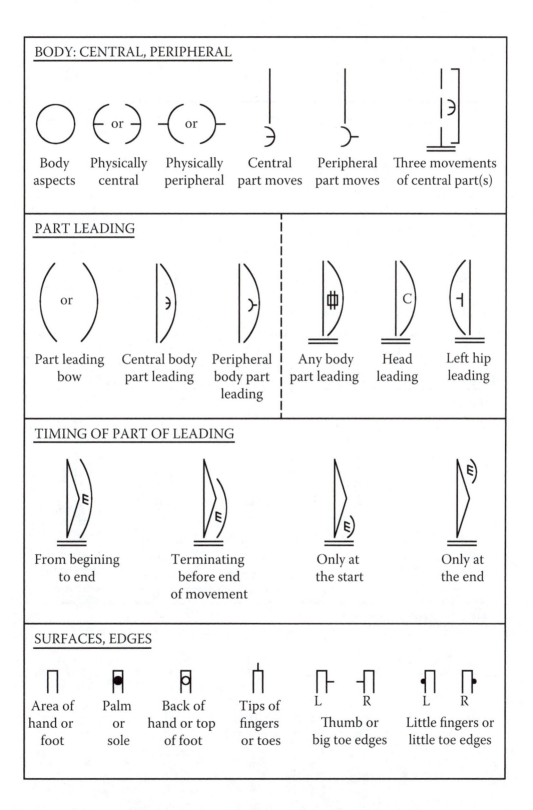

Review for Chapter Thirteen (continued)

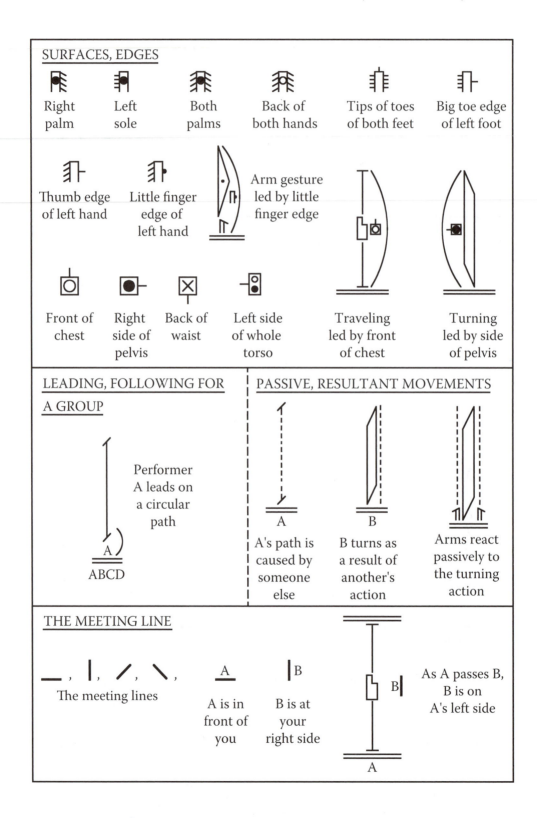

SURFACES, EDGES

Right palm

Left sole

Both palms

Back of both hands

Tips of toes of both feet

Big toe edge of left foot

Thumb edge of left hand

Little finger edge of left hand

Arm gesture led by little finger edge

Front of chest

Right side of pelvis

Back of waist

Left side of whole torso

Traveling led by front of chest

Turning led by side of pelvis

LEADING, FOLLOWING FOR A GROUP

Performer A leads on a circular path

ABCD

PASSIVE, RESULTANT MOVEMENTS

A

B

A's path is caused by someone else

B turns as a result of another's action

Arms react passively to the turning action

THE MEETING LINE

— , | , / , \ ,

The meeting lines

A

A is in front of you

B

B is at your right side

B

A

As A passes B, B is on A's left side

CHAPTER FOURTEEN

One-Sided Gestures; Gestural Pathways; Gathering, Scattering

This chapter investigates further details concerning the manner of performing gestures, their intention and expression.

ONE-SIDED GESTURES—ESTABLISHMENT OF STANCE FRONT

In the progression from movement involving the body-as-a-whole to specific gestures of a particular limb, we discover the need to designate one-sided actions without specifying arm or leg, or involvement of right or left hip or shoulder. The instruction in 14.1a can be performed in many ways. Gestures forward low may be symmetrical or there may be an intentional lack of symmetry with emphasis on one side of the body. One-sided actions have a focus or an impact quite different from two-sided, symmetrical actions. The expression of 14.1b is significantly different from that of 14.1c.

When only one arm or one leg gestures into a sagittal direction, inclusion of one side of the body can augment the action and hence the expressiveness. In 14.1b, the left arm gesture forward low is accompanied by a postural inclination into that

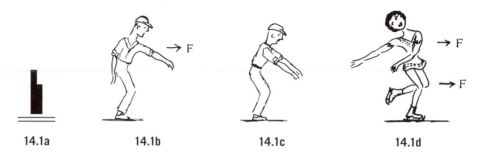

14.1a   14.1b   14.1c   14.1d

direction. This inclusion of the upper torso involves both inclining and twisting, but these actions are not important in themselves. The tilt forward and the twist to the right are resultant, by-products of the main movement. Note that in these drawings "F" (forward) represents the established Front, the direction previously faced. This previously established Front is called Stance, since the feet (stance) usually have retained that front. (See Chapter 21.)

In 14.1d, a backward tilt and a twist to the right enlarge the backward low arm gesture and make it more comfortable to perform. Because the feet have maintained the original Front, the movement is seen as one away from that Front, i.e., backward. This idea of Stance-forward and Stance-backward can be seen in archery, in which a definite twist in the body occurs but does not affect the sense of the forward-backward directions. Bowling or pitching a ball also involves maintaining the Stance direction as forward despite tilting and twisting.

In 14.1e a step backward has been added to the movement of 14.1d, but the head remains looking forward and thus is a strong factor in maintaining that direction. If the head joins the direction of the arms, as in 14.1f, only the left leg retains Stance and this may not be enough to prevent the impression of a sideward movement following an unstressed quarter turn to the right. If, after performing 14.1f, the dancer returns to the Stance front, as in 14.1g, the relation of the action of 14.1f to that front is clear. Any turning that occurred was resultant, taking place only to augment the main backward downward gesture. Therefore, in the context of the event, there has been no change of Front, no facing a new room direction.

14.1e   14.1f   14.1g

INDICATION OF RIGHT OR LEFT SIDE

Until now we have been concerned with general actions of the body-as-a-whole. When nothing is specified, general indications are usually interpreted as general body actions; therefore the sign for "body-as-a-whole," 14.2a, has not been needed. In the progression toward a more specific description, we arrive at the need to localize an action to the right or left half of the body. For example, an action may feature, or be concerned with, the right arm, right leg, right shoulder, right hip, or right side of the torso. We indicate right or left sides by using the sign of 14.2b. This sign represents the three line staff used in structured movement descriptions. By extending the center line, which represents the center line in the body, we can indicate right and left sides, 14.2c. Thus, indications placed on the right of this center line are to be performed by the right side of the body, those placed on the left, by the left side. In 14.2d, an action backward for the right side of the body is followed by an action up for the left side. As the center line then terminates, shown by the inverted staff sign at the top, the following action forward is one of the body-as-a-whole. It will be found that in selecting movement patterns and establishing sequences, use of only one or the other side of the body is more likely to occur occasionally, rather than continuously, hence the need for "signing off" the center line of the body.

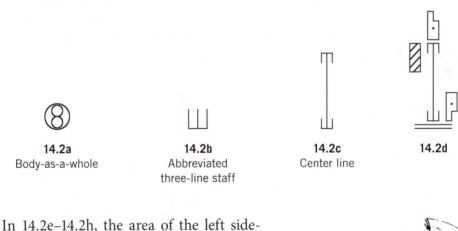

14.2a
Body-as-a-whole

14.2b
Abbreviated
three-line staff

14.2c
Center line

14.2d

In 14.2e–14.2h, the area of the left side-ward direction is used first by the left side of the body, the "open" side, as shown in 14.2e, which is illustrated in 14.2f.

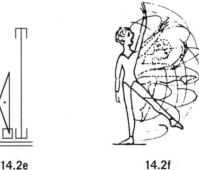

14.2e

14.2f

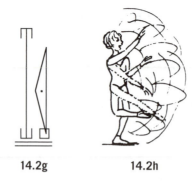

14.2g   **14.2h**

Then this same left side area is used by the right side of the body, 14.2g, showing movement in the "crossed" or "closed" side illustrated in 14.2h. Crossing the center line of the body will be more effective if some body inclusion is used. In doing so, it is important that the standing foot and perhaps the face retain the original front so that there is no suggestion of a turn of the whole body.

CONTINUING THE CENTER LINE

As previously shown in 14.2d, the center line indication is terminated with the addition of the "cap" on the top. When the center line indication is required for a longer span, as in 14.3a, it is visually helpful to state its termination at the end of one staff and then repeat it at the start of the next staff. The termination of the center line before the last movement of 14.3a clearly separates it from the next action indication centered on the staff.

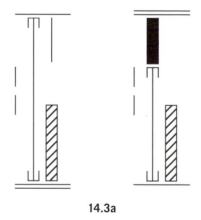

14.3a

READING STUDIES NOS. 42–44

ONE-SIDED ACTIONS

Perform this sequence first at a slow tempo, enjoying the fullness of the space patterns and allowing body inclusion to occur. Then with music track 43, try it at an intermediate pace, and finally at a faster pace with music track 44, observing the resulting changes in expression affecting both performer and observer. After enjoying the study as pure space pattern, imagine a situation in which these actions might have a story to tell. For this, you may wish to vary the timing of measures 1–4, making them uneven, as illustrated in Version B. In Version C the movement starts before the first bar line so that the upward action is given emphasis. Note that in measure 7, the backward low directional action may disappear as there is no retention symbol to maintain it while traveling.

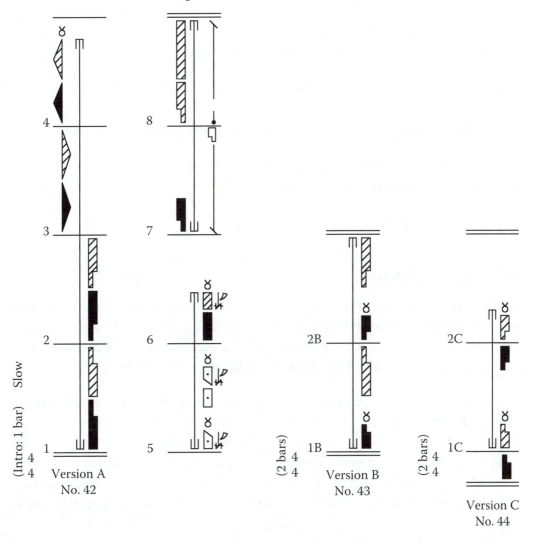

PATHS FOR GESTURES

This book started with exploration of traveling, of paths for the whole body. Let us now look at other kinds of paths. When a limb moves through space, the intention or expression of the movement may be that of describing a path in the air with the extremity. All paths are composed basically of straight or curved lines. The curves may be arcs, complete circles, or wavy, undulating "s" curves, loops, spirals, etc. Straight lines, if they are short, may produce zigzag patterns. In dance, the concept of paths for parts of the body is behind many actions: for example, the straight path for the sideward shifting head movement, often the Sundarï, in Bharata Natya dance, or the horizontal figure eight path of the hips in the Tahitian pelvic gyrations; or the somersault paths for the rib cage met in certain African dances. These subtle movements are generally unfamiliar to Western dance; let us therefore begin with simple obvious actions.

In considering gestural paths, we find three distinct forms, which, although related, have particular characteristics producing different movement sensations and expressions. All are concerned with the limbs moving through space. They are:

1. Straight, curved, and circular paths concerned with the direction of the progression
2. Trace forms, lines in the air producing particular designs, i.e., design drawing
3. Gathering and scattering gestures that "sculpt" space, space being experienced almost as a "tangible" entity

We will begin with the first of these forms.

STRAIGHT PATHS

Gestures in which the extremity follows a straight path may be functional, may mimic functional actions (as in pantomime), or may be purely decorative. A good example of straight path gestures in mime is that performed by Marcel Marceau as he feels with his hands along nonexistent walls, seeking an opening.

A good example of a functional straight path action is 14.4a, which illustrates a punch in boxing. This same path from the center out can occur for many other reasons and also for pure spatial design. Example 14.4b is comparable to 14.4a, being a kick forward, the foot following a straight path. Contact with a flat surface automatically governs the path of a gesture as when the edge of a table is dusted, 14.4c, or a vertical line is drawn on a blackboard, 14.4d. Each of these movements requires a degree of flexion and extension in order to achieve the straight path for the extremity, as does 14.4e in which a zipper on a tent is pulled down.

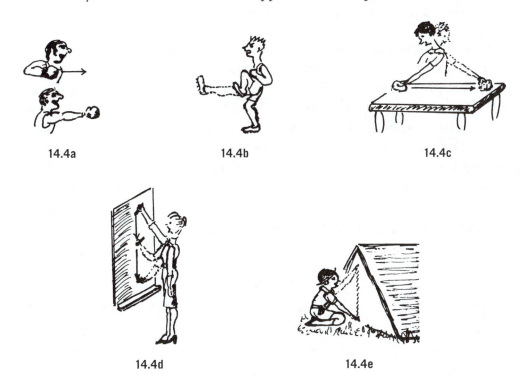

14.4a

14.4b

14.4c

14.4d

14.4e

Straight-line gestures may start from, return to, or pass near the center of the body or base of the limb, or they may lie more on the periphery. Penetrating actions often use straight lines as, obviously, do gestures which describe imaginary square or rectangular objects: pulling a thread, measuring a picture, and so on. While one is sitting on the floor, pulling the legs in and extending them in the same direction will produce straight-line gestures for the feet. For a straight-line leg gesture in the air when standing with the feet together, the simplest form is to draw the foot up toward the hip along the other leg and return it to the floor, thus describing a vertical straight line with the foot. More difficult is a forward-backward straight line for the foot, 14.4f, or a side-to-side line. These gestures require concentration and practice to achieve the right degree of leg flexion to avoid a curved line.

14.4f

CIRCULAR AND CURVING PATHS

Anatomically the structure of the body's joints produces arcs, curved paths for the extremities of the body segments. An example is elbow flexion that produces an arc for the lower arm. Nothing makes such curves more visible than extending the arc through using a prop—a cane perhaps, or a sword. Whole arm, whole leg, and whole torso movements produce the largest arcs, the range being increased when an arm gesture is augmented by torso inclusion.

With the help of flexibility in the upper spine, the arms can perform a great number of interesting and enjoyable circular paths around the body. A simple lateral circle (a cartwheel-like path) is illustrated in 14.5a; 14.5b shows a backward sagittal circle (like a backward somersault path); and 14.5c shows a clockwise horizontal circle. Smaller replicas of these dimensionally based circles can occur all around the body. In 14.5d, a figure eight is described in front of the body using cartwheel paths, right and left. In 14.5e, a small forward somersault path is described with the arm out to the side, while in 14.5f a small horizontal circle is being outlined overhead. The extremity of the torso, that is the head, can also describe circular paths as in the clockwise arc produced by the tilted torso in 14.5g.

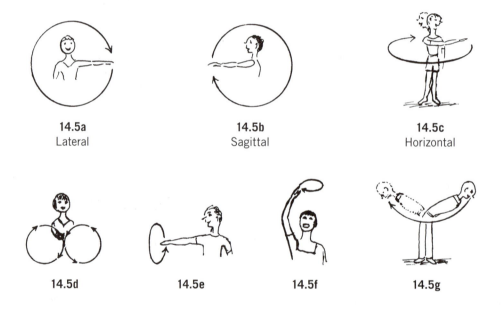

14.5a
Lateral

14.5b
Sagittal

14.5c
Horizontal

14.5d   14.5e   14.5f   14.5g

Combinations of the forms in 14.5a–14.5g used freely can produce a variety of curving paths for the arm, as illustrated in 14.5h and 14.5i.

14.5h

14.5i

Use of rotation helps to produce three-dimensional designs. Gestural paths are augmented visually and the air design expanded by use of objects such as ribbons, soft flowing silk, etc. Choreographers such as Alwin Nikolais have made effective use of a variety of props to extend air designs made by the limbs, in both angular and curved paths. Free, flowing movement may naturally take the form of circular designs. Circular patterns and curving paths allow for long, unbroken movement phrases.

INDICATION OF PATHS FOR LIMBS

The path signs we have used so far described traveling of the whole body. When a limb describes a path, we are aware of the path made by the extremity traveling through space; the base of the limb (the point of attachment) makes no path. The same path signs are modified for Motif Description to indicate this limitation and make clear that it is a gestural path.

As explained earlier, 14.6a indicates an action, a general movement, usually for the body-as-a-whole. When the retention sign: ○ is added at the base of the action stroke, the indication refers specifically to an action of a limb, a part of the body one end of which is attached, hence the retention sign at the base of the movement indication. Thus 14.6b expresses a gesture of a limb. By placing the hold sign at the base of a path sign, 14.6c, we show that one end of the limb is held, it is the free end which describes the path. Thus this example indicates "any" gestural pathway.

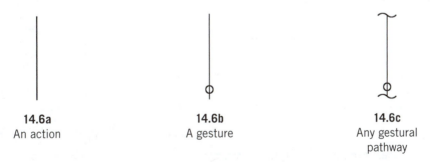

14.6a	14.6b	14.6c
An action	A gesture	Any gestural pathway

Example 14.6d indicates a straight path gesture, no particular direction being indicated; 14.6e and 14.6f show horizontal circular gestural pathways, counter-clockwise and clockwise respectively, while 14.6g indicates the choice of a horizontal circular path in either direction.

Example 14.6h and 14.6i illustrate sagittal circles—a forward somersault path and a backward somersault path, 14.6j providing the sign for the choice of a sagittal circular pathway in either direction.

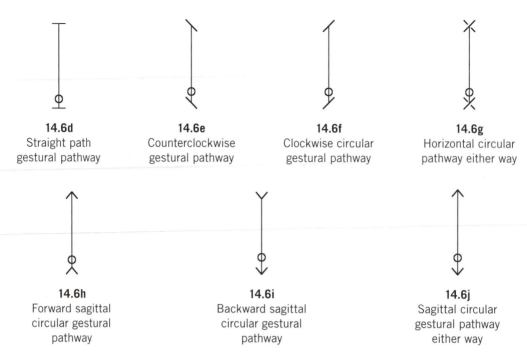

14.6d
Straight path
gestural pathway

14.6e
Counterclockwise
gestural pathway

14.6f
Clockwise circular
gestural pathway

14.6g
Horizontal circular
pathway either way

14.6h
Forward sagittal
circular gestural
pathway

14.6i
Backward sagittal
circular gestural
pathway

14.6j
Sagittal circular
gestural pathway
either way

In the lateral plane, the cartwheel path sign of 14.6k is usually simplified to 14.6l for a cartwheel path to the left; 14.6m, a cartwheel path to the right, is commonly simplified to 14.6n. To provide the choice of direction for a cartwheel path, the ad lib. sign is added to the right (or the left) lateral gestural path sign, as in 14.6o and 14.6p. As is customary, the length of the symbol indicates the duration of time to perform the gesture.

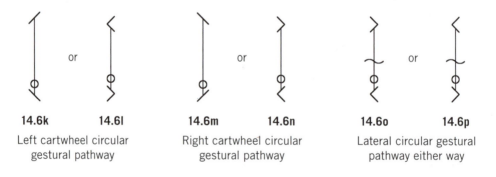

14.6k   **14.6l**
Left cartwheel circular
gestural pathway

14.6m   **14.6n**
Right cartwheel circular
gestural pathway

14.6o   **14.6p**
Lateral circular gestural
pathway either way

Curving paths in the air, as illustrated in 14.5h and 14.5i, are shown with the sign of 14.6q; for gestures, these paths can be two- or three-dimensional. The random, meandering, free-form gestural pathway indicated in 14.6r allows total freedom for improvisation. No specific form has been stated. In 14.6d–14.6r no statement is made concerning size, distance, or degree of circling. Small circles may be performed close to the body or at the periphery of the kinesphere. Patterns may include circles on planes, arcs, and cone shapes of different sizes placed to the right or left, in front or behind, or above the body. Below the body is more limited but can also be implied.

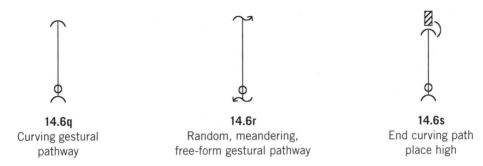

14.6q
Curving gestural
pathway

14.6r
Random, meandering,
free-form gestural pathway

14.6s
End curving path
place high

A special destination for a gestural path can be shown as in 14.6s. The direction symbol being linked to the end of the path sign.

INDICATION OF SPECIFIC LIMB

Stating which limb performs a gestural path is the next step in progressing from general to specific. Example 14.7a, the sign for "a limb," is modified to show a specific limb. The arm is the limb below the shoulder; the leg is the limb below the hip, as indicated in Examples 14.7b–14.7g.

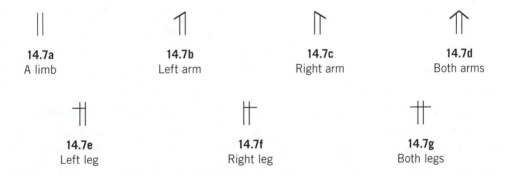

14.7a
A limb

14.7b
Left arm

14.7c
Right arm

14.7d
Both arms

14.7e
Left leg

14.7f
Right leg

14.7g
Both legs

For both legs to make gestural paths one needs to be sitting, lying, in a shoulder stand, held by a partner, or springing high off a trampoline. One leg and both arms may create spatial paths while the performer is standing. Similar or dissimilar patterns may occur at the same time or in sequence. The variety of possibilities provides a rewarding movement exploration. As each limb is stated and the kind of path used is defined, we move closer to a Structured Description. Try the possibilities shown in 14.7h–14.7l.

For these simple indications, it is expected that the rest of the body will participate in producing a fluent, comfortable action. For example, if 14.7h is to be

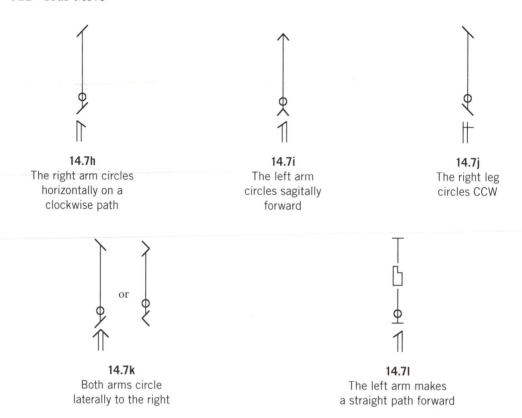

14.7h
The right arm circles
horizontally on a
clockwise path

14.7i
The left arm
circles sagitally
forward

14.7j
The right leg
circles CCW

or

14.7k
Both arms circle
laterally to the right

14.7l
The left arm makes
a straight path forward

performed as a large circle around the body, the torso will probably bend and twist passively to allow the arm to continue the circular path behind the body. For a low level horizontal arm circle, the body is definitely in the way; however, the impression of performing such a circle can be achieved in the following ways: one arm can start the circle and the other can take over to continue the line of movement or the arm can travel as far around as possible and then, by means of a quick turn in the same direction, the arm can spatially pick up the circle and continue the line of progression. If emphasis is placed on the circular path of the arm, the unemphasized turn can be seen as a facilitator of the path and not as an important movement in its own right.

Depending upon the starting location it may be difficult to determine the direction of sagittal and lateral circles. By starting from place high, the direction can be easily determined.

Lateral and sagittal arm circles appear in many movement contexts. For example, in cricket, over-arm bowling employs a sagittal circular path. Swinging an object often involves multiple circles as in the Chinese Ribbon Dance. Windmill-like sagittal circles occur in George Balanchine's *Serenade*, circles for each arm following one another. The motivation, the manner of performance, and the emphasis can all vary, but the shapes of the gestural pathways remain.

SPATIALLY CENTRAL AND PERIPHERAL

Let us consider, as an added component, where gestural pathways can be performed in the kinesphere. Central and peripheral aspects relating to the body were explored in Chapter 13. Here we focus on spatial aspects. In the kinesphere, spatially central movements occur in "near space," i.e., close to the body. Spatially peripheral movements occur in "far space," in the outer reaches of the kinesphere, i.e., away from the body.

NOTATION OF CENTRAL, PERIPHERAL

A diamond, 14.8a, represents spatial aspects for certain notation indications. To indicate central and peripheral, the diamond is divided vertically, as in 14.8b. Short horizontal strokes pointing inward indicate central spatial aspects, 14.8c. For peripheral indications, the short strokes point outward, 14.8d. Only one half diamond is needed to specify these usages; generally it is the right half diamond which is indicated. However, when more practical, the sign can be placed on the left of the staff, in which case the left half diamond is used.

| **14.8a** | **14.8b** | **14.8c** | **14.8d** |
| Aspects of space | | Spatially central | Spatially peripheral |

SPECIFYING A CENTRAL OR PERIPHERAL ACTION

To identify an action as spatially central or peripheral, the appropriate sign is placed in an addition (vertical, angular) bracket alongside the movement it modifies. Example 14.9a indicates the choice of an action that is to take place in a peripheral location. In 14.9b, the action is to occur near the body, i.e., spatially a central placement. A straight gestural path close to the body is shown in 14.9c.

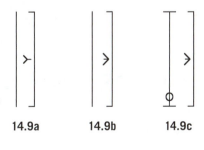

14.9a   **14.9b**   **14.9c**

In 14.9d, the lateral gesture circling to the left is to occur near the periphery of the kinesphere. Statement of spatial placement can also be indicated on the left, as illustrated in 14.9e, where the forward sagittal circle occurs in peripheral space.

In 14.9f, the first sagittal circular path lies on the periphery, the second continues without a break but close to the body.

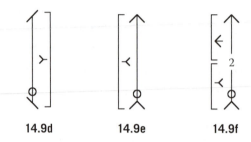

14.9d   14.9e   14.9f

READING STUDY NO. 45

SPATIALLY CENTRAL AND PERIPHERAL PATHS FOR GESTURES

Try the Reading first with the basic path instructions, then reinterpret the reading by exploring the use of spatially central or peripheral locations. An unemphasized transition may be needed to prepare for a change in spatial placement. Note, in measure 4, the curving path has a place high destination. A destination is given for a number of the gestural movements. When choice of limb is left open, it may be leg, arm, hand, or head. One or both arms are usually preferred because of the greater range of movement.

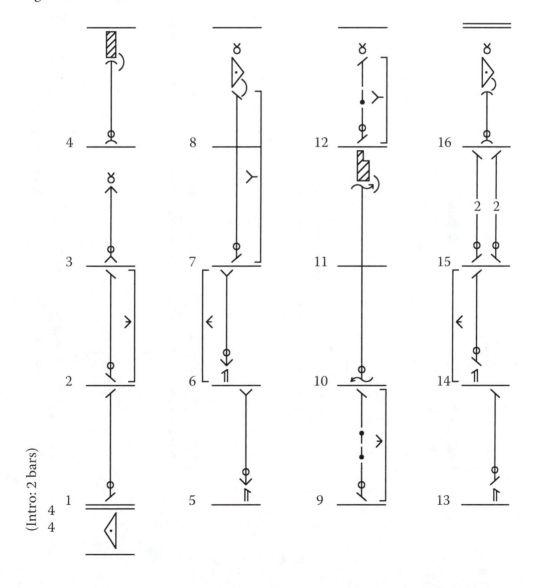

(Intro: 2 bars)

$\frac{4}{4}$

READING STUDY No. 46

GESTURAL PATHS WITH DIRECTIONS AND TRAVELING

In this study, direction for straight gestural paths has been added by placing the appropriate direction symbol in the path sign. The number of circles to be described is indicated by placing the appropriate number within the circular path. A transition before measure 9 may be required to enable the performer to move comfortably into an extended state for the sagittal path. Note that while indication suggests unison for the arms, use of left and right arm symbols suggests both arms in action but used independently.

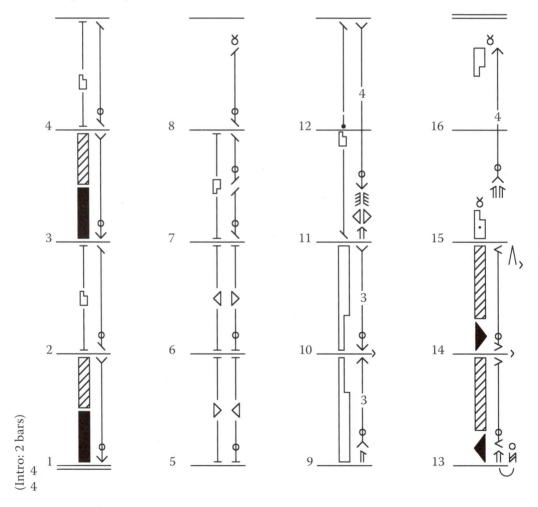

(Intro: 2 bars)

4
4

DESIGN DRAWING

Paths for gestures may take many forms. In pantomimic gestures, the aim may be to describe an object or to perform an activity which is familiar in daily life without the actual tools in hand. Some designs in the air are tracings that suggest writing or drawing on an imaginary wall. The shape, the pattern these tracings make, is the focus of the movement, therefore, these patterns are represented on paper as they appear in the air. This form of gestural paths is called Design Drawing (also known as Trace Forms) and is given a special path sign to distinguish it from other forms of paths.

Example 14.10a shows the sign for "a shape;" in 14.10b the symbol is divided. The path sign derived from this sign, 14.10c, shows the path of a design in the air. The desired design is drawn in the center of the path; in 14.9d any design is stated. A design may be shown but with no indication of where to start, as in 14.10e, the gesture may start at either end of the design indicated.

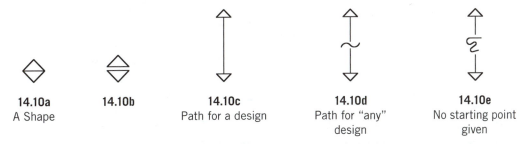

14.10a
A Shape

14.10b

14.10c
Path for a design

14.10d
Path for "any" design

14.10e
No starting point given

For specific designs, a black dot indicates where the design begins. Example 14.10f describes an inward spiral pattern, while 14.10g illustrates a wavy line traveling from left to right. Exact performance is not important at this stage, the "message" is the design itself. Spatial placement of the design, i.e., whether it is in front of you, overhead, at your right side, etc., can be shown by stating the spatial placement of the limb performing the design. In 14.10h, the arm starts forward high. In 14.10i, the head starts upright to perform the figure eight pattern, while in 14.10j, the left arm starts across to the right to perform the series of loops traveling to the left.

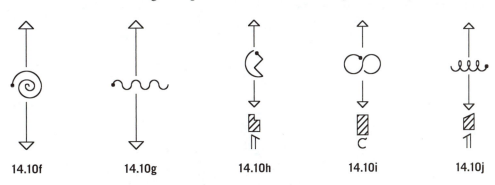

14.10f

14.10g

14.10h

14.10i

14.10j

No indication has been given as to where around the body the design should be drawn. In exploring these possibilities, the tendency is to use the surface in front of the body. Other placements and surfaces can be tried.

SURFACES

Additional information can indicate the surface on which the design is drawn. Example 14.11a is the sign for "a surface." Example 14.11b is a surface in front of you, which is like writing on an imaginary blackboard. Using the surface below, 14.11c, is like writing on the floor below or on a table. The surface above can be like drawing on the ceiling, 14.11d. For surfaces to the left or right, imagine the side walls on each side of you, 14.11e and 14.11f. The surface behind you is indicated as 14.11g. Because it is awkwardly placed, this surface is rarely used. Example 14.10h indicates a figure eight design, drawn as if on the ceiling. Note the placement of the surface indication before the design in the design pathway sign.

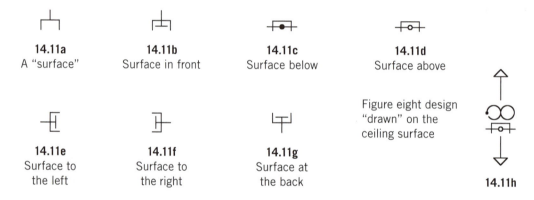

14.11a	14.11b	14.11c	14.11d
A "surface"	Surface in front	Surface below	Surface above

14.11e	14.11f	14.11g
Surface to the left	Surface to the right	Surface at the back

Figure eight design "drawn" on the ceiling surface

14.11h

Greater details in exact placement of the design and of its size will be indicated when needed in a full Structured Description. For now, we are concerned with exploring all possibilities, using the freedoms which this movement idea presents. Experiment with both pantomimic designs and also decorative designs of different sizes and placements. The results should be given scope and style through accompanying general body movements.

READING PRACTICE N (NO MUSIC)

DESIGN DRAWING

Length of the design path indicates the length of time available in which to draw the design. A rich source of design drawing examples are found in the pantomimic gestures in Hawaiian dance where hand gestures represent rippling waters, raindrops, water falls, the sun passing across the sky, etc. Some of these ideas are included here. Note the destination given for some of the design paths. Experiment freely with the ideas given here.

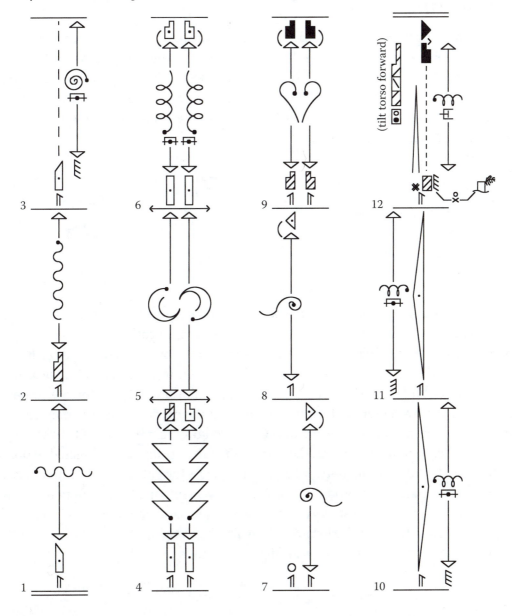

GATHERING AND SCATTERING

As mentioned earlier, gathering and scattering are gestures which "sculpt" space, space being experienced as having volume, i.e., as a "tangible," almost "malleable," entity. These very expressive movements incorporate curved paths with movement "toward" and "away" from the body. Dictionary definitions are not very helpful when it comes to determining what movement must happen to make a gathering action or a scattering action. Let us start with investigating gathering, since scattering is its reverse in idea and spatial usage.

GATHERING

"Draw limbs together," "bring closely together," "take into possession," "contraction, accumulations, assemblage": these dictionary words for the meaning of "gathering" provide no direct image of the desired movement pattern. Yet gathering a dozen fluffy chicks to you, 14.12a, or collecting a pile of autumn leaves into your arms gives the basis of the action very clearly. How does the simple act of taking, 14.12b and 14.12c, differ from gathering?

14.12a	14.12b	14.12c	14.12d
Gathering			Gathering
	Taking		

Taking is a straight line action. The arm starts extended, then draws in to the body on a straight line. It is a simple, direct movement. In gathering, the arm starts more open, often as wide as possible to allow for a greater degree of gathering. It then moves in toward the body on a curved path, an inward spiral ending near the torso, 14.12d (bird's-eye view). This relation of the movement to the torso is important; there is a strong sense of "to me," "mine," in the expression of the movement. An accompanying slight outward lower arm rotation may be present. In theory, one would expect an inward rotation to accompany an inwardly directed action, however, outward rotation (outward arm twist) places the palm in a more functional position. Inward rotation produces a stylized movement, one which might occur in gathering if the palm were sticky and the back of the hand had to be used—a use of the hand seen in the Sailor's Hornpipe, in which hitching up the pants is done with the back of the hand, as if palms and fingers were tarry.

The pathway in gathering may be horizontal or may curve upward or downward. Another term for gathering is "scooping," which suggests a definite downward motion on the way, an undercurve.

Scattering

The simple action of giving (the opposite of taking) also usually makes use of a straight line, 14.13a. But scattering is quite another idea; it is spatially a "generous" action in that it sweeps out from near the body on a curved arc which may end diagonally backward. Example 14.13b illustrates the familiar sowing of seed. The line of the movement is an outward spiral, 14.13c. Another term for this action is "strewing." One can imagine a person searching a basket for the right pair of tights and throwing out garment after garment, strewing them all over the room, 14.13d.

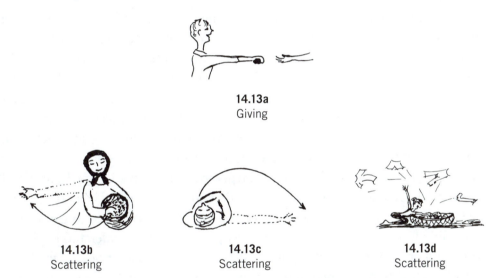

14.13a
Giving

14.13b
Scattering

14.13c
Scattering

14.13d
Scattering

Gathering and scattering actions may express sharing feelings with other people, sharing in an activity or sharing space. "Come, all of you, gather around to share these ideas!" may be expressed by double-sided scattering (for "all of you") followed by gathering. A wide opening of the arms at start or finish expresses generosity and warmth; the expression of these feelings is heightened by opening or closing the arms on a curve.

In dance, gathering and scattering may occur purely as design and often in a highly stylized manner. Waltzing steps are often accompanied by gathering or scattering arm gestures; only one arm may be featured or both may move in a symmetrical or parallel manner. A forward or backward *balancé* is often performed with a slightly stylized scattering on the forward sway and gathering on the backward. In certain lyric forms of modern dance gathering and scattering are used abstractly as movement design and usually incorporate an ebb and flow in energy. Use is made of the falling action toward gravity by tracing a figure eight–like pattern which comes toward the body on the gathering before swinging out and away on the scattering, 14.13e. In this diagram the dotted lines show the unemphasized transitions.

14.13e

The larger movements of gathering and scattering performed by the arms for functional or expressive purposes can be localized in the hands alone. Such movements occur in Spanish dance where they are augmented by rotation of the lower arm and sequential use of the fingers. Usually, the little finger leads the action, the other fingers following in sequence.

Expressive use of gathering can center on the concept of inwardness, of bringing the energy and the line of movement or "a volume of space" to the self. Similarly, expressive use of scattering can be concerned with sending the energy or the line of movement away from the self, of pushing "a volume of space" outward and away from one's center. In these actions, as in many others, space can be experienced as something tangible. This tangibility of space can best be experienced if one imagines oneself to be in a thick fog or in air that is heavily laden with smoke—at which times one can actually see the result of sweeping body movements. Smoke swirls when one waves one's arms; the sensation of an airplane cutting through low-lying clouds provides an awareness of the existence of air and space around. Another useful image is to think of space as a huge mass of foam; then actions such as gathering it up, dispelling it, containing it, pushing it away can be better understood. All such actions could be performed with quite a different focus or intention, in which case they would have different expressions. Abstract movement can be given a particular expression if space is regarded as an entity with which to deal. Space is more than just a practical fact of life.

Once these explorations with the arms are comfortable, gathering and scattering with the legs should also be tried—not an easy task, as the legs have a more limited range of movement. Several possibilities exist, however, that use the necessary enfolding and the reverse. Small details, such as how the foot is used, can strengthen the expressiveness of the movement. Some modern dance techniques make use of leg swings that can easily become gathering and scattering movements. An example of a gathering movement of the leg is the gesture a Spanish dancer makes when she whips the cola (the long ruffled train) behind her to get it out of the way as she turns to face another direction.

INDICATION OF GATHERING AND SCATTERING

As the ideas of gathering and scattering are simple and fundamental, simple signs have been chosen to represent these composite actions.

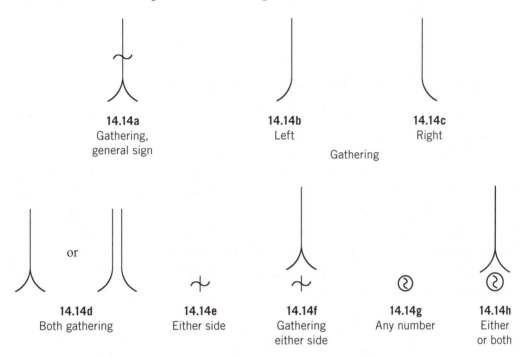

14.14a	14.14b	14.14c
Gathering, general sign	Left	Right

Gathering

14.14d	14.14e	14.14f	14.14g	14.14h
Both gathering	Either side	Gathering either side	Any number	Either or both

Example 14.14a is the general sign for gathering. Gathering for the left side of the body is 14.14b; for the right side it is 14.14c. The two signs combined together, or side by side, 14.14d, indicate both sides gathering. To show either side, leaving the choice open, the sign for "either side," 14.14e, is added below the combined sign of 14.14d, producing 14.14f. Use of the "any number" sign of 14.14g, allows choice of either side or both, 14.14h.

Scattering, the reverse sign, is handled in the same way. Example 14.14i shows the general sign for scattering. Scattering for the left side of the body is 14.14j; for the right side it is 14.14k.

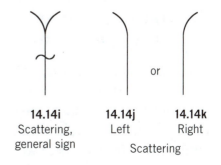

14.14i	14.14j	14.14k
Scattering, general sign	Left	Right

Scattering

The two signs combined together, or side by side, 14.14l, indicate both sides gathering. To leave the choice of side open the sign for "either side" is added to produce 14.14m. The choice of either side or both in shown in 14.14n.

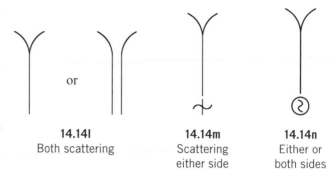

14.14l
Both scattering

14.14m
Scattering
either side

14.14n
Either or
both sides

ANALYSIS OF GATHERING AND SCATTERING

In analyzing the movements just explored, it is possible to spell out the component parts which produce a gathering action. For the one-sided gesture of the right arm the simple gathering sign of 14.15a represents the composite information of 14.15b: approaching the body on a spiral pathway, accompanied by some degree of natural outward rotation together with some degree of flexion, the specific form being that of folding (see Chapter 17). For scattering, the simple sign of 14.15c represents the elements of 14.15d: spiraling away from the body accompanied by a degree of inward (or it may be outward) rotation combined with extension; the form of extension being that of unfolding. It is interesting to note that the terms "scooping" and "strewing" have also been applied to these actions.

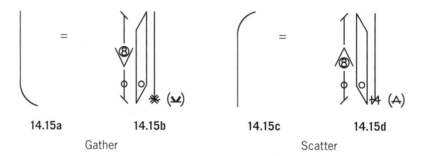

14.15a   **14.15b**

Gather

14.15c   **14.15d**

Scatter

GATHERING AND SCATTERING COMBINED WITH OTHER ACTIONS

Any of the basic movements that we have explored so far may be accompanied by gathering or scattering actions. Examples 14.16a–14.16j can be interpreted in several ways while still adhering to the instructions given. At the beginning of the turn, in 14.16a, gathering takes place with the left side, while in 14.16b it is a scattering action on the right side. Note that two-sided scattering may be written as 14.16c or 14.16d. The same choice is open to gathering, 14.16e, 14.16f.

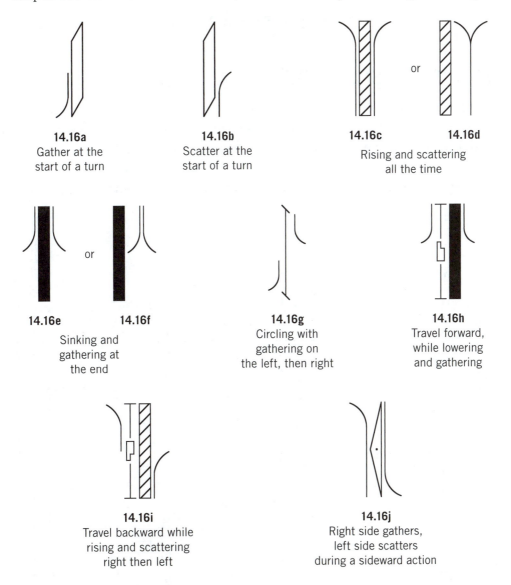

14.16a
Gather at the
start of a turn

14.16b
Scatter at the
start of a turn

14.16c   **14.16d**
Rising and scattering
all the time

14.16e   **14.16f**
Sinking and
gathering at
the end

14.16g
Circling with
gathering on
the left, then right

14.16h
Travel forward,
while lowering
and gathering

14.16i
Travel backward while
rising and scattering
right then left

14.16j
Right side gathers,
left side scatters
during a sideward action

READING STUDY NO. 47

GATHERING, SCATTERING

Gathering and scattering patterns in this study explore isolated, simultaneous, and overlapping actions. In measure 4, even though both limbs are doing the same action of scattering, the manner of performance need not be identical; the space and body patterns may be different. The three scattering actions of measure 15, need to have some unemphasized preparation for the limb to be ready to scatter again.

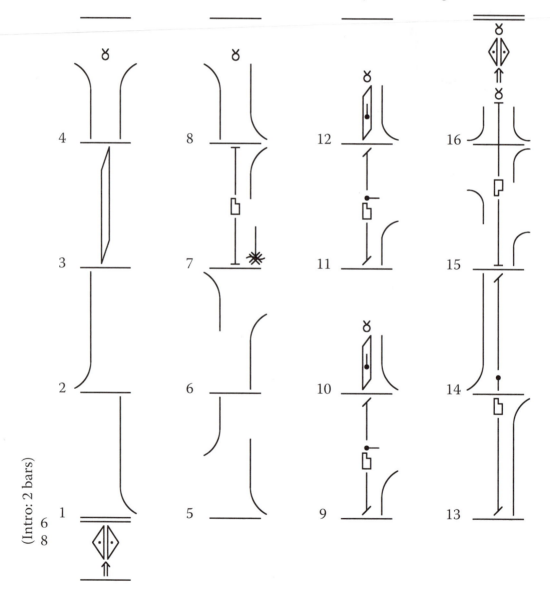

REVIEW FOR CHAPTER FOURTEEN

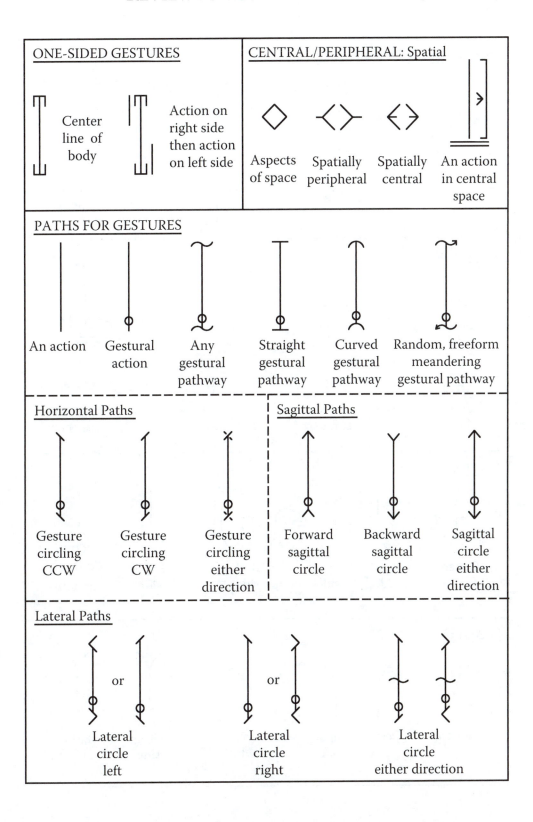

ONE-SIDED GESTURES

Center line of body

Action on right side then action on left side

CENTRAL/PERIPHERAL: Spatial

Aspects of space

Spatially peripheral

Spatially central

An action in central space

PATHS FOR GESTURES

An action

Gestural action

Any gestural pathway

Straight gestural pathway

Curved gestural pathway

Random, freeform meandering gestural pathway

Horizontal Paths

Gesture circling CCW

Gesture circling CW

Gesture circling either direction

Sagittal Paths

Forward sagittal circle

Backward sagittal circle

Sagittal circle either direction

Lateral Paths

or

Lateral circle left

or

Lateral circle right

Lateral circle either direction

Review for Chapter Fourteen (continued)

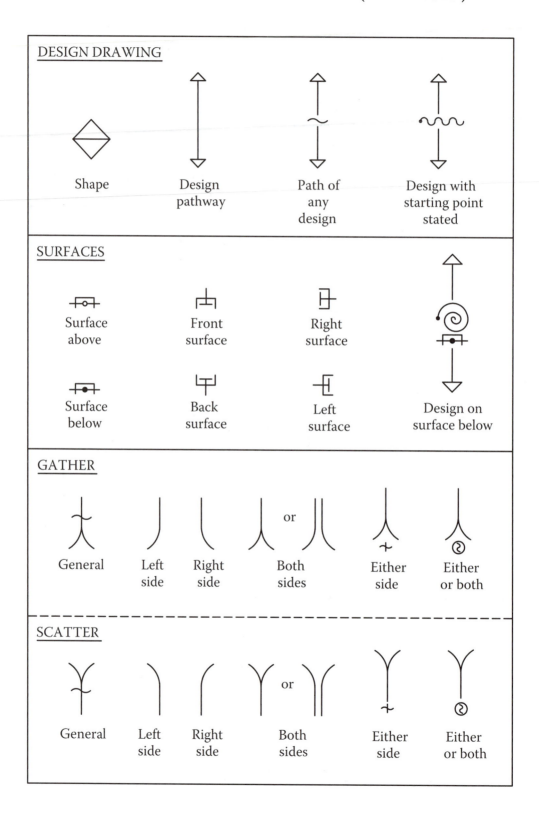

DESIGN DRAWING

Shape

Design pathway

Path of any design

Design with starting point stated

SURFACES

Surface above

Front surface

Right surface

Surface below

Back surface

Left surface

Design on surface below

GATHER

General

Left side

Right side

Both sides

or

Either side

Either or both

SCATTER

General

Left side

Right side

Both sides

or

Either side

Either or both

CHAPTER FIFTEEN
Directions: The Diagonals

It would seem unnecessary to devote a chapter to diagonal directions, yet they can pose a problem because of the lack of a universal terminology in movement study. The crux of the matter is the difference between room diagonals and the diagonal directions taken from the performer's body. The "room" diagonals are further confusing because of reference to the diagonal directions in the Constant System of Reference (see Chapter 21) and the diagonal lines which connect one corner of a room or stage (of any size or dimensions) to its opposite corner. These three types of diagonals must be understood in the mind as well as in the body. Use of clear, appropriate terminology can clarify the difference.

Between the sagittal and lateral directions, 15.1a, lie the four diagonal directions, 15.1b. The term "diagonal" is used by some people to mean a line slanting upward or downward. In the analysis of movement presented here, the word is used only in connection with the directions illustrated in 15.1b. The right-front diagonal of 15.1c, used by the right side of the body, combines both forward and sideward aspects in one action, 15.1d and 15.1e.

| 15.1a | 15.1b | 15.1c | 15.1d | 15.1e |

PERFORMANCE OF DIAGONAL GESTURES

OPEN DIAGONALS

The expression of actions in the diagonal directions is a blend of forward and sideward, or backward and sideward; a diagonal gesture is therefore, in certain respects, richer and subtler than pure forward or pure sideward movement. A right arm gesture into the right front diagonal direction relates less directly to a person in front of you; the relationship is strengthened when both arms are used symmetrically. To express "Welcome!" which would you choose, 15.2b, 15.2d, or 15.2f?

The forward action of 15.2b relates more directly to the person being addressed; it is narrower in that it focuses only on that person. The open gesture of 15.2d could express welcoming a group; it is expansive and hence less personal. Example 15.2f combines the personal with the open welcome.

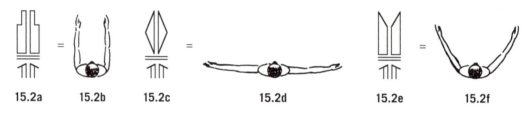

| 15.2a | 15.2b | 15.2c | 15.2d | 15.2e | 15.2f |

CROSSED DIAGONALS

Crossed diagonal directions for arm gestures may be expressive or functional. Both arms in the crossed diagonals express self-enclosing, especially if the arms are rounded. In folk dances, crossing the arms when holding hands in a small circle is not uncommon, 15.3a. Because each arm balances the other, there is no tendency to turn the body as can easily happen when only one arm is used. If the body is allowed to turn, as in 15.3b, the movement becomes a forward gesture (forward from the chest of the performer, from where directions of arm gestures are judged), 15.3c. As a result, the expression contained in a diagonal gesture is lost. Example 15.3d is the correct performance of 15.3e.

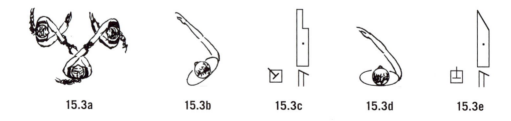

| 15.3a | 15.3b | 15.3c | 15.3d | 15.3e |

The range of expression in using diagonal arm gestures at different levels should be explored. Circular arm gestures which lie on a diagonal, for example a sagittal circle which has been moved 45° laterally, appear in many dance forms, such as in Spanish dance brazeos in which the arm circle comes across the body.

PERFORMANCE OF DIAGONAL STEPS

When no key or other instruction is given, directions are judged from the body's front, i.e., from where the performer is facing. Step direction is judged from the front of the pelvis, arm gestures from the front of the shoulder area. Advancing toward someone may require an open diagonal step, possibly for the practical reason such as passing a person in front of you, 15.4a. Any step which crosses the center line of the body has a narrowness, a feeling of being enclosed, of being spatially "tight." Although this feeling is even more marked in crossed sideward steps, it is also a component of crossed diagonal steps. For diagonal steps, it is essential that the hips do not turn; the established direction into which the body is facing must be retained. With the hip direction unchanged, the crossing leg produces a tension which adds to the style of the movement as a whole. In dances such as the Tango, crossing steps add to the dynamics of the performance.

15.4a

In the following illustrations a black pin represents the performer. To clarify the analysis, interpretation, and performance of diagonal steps, the person is shown as facing into three different directions.

A movement diagonally right-forward as in 15.4b, will produce the movement illustrated in 15.4c, 15.4d, or 15.4e. Facing a different stage direction does not affect the diagonal direction because it is judged in relation to the person's front. A left-forward diagonal movement, 15.4f, is performed as 15.4g, 15.4h, or 15.4i.

15.4b   c   d   e   **15.4f**   g   h   i

Similarly a right-back diagonal movement, 15.4j, would produce 15.4k, 15.4l, or 15.4m. A left-back diagonal movement, 15.4n, would result in 15.4o, 15.4p, or 15.4q. Only three of the eight possible main directions which can be faced are shown here; the same analysis of movement applies to all.

A crossing step into a forward diagonal naturally crosses in front of the other leg, just as a crossing step into a backward diagonal naturally crosses behind the other leg. Occasionally, for a special effect, a step will go the "long way around" and cross the unusual way; such as the leg crossing in front to step into a back-crossed diagonal. This diagonal crossing step occurs in Spanish dance as a preparation before a pivot turn on both feet.

WALKING "FORWARD" IN A CIRCLE

In folk and historical circular dances, when performers hold hands and are instructed to walk "forward" in the line of the circle, they will walk into the direction of the circling but the steps are seldom true forward from the hips. As a result of holding hands, the dancers do not turn the whole body to face the circling direction, thus the steps become a more comfortable in-between direction, a diagonal line to the body, as illustrated in 15.5a–15.5f.

Example 15.5a shows a circle of performers, not holding hands, traveling with forward steps on a clockwise (CW) path, 15.5b. In 15.5c because they are holding hands (indicated on the floor plan by the curved lines for the arms, the small dot representing the hands), the performers are taking the diagonal steps shown in 15.5d. The next examples, 15.5e and 15.5f, illustrate a bird's-eye view of the dancer's relationship to the center of the circle, the focal point for circular dances; indicated by: •. Relationship to this point helps to determine orientation. In 15.5a, each performer's right side is toward the focal point, as illustrated in 15.5e. In 15.5c, the focal point is on the performer's right-forward diagonal line, as illustrated in 15.5f.

Traveling on a Circular Path

When you travel on a circular path, it is helpful to remember that the relationship of the line of travel, i.e., the direction of the steps is always at a right angle (90°) to the focal point, the center of the circle, as illustrated in the diagrams of 15.6a–15.6c.

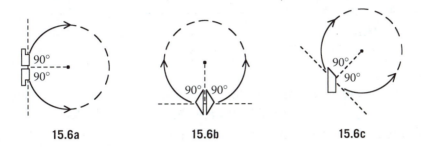

| 15.6a | 15.6b | 15.6c |

Example 15.6a shows circling CW taking forward steps, or circling counterclockwise (CCW) with backward steps. In both cases, the focal point lies at your right side. In 15.6b, sideward steps are taken circling CW or CCW for which the focal point lies in front of you (at 90° to the sideward steps). In 15.6c, the left-forward diagonal steps are taken circling CW. In this case, the focal point lies at your right-forward diagonal direction. It should be noted that this diagonal step direction lies between your forward and left side directions, thus the focal point lies between your forward and your right side directions.

CONSTANT DIRECTIONS

In progressing from diagonal directions as judged from the build of the body, we move to diagonals in the room for which two distinctly separate reference possibilities exist. In speaking of "stage" directions (or "room" directions—both mean the same thing), there are two possible systems of reference, parts of the stage itself or the established Constant Directions. We will deal with the latter first.

The most frequently used directional reference that is not based on body directions is to the Constant Directions. For this, the audience is always Front, even when the performer turns to face other directions. In a studio, one wall is designated as the Front; often this is where the mirrors are located, but another wall can be selected. (Note that this kind of Front is written here with a capital "F" to distinguish it from the front of the body.) With this Front established, the other facing directions fall into place—Constant side-right (stage right), Constant side-left (stage left), Constant backward (upstage), and the diagonal directions in between. This set of directions is comparable to the settings on a compass. The direction

North is constant. A person may turn and face another direction, but North, South, East, and West remain unchanged.

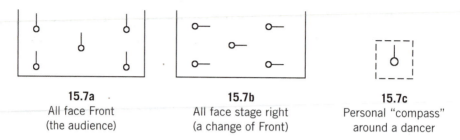

15.7a	15.7b	15.7c
All face Front (the audience)	All face stage right (a change of Front)	Personal "compass" around a dancer

From the above, it can be seen that, no matter where on stage the dancers are placed, when the same Constant Direction is the reference, the facing directions are the same, the performers are parallel, as shown in 15.7a and 15.7b. In this instance, it is as if each performer stands in a small square area, 15.7c. Centered in this square is a cross of directions, like a compass, 15.7d, in which "F," the Constant forward direction is unchanging. When the performer is facing Front, all of his/her directions—right, left, backward, etc.—are the same as the Constant Directions, 15.7e. Hence the name Constant Cross of Directions for this set of directions. It is important to remember that these directions are centered in each performer and move with the performer as s/he travels and turns.

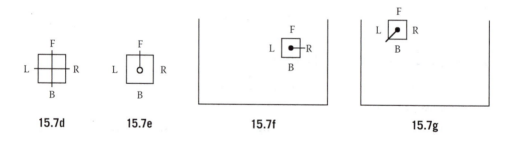

15.7d	15.7e	15.7f	15.7g

In 15.7f, the man in his box is facing the right side of the stage but the Constant Directions remain as before—Front (F) is always to the audience. In 15.7g, he is in the downstage left area, but now facing the left-backward diagonal Constant Direction. The Constant Directions have traveled with him, but, although he turned to face another direction, the Constant Directions did not turn; the audience remains Front, downstage, Constant forward.

Key for Constant Directions

A key is used to indicate when a direction refers to this constant system of reference. This key, 15.8a, is a cross placed on the sign for an area. It is used to indicate that a direction symbol is to be performed in accordance with the Constant Directions. In 15.8b, the forward path is forward of where the performer is facing, forward of his/her pelvis. The path in 15.8c travels Constant forward, i.e., toward the audience, whatever the facing direction of the person or wherever s/he is located. Note the resulting parallel paths in 15.8d.

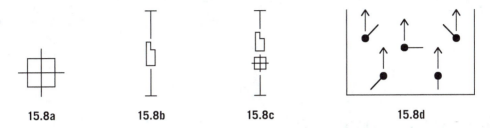

15.8a   15.8b   15.8c   15.8d

THE FRONT SIGNS

"Where in the room are you facing?" This question frequently needs to be answered. The performer's orientation in relation to the Front of the room (stage) needs to be clearly indicated. The individual Front signs are derived from the key for the Constant Cross, 15.8a. Example 15.9a shows the main Constant Directions into which performers face. These signs are placed at the left of the movement notation staff to indicate where the performer is facing at that moment, **i.e., where his/her personal front is in relation to the Constant Directions.** These Front signs are also placed at the beginning of a movement sequence. When any change of Front, of orientation, occurs, the new Front is stated. Note that when you face Front, body directions and Constant Directions are the same. In 15.9b, the movement sequence starts facing back (upstage); in 15.9c it starts facing the right-forward diagonal direction. In 15.9d the performer starts facing side-left (stage left); **after** the half turn the new Front (facing orientation) is side-right (stage right). Note that a turn or circular path may establish a new direction faced so a new Front sign is written after the turn or pathway is completed to indicate the new Front.

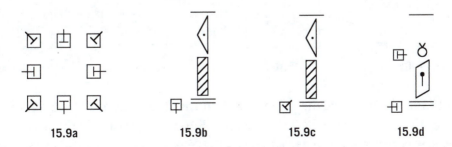

15.9a   15.9b   15.9c   15.9d

In 15.9e and 15.9f, the stage plans illustrate the interpretation of the Front signs, stated at the left, for a group of performers spread around the stage. In 15.9e, each dancer is facing his/her own personal Constant left-forward diagonal direction; in 15.9f they are all facing the Constant diagonal left-back. Their facing directions are therefore all parallel.

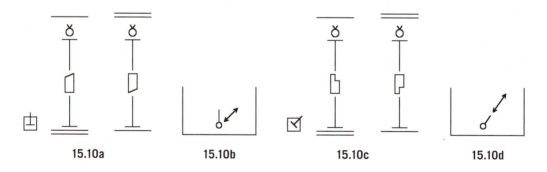

15.9e   15.9f

DIAGONAL TRAVELING

In taking diagonal steps in relation to the front of the body, there is a natural, unintentional tendency on the part of the performer to make a slight turn and to walk forward (or backward) from the hips (pelvis).

Example 15.10a shows a sequence in two parts in which diagonal traveling moves in the forward-right and backward-left diagonal directions while the performer faces Front (the audience) all the time. Example 15.10b illustrates the resulting path. This sequence provides interesting changes from open to crossed diagonal steps such as might occur in a Tango. Example 15.10c is spatially similar, but, while traveling on the same diagonal pathway, all the steps are forward or backward from the hips, produced by the different Front. The performances of 15.10a and 15.10c are different in that in 15.10c, the tension of crossed steps is lost.

15.10a   15.10b   15.10c   15.10d

In 15.10e, the traveling direction is written with the Constant Direction key; this produces the same path as both 15.10a and 15.10c, but physically the performance must occur with sideward steps, shown in 15.10f. Note the arrowhead at each end of the pathway to show retracing the line of travel. When another Constant direction is faced, as in 15.10g, the sideward Constant direction for traveling will produce forward steps, illustrated in 15.10h.

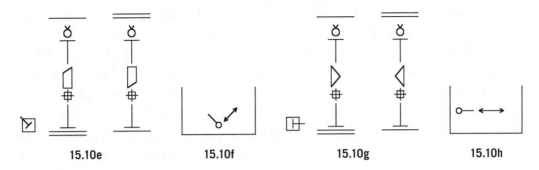

15.10e   15.10f   15.10g   15.10h

THE "DIAGONAL" AREAS (CORNERS) OF THE ROOM/STAGE

Quite another matter in considering diagonal directions is relating to the actual corner areas of the room/stage (see Chapter 11, 11.12b for the stage area signs). Here we are concerned with the build of the stage itself. Whatever the size or shape, reference may be to the center of the stage, a corner area, the center back area, etc. Note that we are dealing here with the standard proscenium stage. Whatever the shape of the room/stage, the diagonal areas are at the corners, as illustrated in the 15.11a, 15.11b, and 15.11c. Be aware that some performance areas may be square, 15.11a, and others wide and shallow, 15.11b. Example 15.11c is a more usual ratio.

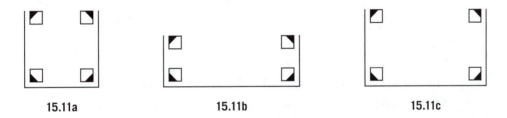

15.11a   15.11b   15.11c

EVERYDAY TERMINOLOGY

Words used in the classroom or in the studio can be misleading. We tend to rely more on what we see, the demonstration or the direction indicated by a gesture. Does "Take three steps to the right" mean to your right side (wherever you are facing) or to the right side of the room? If the command had been "Three steps to stage right" the meaning is clear and all will walk toward stage right, no matter where they are on stage or into which direction they are facing. References such as "toward the audience," "toward upstage," "to stage right," "to stage left" are usually understood to refer to what we specifically call the Constant Directions.

The term "Constant Directions" is not in general studio use. The idea, the fact that movement can relate to those directions exists, but the word "Constant" is unfamiliar. Although it may seem unnecessarily wordy to speak of "Constant forward," "Constant side-right," etc., there is no ambiguity about the designation. Alternatively, if a performer should face a physical location on the stage, then the instruction should include the word "corner" or "area." "Room diagonal" also clearly refers to a diagonal line in the room between opposite corners. By separating these different directional references and by using specific terms and symbols we are at an advantage.

The common instruction, "Face downstage right," may produce two distinctly different results. The instruction, "Face Constant downstage right," will result in all performers using the Constant Directions centered within themselves to produce the parallel facings illustrated in 15.12a. In contrast, the instruction "Face the downstage right corner," will clearly refer to the physical area of the room and consequently produce the converging performer facings as in 15.12b, i.e., using the corner as a focal point.

15.12a   15.12b

When "diagonal steps" or "walking on the diagonal" is the instruction, what is wanted? As we have seen, there are three possible interpretations:

1. Diagonal steps from the front of the body as in 15.12c;
2. Constant diagonal steps, as in 15.12d;
3. The diagonal line in the room, such as between the upstage left and the downstage right corners, as in 15.12e.

Hence, clarity of wording is essential to produce the desired result.

Depending on the shape of the stage, the stage line may be rather flat, as in 15.12f or rather steep, as in 15.12g.

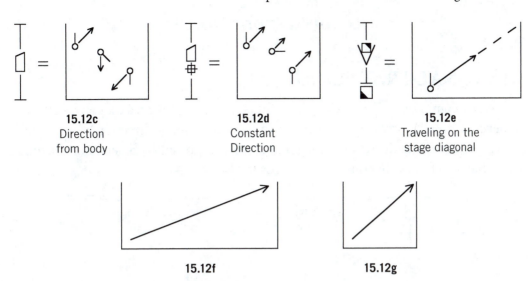

15.12c
Direction
from body

15.12d
Constant
Direction

15.12e
Traveling on the
stage diagonal

15.12f

15.12g

READING STUDY NO. 48

DIAGONAL TRAVELING

This study combines different diagonal Fronts with traveling on a diagonal pathway, achieved through forward, sideward, and backward body-direction steps. Then, walking a square with forward diagonal steps is followed by a series of diagonal steps that also follow diagonal paths across the floor.

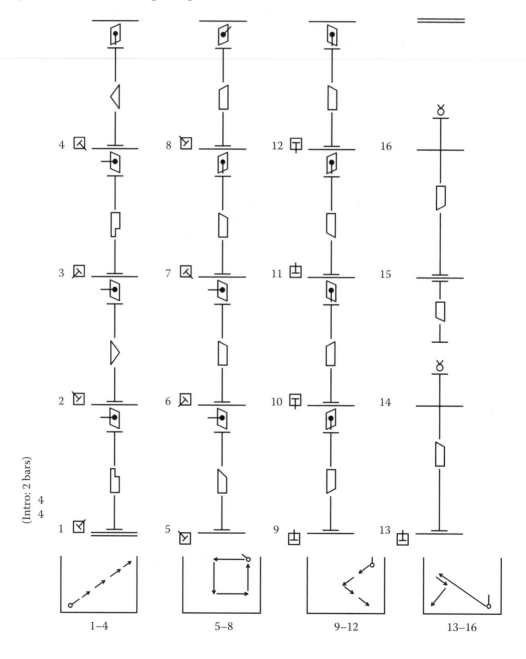

CONSTANT DIRECTIONS AND STAGE AREAS

In **Part I** of this study, the performers all face the same diagonal Front. To walk a square floor pattern, illustrated on the floor plan, they all use diagonal steps. **Part II** shows the Constant Directions they would travel to achieve the same result as Part I. In **Part III,** the performers, labeled "A," "B," and "C," who start facing different directions, travel first together then individually toward different stage areas, as illustrated on the floor plans.

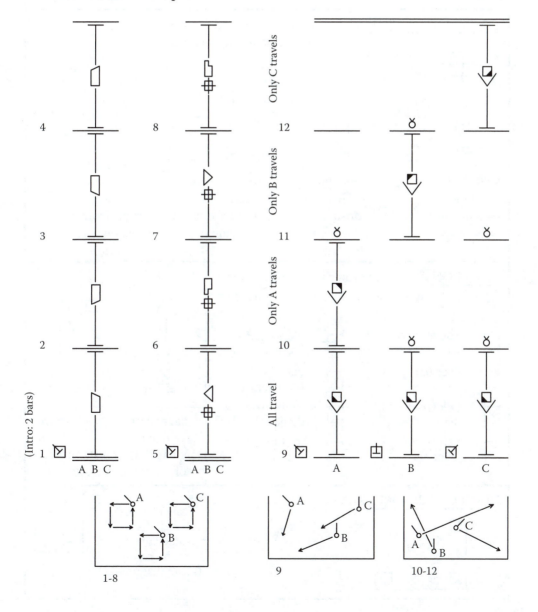

1-8   9   10-12

Review for Chapter Fifteen

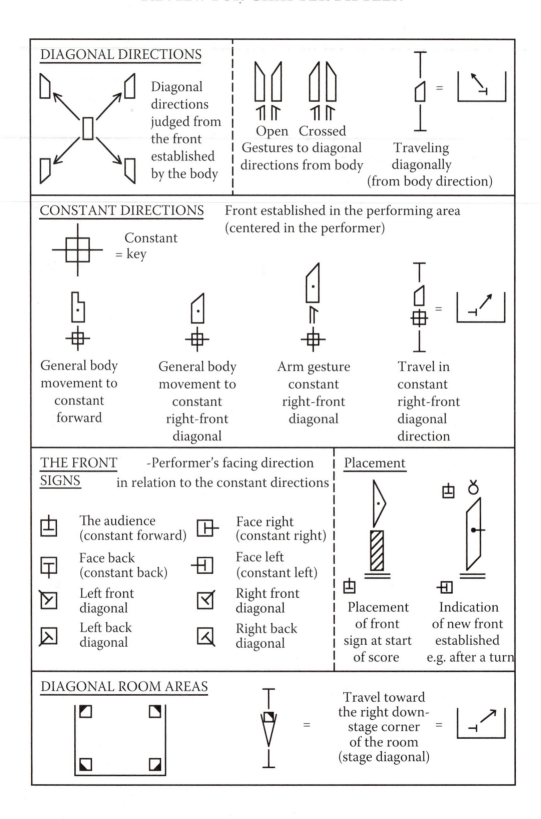

DIAGONAL DIRECTIONS

Diagonal directions judged from the front established by the body

Open   Crossed
Gestures to diagonal directions from body

Traveling diagonally (from body direction)

CONSTANT DIRECTIONS   Front established in the performing area (centered in the performer)

Constant = key

General body movement to constant forward

General body movement to constant right-front diagonal

Arm gesture constant right-front diagonal

Travel in constant right-front diagonal direction

THE FRONT SIGNS   -Performer's facing direction in relation to the constant directions

The audience (constant forward)

Face back (constant back)

Left front diagonal

Left back diagonal

Face right (constant right)

Face left (constant left)

Right front diagonal

Right back diagonal

Placement

Placement of front sign at start of score

Indication of new front established e.g. after a turn

DIAGONAL ROOM AREAS

Travel toward the right down-stage corner of the room (stage diagonal)

CHAPTER SIXTEEN

Turning of Body Parts: Unit Rotation, Twist

The basic action of rotating as a unit is the usual form for some objects and some parts of the body; for others turning takes the form of a twist. Twisting, a familiar movement pattern, takes various forms in the world around us. How do these forms relate to movement? What have we to learn from these forms that can enrich our understanding of similar patterns in the body? First let us see what nature provides.

A rapid rotary motion around a central axis, a spiral, occurs in whirlpools, water spouts, whirlwinds, maelstroms, vortices, cyclones, and tornadoes. Often covering a wide area, a tornado whirls inward to a narrow center. The spiraling center may move across miles, the rotary action continuing all the time. In dance we see a spiral action starting in the body, progressing into turning and whirling through space, the effect of the action being especially marked when a flowing costume is worn. In a group dance the same pattern can emerge, the spiraling out into space being seen in the circling and spreading out of many performers. Conversely, they may be spiraling in. In both cases an interesting and often exciting movement effect is produced. Smaller but equally interesting are the patterns made by twirling objects held in the hands, these being manipulated through twisting, circular motions of the wrists and lower arms.

16.1a
Elizabethan chimney

16.1b
Multi-stranded rope

In a gentler vein we see tendrils coiling, entwining, winding, a loose enclosing which ends with a tighter twisting around an object. Helical shapes, twisted spiral designs in furniture and architecture are often functional as well as decorative. The winding of fibers into a rope produces greater strength than the same number of straight strands. A twist produces resiliency as in coils of wire.

A three-dimensional spiral (a coil, like a chair spring)

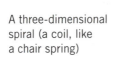

16.1c

A helix (the diameter does not diminish)

16.1d

Coils, 16.1c, may be two- or three-dimensional. A helix, 16.1d, is a coil in which the diameter does not diminish, thus we see that in fact a so-called spiral staircase is actually helical rather than spiral.

Twists in the body have functional as well as expressive use in movement. A twist may be in the same spatial volume, or one of closing in to a center, or one of opening out from a center as the twisting occurs. Motivation for twisting movements may vary considerably; the following words may evoke an image of what is wanted: gyrate, writhe, wring, contort, wind, intertwine, wreathe. Each contains particular elements which gives it its identifying character. Counterparts of everyday meanings exist in gymnastics, swimming, and skating as well as in dance. Such diverse disciplines as South Asian dance and modern jazz introduce many examples of rotations/twists of body parts in their basic training. Turning of body parts may be isolated actions or combined with other movements.

TERMINOLOGY FOR TURNING, ROTATION

In the category of rotation of the body (revolving, turning), the term in general use is **Turn**. Turning can be: (1) revolutions, rotations of the body-as-a-whole, or (2) rotations of parts of the body, the latter having two subdivisions. These subdivisions are: (a) a turn of a body part as a unit, i.e., in one piece; for this the term **Unit Rotation** is used; and (b) a turning action within the torso or other body part in which the extremity achieves a greater amount of turn than the base. For this the term **Twist** is used. Note the following list of terms:

1. **Revolution, Rotation, Turn:** the terms generally in use.
2. **Revolution, Rotation of the Body-as-a-Whole:** the whole body turning, revolving, as in a pivot turn, somersault, cartwheel or wheeling.
3. **Turning a Body Part as a Unit:** each part turns an equal amount, the limb or area turns in one piece, **Unit Rotation**.
4. **Twisting the body-as-a-whole** or **within a Body Part:** the free end turns more than the base, **a Twist**.

The chart in 16.1e illustrates the choice of specific terminology and the symbols that have been selected, when needed, to differentiate the forms.

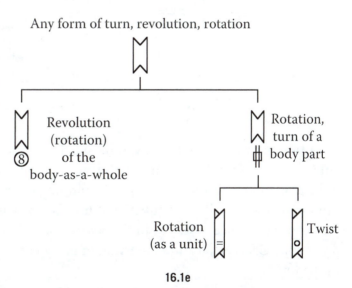

16.1e

TWISTING ACTIONS: FUNCTION AND EXPRESSION

A twist in the torso may be functional in that it may be a preparation for a turn of the whole body as, for example, in skating where a torso twist, leading into a slight lift of weight produces the smooth change from traveling forward to traveling backward. In diving, half twists and full twists are familiar forms. Throwing an object usually involves a preparatory torso twist in one direction, the follow-through being into the other.

Such twists in the body-as-a-whole are illustrated clearly in a golf drive, the preparation being a twist to the right and the follow-through a twist to the left. Change of weight from right foot to left allows a greater range of twist than would be possible on just one foot or if both feet were stationary on the ground. The preparatory twist, then untwist allow for a smooth transition at the moment of impact with the golf ball.

In dance, every *pirouette* or aerial turn starts with some degree of twist. In ballet, the twist preparation in the opposite direction to the turn is usually hidden, occurring in the muscles of the torso. As the turn starts, it begins as a twisting action which soon becomes a turn of the body-as-a-whole. The movement is so fast and the twisting action so brief that only in slow motion films can the twist itself be observed. A familiar form of twist is that in which the feet are apart, the arms outstretched and the body is twisted from side to side, 16.2a. With only one foot supporting, a greater degree of twist can be achieved, the twist going down into the foot.

A twist through the body from supporting foot to head

16.2a

A twist in the torso, called a "spiral," starting from the base and moving sequentially up, is a central feature of the Martha Graham technique. The student trains to be able to extend the range of this spiraling as much as possible for both its expressiveness as well as its functional use. Torso twists occur in many forms of contemporary dance as well as in jazz and African dance. The Twist, made famous by Chubby Checkers, featured twisting in every part of the body—the more parts, the better.

    16.2b   **16.2c**   **16.2d**   **16.2e**

How do twists affect the expressiveness of an action? An increased degree of twist produces a torsion with an inevitable accompanying tension. Relax the muscles and the significant twist will disappear, the limb will return to its normal alignment, the untwisted state. Tension accompanying a twist can be exaggerated by bringing the antagonist muscles into play, i.e., resisting the twist but at the same time allowing it to continue or to be maintained.

ANALYSIS OF UNIT ROTATION, TWIST

Somersaults and cartwheels are examples of rotations (revolutions) of the body-as-a-whole moving in one piece. In a spinning turn, such as a *pirouette*, the whole body turns as a unit, 16.3a. In logrolling (turning while lying on the floor), the body also usually turns in one piece, 16.3b.

16.3a   **16.3b**

A turn of a body part in one piece is expressively and functionally different from a turning action within a body part, i.e., a twist. In our further investigation into the function of, and the expression in, such turning actions, we will consider the main parts of the body separately and observe whether the part naturally rotates in one piece (unit rotation), as illustrated in 16.3c, or whether a twist naturally occurs within that part, as shown in 16.3d.

16.3c   **16.3d**
Unit rotation   Twist

The Whole Torso

The torso can both twist and unit rotate (rotate as a unit); let us begin with twisting, the more usual form. Twists in the torso, slight or marked, may express strong feelings, positive or negative. The latter may be based on fear, conflict, antagonism, aversion, disdain, suspicion, or secrecy. Spatially a twist often occurs to enlarge the range of movement around the body, extending the scope of gestures by bringing into use space behind the body and facilitating performance of gestures across the torso, as in 16.4a and 16.4b.

A twist may start at the extremity and successively move to the base, or vice versa. A return to normal carriage may also start at the base or the extremity and move part by part through the spine, particularly when the movement is slow. Such a successive progression is less observable at speed. Explore twists of the torso by themselves and also twists combined with other forms of movement to discover the expressive possibilities. Next, we will consider how specific twists occur.

16.4a   16.4b

The following illustrations analyze first a twisting with the base, the feet, as the static part and then twisting with the extremity, the head, as the static part. If from the untwisted state, 16.4c, a pivot turn is attempted with the feet glued to the floor, the result will be a twist in the body, 16.4d. The head would turn the most, shoulders less, and so on. Or it could be that the head is the fixed end and the rest of the body turns away, the legs (feet) achieving the greatest degree of turning, as in 16.4e.

16.4c   16.4d   16.4e

Compare twisting of the torso with unit rotating, that is, the torso from pelvis to shoulders turning equally. Example 16.4f shows a unit rotation of the whole torso; chest and pelvis face the same direction; 16.4g shows a twist within the torso, the shoulders turning farther than the hips. Each of these actions involves some twist in the leg(s). Indeed, it is this twist in the leg(s) that makes a unit rotation of the torso possible. Degree of such unit rotation is limited to how far the pelvis can rotate; beyond that, further turning can only be achieved through twisting in the upper part of the torso, the chest, and shoulder section.

16.4f   16.4g

The Head

Turning the head is such a familiar everyday action that we may not be aware of how many different expressions this simple anatomical action can produce. We turn the head to look, to focus our attention on something or someone, or the reverse—to look away. The head may turn to test freedom in the neck as when recovering from a stiff neck. We "shake" the head to say no, to express dismay, sadness, etc. Even though quite small, these are rotary actions.

Though the muscles on the face may twist, the head itself is a solid mass which only unit rotates through the twisting action in the neck, 16.5a. Though it is essentially a neck movement, the focus and awareness of the action is on the head and so it is usually described and written as a turn of the head. The neck can only twist. By combining head rotations with tilting and shifting actions we are able to express many different thoughts and emotions.

16.5a

The Chest

Torsion in the body may focus on the rib cage (the thorax). Unit rotating and twisting the upper part of the torso is a movement that jazz dance would hate to be without. Reacting to a basic beat in the music may take the form of isolated chest twists which may be spatially quite small or may grow to become thrusting actions. Often chest twists initiate other movements. Or a chest twist may occur to augment the range of movement for arm gestures. It may also happen in sitting when change of Front takes place for the upper part of the body without affecting the lower.

Unit rotation of the chest in one piece, from bottom ribs to the shoulders, occurs through a twist in the waist area, 16.6a. The amount of turn possible for the chest in one piece depends on the length and flexibility of the waist area of the spine. The degree is usually small; attempting a large amount of unit rotation inevitably produces a twist in the chest itself (i.e., the thoracic spine), the shoulder line achieving the greatest amount of turn, 16.6b. A slight degree of unit rotation may involve just the upper body, the shoulder section of the spine (base of scapula to shoulders). This occurs in a balletic *épaulement*; however, *épaulements* may also be slight chest twists.

16.6a

16.6b

The Pelvis

As an art form, pelvic rotations have been mastered by more than one culture around the world. The rapid figure-eight twisting patterns of the Tahiti dancers is augmented by the resulting swirl of the grass skirt. North African belly dancers wear a costume which spatially augments their hip rotations and it is astounding to see such activity in the lower half of the body while the top remains so calm that a vase, otherwise unsupported, is carried on the head.

These movements require training; what range is there for less trained dancers? Hip rotation can give an ordinary walk an aggressive or a coy look depending on the direction of the rotation in relation to the stepping leg. A sagittal leg gesture pulled out from the body will take the hip with it thus causing a rotation of the pelvis. Balanchine's use of hip thrusts does not usually include lateral rotation; such rotation is more typical of jazz with its undertone of sex. Many people use slight rotation in their ordinary walk. As with the chest, pelvic rotations may mark the pulse or beat of the music. Hands on hips will make one more aware of the direction and degree of pelvic rotations.

The pelvis is a solid body mass and so can only unit rotate, this rotation being produced through a twist in the supporting leg(s) plus a twist in the waist, 16.7a. In a pelvic rotation the chest should be kept still, that is, it should remain uninvolved, but for greater degree of pelvic rotation the lower part of the chest may need to join in the twist at the waist.

16.7a

The Leg, Foot

Leg rotations, particularly when the limb is bent, provide expressive distortion which may serve comedy or pathos. The baleful stance of 16.8a is basically the same as the cheeky Charleston, 16.8b which, of all dances, probably features leg rotations more than most. Leg rotations appear in many jazz steps both for the supporting leg and for the gesturing leg. Russian and Chinese dances feature smooth sideward traveling which is accomplished by symmetrical or parallel leg rotations with change of weight from ball of foot to heel. Classical ballet appears to use constant outward rotation of the legs, but in fact the degree varies with certain steps and parallel legs are used for swift forward running steps (*bourrées*) on *pointe*.

16.8a   16.8b   16.8c

Changes in degree and direction of leg rotation occur frequently in many step and locomotor patterns. When walking in a circle, that is, on a circular path, an unemphasized rotation of the legs into the direction of the circling occurs on each step. The fewer the steps for a full circle, the more the preparatory rotation is evident. As each step is completed, the body "catches up" with the degree of rotation by "untwisting" from the ankle up. Many European folk dances use parallel feet in a closed position but turned out slightly for steps which follow. A slight change in rotational state of the legs will make any known style of dance look wrong; thus rotational state of the legs is an important factor in dance style.

To avoid injury, teachers of physical education and of dance stress the use of unit rotation of the leg (i.e., in one piece), the action taking place only in the hip socket, 16.8d. All too easily a twist in the legs can occur, 16.8e, particularly if the foot is

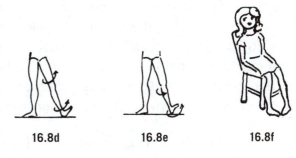

16.8d   16.8e   16.8f

forced outward (or inward) to a degree the thigh cannot match. When the knee is bent, some turning action in the lower leg and foot is possible, 16.8f.

From below the ankle the foot can "roll" through flexibility in the ankle. Such foot rotation produces a support on the outside edge of the foot (inversion), 16.8g, or on the inside edge (eversion), 16.8h. In addition to this rotary action the foot itself can twist, but let us not get too detailed at this point.

16.8g   **16.8h**

The Arms

What of unit rotations and twists in the arms? We are usually unaware that some degree of turning is taking place in everyday actions. Often rotary actions are thought of and described in other terms. We check whether it is raining with an upward facing palm achieved through an outward lower arm twist, 16.9a, or we touch something with palm facing down, 16.9b, without realizing that inward twisting of the lower arm made such palm facing possible. Arms akimbo, 16.9c, requires inward rotation of the upper arm, while outward arm rotation is needed to express bewilderment or lack of knowledge as in the gesture of 16.9d, which could express "I don't know? " or "Where did it go? " or "Who cares?"

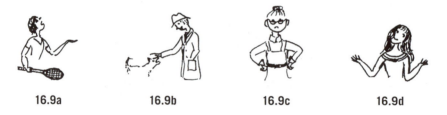

16.9a   **16.9b**   **16.9c**   **16.9d**

Many hidden rotations occur in simple circular patterns of the arms, particularly full circles. Such unemphasized rotations during arm circles are discussed fully later. The sinuous arm ripple of South Asian dance requires rotations in the center of the arm. Hand rotations combined with twists occur in the hand circles used in Spanish dance and in many Asian dance forms. Functionally important arm rotations and/or twists occur in gymnastics and are vital to the accomplishment of particular feats. In a simple cartwheel, placement of the hands (produced by the degree of arm twist) affects the line of travel.

The whole arm moving in one piece (i.e., as a unit) can achieve only a small degree of rotation around its own axis, 16.9e and 16.9f. The rotation is augmented if the shoulder takes part. Rotation of the arm as a unit is less usual than a twist in the arm. Most of this twist occurs in the lower arm. By itself the lower arm can only twist, carrying the hand with it, 16.9g and 16.9h.

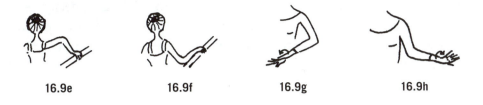

| 16.9e | 16.9f | 16.9g | 16.9h |

The Hands

Rotation of the hand functions like a rotation of the head in that we are more aware of the part turning, the hand, rather than of the adjacent part, the twist in the lower arm, which produces the hand movement. Practical use of such rotation/twist occurs in using a screwdriver, and in changing a light bulb, both of which involve hand rotations produced through twisting movements in the lower arm. Because emphasis and focus is on the hand, the movement is described and written as a hand rotation.

A twist can occur within the hand through the action of the thumb and fingers (the metacarpals and phalanges), 16.10a. The wrist joint itself does not allow for any rotary movement, being built quite differently from such joints as the hip and shoulder which provide much freedom for rotary actions of the leg and arm.

16.10a
Twist within
the hand

ARM ROTATIONS DURING CIRCULAR GESTURES

Circular paths of the limbs involve rotations, which are observed and experienced to a greater or lesser degree. Many performers are unaware that one full arm circle involves one full arm rotation. This rotation may occur gradually throughout the circle so that it is "absorbed" and not generally evident, or the full rotation may occur during a small section of the circle in the form of "getting over the hump." 16.11a and 16.11b are examples for the right arm. In a forward sagittal circle (somersault), 16.11a, a full outward rotation occurs; for a backward sagittal circle an inward rotation takes place. In sagittal circles, the rotation usually occurs between the directions up and backward horizontal. For a lateral circle (cartwheel) to the right, 16.11b, a full inward rotation is needed; for a lateral circle to the left a full outward rotation occurs. In lateral circles the rotation is usually spread out so evenly that many performers are unaware that it occurs.

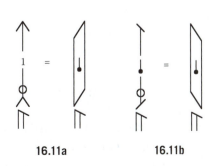

16.11a   16.11b

For a horizontal clockwise circular path, 16.11c, the right arm performs a full outward rotation; for a counterclockwise circle it performs a full inward rotation, 16.11d. In horizontal circles the rotation usually occurs in the section which lies behind the body.

| 16.11c | 16.11d |

Examples 16.11e–16.11i reveal how the rotation occurs in a lateral circle; 16.11j–16.11l illustrate what happens if no rotation at all takes place.

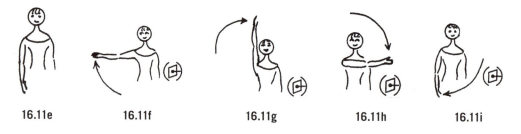

| 16.11e | 16.11f | 16.11g | 16.11h | 16.11i |

Examples 16.11e–16.11i illustrate a familiar lateral circle which starts with the arm down and the palm facing in (the standard rotational state). As the arm lifts to the side the "hidden" rotation brings the palm to face front; as the arm rises to overhead, the hidden rotation brings the palm to face "in" again. When the arm arrives across to the other side, the palm is facing back; on the arm's return to the down position the palm again faces in toward the body. Some people feel that, from the start of 16.11j, it is more "natural" not to change the palm facing as the arm is raised so that, when the arm arrives side horizontal, the palm is facing down, 16.11k. Palms down when the arms are out to the side is common to several movement styles, e.g. gymnastics.

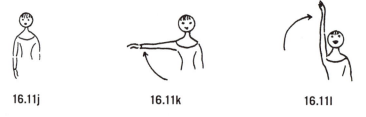

| 16.11j | 16.11k | 16.11l |

If the usage of 16.11k (palm facing down) is carried further with no additional rotational adjustment, the palm will end facing out when the arm is up, as in 16.11l. This carriage can clearly be seen to be a twisted state. As soon as the arm muscles are allowed to relax, the palm will return to facing in, as in 16.11g. Thus 16.11k cannot be taken as the standard carriage for the arms in that direction.

When the arms are down by the side of the body, it is easy to see and feel which direction is inward rotation and which outward. But when the arms are held overhead, what appears to be inward rotation is, in fact, outward rotation, and vice versa. With eyes closed it is easier to feel the inward or outward action, but visually the rotation gives the wrong message.

INDICATION OF TWIST, UNIT ROTATION

In Motif Description, the signs of 16.12a, 16.12b, and 16.12c indicate a pivot turn, a rotation of the body-as-a-whole around its vertical axis.

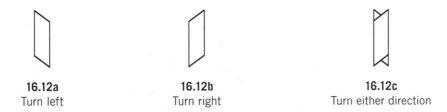

16.12a	16.12b	16.12c
Turn left	Turn right	Turn either direction

These same signs are used to show rotating or twisting within the body, that is, around each part's vertical axis. In a twist, one end of a body part or area is held; the sign for retention, the hold sign is placed within the turn sign near the base, as in 16.12d, 16.12e, and 16.12f. These examples give the general statement for this form of turning. This use of the hold, retention sign near the base of the symbol was applied earlier to gestural pathways.

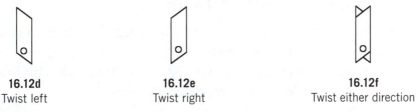

16.12d	16.12e	16.12f
Twist left	Twist right	Twist either direction

When each part turns an equal amount, i.e., rotates as a unit, an equal sign: = is placed within the turn sign, as in 16.12g, 16.12h, and 16.12i.

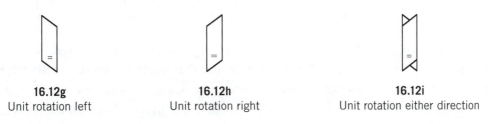

16.12g	16.12h	16.12i
Unit rotation left	Unit rotation right	Unit rotation either direction

OPEN STATEMENTS; UNDERSTOOD PERFORMANCE

When a particular body part has not been indicated, 16.12d, 6.12e, and 16.12f give the general statement for a twisting action, and 16.12g, 16.12h, and 16.12i give the general statement for unit rotation.

STATEMENT OF PART TURNING

Placement of a body part sign before the symbol for a rotation, turn, states what specific part is turning. First we give the general signs to indicate turning for the body-as-a-whole, any body part, any area, any limb respectively, 16.13a–16.13d. Note: for a twist of the body-as-a-whole, the hold sign needs to be added, 16.13e, with the body-as-a-whole pre-sign.

16.13a	**16.13b**	**16.13c**	**16.13d**	**16.13e**
Body-as-a-whole	Any body part	Any area	Any limb	Body-as-a-whole twist

Once a specific body part is indicated, the unqualified turn signs are interpreted as the **form of turning that is natural for that part,** that is, rotation as a unit or twist. Only the opposite, its unusual form, needs to be indicated. The signs for the parts of the body that are unfamiliar are given here.

INDICATION OF PARTS OF A LIMB

To show the different segments of the limbs, the basic sign for a limb, 16.14a, is combined with the appropriate joint sign. The upper arm is the limb above the elbow, 16.14b; the lower arm is the limb above the wrist, 16.14c; the thigh is the limb above the knee, 16.14d; the lower leg is the limb above the ankle, 16.14e.

16.14a	**16.14b**	**16.14c**	**16.14d**	**16.14e**
A limb	Upper arm	Lower arm	Thigh	Lower leg

While turning the lower arm is usually written as a turn of the wrist, the lower arm, 16.14c, can be specified. It should be noted that **parts which naturally rotate as a unit are not capable of twisting**; only the hand is the exception to this fact. A part that normally twists can, with control, be made to rotate as a unit, to indicate this, the sign: = is added within the turn sign. In exploring how specific body parts naturally use the two forms, it may be helpful to refer to the chart on page 370, later in this chapter. For now, let us start with the head.

ROTATIONS OF THE HEAD

The sign for the head is the letter C. Turning the head can be swift, sustained, or somewhere in between. Example 16.15a shows a slow rotation right, then left. As you turn the head slowly, concentrate on the act of turning, not of looking into another direction. Keep the eyes unfocused, perhaps even closed, and feel the turning action, the rotation around the axis of the spinal column. As mentioned before, this action is correctly analyzed as a twist in the neck, so try the movement again, this time with concentration on the neck. When might such an action occur in everyday life? In dance? What motivation might there be for it? A dramatic situation? Would such actions occur just for the enjoyment of moving? As a decorative effect?

16.15a

Having rotated the head alone, by itself, make it now the central movement in a "cluster," that is, support this main action with minor actions in other parts, perhaps an inclination of the body. Try variations in the speed of the movement. Can such head movement occur as pure movement, devoid of meaning?

TURNING THE HANDS

Next, concentrate on the hands, two centers of expression for which turning plays an important part. As you know, 16.16a and 16.16b are the signs for the left and right hands. First try a very slow rotation of the right hand only, 16.16c, then put it into a movement context. What other movements might support this main action? Then rotate both hands symmetrically, 16.16d, at a moderate speed.

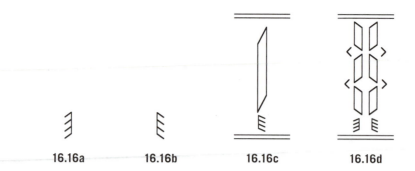

16.16a 16.16b 16.16c 16.16d

How can such movements be set into a dance form? Symmetrical hand rotations occur in certain Russian folk dances, the arms gesturing forward and outward to the audience while the feet repeatedly perform a fast push-off step. The expression is very gay, vivacious and light-hearted. No Lady Macbeth looking at her bloodstained hands, turning them, palms up, in disgust. At a very fast tempo this rotary action of the hands can become a shaking, vibrato movement producing a very different expression, 16.16e.

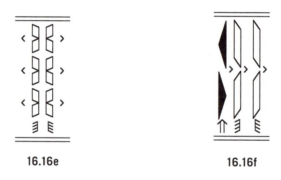

16.16e 16.16f

Quite another effect is produced by parallel hand rotations, as in 16.16f. This relationship may seem unusual, yet at a slower tempo it is used with low side-to-side arm gestures in a lilting *balancé* waltz step, the rotation going into the direction of the path of the arms.

TURNING THE WRIST (LOWER ARM)

Although a change in palm facing occurs through rotation of the hand (lower arm twist), if direction of palm facing is the intention or emphasis of the movement the notation is written with palm indications (see Chapter 18). When emphasis is on lower arm twisting, the hand remains passive; it does not catch the eye of the observer since it is not featured. A common action of this kind is turning the wrist to look at one's watch, an inward twist, 16.17a; or it may be the reverse for the purpose of inspecting the inner surface of the lower arm. Example 16.17b indicates such an action for the right wrist. If attention is to be on the lower arm itself, this can be written as in 16.17 and 16.17d.

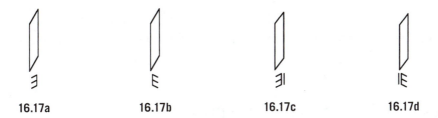

| 16.17a | 16.17b | 16.17c | 16.17d |

LEG ROTATIONS

Small degrees of leg rotation are usually unit rotations; it is the greater degrees which, without training to achieve unit rotation, become twists. For many rotary actions thought need not be given to which form is being used. Parallel or symmetrical leg rotations can occur while standing through swiveling the feet on the floor or when lying on the back when both legs are free to gesture together. Example 16.18a, shows two outward symmetrical leg rotations followed by inward rotations, first slower, then faster. In 16.18b, the rotations are parallel, each leg moving in turn and then both in unison. In the Charleston, symmetrical rotations involve a mixture of one leg supporting while the other gestures. Individually isolated, the upper and lower leg each unit rotate. In 16.18a each additional movement indication, which follows the body part pre-sign, is understood to refer to that same part of the body. If a gap occurs, as in 16.18b, a caret, meaning "the same," 16.18c, can be used to make clear that reference is to the same part of the body. The caret has been used in 16.18b. Some writers prefer to use carets as a matter of course as a constant reminder.

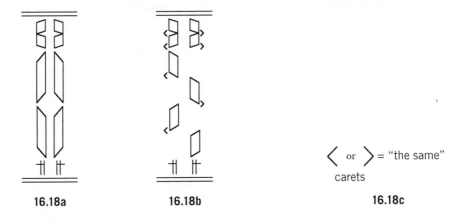

| 16.18a | 16.18b | 16.18c |

ANALYSIS CHART

Unit Rotation, Twist of Parts of the Body

For quick reference, the parts of the body are listed showing which naturally makes use of a twist and which of unit rotation. Note that the sign for the neck is the limb below the head.

Chart of Natural Abilities

Chart 1

Naturally unit rotates	Naturally twists
⊂ Head	Ꝋ Neck
	⊞ Shoulder section
⊙ Pelvis	⊡ Chest
⅌ Upper arm	⊟ Whole torso
	⋔ Whole arm
⅄ Hand	⊫ Lower arm
⋔ Whole leg (when gesturing)	⋔ Whole leg (when standing)
⊩ Upper leg	⊩ Lower leg (slight)
⊨ Foot (when standing)	⊨ Foot

With the exception of the hand, those parts which naturally unit rotate are not able to twist. However, with control, parts which normally twist can achieve unit rotation. Chart 2 indicates these.

Chart 2

Can unit rotate	Can twist
⊡ Chest (limited)	⅄ Hand
⊟ Whole torso	
⋔ Whole arm	
⋔ Whole leg	

The body part pre-sign is included in the timing of the action. In 16.18d, the action takes one count; in 16.18e the actions take half a count.

16.18d   **16.18e**

In Reading Studies Nos. 50 and 51 remember that automatic cancellation is an open choice, resting on the idea that one action has its moment and is then replaced by another. Equally, the result of a previous indication may be retained. Study A uses general indications, therefore the hold sign is needed to show twisting. Study B deals with twist and unit rotation of specific parts.

READING STUDIES NOS. 50 AND 51

UNIT ROTATIONS AND TWISTS

Note that in measure 6, no hold sign is written for the head; therefore it may or may not return to normal at an appropriate time, probably during the twist to the left. The whole sequence could be performed as though by a wary, suspicious person, the twisting and head turns suggesting clandestine activities, or, of course, it could be performed totally as an abstract design.

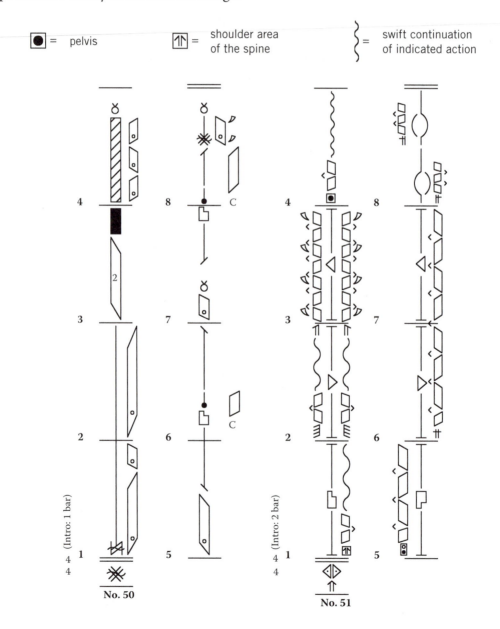

TURNING COMBINED WITH FLEXION, EXTENSION

Many arm gestures combine a flexion or extension with a rotation, a twist. 16.19a–16.19d all illustrate movements for the right arm.

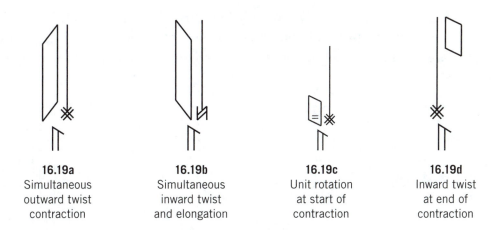

| **16.19a** | **16.19b** | **16.19c** | **16.19d** |
| Simultaneous outward twist contraction | Simultaneous inward twist and elongation | Unit rotation at start of contraction | Inward twist at end of contraction |

The simple material of 16.19a (twist combined with flexion) can be varied in timing and in degree to produce differences in expression, as can the movements in 16.19b and those of 16.19c and 16.19d. Such actions also occur in the legs, though the range is more restricted. The torso may also combine flexion and extension with unit rotating or twisting. Note the centering of the arm sign in 16.19a–16.19d to state that both movement indications refer to the arm.

READING STUDY NO. 52

ROTATION, TWISTS OF SPECIFIC PARTS

The jazzy character of the music should help to inspire an appropriate mood. In measure 25, the white diamond space hold, following the sign for the face, means that the face remains looking into the same direction, despite the accompanying chest twist.

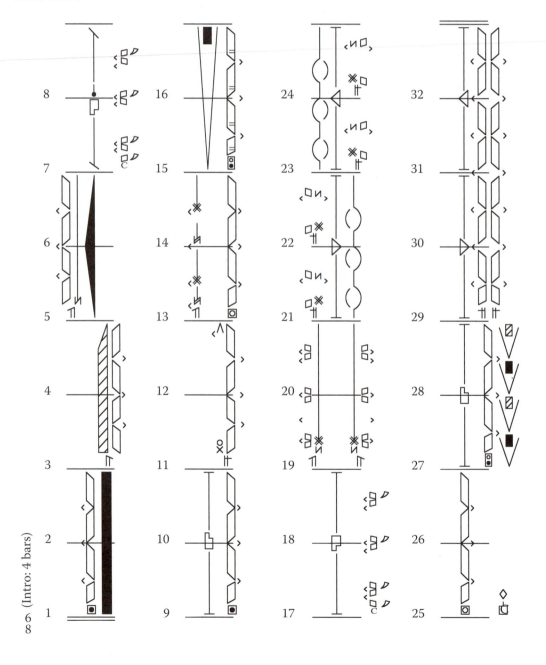

REVIEW FOR CHAPTER SIXTEEN

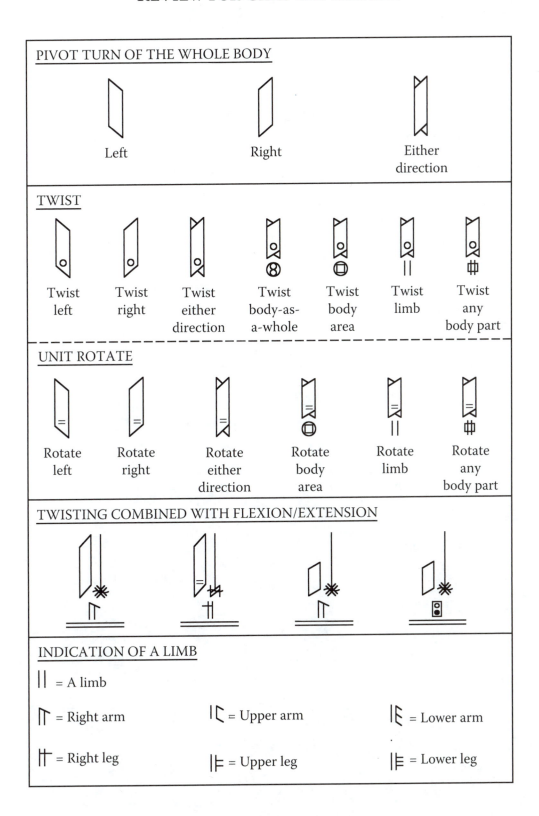

PIVOT TURN OF THE WHOLE BODY

Left   Right   Either direction

TWIST

Twist left   Twist right   Twist either direction   Twist body-as-a-whole   Twist body area   Twist limb   Twist any body part

UNIT ROTATE

Rotate left   Rotate right   Rotate either direction   Rotate body area   Rotate limb   Rotate any body part

TWISTING COMBINED WITH FLEXION/EXTENSION

INDICATION OF A LIMB

|| = A limb

⌐ = Right arm   ⌐C = Upper arm   ⌐E = Lower arm

H = Right leg   ⌐F = Upper leg   ⌐E = Lower leg

CHAPTER SEVENTEEN
Flexion and Extension: Specific Forms

The complex structure of the human body, the different ranges of motion in the various joints, and the many coordination possibilities in using them, add to the richness of movement. Once a clear understanding of the existing forms of flexion and extension is reached, the eye can differentiate between the forms.

In our previous exploration of flexion and extension, several words were found to describe the various possible actions that come under these general headings. Now we will investigate and identify the specific forms, giving consideration to how they function and also to their expressive use.

THE THREE FORMS OF FLEXION

Three distinct forms of flexion are defined by special terminology and signs. Bearing in mind other disciplines and terminology in movement analysis, the Language of Dance® has chosen those terms which have generally proved to be most appropriate. The three forms are:

1. Contract*   2. Fold   3. Join

---

* The terms "contract," "contraction," are here used in their general sense and are not to be confused with the specialized use in the Martha Graham contemporary dance technique.

For each of these terms synonyms exist. Contracting may also be called short-ening, pulling in, retracting, shrinking. Folding may also be experienced as curling, curving, arching, or wrapping. Joining, closing in, may also be overlapping in the lateral or sagittal dimensions, that is, closing in, in relation to the "width" (breadth) or the "depth" of the body part. Adduction is lateral closing.

Our earlier exploration of general flexion included all three forms in expressing movement ideas. Flexion occurs naturally when one is reacting to fear, to a threat. When the body pulls in, it closes up for self-protection, one is not aware of exactly how the action occurs, what form it is taking; it is a reflex action. Similarly, reacting to cold causes the body to contract, to fold up. Or there may be a practical need for folding/contracting such as crouching to pass through a small space or closely inspecting one's toenails. Many tumbling tricks require making the body as small as possible.

17.1a	17.1b	17.1c
In hiding	Pedicure	On the rings

THE THREE FORMS OF EXTENSION

The specific forms of extension relate directly to those of flexion. They are:

1. Elongate   2. Unfold   3. Separate

Elongation involves lengthening, stretching, reaching out. The term "protract," which usually refers to drawing out, lengthening in time, according to Webster's International Dictionary, can also be used in relation to space and is anatomi-cally used for a muscle which extends a part of the body (the opposite of retract). "Protract" might seem to be the obvious opposite of the term "contract," but since it is unfamiliar in this context it is replaced by "elongate," which is the more familiar term. The usual term for the counterpart of "fold" is "unfold," though "unwrap," "unfurl," etc., may be appropriate and descriptive in certain instances. Separating and spreading out occur in the width or breadth of a part of the body, i.e., in its lateral or sagittal dimension. Abducting is lateral opening.

Emotions which produce expansion in the body—great joy, exhilaration, exuberance—will involve general extension with no awareness of how the different forms are being used in different parts of the body. Extension may occur for practical reasons such as in holding outstretched a section of a roll of wallpaper, 17.2a, extending to cast a line when fishing, 17.2b, or in a predicament we hope never to encounter, 17.2c.

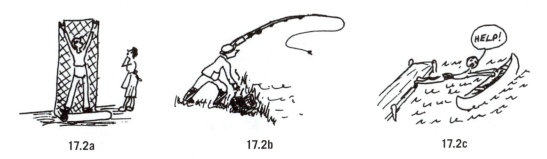

| 17.2a | 17.2b | 17.2c |

By "contracting" and "elongating" we do not mean literally that the body itself shrinks and grows although these are the sensations experienced, but that it makes use of (occupies) less or more space. The following technical exploration of what happens spatially when contraction and elongation occur will be followed by consideration of how these actions are used expressively.

CONTRACTION AND ELONGATION

Contraction means shortening, drawing nearer, and this shortening occurs on an established spatial line. Elongation means drawing out, lengthening on the established line. An inchworm provides a handy example. By bringing its back legs in, it contracts its length (shortens the distance between its extremities); then, to progress, the front legs move forward into the established direction, traveling being accomplished by lengthening on the same spatial line.

CONCEPTUAL ANALYSIS OF
CONTRACTION AND ELONGATION

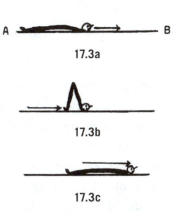

In 17.3a–17.3d, the established direction, A–B is kept all the time. Here it is the direction forward horizontal. The line between the extremities does not change, even though the middle is displaced. The inchworm behaves as though it has only one center joint in its length, the result being similar to contraction of an arm or leg, each of which has only one center joint.

In contrast to the angle produced by the single hinge of the inchworm, a caterpillar, 17.3d, contracts into a rounded hump since it has a multi-jointed "spine." For us, such rounded contractions occur in the torso and in the hand. The diagrams of 17.3e and 17.3f illustrate the spatial results of such contractions. Example 17.3e shows the result for a limb with a single central joint; 17.3f shows the result for a multi-jointed part.

17.3d

One central joint:

17.3e

Multi-jointed:

17.3f

Note the following facts:

Path:	Straight path. The extremity of the body part, "z," draws in toward the base "x" on a straight line.
Line of Direction:	The extremity "z" maintains the same directional relation with the base "x."
Displacement:	The center joint "y" is displaced out of the original line of direction.
Involvement of Joints:	When the whole arm contracts, articulation occurs in both shoulder and elbow joints (i.e., in "x" and "y"). The same is true for the leg in regard to the hip and knee joints.

Elongation is the reverse process; the limb lengthens along the same line. Everyday examples of elongation and contraction include pushing and pulling a door or other object, contraction of the legs in a deep knee bend (a squat) and the subsequent rising and straightening. In sports, the leg and arm actions which occur in rowing a scull, 17.3g and 17.3h, are basically contraction and elongation, as are the actions of lifting a weight with the legs while in a shoulder-elbow stand, 17.3i and 17.3j. The path of the movement in this last example is on the vertical line because of balance and the force of gravity.

| 17.3g | 17.3h | 17.3i | 17.3j |

Specific Signs for Contraction

The general signs for flexing used so far: a small degree, 17.4a, and a greater degree, 17.4b, included the horizontal ad lib. sign 17.4c, to establish the statement of **any form.** Without the horizontal ad lib. indication, these signs, 17.4d and 17.4e, represent **contraction**, two-dimensional closing in along the longitudinal axis of the limb or torso, as in 17.3e and 17.3f.

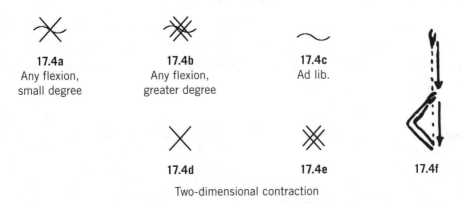

| 17.4a | 17.4b | 17.4c | |
| Any flexion, small degree | Any flexion, greater degree | Ad lib. | |

| 17.4d | 17.4e | 17.4f |
| Two-dimensional contraction | | |

The range for a small degree of contraction and that for a greater degree is illustrated in 17.4f. A right angle in the limb is the general reference point for distinction between these two main degrees. When the open statement of "any degree" is needed, a small vertical ad lib. sign, 17.4g, is centered under the lower part of the symbol, 17.4h. With the addition of a duration line, connected to the flexion sign, this small ad lib. sign is easy to read, 17.4i.

| 17.4g | 17.4h | 17.4i |
| Any | Any degree of flexion | Any degree of contraction |

Shrinking, three-dimensional contraction, is shown by adding a straight horizontal line representing the third dimension, 17.4j and 17.4k, the latter being illustrated in 17.4l. Only hands, chest, and belly, as well as the body-as-a-whole, have the ability to expand and to contract two- and three-dimensionally. One may think of the air going out of a balloon and the balloon collapsing three-dimensionally.

17.4j   **17.4k**   **17.4l**
Three-dimensional contraction   A body "fist"

Specific Signs for Elongation

The general signs for extension (any form of extension) are: 17.5a for a small degree and 17.5b for a greater degree. Without the horizontal ad lib. sign, 17.5c and 17.5d mean elongation, two-dimensional lengthening along the longitudinal axis of the limb or torso.

17.5a   **17.5b**   **17.5c**   **17.5d**   **17.5e**
Any extension small degree   Any extension greater degree   Two-dimensional elongation   Any degree of elongation

The two main degrees of elongation for the arm are illustrated in Chapter 7, in 7.2i and 7.2j. As indicated, the greater degree of elongating involves pulling out from the body. The vertical ad lib. sign can be used to state any degree of extension, 17.5e. Three-dimensional extension, expansion, is indicated by adding a horizontal line representing the third dimension, 17.5f and 17.5g, illustrated in 17.5h.

17.5f   **17.5g**   **17.5h**
Three-dimensional elongation

PHYSICAL ANALYSIS OF CONTRACTION, ELONGATION

Contraction, Elongation of the Legs

Because bending the legs happens in a variety of circumstances, the form used and the basic direction involved are not always immediately evident. Therefore, an exploration into many of the possibilities may be helpful. In 17.6a, 17.6b, and 17.6c, the notation states the leg direction and state of contraction or elongation for each figure.

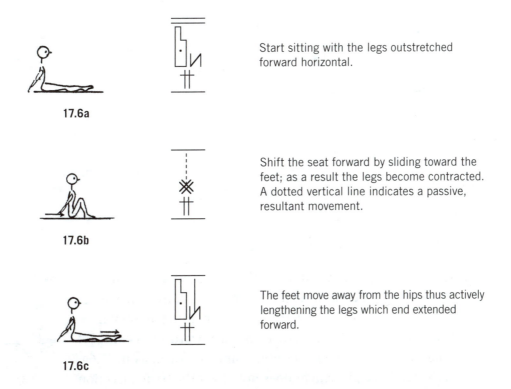

17.6a Start sitting with the legs outstretched forward horizontal.

17.6b Shift the seat forward by sliding toward the feet; as a result the legs become contracted. A dotted vertical line indicates a passive, resultant movement.

17.6c The feet move away from the hips thus actively lengthening the legs which end extended forward.

In a way similar to the inchworm moving forward or backward, we can "inch" along while sitting on the floor by contracting and elongating the legs. The movements of 17.6a, 17.6b, and 17.6c produce traveling forward.

The action of 17.6a, 17.6b, and 17.6c is the same as 17.3a, 17.3b, and 17.3c; the basic direction for the legs has not changed. The legs contract as the hips move toward the feet; they lengthen as the feet move away from the hips. By repeating this action, the performer gradually inches forward along the floor. The fact that the knees "bulge" out into another direction when the legs contract does not change the line between the extremities, the feet and hips; it is still forward.

In 17.6d, 17.6e, and 17.6f, the reverse process produces traveling backward. The basic direction for the legs remains forward middle.

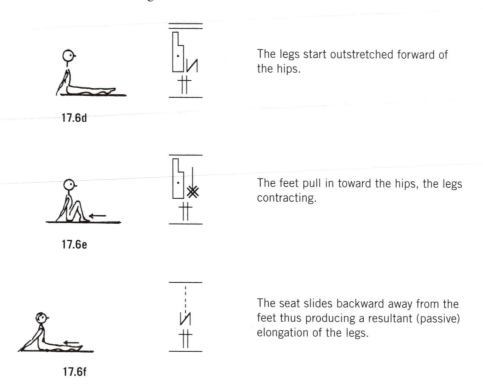

The legs start outstretched forward of the hips.

17.6d

The feet pull in toward the hips, the legs contracting.

17.6e

The seat slides backward away from the feet thus producing a resultant (passive) elongation of the legs.

17.6f

A change in the rotational state of the legs produces a different look to the movement. In every leg contraction, the center joint, the knee, must flex and be displaced spatially. If the legs are parallel as they have been in 17.6b and 17.6e, the knees will point toward the ceiling. If outward rotation is used, the knees will point sideward, as in 17.6g. This difference in knee placement does not affect the basic direction established for the leg as a whole.

17.6g

Examples 17.6h, 17.6i, and 17.6j shows a familiar exercise in contracting and elongating the legs, the hips remaining where they are. Next to each figure illustration is written the position reached. Example 17.6k shows the exercise written as a movement sequence; note the starting position.

Let us now take a similar movement for the leg that occurs in the air in the forward middle direction while you are standing on one leg. We get exactly the same spatial pattern, but without the floor under the gesturing limb to facilitate retention of the basic forward horizontal direction. If, in the sequence of 17.7l, 17.7m, and 17.7n, outward rotation is used, this line between foot and hip would still be retained.

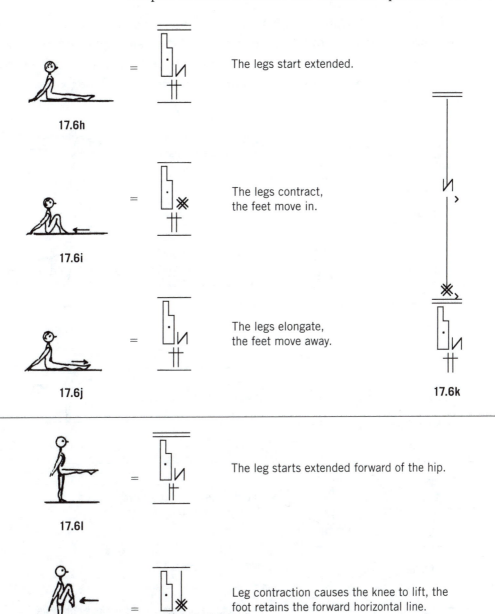

17.6h

The legs start extended.

17.6i

The legs contract,
the feet move in.

17.6j

The legs elongate,
the feet move away.

17.6k

17.6l

The leg starts extended forward of the hip.

17.6m

Leg contraction causes the knee to lift, the
foot retains the forward horizontal line.

17.6n

Elongation straightens the leg, knee returns to
forward middle line.

Now we examine this same contraction—elongation when the leg is sideward horizontal. Examples 17.6r, 17.6s, and 17.6t illustrate exactly the same leg pattern performed with one leg in the air while the other is supporting. In certain barre stretching exercises a similar basic action occurs but with the hip moving toward the foot.

17.6o

Here the right leg is side horizontal, resting on the floor.

17.6r

17.6p

As the foot draws in to the hip, the leg contracts; the foot remains to the side of the hip.

17.6s

17.6q

The leg elongates in the side middle direction, increasing the distance between foot and hip.

17.6t

17.6u

The right leg is on the barre, the foot is side middle from the hip.

17.6v

The foot remains where it is, it does not move from the spot. As the leg contracts, the hips move toward the foot and the knee is displaced upward.

17.6w

As the hips return to where they started, the leg passively extends. The basic leg direction remains the same, i.e., side middle.

The above notations focus on the leg activity, not on the total picture of the body as would be spelled out in the Structured Description of Labanotation.

Next we explore contraction and elongation of the legs in the downward direction. A very good example occurs in *Petroushka*, the ballet in which the dolls are supported by a bar under the armpits, allowing their legs to move freely because they are not needed as supports, Examples 17.7a, 17.7b, 17.7c.

The parallel legs in 17.7g, 17.7h, and 17.7i produce a different look and the feel of the movement is different, but the spatial relationship is the same.

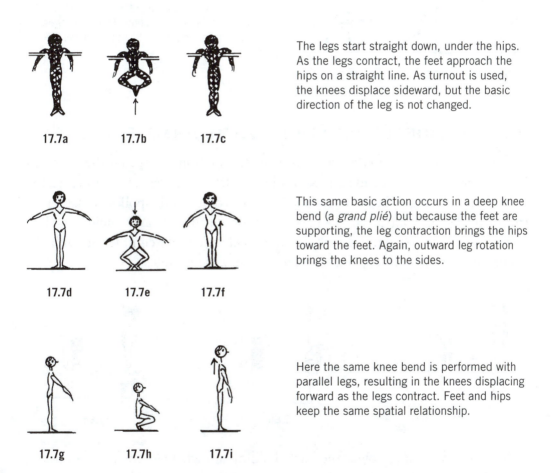

The legs start straight down, under the hips. As the legs contract, the feet approach the hips on a straight line. As turnout is used, the knees displace sideward, but the basic direction of the leg is not changed.

17.7a   17.7b   17.7c

This same basic action occurs in a deep knee bend (a *grand plié*) but because the feet are supporting, the leg contraction brings the hips toward the feet. Again, outward leg rotation brings the knees to the sides.

17.7d   17.7e   17.7f

Here the same knee bend is performed with parallel legs, resulting in the knees displacing forward as the legs contract. Feet and hips keep the same spatial relationship.

17.7g   17.7h   17.7i

Comparable contraction in the backward direction is less familiar, as shown in 17.7j–17.7l.

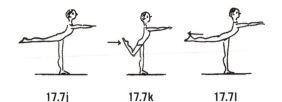

17.7j   17.7k   17.7l

With legs parallel, the free leg is backward horizontal. As the leg contracts, the knee drops down and the foot approaches the hip. The line from hip to foot is still back middle.

For 17.7k, outward leg rotation would bring the knee out to the side, as in an attitude.

17.7m   17.7n   17.7o

Low or high level gestures follow the same logic, the line of direction between base and extremity is maintained. The right leg is shown contracting and elongating in the side low direction.

CONTRACTION, ELONGATION OF THE ARMS

Greater freedom in the shoulder joint and greater rotational scope for the arm provide a wider range of directional possibilities for flexed arm gestures. However, the same understanding of basic directions for a flexed arm still applies. Whether an arm is stretched or contracted, the basic direction for the arm as a whole is the line between shoulder and hand. Examples 17.8a–17.8i illustrate contraction with the arm down, with the arm up, and with the arm forward middle.

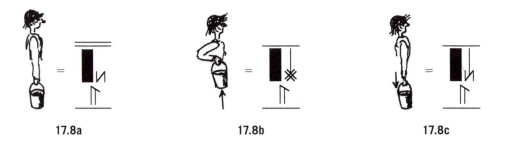

17.8a   17.8b   17.8c

In 17.8a, the arm is down, the hand holding a bucket. As the arm contracts, lifting the bucket, the hand and bucket remain below the shoulder and the elbow displaces backward. The arm then lengthens in the same direction.

In the next example, the arm is up, holding a ball in 17.8d. As the arm contracts, bringing the ball closer to the shoulder, hand and ball remain above the shoulder. The basic direction for the arm remains up. The arm then stretches (elongates) up into the same direction.

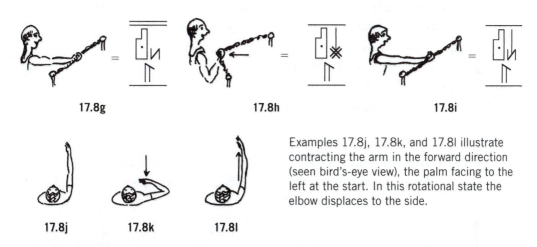

17.8d   **17.8e**   **17.8f**

In 17.8g, the arm starts forward, grasping a rope. As the arm contracts, pulling the rope toward the body, the hand retains the same directional relationship to the shoulder. Because outward rotation is used, the elbow drops downward, but this drop does not change the direction for the arm as a whole. The arm then extends (elongates) on the same line.

17.8g   **17.8h**   **17.8i**

Examples 17.8j, 17.8k, and 17.8l illustrate contracting the arm in the forward direction (seen bird's-eye view), the palm facing to the left at the start. In this rotational state the elbow displaces to the side.

17.8j   **17.8k**   **17.8l**

Notice what happens when the arms are in an open side-high position, with the palms facing upward.

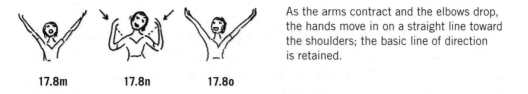

As the arms contract and the elbows drop, the hands move in on a straight line toward the shoulders; the basic line of direction is retained.

17.8m   **17.8n**   **17.8o**

CONTRACTION, ELONGATION OF THE HANDS

Because the hand has additional joints, contraction usually produces curves rather than angles. Hand movements can be quite complex; we will deal only with a simple contraction and elongation here.

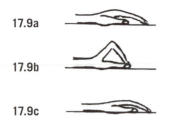

17.9a

17.9b

17.9c

The hand is forward, resting on a table. As the hand contracts, the extremity (fingertips) draws in to the base (heel of the hand) the center joint (knuckles) is displaced upward from the original line. As the hand lengthens, the fingertips travel on the same line and the knuckles return to that line.

CONTRACTION, ELONGATION OF THE TORSO

To investigate the action of the torso when it contracts, let us once more look at our friend, the caterpillar. Once again we must remember that this is a general, basic movement of contracting, and not the highly stylized version central to the Graham technique. This caterpillar starts backing down, the head traveling downward through contraction of the body, i.e., the head extremity approaching the base. It then elongates, the head moving upward to return to the original location. No matter how much it arches, the basic direction, the vertical line, remains the same.

17.10a   17.10b   17.10c

In a torso contraction, the free end (the shoulders) approaches the base (the hips) on the vertical line. To accomplish this, the waist bulges backward, comparable to the bulging outward of the caterpillar, 17.10b

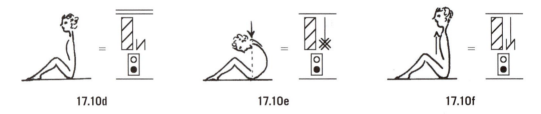

17.10d   17.10e   17.10f

Examples 17.10d, 17.10e, and 17.10f illustrate a torso contraction. The result of the contraction is that the pelvis (upper rim) changes its line of direction, tipping more and more backward as the contraction increases. In straightening (elongating), the free end lengthens upward, the bulge disappears and the waist returns to the vertical line maintained between the shoulders and hips.

It is important to note that for torso contractions we are concerned with the direction of the extremities of the torso—shoulder line to hip joints. The head is not considered part of the torso; it reacts passively in that it retains its relationship to the torso, continuing the curve established in the rest of the spine without making any special movement of its own.

The most natural contraction of the torso occurs over the front surface as in the examples above. It is possible, however, to contract over the back surface and also over the sides and the diagonals. In each of these contractions, the pelvis tilts, that is, it changes its line of direction as did the upper arm in arm contractions.

Contractions of torso or limbs often occur in conjunction with a change of direction for that part. When this change happens, the new direction, stated alongside, becomes the line of direction for the extremities. Example 17.10g shows the use of a small horizontal bow to link the contraction indication to the direction symbol. In 17.10h, the symbols are centered over the torso sign.

17.10g   **17.10h**

EXPRESSIVENESS OF CONTRACTING AND ELONGATING

We have investigated the basic facts regarding specific forms of contraction and elongation, i.e., their practical, functional use; but what of their expressive use in dance?

Jabbing actions of the limbs, particularly of the arms in jazz sequences, express an "out-in" thrusting penetration piercing the air, the space around the performer. These actions move in a spoke-like manner out from the center of the body and in again. If the kinesphere were a huge bubble, it would burst as its "skin" was reached. Expressively, the strength of such actions lies in their directness. The arms usually start with the hands near the shoulders to provide the greatest range in piercing space. The body often accompanies the gesture, thus augmenting the reach, or it may "set off" the movement by a simultaneous motion in the opposite direction. Though sharp, sudden movements are typical for this kind of action, the same patterns may take place with smooth gliding, with sustained pressure, or with an interrupted, jagged progression. Such details add to the expression, change the style, and enrich the basic activity of contraction and elongation.

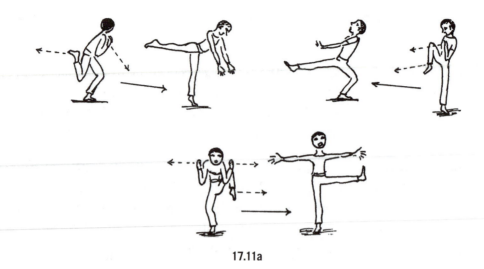

17.11a

READING STUDY No. 53

CONTRACTION, ELONGATION

No directions are given for these actions, the choice of direction is up to the performer. The actions must still clearly contract and elongate on a straight path. After each contraction, elongation can take place into a different direction, the choice being left open. The double elongation can be interpreted as pulling out from the body, i.e., allowing an inclusion of the body to occur.

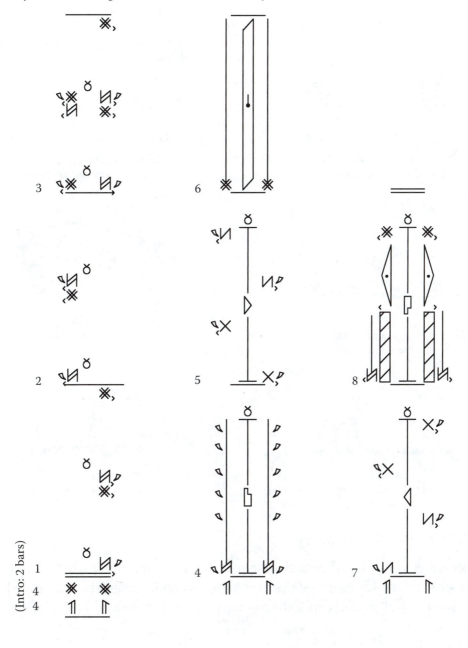

FOLDING AND UNFOLDING

What is folding? The dictionary defines it as "Putting one part of a thing over another, laying one section over another, bending into a fold." Unfolding is, of course, the reverse process. Let us look at some typical examples from everyday life.

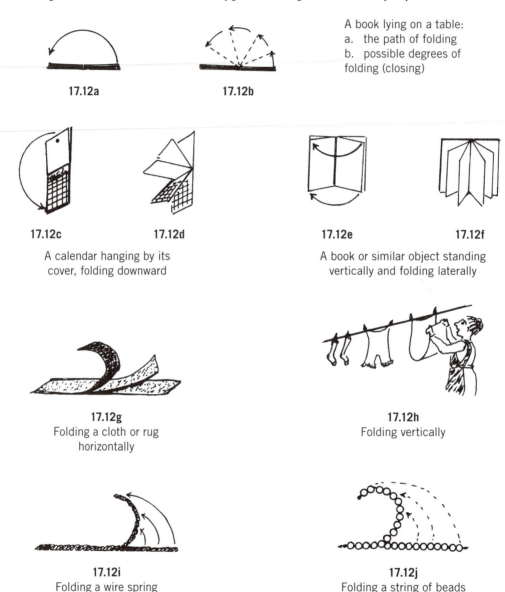

A book lying on a table:
a. the path of folding
b. possible degrees of folding (closing)

17.12a

17.12b

17.12c   **17.12d**

A calendar hanging by its cover, folding downward

17.12e   **17.12f**

A book or similar object standing vertically and folding laterally

17.12g
Folding a cloth or rug horizontally

17.12h
Folding vertically

17.12i
Folding a wire spring

17.12j
Folding a string of beads

ANALYSIS OF FOLDING

When an object is folded, usually one part is moved and one part stays still. **The part which does not move retains the basic direction established for the object.** This is the "base" toward which the free part moves. In the case of a stiff object such as a book, there is only one joint, a hinge at the center. The free end approaches the base on a curved path. In 17.13a, 17.13b, and 17.13c (reading upward), line A–B is the fixed part which does not move, and C is the extremity of the moving part, the free end. Thus C approaches A on a curved path while B (the mid joint) folds. In a many-jointed object—such as a wire spring or a string of beads—a curve is produced in the object instead of an angle. Examples 17.13d, 17.13e, and 17.13f illustrate the extremity C approaching the base A (the last fixed segment) in a many-jointed object.

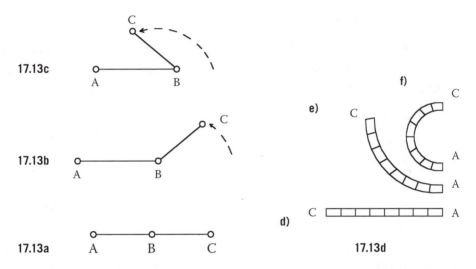

According to the part of the body involved, the words "curving," "curling," or "arching" may be applicable to this action.

Folding the Leg

Let us look first at actions of the leg.

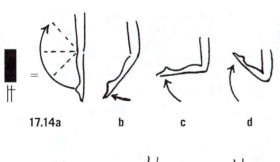

17.14a   b   c   d

The basic direction for the whole leg is down. The lower leg, hinging at the knee joint, folds backward. There is no movement for the thigh.

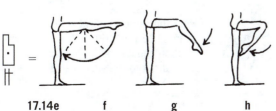

17.14e   f   g   h

The whole leg is forward. As the knee folds, the lower leg moves closer to the base, i.e., the hip joint. Compare this example with the leg contraction in 17.6l and 17.6m.

In the next example, 17.14i, the leg starts at the side with outward rotation.

The whole leg is side middle. The leg folding at the knee causes the foot to approach the supporting leg on a curved path.

17.14i   j   k   l

Folding the Ankle

The action of folding the ankle brings the extremity of the foot, the toes, closer to the lower leg. The toes describe an arc in the air. Examples 17.15a–17.15f illustrate this action in two different locations.

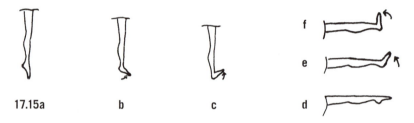

17.15a   b   c   d

Folding the Arm

Examples for the arm follow an identical pattern but, because of the greater range of movement and the possible degrees of rotating and twisting, analysis of what is occurring may not be so easy. Like the knee, the elbow (center joint of the arm) can only fold in one physical direction, i.e., "forward," with, for some people, the exception of hyperextension which is a backward folding, i.e., "over the back."

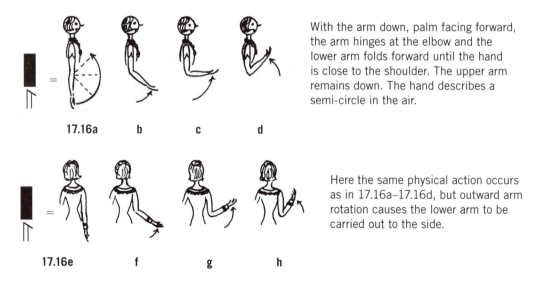

With the arm down, palm facing forward, the arm hinges at the elbow and the lower arm folds forward until the hand is close to the shoulder. The upper arm remains down. The hand describes a semi-circle in the air.

17.16a   b   c   d

Here the same physical action occurs as in 17.16a–17.16d, but outward arm rotation causes the lower arm to be carried out to the side.

17.16e   f   g   h

With the whole arm forward middle at the start, palm facing up, the folding action in the elbow brings the hand on a circular path toward the shoulder.

17.16i   j   k   l

Next, the arm starts forward middle, palm facing side left (bird's-eye view).

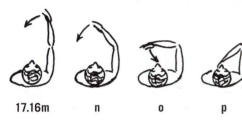

Folding the elbow produces a spatial displacement different from 17.16i–17.16l, but within the arm, the action is the same.

17.16m   n   o   p

As can be seen from 17.16a–17.16p, the spatial result of a folding action for the arm depends on the rotational state of the limb.

Folding the Wrist

A folding action of the wrist spatially displaces the hand. Unlike the knees and elbow, the wrist has a greater range of flexion, being able to fold forward and backward, as well as slightly sideward and diagonally. When the wrist folds, the lower arm, its "base," does not change direction. The degree of wrist folding varies among performers. Asian dancers train to develop as great a range as possible.

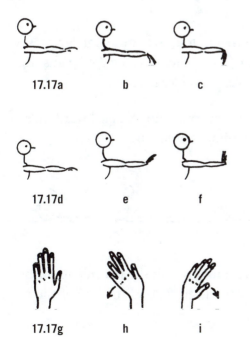

With the arm forward, palm down, a forward fold of the wrist causes the hand to drop toward the floor.

17.17a   b   c

A backward wrist fold brings the hand up to the ceiling. This same physical action occurring in different spatial placements and with different arm rotation produces different directions for the hand.

17.17d   e   f

In 17.17g the left hand starts in line with the lower arm. In 17.17h, the wrist has folded to the left toward the little finger; in 17.17i, it has folded to the right toward the thumb. Both these actions have a rather limited range.

17.17g   h   i

Folding the Torso

The torso, being a multi-jointed part, forms a curve when folding. The base still retains the previously established direction. A curving, folding action of the torso occurs naturally from a supine position. In lifting from the ground, the free end of the torso folds forward. The hips (line of the pelvis) keep the original line of direction, in this case backward horizontal. As soon as the performer sits up, the line of the pelvis has changed, a new torso direction is established by the pelvis, 17.18d.

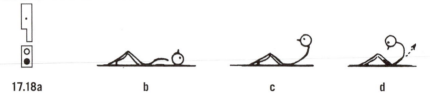

17.18a   b   c   d

Folding the torso forward while sitting is given next. From a vertical sitting position, folding the torso is exactly the same as in 17.18a–17.18d; but here one does not have to battle with gravity, hence it is usually easier to achieve a greater degree of folding. The amount possible will vary according to flexibility in the spine. It is important, however, that the base, the pelvic line, does not change direction, that is, unless a change of direction is stated.

17.18e   f   g   h   i

The flexibility of the spine allows the torso to fold over different surfaces, i.e., over the front, the right side, the back, the left side, and also the diagonal surfaces in between. We will deal with only the simpler examples here.

If one is lying prone, 17.18j, the free end of the torso can fold backward. In some acrobats the degree of flexibility for such bending is amazing.

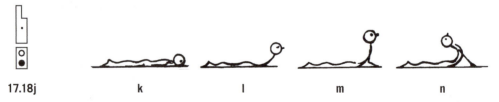

17.18j   k   l   m   n

When lying on the right side, sideward folding is over the left side of the body. Note that in examples 17.18p, 17.18q, 17.18r the head follows the line of the spine unless another direction is stated for it.

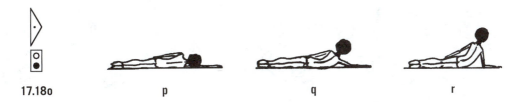

17.18o   p   q   r

These same physical actions can occur while one is standing. The movement (physical change) is the same, but it looks and feels different because of the different relation to the line of gravity and the different "picture" produced.

Folding the Hand

Rest your hand on a surface, palm up. The fingers fold toward the base of the hand ending near the center of the palm, 17.19b–17.19e. The base of the hand, the metacarpus, does not move. This same action can happen for the fingers only, the palm being unaffected, as in 17.19f. Folding the hand in the upright situation (or indeed in any direction) is the same as 17.19b–17.19e. If there is no flat surface to help physically and visually to keep the basic line of direction, care must be taken not to involve the wrist joint.

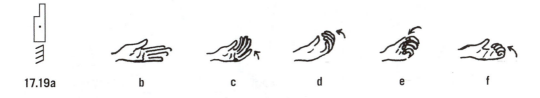

17.19a   b   c   d   e   f

UNFOLDING

Unfolding, as the word implies, is the exact opposite of folding; the joint(s) straighten until the part which folded is again in its normal alignment with its base. 17.14a–17.19f need only to be read in reverse to see unfolding take place until the unfolded state is reached.

SIGNS FOR FOLDING, UNFOLDING

The signs for folding are derived from the sign for contracting. In a contraction, two joints are affected (marked point "a" and "b" in illustration 17.20a), and two segments of the body (marked "1" and "2") are spatially displaced. In folding, only one joint "b" moves and only one part "1" is displaced. Note that this analysis is for parts with one central joint; the same symbols are also used for multi-jointed parts.

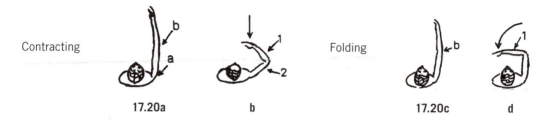

Contracting · · · Folding

17.20a · · · b · · · 17.20c · · · d

The sign for folding is, therefore, half of the sign for contracting. The full contraction sign of 17.20e is cut in half to represent the idea of folding, 17.20f. A greater degree of folding is shown by the doubled symbol, 17.20g.

17.20e · · · 17.20f · · · 17.20g

The sign for unfolding, 17.20h is the reverse of folding. It means a return to the normal alignment of the limb in the established direction; it is used for each of the possible directions and degrees of folding. It has not been necessary to give specific degrees of unfolding; however, the idea, the intent of **approaching unfolded** can be expressed as 17.20i.

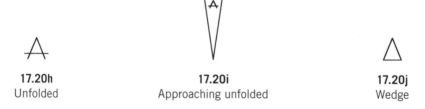

17.20h
Unfolded

17.20i
Approaching unfolded

17.20j
Wedge

Because the unfolding sign is related to the sign for away, the symbol should theoretically be drawn as in 17.20j. However, this sign resembles a wedge, therefore the base line is drawn slightly higher, as in 17.20h; it is not drawn like a letter A.

DURATION OF FOLDING, UNFOLDING

Duration is shown by the addition of the duration line. As with the other flexion and extension symbols, it is important that the line connects directly with the folding or unfolding symbol.

17.21a · · · 17.21b

EXPRESSIVENESS OF FOLDING, UNFOLDING

In contrast to the directness of contraction and elongation, folding and unfolding seek to encompass or enclose the space around you. A large circular movement of the arm may conclude with a folding in the elbow and perhaps also in the wrist. This movement will often be followed by an unfolding that develops into a sweeping, opening circular gesture around the body. Many of Isadora Duncan's gestures were of this type. By varying the space patterns and the rotations used, and adding body inclusion, "rich," "generous" movement can result. The outer reaches of the dancer's space are not "punctured" but are stroked, caressed, or swept along into curved arcs. The curved nature of the gestures allows for softness and gracefulness. Examples 17.22a–17.22d illustrate some examples. Flowing spatial patterns are much augmented by use of scarves and draperies. In certain Asian dances, a folding and unfolding action of the hand and wrist is augmented spatially by manipulation of a long sleeve, as in Japanese dances; or light silk scarves hanging from the waist as in Javanese dances.

| 17.22a | 17.22b | 17.22c | 17.22d |

SPECIFIC DIRECTIONS FOR FOLDING

By selecting the way of dividing the contraction symbol in half, we indicate the physical direction of the folding movement, i.e., toward which surface the folding occurs: front = volar (ventral) surface; back = dorsal surface.

The open choice for direction of folding, indicated by use of the horizontal ad lib. sign, is shown in 17.23a.

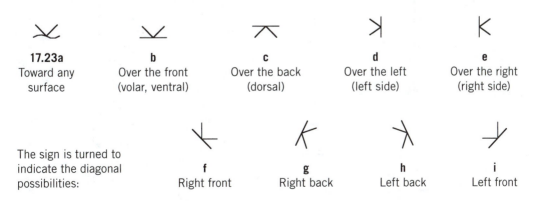

17.23a	b	c	d	e
Toward any surface	Over the front (volar, ventral)	Over the back (dorsal)	Over the left (left side)	Over the right (right side)

The sign is turned to indicate the diagonal possibilities:

	f	g	h	i
	Right front	Right back	Left back	Left front

READING STUDY NO. 54

FOLDING, UNFOLDING

Because no directions have been stated for this study, much leeway exists in how and where folding and unfolding occur. Find variations in how these simple actions are performed to add interest to the study.

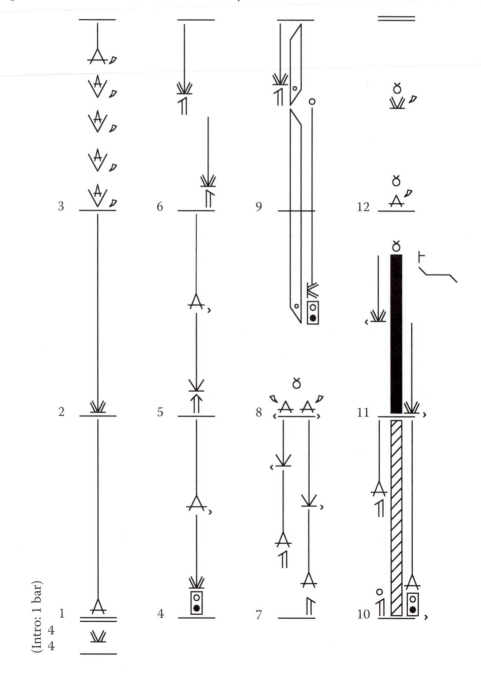

READING PRACTICE O (NO MUSIC)

FOLDING IN DIFFERENT DIRECTIONS

The flexibility in the spine allows bending (folding) to occur over different body surfaces. This study explores ideas for a modern dance study, Limon-style.

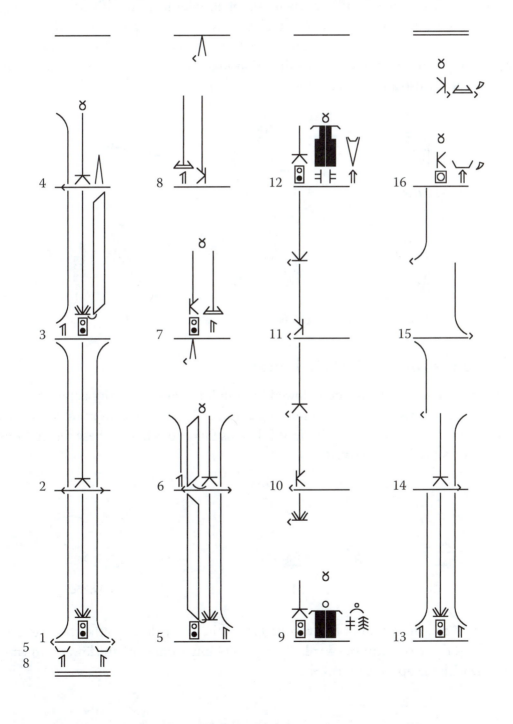

FLEXION, EXTENSION: MIXED FORMS
ANALYSIS OF DIRECTION FOR A BENT LIMB

In 17.24a the arm is bent with the hand in line with the shoulder. In terms of contraction, the arm direction and level is forward middle, but with a large amount of contraction. If, from here the arm elongates, it will follow the forward horizontal line, 17.24b, arriving at 17.24c. In terms of unfolding from this same starting position, the direction for the arm, established by the upper arm is forward low with a large degree of folding, 17.24d. Unfolding from this position, 17.24e, will carry the lower arm to forward low, i.e., the direction maintained by the upper arm, 17.24f. This analysis also applies to the torso and other limbs.

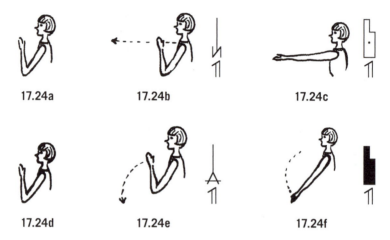

17.24a	17.24b	17.24c

17.24d	17.24e	17.24f

MIXED FORMS: ARMS, TORSO

A contracting action may be followed by unfolding and a folding action may be followed by elongation. Is such a mixture common? What happens spatially? Let us take a simple example in which the arm begins forward middle. These illustrations are seen from a bird's-eye view.

17.25a	17.25b	17.25c

In 17.25a, the action of contracting brings the hand closer to the shoulder and displaces the upper arm sideward, 17.25b. Unfolding from here, the lower arm ends in line with the upper arm, 17.25c.

In 17.25d, the arm starts side middle. The lower arm folds in, 17.25e. The directional relationship now established between the hand and shoulder dictates the line into which the limb elongates, 17.25f.

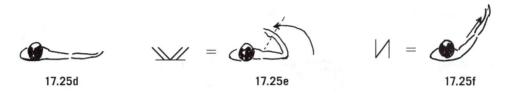

| 17.25d | 17.25e | 17.25f |

Such switching from one form to another may seem strange, but in fact it is not uncommon, particularly where exactness in spatial placement is not primary and the specific actions of flexion and extension are being featured. A good example involving the torso occurs in modern dance exercises where the line within the torso is more important than the spatial direction achieved. Examples 17.25g–17.25k give one version of such a torso exercise.

| 17.25g | 17.25h | 17.25i | 17.25j | 17.25k |
| | Fold | Elongate | Contract | Unfold |

The torso starts vertically up, elongated, 17.25g. It then folds over forward as much as possible, 17.25h. The degree of such folding varies according to the build and flexibility of the performer. The torso then elongates, lengthening along the line established between the shoulders and hips, 17.25i. There follows a contraction along this new line, 17.25j. Finally the torso unfolds to the line established by the base (the pelvis), returning to the upright sitting position, 17.25k.

A series of folding movements, each followed by an elongation, will gradually completely change the spatial placement of a limb. The same is true of a series of contractions followed by unfolding; there will be a constant change in spatial placement of the limb or torso. The build of the body imposes limitations on such sequences, unless the degrees are small. For spatial precision exact degrees for contraction and folding would need to be known. The full scale is not being investigated here.

DÉVELOPPÉ, ENVELOPPÉ

The movements of *développé* and *enveloppé* are familiar in ballet, contemporary dance, jazz, etc., and are usually part of basic Western dance training. Yet one must investigate to discover how differently the leg functions in doing these movements according to which direction is used—forward, sideward, or backward, and whether the leg is turned out or parallel. It will be found that sometimes a *développé* uses elongation, sometimes unfolding. Similarly sometimes an *enveloppé* uses contraction and sometimes folding. Let us investigate to be sure these differences are clear.

17.26a   17.26b   17.26c   17.26d   17.26e

Example 17.26a illustrates *développé* and *enveloppé* in the forward direction with the legs parallel. First the leg contracts, 17.26b, followed by unfolding 17.26c. It then folds, 17.26d, and then elongates, retracing its path, 17.26e. This same sequence occurs when the leg is turned out and moving to the side (a sideward *développé* and *enveloppé*).

When the legs are turned out, 17.26f, and a forward *développé-enveloppé* occurs, the initial contraction of the leg, 17.26g, is followed by elongation into the forward direction, 17.26h. At the start of the *enveloppé*, the leg again contracts, the foot coming in on a line toward the hip, thus causing the knee to move to the side, 17.26i. The end of the *enveloppé* uses elongation to return to the starting position, 17.26j.

17.26f   17.26g   17.26h   17.26i   17.26j

A *développé* to the side with outward leg rotation involves an initial leg contraction, 17.26k, followed by unfolding at the knee, 17.26l. The leg then folds, 17.26m, before elongating to return to the starting position, 17.26n.

17.26k   17.26l   17.26m   17.26n

Not used in ballet, but appearing in other movement forms, is a Karate kick, a sideward parallel leg action which involves contraction and elongation. Different spatial placement and rotation of the legs produce a range of such actions of flexion and extension.

JOINING, SEPARATING

The third form of flexion and extension is "joining" (closing in, narrowing) and "separating" (opening out, spreading). In anatomical terms, lateral joining and separating are comparable to adduction and abduction. In group arrangements, joining and separating are familiar spatial actions, as they are also with only two performers. Such joining, separating may be from different directions and with different parts of the body. Within the body there is often the intent of one part joining with another.

LATERAL DIRECTION

How does one person make use of this form? Immediately understandable are the separating and joining of the fingers. Such actions can also involve the limbs in relation to each other, e.g., the legs joining or separating, awareness being of each other. Or, awareness may be the relationship of the limb to the center line of the body, that is, moving away from it, 17.27a, or coming in to it, 17.27b. The arms may close in toward each other, 17.27c, or move apart, as in 17.27d when they join and separate overhead.

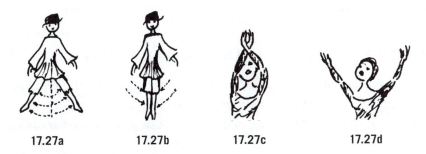

17.27a   17.27b   17.27c   17.27d

Awareness is often of the relationship of the arms to the torso. In moving laterally away from the torso, the arm may be aware of creating space, allowing more air between its inner surface and the side of the torso. An awareness, a slight tension is produced as though stretching elastic cobweb threads between arm and torso, 17.27e. Conversely, the arms may open laterally as though attracted by an outside magnet, 17.27f. There is a sense of the body breathing in, expanding to occupy more space.

17.27e   17.27f   17.27g

In contrast, lateral closing in to the torso can be experienced as pressing the air away, as narrowing the space, as being drawn to the sides of the torso until a pressing of the torso can result, 17.27g. In such movements, the dynamic quality can vary. Arms may hug the body, as in 17.27h in which a 1920s flapper reacts to a mouse. Here the limbs cross the body and each other—a greater degree of joining (adducting). Example 17.27i shows a clown being drenched in a heavy downpour of rain. Note that many of the resulting positions could be described as directional placement for the limbs, but such placement is not the intention, not the motivation of the movement. Emphasis is on the closeness or distance of the limbs in relation to each other or to the torso.

17.27h   17.27i

Signs for Lateral Joining, Separating

The indication for lateral joining (closing) and separating (spreading) are pictorial in that they suggest a base with two "wings" which close and open. Note the doubling of the sign for the greater degree. In general, these signs indicate two-sided joining and separating.

For the signs of 17.28a and 17.28d, it is assumed that both sides are active. In themselves the lateral signs indicate two-sided joining and separating such as usually happens with the fingers. For the arms and legs both arms or both legs open or close laterally. In 17.28g, both arms open laterally, each to its own side, while 17.28h indicates both legs closing laterally. With indication of only one limb, it is clear that this limb will perform the stated action to its own side. In 17.28i the left leg will abduct; in 17.28j the right arm will abduct.

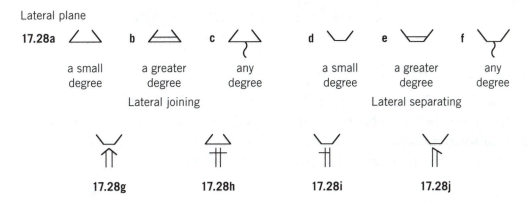

By thickening one side of the symbol, single sided opening or closing can be shown. In 17.28k the opening is to the left, in 17.28l it is to the right. To facilitate reading, 17.28i and j could be written as 17.28m and n.

When open choice is wanted, the symbol for "either side" can be used, thus 17.28o gives the choice of right or left arm. The choice of either or both is expressed in 17.28p; in this case the sign for any number means one or two.

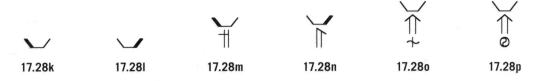

TERMINOLOGY

The terms "opening" and "closing" are in common use and can as well be applied to three-dimensional contraction and extension, to folding and unfolding and also to gathering and scattering. For separating and joining of the legs, as in 17.29, many people would just say "open" and "close" the legs. But separating and joining indicate an awareness of the other part, a relationship different from general opening and closing. The word "widening" is especially applicable to lateral spreading (abducting), as is "narrowing" to the closing in (adducting). The words lateral spreading and narrowing and their signs can also be applied to the chest.

17.29

Reading Practice P (no music)

JOINING, SEPARATING

This simple reading material provides a variety of possibilities. It is important that concentration be on the basic actions described. The manner of holding the limbs, state of rotation, flexed ankle or wrist, etc., are all open to choice so that the performer can give a particular character to the movements.

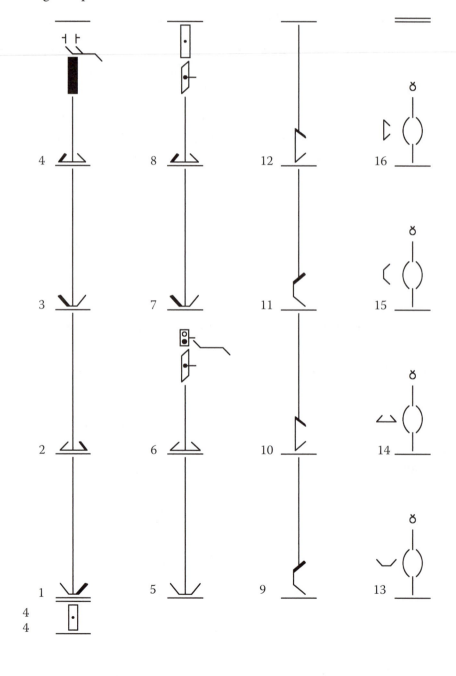

READING STUDY NO. 55

JOINING, SEPARATING WITH SPECIFIC LIMBS

Note the ritardando at the end in measure 12 that indicates the music slows down.

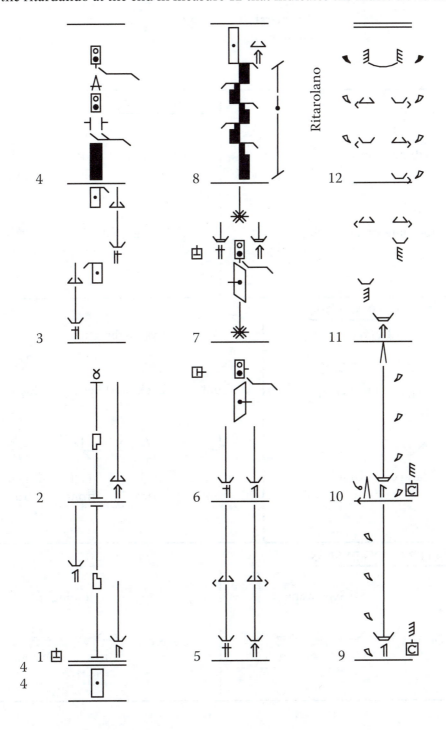

REVIEW FOR CHAPTER SEVENTEEN

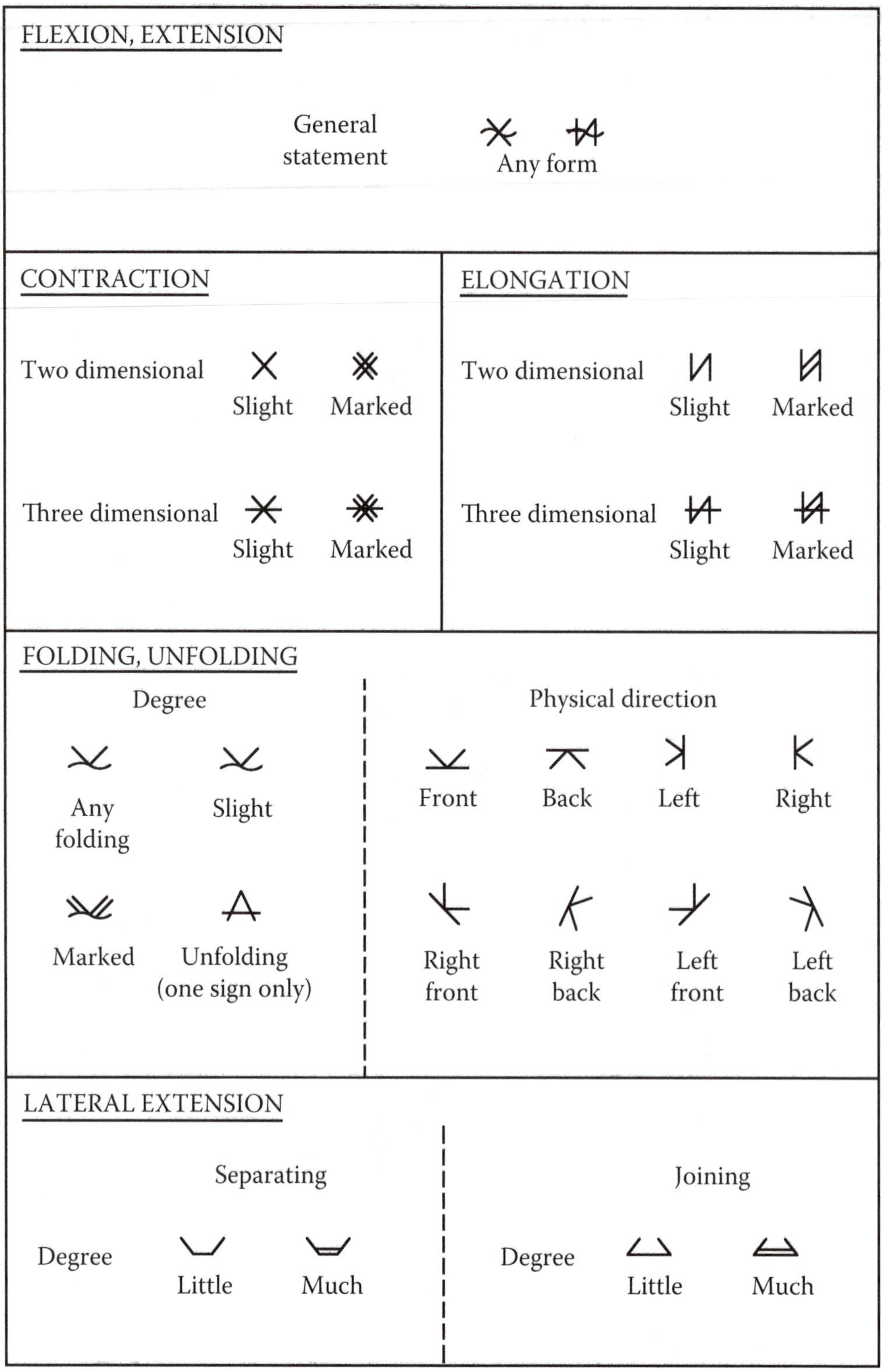

FLEXION, EXTENSION

General
statement ✳ ⟊ Any form

CONTRACTION

Two dimensional   ✕   ✳
Slight   Marked

Three dimensional   ✳   ✳
Slight   Marked

ELONGATION

Two dimensional   Ⲛ   Ⲛ
Slight   Marked

Three dimensional   ⟊   ⟊
Slight   Marked

FOLDING, UNFOLDING

Degree

⌄   ⌄
Any   Slight
folding

⌄   ⋀
Marked   Unfolding
(one sign only)

Physical direction

⌄   ⊼   ⋋   ⋋
Front   Back   Left   Right

⋌   ⋋   ⋋   ⋋
Right   Right   Left   Left
front   back   front   back

LATERAL EXTENSION

Separating

Degree   ⌣   ⌣
Little   Much

Joining

Degree   △   △
Little   Much

REVIEW FOR CHAPTER SEVENTEEN (CONTINUED)

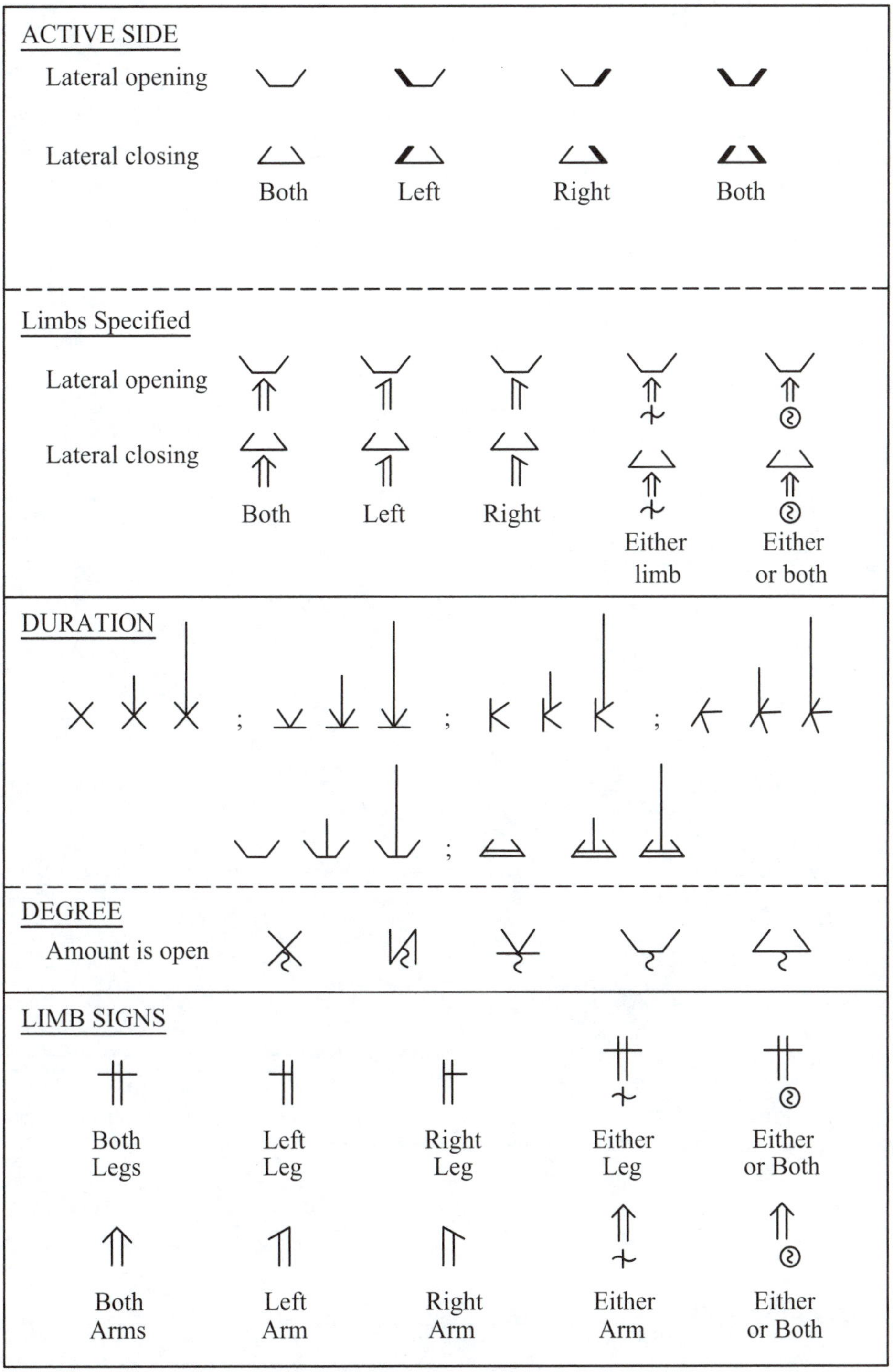

ACTIVE SIDE

Lateral opening

Lateral closing

Both   Left   Right   Both

Limbs Specified

Lateral opening

Lateral closing

Both   Left   Right   Either   Either
                          limb   or both

DURATION

LIMBS SPECIFIED (additional symbols shown)

DEGREE

Amount is open

LIMB SIGNS

| Both Legs | Left Leg | Right Leg | Either Leg | Either or Both |

| Both Arms | Left Arm | Right Arm | Either Arm | Either or Both |

CHAPTER EIGHTEEN

Relationship: Situations in Meeting; Looking

SITUATIONS IN MEETING

Exploration of relationship, investigated in Chapters 11 and 12, must also include how two people stand in relation to one another. In everyday life when two people meet we expect that they will face one another; when walking together they will usually be side by side, and so on. Obviously, more possibilities present themselves when three, four, or more people are involved. But for our purposes, two provide enough variations to establish the possibilities and how they are indicated. Let us investigate such relationships and the possible meanings each might have.

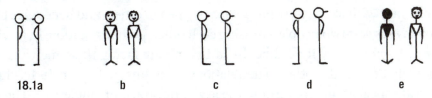

18.1a   b   c   d   e

In 18.1a, two people face one another. They may be deep in conversation as close friends or they may be confronting one another in a head-on dispute. The placement of 18.1a commonly suggests an equal status, as does 18.1b in which two people are side by side, a relationship expressing equality or a belonging together, a sharing, a mutual stance in facing the world. Generally speaking, it makes no difference on which side each stands, although man and woman relationships in folk dances have traditionally placed the man on the woman's left. Placement one behind the other as in 18.1c expresses an unequal relationship. It may be a follow-the-leader situation in which the one in front knows the way and therefore is the dominant one. The one in front may be ignoring the other or may be acting as a protector. The one behind may be in a weaker, subservient position, being perhaps less sure, less knowledgeable. However, there is a mutual interest in that they are both facing and perhaps traveling in the same direction. In 18.1d, the back-to-back situation suggests differences of outlook, a non-sharing, possibly a mutual rejection, a dispute, or it could be mutual protection: keeping a look-out in both directions. In 18.1e, the two people are side by side but facing in opposite directions. This situation has a sense of transience, of a moment in passing, rather than of a relationship which might last for some time. There is no real sense of sharing: they might be two people passing in the street, having a quick word without changing the direction they intend to travel. Whether they pass left or right shoulders does not change the meaning of the relationship, though certain dances have a "rule of the road" to pass on the right.

Placements involving combinations of these five main, straightforward situations, may combine the meanings, generally making them more casual, less clearly defined, as illustrated in 18.1f, 18.1g, and 18.1h.

18.1f   18.1g   18.1h

Example 18.1f shows two people facing one another but on a diagonal line, a mixture of 18.1a and 18.1e. Such a relationship occurs often at a social gathering where one may wish to converse but also to be open to others and hence able to move away. It may suggest two people assessing each other, perhaps cautiously, leaving the path open to move away if need be. In 18.1g both are facing the same way, but one is diagonally behind the other. The relationship is unequal, as in 18.1c, the front person still appears more important, the leader or protector, but less so. The person behind could be threatening; he is more in the picture than he is in 18.1c, and could easily move alongside to an equal position. In 18.1h, we have a mixture of 18.1d and 18.1e. It is as though they have drawn away from the 18.1e situation but have paused, perhaps to reconsider their relationship; there is not the degree of negation inherent in 18.1d. In each of 18.1f, 18.1g, and 18.1h the positioning could be on the other side with no change in meaning. A summary of these relationships is given in 18.1i–18.1p using the standard floor plan pins for people: a white pin for a female, a black pin for a male. The examples here illustrate one sex only to avoid any male-female connotations. Note: Here, "equal" means equal status.

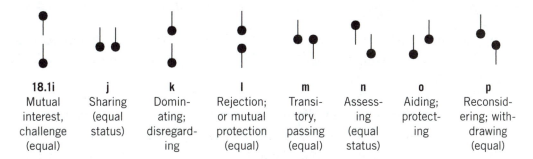

18.1i	j	k	l	m	n	o	p
Mutual interest, challenge (equal)	Sharing (equal status)	Domin-ating; disregard-ing	Rejection; or mutual protection (equal)	Transi-tory, passing (equal)	Assess-ing (equal status)	Aiding; protect-ing	Reconsid-ering; with-drawing (equal)

Note that in these relationships, except for 18.1k and 18.1o, the two people have the same relationship to one another. In partner work, if the female is in front of the male, she may be in eight clear relationships to him, as illustrated in 18.1q–18.1x.

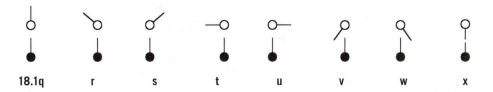

18.1q	r	s	t	u	v	w	x

Such relationships also occur between a performer and an object. Both dramatic and humorous possibilities may be explored. A story line can be developed, other movements being added to provide color and meaning, or changes may be based on design or developing shapes.

INDICATION OF SITUATIONS IN MEETING

To understand how these situations are written, imagine yourself inside a black-edged box, the front of the box being where you are facing, i.e., your front, 18.2a. The edges (the black lines), 18.2b, are the meeting lines used individually to represent you, the performer. In the illustrations below, your partner "P" is represented by a faceless circle since where P is facing may vary and does not affect his/her spatial relationship to you, i.e., P may be turning and yet still remain in front of you.

18.2a   **18.2b**
Meeting Lines

18.2c	**18.2d**	**18.2e**	**18.2f**
Partner in front	Partner at your right	Partner behind you	Partner at your left

In 18.2c, your partner is in front of you; in 18.2d, P is on your right. Example 18.2e shows P to be behind you, while in 18.2f, P is on your left. A separate statement is needed to indicate where P is facing.

The diagonal situations are indicated in a similar way; the box has now become a black-edged diamond, 18.2g, the slanting lines represent you, the performer, 18.2h. In 18.2i, P is on the diagonal line in front and to your right, while in 18.2j, P is diagonally behind and to your right. In 18.2k and 18.2l) the left-front diagonal placement and the left-back diagonal placement are illustrated.

18.2g

18.2h
Diagonal meeting lines

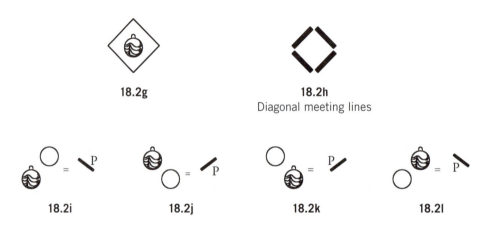

18.2i	**18.2j**	**18.2k**	**18.2l**

Indication of your partner's relationship to you as well as your relationship to him/her (his/her point of view) gives the total picture of where each of you is situated in relation to the other. **The meeting lines, as they are called, do not give information as to where in the room you are placed, nor do they give the room direction faced.** You may travel and yet keep the same relationship to your partner; you may turn and still maintain the same relationship. Because of the many different possibilities these indications are kept separate.

Example 18.2m states traveling for performers A and B with the destination that each ends with the other on the right side. As no other information is given, we do not know where they started, whether each traveled with forward steps, etc. We only know what their destination must be in relation to each other. Therefore, the room direction faced could be any of the possibilities given in 18.2n–18.2q.

Meeting situations are needed when people are near each other; the other person could, however, be at some distance. But distance between people is a separate statement; it is not given here.

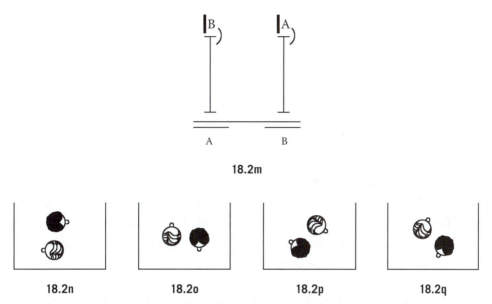

18.2m

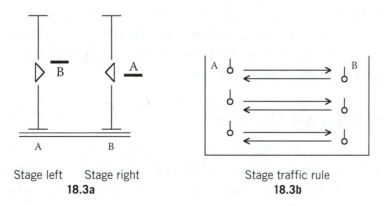

18.2n   **18.2o**   **18.2p**   **18.2q**

Variations in room orientation for partners on each other's right

PATHS CROSSING

When traveling involves passing someone and there is a need to state the relationship to the other person, the meeting line is used to show on which side people pass one another when crossing. In 18.3a, two lines of dancers (A and B) travel sideward across the stage, line A passing in front of line B. This is illustrated in the floor plan of 18.3b. The stage traffic rule established long ago in Russia is for people on stage left to pass in front of those on stage right. This rule is shown on the floor plan here and also next to the path sign at the moment of passing.

Stage left   Stage right

18.3a

Stage traffic rule

18.3b

Many instances of passing occur in folk dancing. In 18.3c–18.3f the directions faced at the start are given and also the direction of traveling, but other performance details are left out. In each example A starts stage left, B stage right.

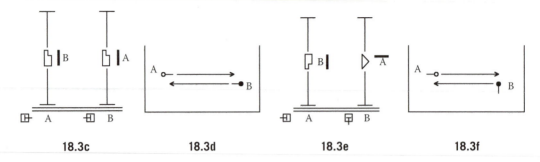

| 18.3c | 18.3d | 18.3e | 18.3f |

In 18.3c, B starts facing stage left, A facing stage right. They travel forward passing right shoulders, illustrated in 18.3d. Example 18.3e shows an asymmetrical pattern. A starts facing stage left and travels backward while B faces upstage and travels to his right. A has B on her left as they pass each other, whereas B has A behind him at that moment. Note indication of this on the floor plan, 18.3f.

When paths literally cross, the arrow on the floor plan is broken for the person who passes behind. In 18.3g the men pass behind the women as each group travels diagonally across the stage.

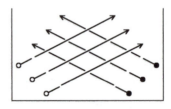

Stage left passes in front
18.3g

Because floor plans can indicate the situation and relationship of performers, they may seem to make the meeting line redundant. However, the addition of the meeting line gives information that is helpful in working out what is intended as well as the moment when passing occurs.

RELATING TO AN OBJECT

Relationship to an object may also need to be indicated. A path may end close to an object, or a performer may pass an object or relate to it while traveling. In these examples, a chair is the object and floor plans are provided to illustrate one possible interpretation.

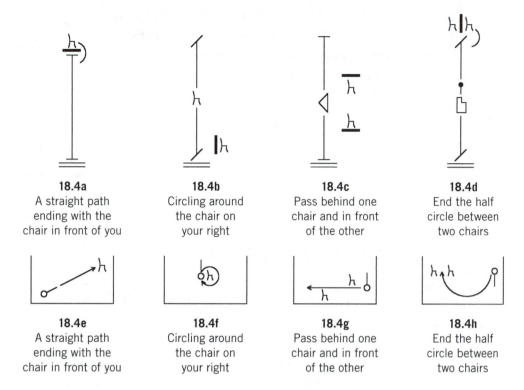

18.4a	18.4b	18.4c	18.4d
A straight path ending with the chair in front of you	Circling around the chair on your right	Pass behind one chair and in front of the other	End the half circle between two chairs

18.4e	18.4f	18.4g	18.4h
A straight path ending with the chair in front of you	Circling around the chair on your right	Pass behind one chair and in front of the other	End the half circle between two chairs

In many folk and national dances, couples weave in and out and exchange places. Usually passing right shoulders is the established rule but in less traditional dances many variations are possible and with any large group it may be important to know who is passing whom at any given moment. The meeting line provides such information in a simple, practical way.

RELATING TO A FOCAL POINT

When performing outdoors, there may be no clear Front for the performers to relate to, so a focal point needs to be established. For any circular dance, the center of the circle is the understood focal point. In the case of a Maypole dance, the pole itself is obviously a focal point and so use of relationship to that central point is obvious. The focal point in the figures is represented by a small black circle. Basic orientation can be shown by using the meeting line.

In 18.5a you face the focal point. In 18.5b your back is to the focal point. Right side to the focal point is shown in 18.5c, while in 18.5d, the focal point is at your left. Diagonal relationships follow those given in 18.2i–18.2l.

18.5a	18.5b	18.5c	18.5d

A statement of the relationship to a focal point can be given at the start of a score. Example 18.5e starts with the performer's back to the focal point. After turning to the left, the orientation is to have the left side to the focal point. After the stillness, the turning spring ends with the person's right side to the focal point.

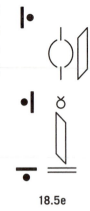

18.5e

NOTES FOR READING PRACTICE Q

In this folk dance-like piece, a circle around a pin represents a person, as shown below. The number adjacent to these pins relates to the number of the dancer on the floor plan.

= lady   = man   1 = lady no. 1   P = person   C = head nod

Because the first four measures are repeated, the numbers for the repeated measures are shown in parenthesis (5) at the start of the repeat and (8) at the end. The ending of the repeat is different for the second time, though; therefore the first and second ending need to be shown. These are handles as in music, but placed vertically.

    Second ending
    First ending

On this second ending at the end of measure 8, each person makes a ¼ turn to face into the direction shown on the next floor plan, ready to start the hey-like weaving. Man no.1 and ladies 2–4 turn ¼ left, while lady no.1 and men 2–4 turn ¼ right.

At the end of measure 12, lady no.1 turns ¼ right and man no.1 turns ¼ left, as indicated at the left of the staff. Turning for the rest of the ladies and the men is shown on the right of the staff.

READING PRACTICE Q (NO MUSIC)

PATHS CROSSING, MEETING, RELATING TO PEOPLE

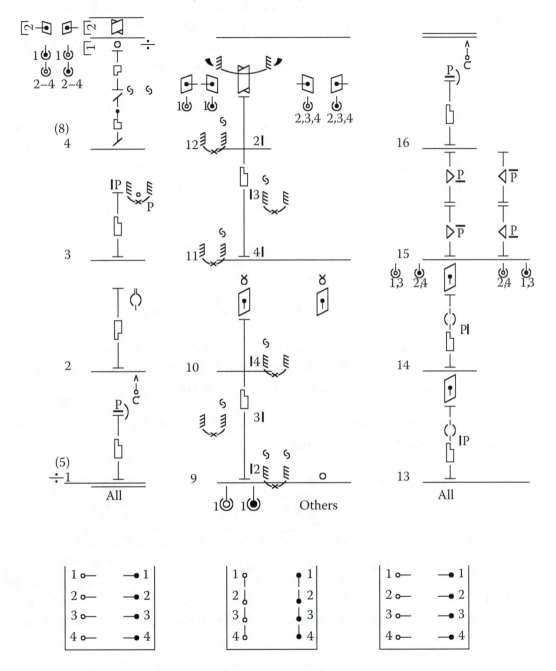

ADDRESSING WITH THE FACE AND EYES

When turning the head, it may not be the turning itself that is important, but the result—looking to the side. The action of looking needs then to be directly stated, hence there is a separate indication for it. Looking is, of course, an important form of addressing which in some respects is so familiar it would seem to need no investigation. Yet we need to be quite clear about how the eyes are used in the act of looking. We see with our eyes, but it is not just the eyes that move when we look, in most instances it is our full face that addresses the direction, person, or object. We are most comfortable when the eyes and nose are in the same direction. This is what happens when there is nothing to hide. The more secretive the looking, the more it becomes a movement of the eyes alone. To enable us to distinguish between eye movements and the usual looking, two terms are provided—"looking" being for the standard action and "gazing" when eyes alone are involved. This terminology is not universal but no other exists, therefore these are used to serve our purposes. We will begin with an investigation of looking.

LOOKING WITH THE FACE

What more expressive action is there than looking? A change of focus for the face can alter the meaning of an action. Where a look is directed may significantly affect the expression and hence the message being conveyed. The point of interest in a movement is usually clearly indicated by where the performer looks; however, there may be another point of interest indicated by another part of the body.

In the simple illustrations in 18.6a–18.6f, only the head is changed, that is, the direction into which the walker is looking.

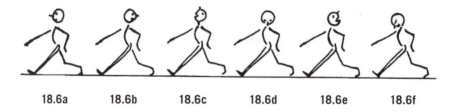

| 18.6a | 18.6b | 18.6c | 18.6d | 18.6e | 18.6f |

In choreographed actions, the focus for the face, the concentration of the looking, is very significant in its relation to the whole. Different messages are conveyed by a change in looking, as illustrated in 18.6g, 18.6h, and 18.6i.

When a torso tilt, as in 18.6j, should express the forward horizontal direction, the use of the face is important. Without the direction forward for the face, this torso movement may well express downward. Example 18.6k is more expressive

| 18.6g | 18.6h | 18.6i |

of forward horizontal than 18.6j as a result of this forward focus. It is interesting to note that the more casual stance of 18.6l contributes to the expression of forward horizontal.

| 18.6j | 18.6k | 18.6l |

INDICATION OF LOOKING

The face, indicated by 18.7a (the front surface of the area of the head), is used for looking in a particular direction. Example 18.7b states the face addressing forward middle, the normal direction for the face. In 18.7c, the face is looking up, while in 18.7d it is looking to the right.

18.7a	18.7b	18.7c	18.7d
Sign for the face	Normal looking direction	Looking up	Looking to the right

Experiment with variations in looking combined with a simple action. Sense the different feeling and observe the different resulting expression when others improvise on this aspect of movement. Travel in different directions with changes in facial focus. Compare the resulting different expressions when the movement examples in 18.7e–18.7j, are performed: lowering (sinking) while looking down; lowering while looking up; and lowering while looking sideward.

Changes of focus while rising will also give very different results to a simple basic action.

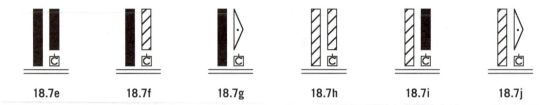

| 18.7e | 18.7f | 18.7g | 18.7h | 18.7i | 18.7j |

The "spelling" of addressing a direction, of looking, stated in 18.7b, 18.7c, and 18.7d, has been abbreviated to the general indication of a direction symbol following the sign for the face, the action of looking into that direction being understood. Any surface indication for a body part, followed by a direction symbol, always means facing that direction, as illustrated for the face, 18.7e–18.7j.

Gazing; Independent Action for the Eyes

We have spoken of looking with the face, the front surface of the head; of course it is the eyes which do the actual seeing, the looking, focusing on a person, object, or direction. But the eyes can move and focus on a person, object, or direction other than that toward which the face is directed. Given the choice, we turn the head so that the eyes are in their normal alignment in the face (or nearly so). To distinguish between an ordinary "face looking" and an independent eye action we use the term "gazing" when seeing involves only the eyes. Observe the differences between the illustrations in 18.8a–18.8f.

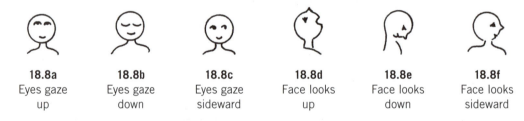

| **18.8a** | **18.8b** | **18.8c** | **18.8d** | **18.8e** | **18.8f** |
| Eyes gaze up | Eyes gaze down | Eyes gaze sideward | Face looks up | Face looks down | Face looks sideward |

Looking with the face involves a rotation or a tilt (inclination) of the head, sometimes both, but these actions are the means used to look and are not the purpose of the movement.

Indication of Eye Movements for Gazing

The sign for the eyes, 18.9a, is combined with the addressing sign to show gazing (moving eyes only). As with the face, this indication can be abbreviated to the use of a direction symbol without the addressing sign.

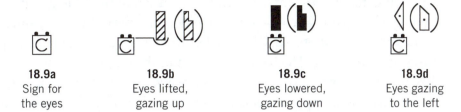

18.9a	18.9b	18.9c	18.9d
Sign for the eyes	Eyes lifted, gazing up	Eyes lowered, gazing down	Eyes gazing to the left

In 18.9b the eyes are written as addressing (being directed) up. In fact they cannot totally achieve that direction without some change in the head alignment, so forward high (as indicated in brackets) might seem a more appropriate description. However, the effort to look up rather than forward high does produce a slightly different expression and this difference may be important. Therefore, we sometimes write what we have in mind, the aim or the intention, rather than a more limited degree that is likely to be achieved. In 18.9c and 18.9d, the description has been simplified. Again the direction actually achieved for the eyes is shown in brackets.

PALM FACING

Many expressive gestures center on or feature a particular spatial placement of the palm. As Doris Humphrey, the renowned American choreographer, pointed out, the palm choreographically is the "face" of the arm and can be very expressive in a way similar to the face. Humphrey often spoke of the "greeting" hand, 18.10a, in which the palm addresses the audience. Conversely, it is with the palm that we stop people from advancing toward us, 18.10b. The priest supplicates with palms up, 18.10c, blesses with palms down, 18.10d. The palms facing forward was used by Sigurd Leeder for the two ghostly "pale sisters" who glide colorlessly across stage in his ballet *Danse Macabre*, 18.10e.

18.10a
Greeting

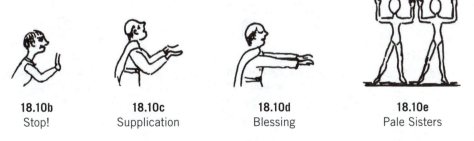

18.10b	18.10c	18.10d	18.10e
Stop!	Supplication	Blessing	Pale Sisters

A change in palm facing direction is achieved through a twist in the lower arm, a wrist flexion, or both. The aim of the movement, however, is neither rotation nor flexion but palm facing, which has a very strong expression of its own.

In palm facing, there is a slight heightening of tension in the hand and usually a slight widening of the palm. Such hand reaction does not mean that the palm is flat or the fingers particularly stretched. Observe the familiar gesture of turning the palm upward to see if it is raining. The hand is not held in the same way as when it rests on your lap or hangs down by your side. You have given the hand no instruction to "be alert," yet alertness seems automatically to be included when the palm "faces" a direction, person, or object. Many such gestures are understood and accepted as the norm without ever being specifically analyzed. A change in palm facing may provide a positive or a negative message. Without appropriate palm facing, a gesture may be meaningless. It is, therefore, important to choose carefully the appropriate description for an action, both in notating and in calling out movement instructions.

INDICATION OF PALM FACING

The sign for the palm surface of the hand is 18.11a. This is followed by an addressing sign plus the appropriate direction, 18.11b. As with the face, this statement is usually abbreviated to use of the direction sign only, as in 18.11c. The palm sign is a surface sign and surfaces "face" or "look at" the direction stated, as in 18.11d.

18.11a	**18.11b**	**18.11c**	**18.11d**
Sign for palm	Palm surface faces up	The same abbreviated	Palm faces forward

The reading examples which follow describe some everyday movements in which the palm is used expressively. Examples 18.11e, 18.11f, and 18.11g show a few unfamiliar signs used in these examples. The sign for the forehead, 18.11e, is composed of the head sign with a forward pointing white pin indicating the forward high part of the head, in other words, the upper part of the face, the forehead.

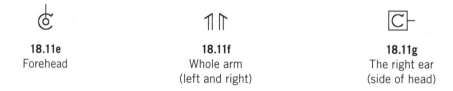

18.11e	**18.11f**	**18.11g**
Forehead	Whole arm (left and right)	The right ear (side of head)

READING EXAMPLES FOR PALM FACING

Example 18.12d contains the following information: palms backward, hands near face, eyes down. More detail could be added to achieve an exact position, but the main ingredients are there. Examples 18.12a–18.12l show various pantomimic gestures in a simple form.

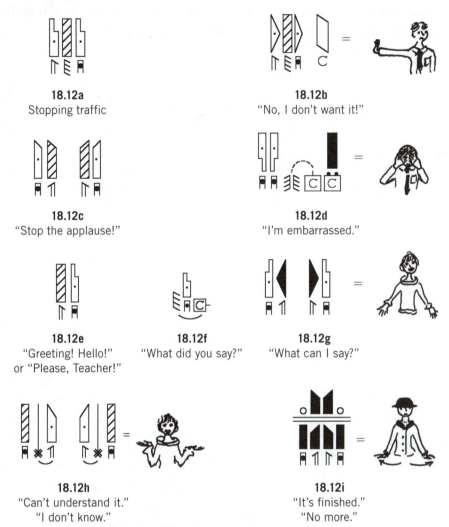

18.12a
Stopping traffic

18.12b
"No, I don't want it!"

18.12c
"Stop the applause!"

18.12d
"I'm embarrassed."

18.12e
"Greeting! Hello!"
or "Please, Teacher!"

18.12f
"What did you say?"

18.12g
"What can I say?"

18.12h
"Can't understand it."
"I don't know."

18.12i
"It's finished."
"No more."

In the gesture of 18.12i, the hold sign for the palms indicate physical retention of that direction. Note the differences in meaning among 18.12j, 18.2k, and 18.12l. In each, the hand contacts the forehead but each time produces a different message according to the facing direction of the palm.

18.12j
Peering into
the distance

18.12k
"It's awful!"
"Woe is me."

18.12l
"Let me think."

It is important to remember that, out of context, the sign of 18.12m can refer either to the palm or the sole of the foot. In the examples of arm gestures above, the context easily identifies facing of the palm. In some cases it may not always be clear so the specific identification of foot or hand can be helpful. The possibilities for the hand are repeated here as a reminder.

| **18.12m**
Palm or
sole of
the foot | **18.12n**
Palm of
the left
hand | **18.12o**
Palm of
the right
hand | **18.12p**
Both
palms | **18.12q**
Either left
or right
palm | **18.12r**
Either left,
right, or both
palm(s) |

READING PRACTICE R (NO MUSIC)

LOOKING, GAZING; PALM FACING

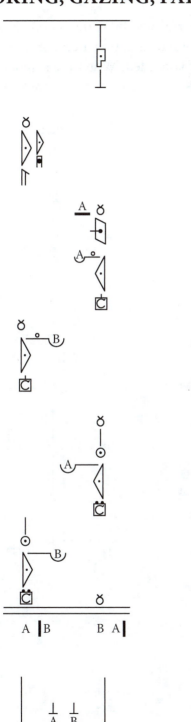

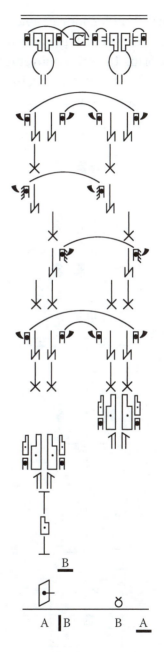

Note: the sign: ⊙ means
       return to the normal
       state for that part.

READING PRACTICE S (NO MUSIC)

SITUATIONS IN MEETING; LOOKING

This study for four people (which could be performed by many more) suggests a primitive ritual dance around a fire to a drum beat or chanting. Because each person performs the same movement, only one staff is needed. When the symbol "X" is placed in a path sign, as in measures 2 and 18, it refers to distance traveled, i.e., a little, short distance.

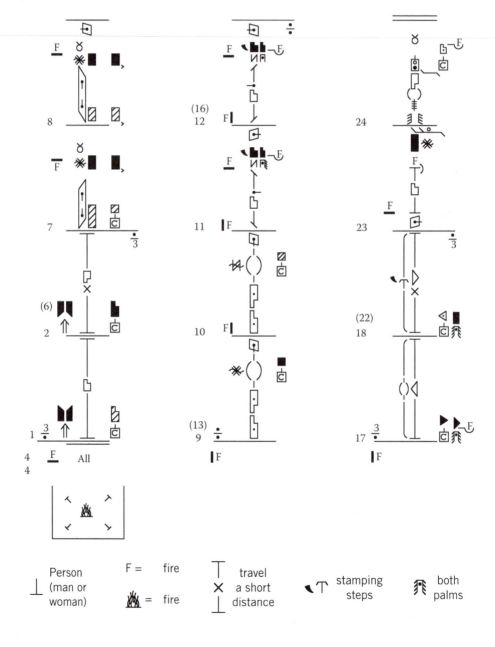

DYNAMICS: EMOTIONAL INTENSITY

Physical energy may be expended in hitting a heavy object, shaking a cloth, digging a hole, etc., or focus may be on the body itself in strengthening or relaxing the muscles. In contrast to these, many dynamic actions stem from the emotional state of the individual. A forceful gesture may result from anger or the elation of victory; a dropping of energy may be caused by despair or a sense of relief when fear is dispelled. In some cultures stamping on the ground has the purpose of hardening the surface; strong, rhythmic stamping in Spanish dance reveals the skill and authority of the performer; in an emotional situation, stamping can express frustration. In dance, the emotional feelings of the performer, particularly in portraying a character, will affect the quality of the movements. The difference between functional uses of energy and changes in energy level that result from the feelings of the individual are important.

INDICATION OF EMOTIONAL INTENSITY

The original idea of showing feelings by placing indications within a heart-shaped symbol, 18.13a, developed into opening the heart shape of 18.13b into a curved bow, 18.13c. Indications placed in the vertical angular addition bracket indicate physical facts. In 18.13d muscular, physical strength is shown. Strong feeling producing a strong expression is indicated in 18.13e. The physically relaxed quality of 18.13f becomes little feeling, little expression in 18.13g. A total lack of physical energy, 18.13h, is, in terms of feeling, 18.13i, no feeling at all, a robot-like state. The slight fighting gravity, shown in 18.13j, indicates raised spirits when in the curved bow, 18.13k. Physical use of gravity in sensing weight, shown in 18.13l, becomes dispirited, losing heart, in 18.13m. These are some examples; in Chapter 22 the Dynamic Chart gives many more.

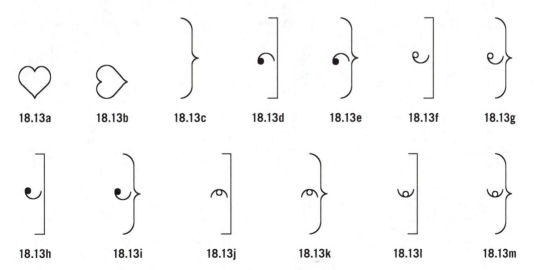

18.13a   18.13b   18.13c   18.13d   18.13e   18.13f   18.13g

18.13h   18.13i   18.13j   18.13k   18.13l   18.13m

READING PRACTICE T (NO MUSIC)

EMOTIONAL EXPRESSION, FEELING

These brief studies explore a few of the emotional dynamic possibilities. In A the letter "S" represents a stranger. In B the robot-like state (maybe like the doll in *Coppélia*?), given at the start, changes briefly and becomes human at the start of the second measure. Example C ends with physical as well as emotional intensity.

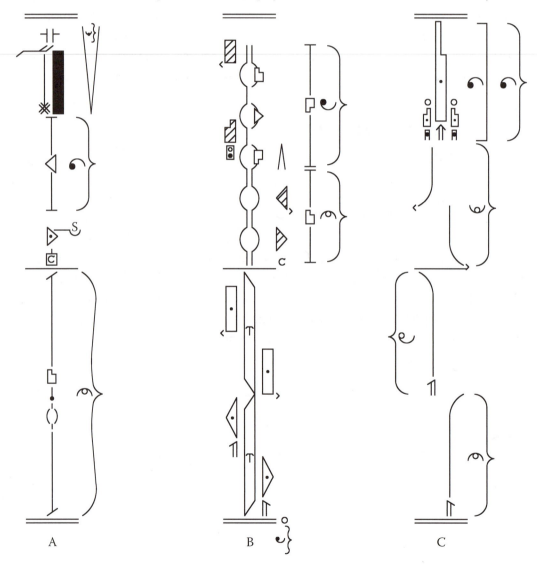

A B C

REVIEW FOR CHAPTER EIGHTEEN

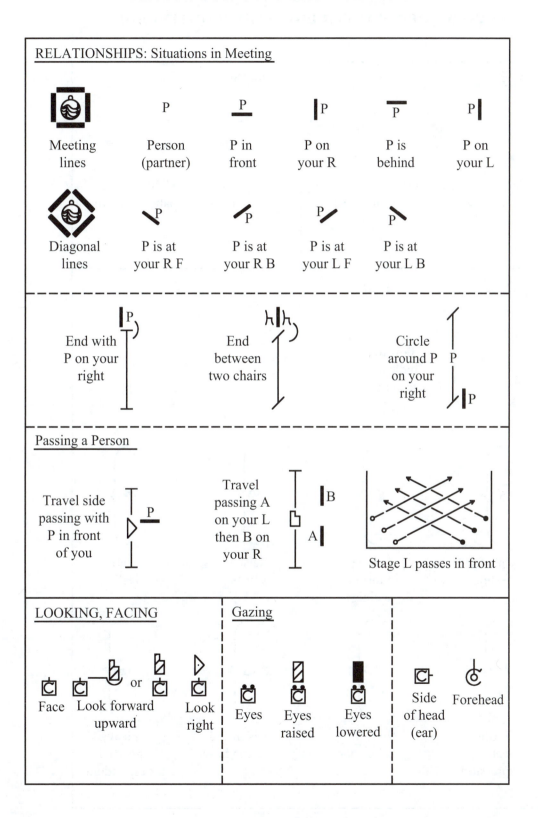

RELATIONSHIPS: Situations in Meeting

Meeting lines

Person (partner)

P in front

P on your R

P is behind

P on your L

Diagonal lines

P is at your R F

P is at your R B

P is at your L F

P is at your L B

End with P on your right

End between two chairs

Circle around P P on your right

Passing a Person

Travel side passing with P in front of you

Travel passing A on your L then B on your R

Stage L passes in front

LOOKING, FACING

Face   Look forward upward   or   Look right

Gazing

Eyes   Eyes raised   Eyes lowered

Side of head (ear)   Forehead

REVIEW FOR CHAPTER EIGHTEEN (CONTINUED)

Palm Facing			Specific Signs		
Palm	Palm up	Palm forward	Left palm	Right palm	Both palms

DYNAMICS—Emotional Intensity

{ or } Bow to indicate feelings

Heightened feeling	Strong emotion, feeling	Raised spirits	Elated feeling

Little feeling, expression	No feeling, robot-like	Dispirited, loosing heart	Heavy hearted, despondent

CHAPTER NINETEEN
Specific Directional Actions

Directional movements may be of several kinds. The body-as-a-whole makes use of and expresses directions, or the torso or a limb may use a direction as its focus. The limbs and torso may approach a direction or may travel along the line of a direction, as in extending into that direction. The general statement of movement into the side high direction, 19.1a, may be interpreted as a movement of the body-as-a-whole, 19.1b, or it may be interpreted as a gesture of a limb related to that direction, 19.1c. In 19.1d, the limb is specified as being the right arm. This side high movement may be interpreted as a gesture approaching the side high spatial point, 19.1e, or one of arrival at that point, 19.1f. While in 19.1f, the hand arrives at the side high point, the emphasis may be on the slanting line of the arm, i.e., the arms embodiment of that direction.

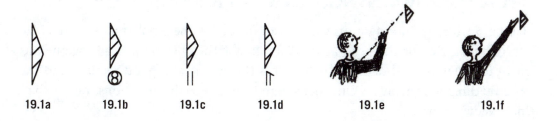

| 19.1a | 19.1b | 19.1c | 19.1d | 19.1e | 19.1f |

| 19.1g | 19.1h | 19.1i |

Let us take an example of the arms embodying, i.e., "becoming" the stated direction. In Semaphore, the lines of the arms holding the flags state the number or letter to be conveyed to the observer. A static spatial design is established, 19.1g, 19.1h, and 19.1i. Such establishment of lines in the body by limbs, torso, or body-as-a-whole is architectural in effect. The limb or torso "becomes" that direction. It physically "takes" that direction, so to speak. This idea that the limb itself represents that direction, rather than that a movement ends in that location, is an important concept that needs a separate statement. This specific form of directional movement for a limb or the torso, that of **tilting** (also called inclining) is sometimes called "**taking a direction**." The part of the body involved may be seen or experienced as aligning itself with that direction. The word tilting pertains, in particular, to the head and torso, but is applicable to any part. "Taking a direction" means placing the limb or part of the body so that its longitudinal axis is on the stated directional line. Examples 19.1j–19.1n show some familiar examples for the arms; concentration is on the line produced by the angle which the head or arms make in relation to the horizontal and vertical axes of the dimensional cross. Thus "taking a direction" is a destinational action, the design or picture achieved being important.

| 19.1j | 19.1k | 19.1l | 19.1m | 19.1n |

TILTING, INCLINING, "TAKING A DIRECTION"

Tilting, inclining, "taking a direction" can occur for the whole torso as in 19.2a, 19.2b, and 19.2c, for the head as in 19.2d, or for the chest and head together, as in 19.2e. Later we will define which part is tilting, or taking a direction, and the specific direction involved. Our focus here is on the main directions, rather than intermediate points.

19.2a   19.2b   19.2c   19.2d   19.2e

ANALYSIS OF TILTING, INCLINING

As an illustration of tilting, inclining, let us take a book and note its changing spatial alignment. From a vertical situation, 19.3a, the book can incline away to a slight or greater degree, as in 19.3b and 19.3c. If the book is lying down horizontally, as in 19.3d, a tilting action occurs as it is being raised, 19.3e. The slanting line achieved in relation to the vertical or horizontal is important; the direction of the movement which produces the result is not of significance here.

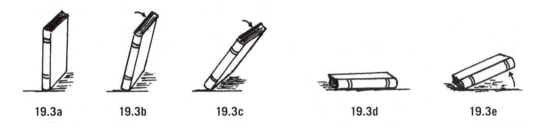

19.3a   19.3b   19.3c   19.3d   19.3e

Next, explore other possibilities for the whole torso, remembering that, since the torso hinges at the hip joints, direction and level for the free end (the line of the shoulders) are judged from there (the head goes along for the ride). For horizontal tilts, the longitudinal line (axis) of the torso must be parallel with the floor. Examples 19.3f–19.3m are illustrations of tilting the torso, an analogy being made with tilting a chair. This same analogy applies to the head, chest, and pelvis, although these are smaller units. In 19.3i, hinging is at the knee joint; for most people the hip is not flexible enough to produce such backward tilting without bent legs.

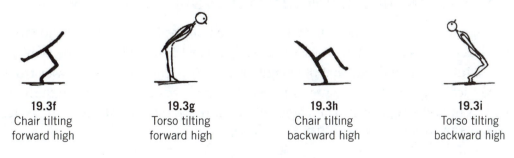

19.3f
Chair tilting
forward high

19.3g
Torso tilting
forward high

19.3h
Chair tilting
backward high

19.3i
Torso tilting
backward high

| **19.3j**
Chair tilted
forward horizontal | **19.3k**
Torso tilted
forward horizontal | **19.3l**
Chair tilted
side horizontal | **19.3m**
Torso tilted
side horizontal |

The normal situation for the torso is straight up, i.e., place high, this is also true for the pelvis, chest, and head. Usually, torso tilts are in the high level. Only when it is horizontal, parallel with the floor, has it reached middle level. Experiment with forward or sideward low level tilts (slanting downward). From a standing position, backward torso tilts are limited.

Tilting, inclining actions for the head can also express an architectural line. The head inclines through the flexibility in the neck, direction being judged from the relationship of the top of the head (free end) to the base of the neck (point of attachment). The head is normally up (place high) when one is standing upright. From there it can easily incline forward, backward, and sideward in high level (slanting upward from the base of the neck). For the head to achieve horizontal level the upper spine usually has to take part.

Inclining the chest (rib cage) can have the feeling of that part "taking a direction," moving as a unit, as an area, rather than as a flexion of the spine, a curving of the vertebrae.

Next, explore the full range of "taking a direction" for the arms and legs. Such actions (particularly for the arms) may be more familiar since they can occur in everyday life. Be consciously aware of the direction used. Combine arm and leg gestures to produce an architectural effect. Find variations in use of one, two, or three limbs at the same time.

INDICATION OF TILTING, INCLINING

The sign for tilting, "taking a direction," is based on the blank rectangle (no level) which represents the vertical line, 19.4a. The stroke: \ is placed inside the symbol, shown in 19.4b, to indicate that the longitudinal axis of the body part is away from the vertical alignment. The slanted stroke is drawn in opposite direction to the lines used to indicate high level. The choice of any direction can be stated as in 19.4c. Example 19.4d states a forward tilt at any level.

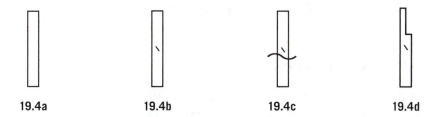

19.4a	19.4b	19.4c	19.4d

In tilting (inclining,"taking a direction") the body part involved "becomes" that direction. To achieve the appropriate expression, the limb/body part needs to be normally extended, i.e., not contracted or folded. The line of the direction must be clear. At times this line may be formed by just the upper arm, led by the elbow, or by the thigh, led by the knee. A lower limb may also indicate a direction, the distal end forming the line to "become" the direction stated.

General Statement of Part Tilting, Taking a Direction

The sign of 19.5a provides choice as to which area (torso, pelvis, chest, or head) to use. Example 19.5b is the sign for a (any) limb. Open choice in use of body part is shown in 19.5c, i.e., use of any body area or limb. The simplified, preferred version of 19.5c is 19.5d.

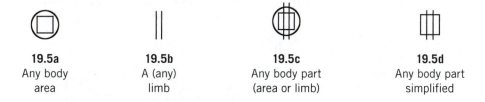

19.5a	19.5b	19.5c	19.5d
Any body area	A (any) limb	Any body part (area or limb)	Any body part simplified

READING STUDY NO. 56

TILTING, INCLINING

This study explores tilting actions of body areas, of limbs, and of the two combined. For a limb, "taking a direction" is a better term.

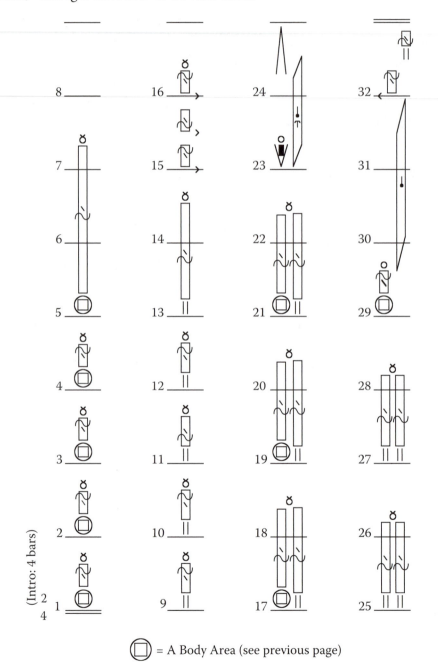

⬚ = A Body Area (see previous page)

DIRECTIONS FOR TILTING, INCLINING

In describing tilting, the next step after freedom in choice of direction and part of the body, is to state a specific direction. This is done by placing the slanting stroke: \ in the appropriate direction symbol. Examples 19.6a–19.6h illustrate direction with no level stated, this being open to choice.

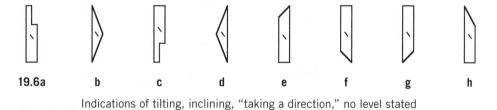

| 19.6a | b | c | d | e | f | g | h |

Indications of tilting, inclining, "taking a direction," no level stated

When level is added to the general indication of tilting, inclining, room must be allowed within the symbol for the slanting stroke. For low and high level, a gap is inserted in the center of the symbol. Examples 19.6i, 19.6j, and 19.6k illustrate how the slanting stroke is placed in high, middle, and low level direction symbols.

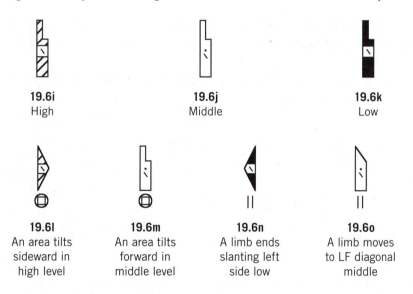

19.6i
High

19.6j
Middle

19.6k
Low

19.6l
An area tilts
sideward in
high level

19.6m
An area tilts
forward in
middle level

19.6n
A limb ends
slanting left
side low

19.6o
A limb moves
to LF diagonal
middle

INDICATION OF SPECIFIC PART

By placing the appropriate part of the body sign before a direction symbol, we state which part tilts, inclines, or "takes a direction." Example 19.7a shows the torso tilting right side high of its normal place high situation.

19.7a

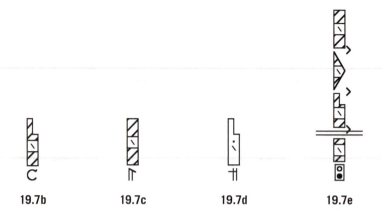

19.7b   19.7c   19.7d   19.7e

In 19.7b the head inclines forward high, while in 19.7c the right arm takes the vertical line of place high. The left leg indicates the forward horizontal line in 19.7d. In 19.7e, the torso starts in its normal place high situation. After tilting forward, it then tilts to the right of its normal placement, and then returns to its place high centered alignment.

Where movements are quick and symbols small, the slanting stroke can be placed in an addition bracket alongside the symbols, as in 19.7f.

The use of a caret: < or > means "the same," thus the limb, body part, or area pre-sign need not be repeated.

19.7f

Reading Study No. 57

SPECIFIC TILTING, INCLINING, "TAKING A DIRECTION"

This reading, a mechanical doll dance, starts with arms folded across the waist. All directions for the limbs are tilting ("taking a direction"). Note the Front sign at start and changes of Front during the study. Slight turns to face another direction are not indicated, such turns being unemphasized and taken for granted.

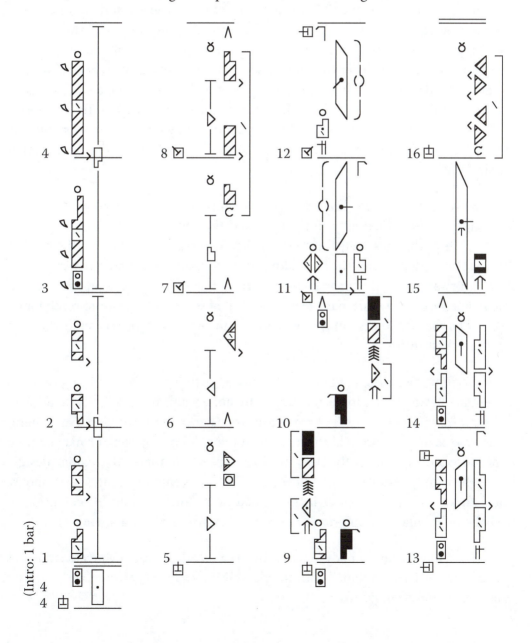

SHIFTING BODY AREAS

The action of a body area shifting out of its normal alignment is usually a displacement of that part on a straight path. When standing upright, most such body shifts are horizontal though upward/downward slanting shifts occur occasionally. The part in question may displace very slightly or a great deal. Shifts of head, chest, and pelvis appear in modern jazz, either in isolation—often with a particular rhythmic pattern—or as part of a general movement pattern serving stylistically to augment or embellish the main action.

What can shifting express? Shifting the head may have a practical function as when one peers forward to see better. In the theater, a sideward head shift may be necessary in order to see when a tall person is sitting in front of you. A sideward shift may also occur in order that one may hear better. A backward head shift may be caused by disapproval or by a negative reaction to something such as a nasty smell. A comic effect may be provided by the "pecking" action of the head as it shifts forward and backward. Or, shifting actions may be decorative, seductive, or may express valor or wonder, as in the lateral head shifts seen in South Asian classical dance.

A body area is able to shift through flexibility in the area of attachment. The head shifts through flexibility in the neck and the chest through flexibility in the waist. Shifts of the chest may function for the same reasons as those of the head in that the chest often carries the head along as it shifts and thus may augment a head shift. A forward chest shift may express warmth toward a person who is in front of you. A sideward chest shift may occur to get out of someone's way or to reach for an object. The very fluid torso movements in certain African dances often include, or focus on, chest shifts.

In performing shifts, the pelvis is "trapped" between waist and hip joints and is therefore more limited in performing truly horizontal shifts. Slightly bent knees and some "give" in the legs help to increase the distance of a pelvic shift. In contemporary dance and in jazz, a hip shift may augment a lunging step, or may be used to produce a distortion in the natural alignment of the torso, an angular design. Pelvic shifts may result in the stylized hip displacements used in cabaret shows. Interestingly, pelvic shifts were incorporated by Balanchine into his extension of the ballet vocabulary, often proceeding a *piqué* to *arabesque* or a lunge *en pointe*.

Shifting movements of body areas, as in 19.8a–19.8d, are usually practiced first as isolated actions, later combined with simple walking and arm gestures, and still later as part of composite movements.

| 19.8a | 19.8b | 19.8c | 19.8d |

ANALYSIS OF SHIFTING

To understand the basic action of shifting, let us consider a pile of books. In 19.9a, the librarian is pushing the whole pile forward horizontally across the table, the end position being shown in 19.9b. Note that each book has traveled the same amount. In 19.9c the top books have been moved horizontally (shifted) while the bottom books have not moved. In 19.9d, several books in the middle have been shifted while the top and bottom books remained in place. How do these examples relate to movement of the body-as-a-whole and to movements of its parts?

19.9a	19.9b
19.9c	19.9d
19.9e	19.9f	19.9g	19.9h

Example 19.9e illustrates a progression, a path forward for the body as a whole. Such moving to another place on a straight path occurs in walking and is comparable to 19.9b. In 19.9f, only the head "travels," shifting forward on a straight path while

remaining upright. In 19.9g, the chest has shifted, in this case carrying the head with it. A pelvic shift forward is shown in 19.9h, the chest remaining behind, which is comparable to 19.9d above. Degree of displacement for shifts varies according to the build of the body, that is, how a particular part is attached, and to the flexibility and training of the performer.

INDICATION OF SHIFTING

Because a shift for a body area can be analyzed as a path (albeit somewhat limited in range) the movement could be (and sometimes has been) described with a straight path sign for the area, as in 19.10a, shown for the head. The appropriate direction symbol is placed within the path sign, as in 19.10b. However, because the point of reference for shifts is the natural body alignment to which the part will return, it is more appropriate to indicate the action as one in which each part of that body section is spatially displaced the same amount. This is in contrast to a tilting, inclining action, in which the free end of the torso or limb travels the greatest amount and each part that is closer to the base displaces less, as illustrated for the torso in 19.10c, and for the arm in 19.10d.

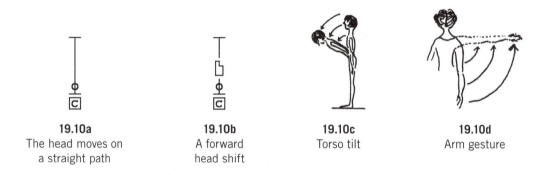

19.10a	19.10b	19.10c	19.10d
The head moves on a straight path	A forward head shift	Torso tilt	Arm gesture

In a shift, each part of the body section moves an equal amount, therefore the equal sign is placed within the direction symbol. Example 19.10e states shifting into any direction. The directional point of reference for shifting is the body part's (head, chest, pelvis, torso) normal centered situation, i.e., place middle, 19.10f. For shifting, this is the point from which shifting directions are judged.

19.10e   19.10f

In 19.10g, the head shifts to right and then to the left of center. In 19.10h, the forward head shift is followed by a return to center, i.e., a shift to place middle. Note that for horizontal shifts the equal sign is placed below the dot. In writing high or low level shifts (shifting upward or downward), space must be left within the symbol for the equal sign, 19.10i and 19.10j. Example 19.10k describes a clockwise "circular" shifting pattern performed by the head.

For shifting actions, the sign for the area of the head is considered more appropriate than the ordinary "C" sign representing the head, though this latter would not be wrong. All parts that are capable of shifting do so as a "block" without inner flexibility.

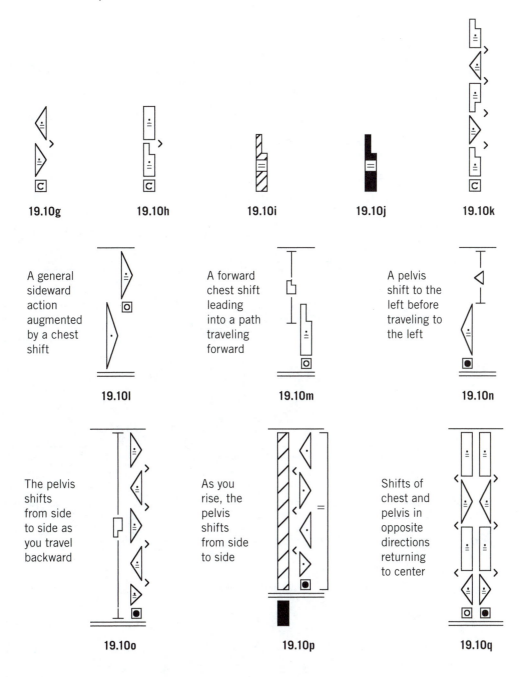

19.10g   **19.10h**   **19.10i**   **19.10j**   **19.10k**

A general sideward action augmented by a chest shift

19.10l

A forward chest shift leading into a path traveling forward

19.10m

A pelvis shift to the left before traveling to the left

19.10n

The pelvis shifts from side to side as you travel backward

19.10o

As you rise, the pelvis shifts from side to side

19.10p

Shifts of chest and pelvis in opposite directions returning to center

19.10q

Note the use of the addition bracket in 19.10p to state that the equal sign for shifting refers to all the adjacent symbols. The following example, 19.10r, features quick chest shifts into side high directions, similar to those used in some African dances. Again, the addition bracket has been used for writing convenience.

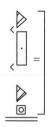

19.10r

READING STUDY NO. 58

SHIFTING BODY AREAS

In this study, no indications are given for the arms; they could be placed on hips, shoulders, or on the head. When a shift is shown to return to center, it is because that is an important action and not an incidental "erasing" of a previous shift. Some shifts are shown to be retained, for others nothing is stated, allowing choice. When stillness follows a shift, the shift will remain.

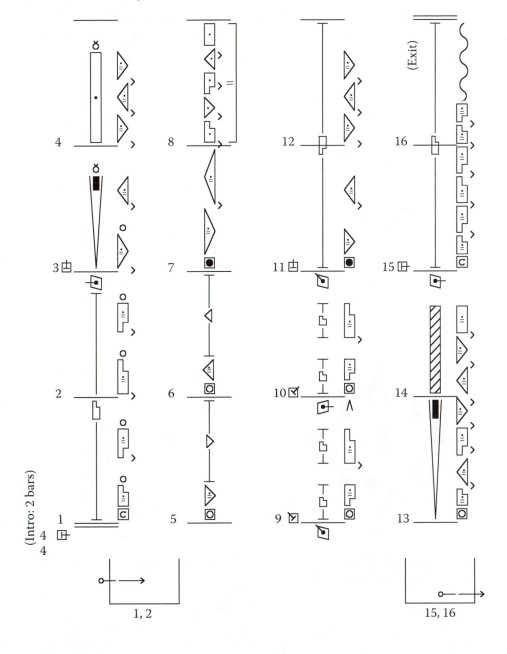

MINOR DISPLACEMENTS

A displacement in space, such as a shift of a part of the body, may be a significant action or may be very small, a minor movement. The main direction symbols indicate major displacements, substantial movement. A pin shows a minor displacement away from an established center, a very slight change. For parts of the torso and the head, the pins show minor displacement away from the normal situation. For extremities of the limbs, e.g., a hand, elbow, etc., the displacement is in relation to the distal center of that part, i.e., at its extremity.

For each of the main directions around the body, there is an equivalent pin to show a spatially comparable minor displacement. In the charts shown in 19.11a–19.11c, each pin is placed next to the main direction symbol to which it relates.

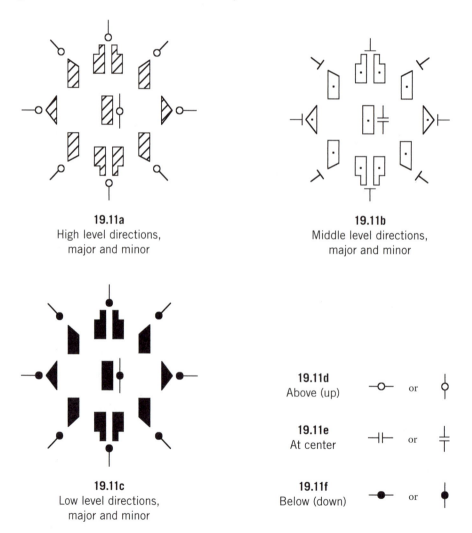

19.11a
High level directions,
major and minor

19.11b
Middle level directions,
major and minor

19.11c
Low level directions,
major and minor

19.11d
Above (up)

19.11e
At center

19.11f
Below (down)

The point of the pin indicates the direction; the head of the pin indicates the level. White pins indicate upward, high level minor displacements; straight pins (often called "tacks") represent middle level (horizontal) minor displacements, and black pins represent downward, low level minor displacements. For the vertical dimension—above, below, or at center—there is a choice in drawing the symbol vertically or horizontally as shown in 19.11d, 19.11e, and 19.11f. The choice depends on what is visually easier to read.

Minor directional changes, though small, may be very expressive. In 19.11g, the lower arm (experienced mainly at the hand, the extremity) moves upward, to slightly above where it was before. In 19.11h, the body (torso and head) moves forward, a slight displacement which may express a sympathetic motion toward someone, an interest in what is there, or conversely, a slight motion away from something behind, as might occur when a pillow is being placed behind your back when the back of a bench is too cold or hard.

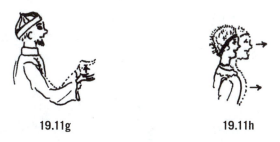

19.11g   19.11h

Minor displacements often come in pairs of opposites which repeat, possibly slowly, but often rapidly. Fluttering of the hands up and down, side-to-side, forward and backward are familiar examples, the direction of the flutter depends on the spatial placement of the arm. Such fluttering or vibrating can be of the whole arm, just the lower arm, or only the hand. Many parts of the body can vibrate, shimmer, or shiver; the pins describe how it is done.

MINOR DISPLACEMENTS OF PARTS OF THE TORSO AND HEAD

The point of reference for minor displacements of body areas—pelvis, chest, and head—is the normal centered situation, as place middle is for shifting. The head displaces forward and backward in 19.12a. Example 19.12b gives sideward displacements (shifts) for the chest.

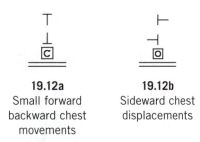

19.12a
Small forward backward chest movements

19.12b
Sideward chest displacements

In 19.12c the minor forward chest movement is followed by a return to center, its normal placement. The shoulders in 19.12d move backward and forward in opposition. In 19.12e, they move in unison.

19.12c
Return to center after small shift

19.12d
Shoulders in opposition

19.12e
Shoulders in unison

MINOR DISPLACEMENT OF LIMB EXTREMITIES

For minor displacements of extremities, the directions are judged from the cross of directions at the extremity, the distal center for the limb. Examples 19.13a–19.13d show such displacements for the hand: up and down in 19.13a; side to side in 19.13b; forward and back in 19.13c; and sideward displacement with the arm down in 19.13d. This last displacement was used repeatedly in Martha Graham's *Steps in the Street* to indicate agitation. Note that a return to the established starting point is indicated by the pin for center, 19.13e.

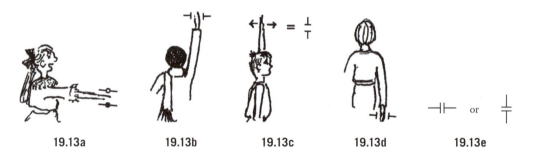

19.13a   **19.13b**   **19.13c**   **19.13d**   **19.13e**

For 19.13f–19.13j we assume that the arms are forward middle. Only a forward displacement occurs in 19.13j.

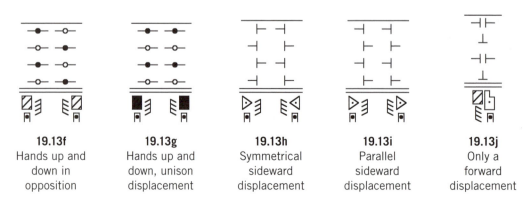

19.13f
Hands up and down in opposition

19.13g
Hands up and down, unison displacement

19.13h
Symmetrical sideward displacement

19.13i
Parallel sideward displacement

19.13j
Only a forward displacement

Repeated rapid minor displacements can be shown to continue through use of a wavy vertical line (the vibrato sign), 19.13k. In 19.13l the knees are shown to be shaking.

19.13k
Sign for
vibrato, tremolo

19.13l
Knees
shaking

READING EXAMPLES

Examples 19.14a–19.14e indicate use of these symbols in connection with some everyday gestures.

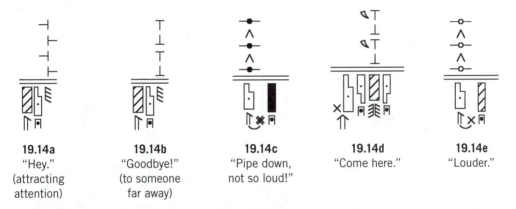

19.14a
"Hey."
(attracting
attention)

19.14b
"Goodbye!"
(to someone
far away)

19.14c
"Pipe down,
not so loud!"

19.14d
"Come here."

19.14e
"Louder."

Note that in 19.14c, 19.14d, and 19.14e two different actions are shown at the same time for the arm: the direction and the contraction. The arm symbol can be centered below both movements, as in 19.14f, or a small horizontal bow can be used to link the additional action to the arm symbol, as in 19.14g.

19.14f

19.14g

READING STUDY NO. 59

MINOR DISPLACEMENTS

For the swift transition needed before measure 7, the arms come in near the shoulders. Note use of the sign for "unemphasized" here, (and also at the start of measure 9) to show that this arm placement is not to be stressed.

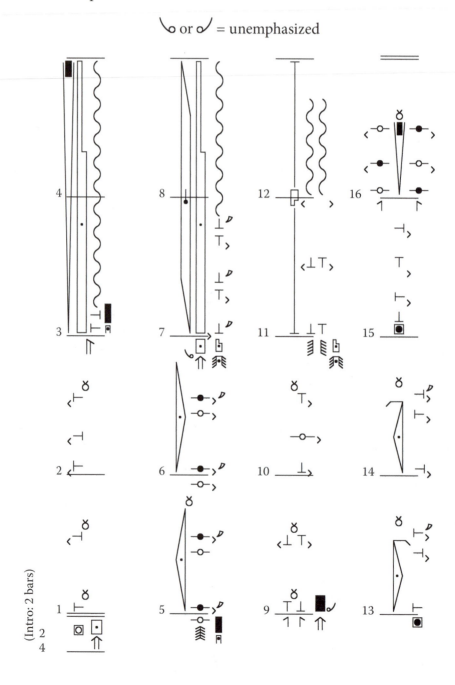

REVIEW FOR CHAPTER NINETEEN

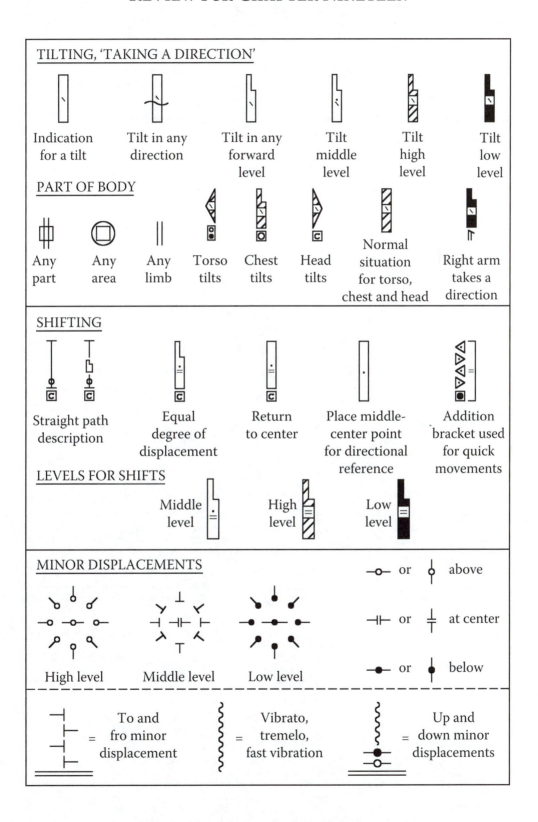

TILTING, 'TAKING A DIRECTION'

Indication for a tilt | Tilt in any direction | Tilt in any forward level | Tilt middle level | Tilt high level | Tilt low level

PART OF BODY

Any part | Any area | Any limb | Torso tilts | Chest tilts | Head tilts | Normal situation for torso, chest and head | Right arm takes a direction

SHIFTING

Straight path description | Equal degree of displacement | Return to center | Place middle-center point for directional reference | Addition bracket used for quick movements

LEVELS FOR SHIFTS

Middle level | High level | Low level

MINOR DISPLACEMENTS

High level | Middle level | Low level

—o— or ⌽ above

—⫟— or ⫟ at center

—●— or ● below

To and fro minor displacement

Vibrato, tremelo, fast vibration

Up and down minor displacements

CHAPTER TWENTY
Destination, Motion

Are the terms "destination" and "motion" familiar as used in relation to physical movement? Does an image come immediately to mind of a movement that is destinational in character? Can you envisage a movement, similar but significantly different, which expresses motion with no destination? These concepts, although touched upon in the course of movement analysis, are rarely investigated in depth.

Let us first give some basic definitions. Motion is the "going," the departure, the sudden desire to leave and go somewhere. Destination is the arrival. Before investigating the movement possibilities that come under the heading of "destination" and "motion," let us look at some everyday situations to see how these can shed light on our investigation.

Driving north is the motion, the process of going; arriving in Toronto, for example, is the destination. When you state "I'll drive to Toronto" the destination is known from the start. In driving north, your destination might be anywhere. You may ignore a logical destination and just keep going. The statement, "At 4 o'clock we will go to the park" is specific. A definite time is given and a definite destination. However the following statement: "After waiting an hour we will leave," is relative. "After waiting an hour" could be at any time (when does one start counting the hour?) and "leaving" is an action or a direction in relation to the starting point but provides no destination. These ideas can be transferred to the body moving in space. Specific movement statements employ actions which have clear destinations. But the relative descriptions of motion often capture the essence, the initiation or concept of the desired movement. The following discussions aim to take a fresh look at these movement possibilities.

Let us start with a child. The earliest movements it makes are pure motion; without conscious thought, the baby explores physically what its body can do. In discovering movements of its hands it is not yet thinking of holding a pen or grasping a golf club, for which certain positions are considered the most efficient. In extending its legs the baby does not have in mind the streamline position required for diving or an extended dance position such as an *arabesque*. For a baby only the body build, the clothing worn, or the surrounding crib limits the range of movement. However, movement soon begins to have an aim: the hand reaches out to grasp an object, the action of extending has a definite point at which it stops, a goal, hence a destination. Although this is an exterior destination, it is not a chosen spatial placement of the limbs that is so often the aim in dance. Depending on the culture, destinational placement of the limbs will gradually come as the child learns to sit cross-legged or to kneel in prayer, palms together, or to assume any of a number of other taught body positions.

Motion is often spontaneous, often unpremeditated, and hence unstructured. A ball comes rolling down the hill, you step aside to avoid it. Such avoidance is motion. Some of the early dance education concepts concentrated on motion. The Laban-based Modern Educational Dance provided movement explorations such as slashing, pressing, flicking, gliding, each of which is pure motion, set in no one choreographed form. Dance for laymen stresses the enjoyment of movement, not how it looks to the beholder. In contrast, theatrical dance must please the observer; hence the much greater emphasis on the creation of "pictures," arriving at a destination. This pictorial emphasis is true of Eastern as well as Western dance. Temple dances require very precise positions of the hands, head, torso, and feet. Classical ballet is full of movement, but even in jumps and traveling actions the limbs are intentionally placed—if only momentarily—to produce an attractive picture.

Conversely, intention is different when the orientation is motional. "Free Dance" often sought to be free from established poses; emphasis was often placed on the continuity of motion, with moments of stillness providing an "ending" that was significant more for capturing a particular quality or expression than for presenting any architecturally interesting form. Dynamic content made such Free-Dance pauses meaningful. The observer enjoys these moments of stillness, particularly when the form and design made by the body is aesthetically pleasing although the resultant shapes from the cessation of motion may not have been specifically planned. Several forms of African dance use motion rather than destination for arm and body gestures. The range of placement of the limbs and torso can vary considerably from one performer to the next, yet the basic impact and expression of the movement remain the same.

Consider an everyday example of motion and destination such as would occur in the following situation: in a classroom, students are already seated. The instruction is given: "Everyone get up and go to quite another part of the room and sit down." The first reaction is to rise (motion away from sitting); then there is often uncertainty and hence various degrees of "milling around" as each decides where to go. A few may wait to see where others go and, while looking for a vacant spot, may move somewhat aimlessly, as in 20.1a. Once a destination is clear, the decision made, the nature of the movement changes; direct paths to a destination result, 20.1b. This experiment illustrates both how people tend to move when they have no immediate aim, no picture of where they should end, and then the change in movement that occurs once a destination has been decided.

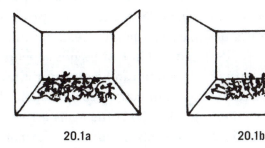

20.1a   20.1b

DESTINATION

Familiar everyday destinations also occur in dance. Before taking concrete examples, let us consider what lies behind destinational actions, what are some typical features, some prevalent attitudes.

AMBITION—PURPOSE—INTENTION—DETERMINATION—DECISION

Destination is premeditated. Before a movement is started the idea of the destination is set, a choice has been made. This decisiveness may show in the eyes of the performer, in the carriage of the head, and in other supporting actions. In dance, a destination may be a situation on stage (a chosen point to which to travel), or a destination for a gesture (a point of arrival to be reached in relation to the body, a clearly defined point in the kinesphere).

Starting positions are mainly destinational because they aim to produce a position. A starting position for a movement sequence is the result of movement, you have to move to achieve that position. Starting positions are usually described with directional statements or degrees of flexion or extension. The motion action of a spring is never indicated in a starting position, nor is a fall or a path sign or a turn. A "toward" or "away" statement does not appear in a starting position; as both are clearly indications of motion.

Of the list of verbs in the Movement Alphabet, which are destinational by nature?

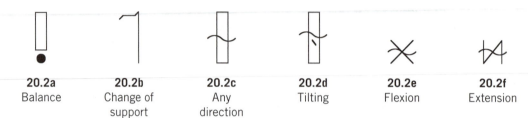

20.2a	20.2b	20.2c	20.2d	20.2e	20.2f
Balance	Change of support	Any direction	Tilting	Flexion	Extension

In our initial exploration of these movement possibilities, much leeway was allowed in interpreting them as motion or destination. Now we consider their basic function. Clearly balance is a destination, a point of equilibrium to be achieved. Transference of weight is also destinational in that it ends supporting on a different body part. Arrival at a specific direction can be seen in tilting or inclining as when the torso arrives at a destinational direction, 20.2g, 20.2h. The same is true of the limbs "taking a direction"; in 20.2i, 20.2j the arms arrive side high. After the freedom given to directional movements in our initial exploration, direction symbols for limbs and torso inherently refer to destinations, arrival at a destinational point. Later, we will present how they can be performed and written as motion. The same is true of the specific actions of flexion and extension which, to be achieved are destinational, but, as we will see, can be performed and written as motion. The exactness in degrees of flexion, which is clearly established in Labanotation, is not stressed in Motif Description. The fact that these indications produce destinations is controlled by the physical structure of the body; the torso and limbs are limited in the degree possible for flexion and extension.

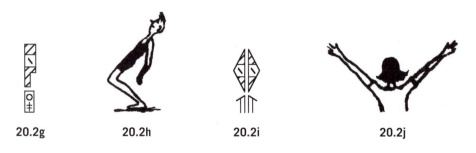

20.2g	20.2h	20.2i	20.2j

Example 20.2k shows the intended destination for an arm gesture; 20.2l illustrates the arrival. Intended destination and actual arrival are also illustrated in 20.2m and

20.2n. The manner of performance, a supporting focus of the head or a clear moment of pause will all contribute to the expression of a destinational gesture.

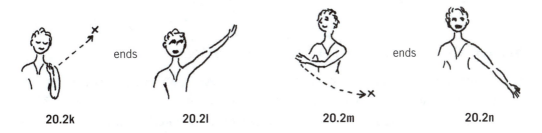

20.2k   **20.2l**   **20.2m**   **20.2n**

What factors contribute to destinational movement? Which are usually present because of the nature of this kind of movement? We will consider how time, space, dynamics, and flow of energy are used.

TIME IN RELATION TO DESTINATION

Whatever the speed of a movement to a destination, there is always at least a brief pause once the destination is reached, this pause having the visual effect of informing the observer that this is the intended point of arrival. Destinational movement embodies enjoyment of arrival. In many everyday situations one travels only to reach a destination; the journey is often not enjoyed, and the traveler can't wait to arrive at the desired place. In certain contexts a dancer has the same attitude and his/her movements reveal it. Whether the action is fast or slow, emphasis in phrasing is on arrival at a conclusion. Such arrival will usually fall on a strong beat in the music, frequently the strong beat immediately after a bar line.

20.3a   **20.3b**   **20.3c**

Any of the time patterns of 20.3a, 20.3b, or 20.3c, is suited to destinational movement, since each ends on the emphasized beat at the beginning of a new measure (bar). In 20.3a, the movement on count 4 leads to the conclusion on count 1. In 20.3b the movement phrase starts earlier, making use of counts 3 and 4 of the previous measure, but the conclusion is still on count 1. Example 20.3c starts even earlier by using count 2 of the previous measure, still concluding on the following count of 1. Ending on a strong beat helps to produce a positive, conclusive statement, an impact. How long the resulting position is held may vary; usually the more definite and final the position, the longer it is held.

SPACE IN RELATION TO DESTINATION

Movement with an aim is by nature direct—why deviate when you know what your goal is? If the path, the progression itself, is not important, why embellish it? The movement tends automatically to go directly to the intended destination. Gestures that move out from the center of the body on a straight, spoke-like path, as in 20.4a, have a final limit—the extension of the limb in that direction.

20.4a   20.4b

The path of a movement can be extended, the limb can be carried further in space by including a movement of the body, as in the torso inclination of 20.4b. The arm can appear to continue to move spatially if the extending gesture leads into traveling, as in 20.4c. It must be realized that movement of the arm itself has ceased, its physical destination has been reached; the limb is moving only in the sense that it is being transported, much as we move through the countryside when we sit still in a car.

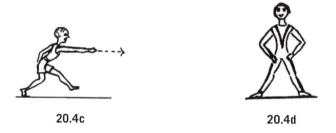

20.4c   20.4d

In many destinational movements, both performer and viewer may be quite unaware of the path of the movement which produced it, that movement may have been so quick or so vague that they are aware only of the final position reached. This position is usually very definite, architecturally clear-cut, as in 20.4d. Strong destinational statements make use of dimensional directions and those at 45° angles to them, as in the examples given in 20.4e, 20.4f, and 20.4g.

| 20.4e | 20.4f | 20.4g |

Taking the starting position of 20.4e, we are not surprised by the finishing position of 20.4f. It is a location for the arms that is familiar in most forms of dance and gymnastics. Therefore, we can register that point in space by a very brief pause before moving on to the destination of 20.4g—another well-established placement. But in the case of 20.4h the alignment is like an indistinctly pronounced word; should it have been as in 20.4f?

20.4h

Intermediate directions are used for aesthetic reasons and, through repeated use, become established as the "norm," the expected destinational points. Classical ballet uses many intermediate directions for the arms. Spatially they are not aligned with the major dimensional directions, but the extremities often relate to a particular part of the body, the level of the eyes, the breast bone, the hips, and so on, illustrated in 20.4i and 20.4j.

Design or "shape" poses, such as in 20.4k, occur in many Asian dances where the idea of display, of presenting stylized and often intricate pictures, is predominant. For some choreographers, picture making is their prime aim, both for the individual dancer as well as for group formations. Movement occurs in changing from one shape to another. Pilobolus Dance Company has explored this aspect of movement with astonishing results.

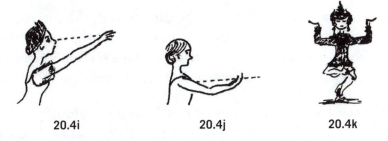

| 20.4i | 20.4j | 20.4k |

DYNAMICS IN RELATION TO DESTINATION

For a destinational action, a slight increase in energy at the moment of arrival serves as punctuation and gives emphasis to the termination. It has the effect of "sealing" the end of the movement. Strong, dramatic gestures such as 20.5a are of this type. Example 20.5b is the sign for strength.

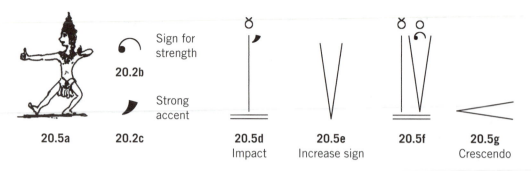

A strong accent, 20.5c, occurring at the end of an action, 20.5d, expresses a pattern ending with a sudden impact, a clear emphasis (or "sealing") for the ending. Such impact movements require a definite spatial point of arrival to be expressive, to establish a clear, strong message. Use of strength may gradually increase during the life of the movement up to its end. Note the sign for strength, 20.5b, combined with the increase sign, 20.5e, to produce the gradual increase of strength shown in 20.5f. The increase sign is derived from the music sign for crescendo, 20.5g.

FLOW IN RELATION TO DESTINATION

In his **Effort** analysis, Rudolf Laban distinguished between bound flow and free flow. He was the first to pinpoint awareness of, and provide indications for, these two important aspects of movement. The term "bound flow" includes guided, restrained, controlled movement, a movement that can be stopped at any point. Degrees of bound flow can be slight or marked; we will not be dealing here with degrees, just the general category.

In carrying a tray filled with water, the care needed, the control, means that bound flow is inevitable. Someone knocks into you and your arms, the tray, and the water go flying—free flow has taken over. Walking on thin ice or sitting down gingerly when muscles are sore are examples where bound flow occurs naturally.

An action may have a bound flow quality from the beginning, or the control may occur only toward the end. In the case of destinational movement an arrested ending often incurs bound flow. Example 20.6a is the sign for bound flow; 20.6b indicates free flow which will be fully discussed later. In 20.6c the action is shown to be controlled throughout; in 20.6d there is an increase in bound flow up to the end.

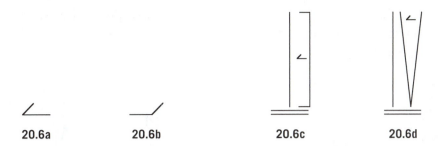

| 20.6a | 20.6b | 20.6c | 20.6d |

A sudden free-flow outburst may end at a clear destination if bound flow takes over. Slower movements to an intentionally clearer destination are likely to incorporate bound flow.

INDICATION OF DESTINATION

The general statement for destination, an action ending with an aim, is given in 20.7a; here the aim is represented by the ad lib. sign. In our first introduction to direction symbols for gestures, interpretation was allowed to be either motion or destination as long as the direction was clearly expressed. This is also true for flexion and extension; focus was on understanding the basic nature of each movement. With a more specific understanding of the possibilities for destination or motion, we need now to consider whether 20.7b, the indication for up, should mean upward motion from where the body or body part is, or whether it should mean arrival at the stated point of place high, the destinational statement. We will first focus on destination.

| 20.7a | 20.7b |

In the specific Structured Description used in Labanotation, all unmodified direction symbols for gestures indicate the point of arrival, i.e., destination. As we have seen, in Motif Description, tilting the torso, or "taking a direction" for a limb mean embodying the stated direction, that is, the body part or limb physically indicates that direction, as illustrated in Chapter 19, 19.1g, 19.1h, and 19.1i. However, awareness of direction as motion is different from the arrival of an extremity at a destinational point. To take a specific example, the illustration of 20.7c can be experienced as either the limb taking a direction, 20.7d, as though it is a cylinder, illustrated in 20.7e. In 20.7f, awareness is on that spatial point, the arm extremity (the hand) arriving at the point directly above the shoulder, i.e., reaching place high, as illustrated in 20.7g.

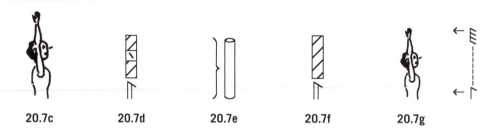

| 20.7c | 20.7d | 20.7e | 20.7f | 20.7g |

Destination for Traveling and Gestural Pathway

There are some actions that, although inherently motion, can be made destinational. We have already met these in previous chapters, but will review them here for clarification. Traveling is the motion of going from where you are along a path, distance may not be known, 20.8a. In 20.8b, the performer has just entered and X marks the spot to which he plans to proceed. In 20.8c, he has arrived at that location. The center stage destination was intended before he started. To indicate destination for traveling, the aim of the path is stated at the end of the traveling sign, as in 20.8d.

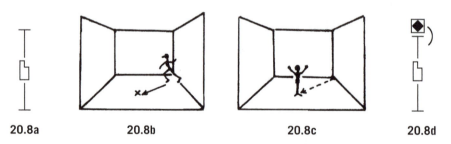

| 20.8a | 20.8b | 20.8c | 20.8d |

As previously met in Chapter 11 in the progression of relating, the destination can be a person as in 20.8e, or a prop, as indicated in 20.8f.

| 20.8e | 20.8f |

This idea of traveling through space with the whole body to a destination also transfers to parts of the body and gestural pathways. We met a gestural pathway for a limb ending in a destination in Chapter 14, Reading Study No. 45.

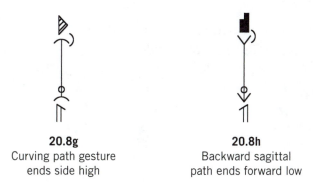

20.8g
Curving path gesture
ends side high

20.8h
Backward sagittal
path ends forward low

READING STUDY NO. 60

DESTINATION

This study uses various destinational actions, and includes a flower as a prop. Note the repeat of measures 9–12 to the other side.

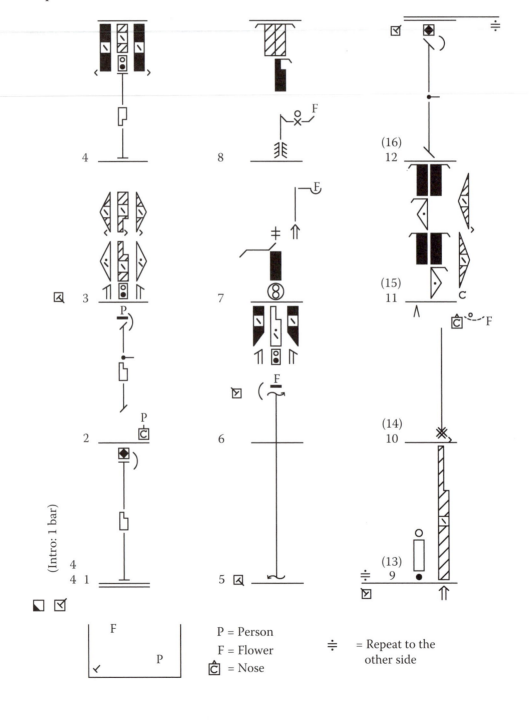

P = Person
F = Flower
Ⓒ = Nose

÷ = Repeat to the other side

MOTION

Dance is concerned with **moving**, with change, with passage from one situation to another. It is this passage which is the actual motion, movement "in flow," the "going" of movement. What are the attributes of motion?

EXPLORING—FREE TO GO—WANDERING—AIMLESS—
ENJOYING THE PASSAGE THROUGH SPACE—INDULGING IN
AWARENESS OF THE MOVEMENT ITSELF

These words evoke the image of the flight of birds, lifted by air currents, soaring, drifting, gliding, enjoying their passage through the air. Such motion cannot be captured in still drawings; hence no attempt at illustration is made here.

Motion as an aimless, indefinite activity may seem to be of a negative type. Motion can also be positive. In many parts of the world, society is goal-oriented; there is an expectation to plan ahead. In some cultures, particularly those affected by hot climates, the lifestyle is often easier, and the indigenous movement styles enjoy many flowing, ongoing patterns of movement. Impulsive flinging actions are seen in contemporary choreography as well as in bursts of energy in certain African cultures.

In exploring motion, we must relinquish the desire for a destination and be concerned with movement for its own sake, enjoying the process of the journey. Examples include enjoying a leisurely walk in a park with no plan of where to go, or milling about an antiques market. A good start is to wish only to move away, away from where you are. Where you go is not important; think only of a change. This "going away" may be just of the limbs moving in space, or of the whole body moving across the floor, going from place to place—exactly where is of no consequence. A dramatic version of such going away is the idea of being chased, which allows for much improvisation both in paths and in gestural actions expressing the reason for fleeing, perhaps fear, perhaps teasing the pursuer.

While sitting on the floor one might decide to change position; perhaps stiffness is setting in and there is a desire to move. A change is needed, but often no new shape or arrival point is in mind, just the desire to move. In a lecture, after a spell of sitting, students may be given a few moments to get up, to stretch, and move around. Stretching and any accompanying actions are usually pure motion performed and enjoyed for its own sake.

Motion may also be toward a destination but without an arrival. In the ballet *Lilac Garden* by Antony Tudor, Caroline, seeing her lover, makes a gesture toward him, but stops short as she knows she must not be seen. Her pause is an arresting of the movement toward her lover, not the establishment of a position, a placement of her limb. A spatial design is the last thing on her mind, and if it were, if she felt the angle of her upper arm, lower arm, and hand were important, it would ruin the dramatic effect of the suspended motion.

What forms of movement best express motion? Which of the list of verbs in the Movement Alphabet belong by their very nature in the category of motion? Consider actions such as turning, traveling, springing, falling, and movements toward and away; by nature, these are motions.

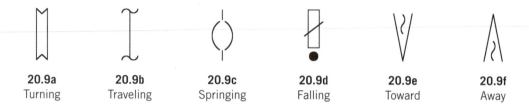

20.9a	**20.9b**	**20.9c**	**20.9d**	**20.9e**	**20.9f**
Turning	Traveling	Springing	Falling	Toward	Away

A turn can continue endlessly, a destination for a turn—where you end facing—is not part of the turn itself, the destination needs to be decided and indicated separately. In itself a turn can never be a position, though a body position can be held while turning. Turning actions of parts of the body, e.g., the head, have physical limits as to how far that part can rotate or twist. These constraints affect the range but do not change the basic nature of the turning action. Turning is always an action of change. As we have seen, the act of traveling is motion; a destination, the place of arrival has to be stated in order to define a destination. A springing, jumping action is pure motion limited only by the pull of gravity and arrival back on the floor. If gravity did not exist, one would continue to propel through space initiated by the push of the takeoff. During a spring, the limbs and torso may take a position, or establish another position on the landing, but this does not change the nature of the spring itself. The same is true of loss of balance, it is the floor or another support which provides the stopping point, a destination. The act of falling itself, as in parachuting, can go on for much longer, the end of falling is a destination forced upon you by gravity and the earth. The actions of toward and away, which relate to a position, person, or location, are innately that of motion.

Of course the motion of traveling may be terminated abruptly, by something suddenly in your way or the command "Stop!" You have stopped moving, it is the end of motion, but no sense of destination was present. A destination may be forced on you, as when you car breaks down or a person steps into your path. These stops are not your choice, they are not the aim of the movement; in this sense the stops are not destination.

TIME IN RELATION TO MOTION

Because motion usually lacks purpose in the sense of arriving at any spatial point, there is frequently an enjoyment of time; a tendency to use more time, to be slower. Though speed may be enjoyed in the passage through space, a sense of hurry, of urgency, is usually absent. Once movement is "set in motion," it has the tendency to keep going (the Law of Inertia). This is particularly true of flinging, throwing movements. When a stop occurs it often results from a petering out of the impetus that caused the movement; a new movement idea has not yet been formed. Or there may be the simple desire to stop moving, a cessation until a new motion is initiated. An abrupt stop may be the result of an outside influence or a change of idea, a stopping in one's tracks to surge off into another direction. Timing itself does not change the basic nature of motion; however, a slower pace allows more awareness and enjoyment of the "goingness." T'ai chi Ch'uan incorporates sustained enjoyment of limbs and body moving through space combined with a clear arrival at a destination.

A motion may begin with a slight impulse, the motion then proceeding on its way, 20.9g. For this reason it may start on the strong beat in the music. In 20.9h the action starts on the first beat after the bar line; in Western music this beat is traditionally stronger.

20.9g   20.9h

SPACE IN RELATION TO MOTION

Because motion is so often based on a positive aimlessness, the enjoyment of an energy flow which carries the body into space, motion has an affinity with indirect paths. When motion is enjoyed for its own sake (not as a by-product of another state) there is usually also an enjoyment of space. Movement is allowed to meander through kinespheric space as well as through the performing area. It is important that no destination be expressed. In place of direct, spoke-like movements for which an intent or aim usually exists from the start and for which there is spatially a physical limitation, motion is better served by arcs, curves, and circles. If an arm rises from its normal situation at the side of the body, 20.10a, how far will it rise?

Where will it stop? By use of continuous curves we may produce endless gestural movement, as in any circular pattern or figure eight design, 20.10b and 20.10c.

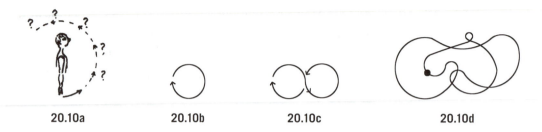

| 20.10a | 20.10b | 20.10c | 20.10d |

In such patterns, there is no obvious destination, no built-in ending point, no place where the movement HAS to stop. 20.10d shows a curving path which could be started anywhere and go on endlessly. It could be a three-dimensional gestural path traced in the air or could be a path walked across the floor. The indulgence in space, which such a space pattern suggests, is well suited to the type of movement which stems from the concept of motion. However, note that gestures in the category of motion can also be spatially direct, making use of straight paths.

DYNAMICS IN RELATION TO MOTION

As we have seen with the idea of being chased, motion can be replete with energy, or, as in T'ai chi, energy used may be almost minimal to produce gently flowing controlled movements. The specific energy pattern or dynamic which specifically fits motion (as opposed to destination) is that of **impulse** (in contrast to **impact** for destination). An initiation from a center of energy results in the movement flowing out, streaming out of the body. The energy in an impulsive movement may soon be dissipated. Example 20.11a shows an action which starts with a strong accent. In 20.11b, an action starts with strength, the strength gradually diminishing, as shown by the "going away" sign of 20.11c, which is related to the musical sign for diminuendo, 20.11d.

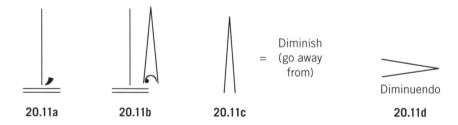

| 20.11a | 20.11b | 20.11c | 20.11d |

Pure motion, which occurs without pre-planning on the part of the mover, may result from an outside force, as when one is pushed or a previous support is no longer there, causing you to travel or fall. Pure motion is less familiar, less conscious than movement to a destination. In one way or another most movement training is goal-oriented. It would be good to give more illustrations of motion, but pictures are static and even when arrows showing motion are used, the end of the arrow suggests a destination. One must return to the image of the passage of a bird enjoying the freedom of the air, floating on the air currents, **before** it spots a morsel of food or decides to return home.

FLOW IN RELATION TO MOTION

The very nature of motion suggests free flow, the ongoingness of it, the lack of planning, of any aim, the movement of a free spirit, unfettered by required patterns and paths. Free-flow movement is unrestrained, unguided, once initiated it goes on its own way, uninhibited until it runs out of "steam," peters out, or meets with an obstacle which stops its path. A strong impulse can start a very free-flowing movement, or a modicum of guidance can come into the picture so that the movement follows a determined path. Certain natural affinities do not mean that other combinations cannot exist. A motion may be performed with bound flow, the enjoyment or need being to control the "goingness" of the movement.

As with bound flow, the sign for free flow can be added to a movement indication; an increase or decrease in the free flow can be shown by the appropriate signs. A consistent quality of free flow is shown in 20.12a; in 20.12b, the movement starts with free flow and then becomes increasingly bound. An increasing quality of free flow is shown for the action in 20.12c. The sudden free-flow outburst at the start of the action ends at a clear destination as a result of bound flow occurring at the end, as in 20.12d.

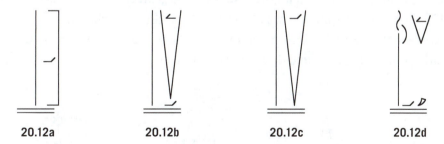

| 20.12a | 20.12b | 20.12c | 20.12d |

INDICATION OF MOTION

In addition to actions that are inherently motion: turning, traveling, falling, and springing, as already covered, motion can be of two kinds: motion toward or away from a directional point, a person/prop or a state, etc., or motion in terms of the

Direction of Progression. We will deal now, more specifically, with motion toward or away.

MOTION TOWARD OR AWAY

The idea of motion toward, i.e., approaching, was given in Chapter 11, Examples 11.8a, 11.8b, and 11.8c. Example 20.13a indicates approaching the place high directional point.

In 20.13b, this direction is being approached by the right arm. How far the movement will progress to that point is not stated; the intention of the dotted lines in the illustration of 20.13c is to suggest this openness. Much depends on the starting point; 20.13b might be interpreted as any of 20.13c or 20.13d. In any case, the arm does not arrive at the place high destination as in 20.7c. Motion toward a direction or person can be very expressive, as we saw in comparing 5.10j with 5.10h, in Chapter 5.

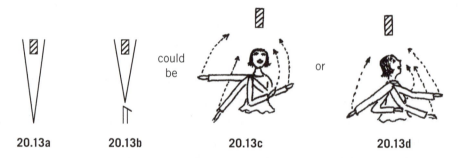

20.13a   20.13b   20.13c   20.13d

In a comparable manner, motion away can be shown, already introduced in Chapter 11, 11.8d–11.8g. Example 20.13e states moving away from the place high point. In 20.13f, the right arms moves away from that location; into what direction and how much is not stated. Possible interpretations are illustrated in 20.13g and 20.13h. But, with nothing specifically stated, there is freedom in choice.

20.13e   20.13f   20.13g   20.13h

MOTION FOR FLEXION AND EXTENSION

As already explained, in Labanotation the indications for flexion and extension are destinational and specific degrees are provided. Here we will continue with just the two main degrees as presented in Chapter 7. The contraction and elongation statements of 20.14a–20.14d could equally be expressed as actions arriving at those destinations, indicated in 20.14e–20.14h; there is no difference in performance. This could equally be true for folding, joining, and separating.

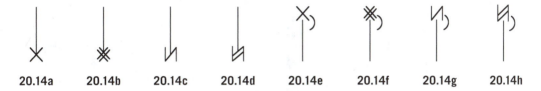

| 20.14a | 20.14b | 20.14c | 20.14d | 20.14e | 20.14f | 20.14g | 20.14h |

The motion of different forms of flexing or extending, the awareness of the process with no degree, no destination in mind, can be indicated as in 20.14i–20.14l.

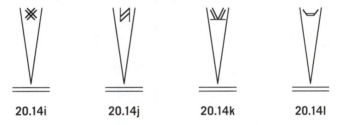

| 20.14i | 20.14j | 20.14k | 20.14l |

Moving away from a flexed or extended state is also possible, 20.14m and 20.14n. Here there is no statement of degree. What is not known from the indications is what state of flexion or extension existed prior to these motion instructions; the resulting movements could vary considerably.

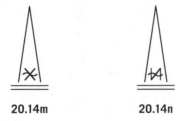

| 20.14m | 20.14n |

Such indications are intentionally indefinite, this is their particular value. We are not interested in the exact movement to be produced. Because of the lack of any clear visual result, i.e., destination, these motions are hard to illustrate with drawings. They need to be explored through movement, to be experienced. As mentioned, symbols for explicit degrees exist and are used in the Structured Description provided by Labanotation.

READING STUDY NO. 61

MOTION

This study features the various actions of motion. At no point is a destination of any kind achieved, thus there is a sense of constant change, of flux. Explore how aspects of space, dynamics, and flow create different interpretations of the study.

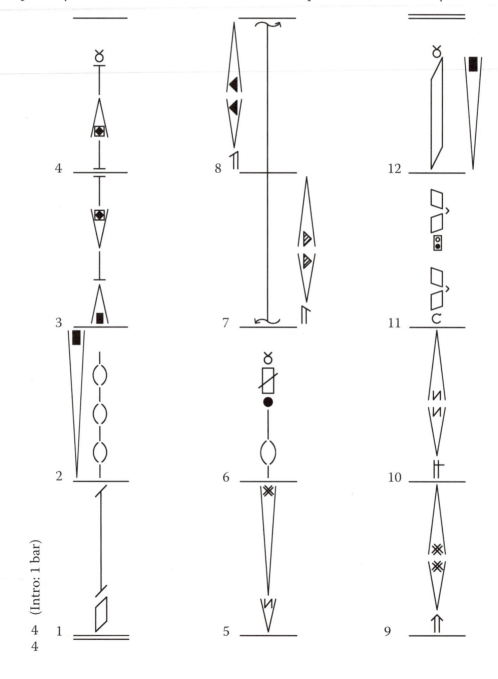

DESTINATION, MOTION COMBINED

This study explores motion toward a destination and arrival at a destination. Note that one arrives at a directional destination and achieves a slight or greater state of flexion or extension. Measures 11–16 show similar movement patterns expressed in terms of destination or motion. The large strong accent sign at the end of measure 16 refers to the whole movement.

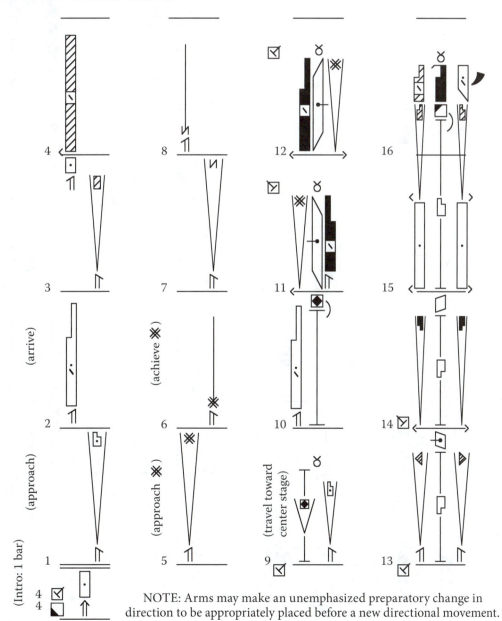

NOTE: Arms may make an unemphasized preparatory change in direction to be appropriately placed before a new directional movement.

READING STUDY No. 63

DESTINATION, MOTION VARIATIONS

This study explores different types of motion and destinational actions; note how the quality of the movement changes accordingly.

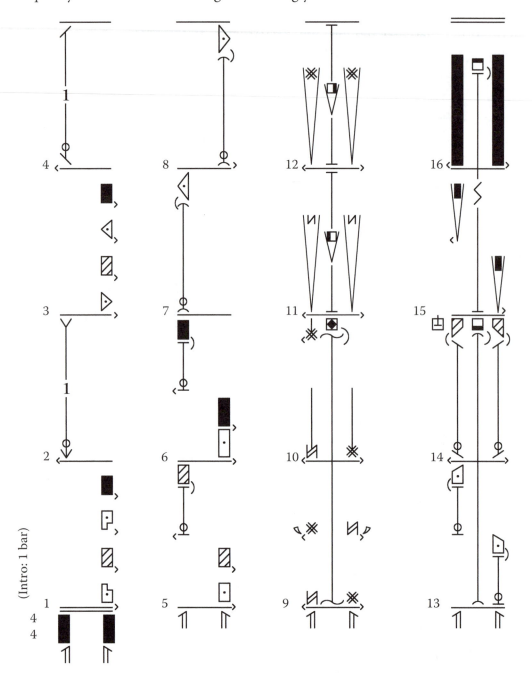

MANNER OF PERFORMANCE

In the field of sports, we see a different kind of goal for movement, the aim to achieve a particular result, usually that of getting a ball into or over a net. In many games it is not important how one kicks or hits the ball; only the result matters and one works to find an efficient way to produce that result. A tennis stroke, for example, is motion even though the aim is to hit the ball over the net. In other sports, swimming for instance, experience and tests have proved that training in specific movement patterns will produce the best results. Swimming may be motion in the sense of continuity, but the movements are channeled into precisely defined paths. In gymnastics and in skating, how the body is held is extremely important and hence it must be highly trained. In moments of stillness, correct positions i.e., physical destinations, need to be shown.

A change of quality takes place when destinational patterns are performed with motion in mind and vice versa. Such an inner feeling or desire affects the performance of material which is opposite in nature to that feeling. In classical ballet, *ports de bras* and *adage* sequences require sustained, flowing movement, but they are based on clear, established positions through which the limbs must pass or at which they must terminate. Too often, the image of destination (a necessary image during the early training stages) produces a stilted quality of movement. With a sense of motion in mind, the performer can observably change the manner of executing such established patterns. Conversely, movement patterns which should be flowing motion will be subtly changed if inner thought or feeling is concentrated on seeking a destination, for example, someone walking around looking for a partner at a ball but trying not to let that be obvious; a foot reaching down to find the next step when your arms are full and you can't see; or perhaps groping to find a light switch in the dark. Subtle changes occur which do not need to be "spelled out" or analyzed fully. Long before any deep study of dynamics (the ebb and flow of energy in the body) is undertaken, appropriate images can produce a desired change in movement quality. Focus again on the previous study with these ideas in mind.

MOTION: DIRECTION OF THE PROGRESSION

A specific motion concept is describing the path of a gesture **in relation to the point of departure**, the placement or situation of a limb **before** motion begins. In relation to the starting point, the part of the body progresses forward, sideward, upward, and so on. This description of movement is exactly comparable to that used for ordinary walking, i.e., progression across the floor. For each step, the direction is judged from the point where you are before the step begins. After the step is completed, a new point has been established from which the next step direction is judged. So it is when you describe the direction of progression for a gesture. The progression is judged from the extremity of the limb, the whole arm moves, but one is conscious of the path the hand takes. Where the hand is in space, its point of departure becomes a "satellite center" and direction and level are judged from that distal "center." Example 20.15a illustrates such a distal "center"; from that point, progression can be in any direction. Here the dimensional directions are shown. In 20.15b a motion sideward horizontal is followed by a vertical rising.

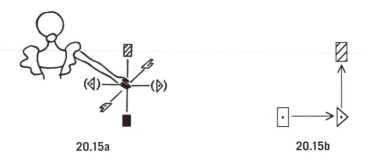

20.15a   20.15b

The reference for these directions is usually the Standard Key (see Chapter 21), i.e., directions related to the performer's front and to the line of gravity. Any motion which progresses parallel with the floor is in horizontal level; any motion that travels vertically up or down from the starting point is so described. When these key directions are kept in mind, motions forward, backward, side, etc., fall into place.

An arrow, 20.15c, is the general sign for the direction of progression. It is familiar from its use on floor plans to state "Progress from here to there." For practical reasons, the arrow placed within a direction sign **always points forward** (toward the top of the page) regardless of the direction of the movement; thus it is a concept represented by the symbol rather than a pictorial indication. When used within a main direction symbol, it indicates the direction of the progression stated by that symbol. Example 20.15d shows the basic key for the concept of the direction of progression. Example 20.15e states a progression up from the point of departure, 20.15f a progression down from the point of departure. In 20.15g the motion is forward horizontal. In 20.15h, the direction of progression is right side horizontal.

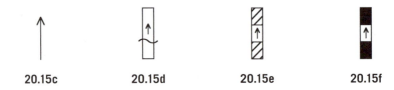

20.15c   20.15d   20.15e   20.15f

20.15g   20.15h   20.15i

An empty direction symbol with the arrow inside, 20.15i, gives no indication of level, this is left open to the performer's choice. For middle level the dot is usually placed above the arrow, 20.15g; for high and low level symbols, space must be left in the center of the symbol for the arrow, as illustrated in 20.15e and 20.15f.

Example 20.15j illustrates one setting for a progression vertically up; the arm as a whole rises but we are aware of the path of the extremity from its starting point. In 20.15k, the direction of the progression is forward horizontal from the starting position. In 20.15l, the movement is on a horizontal path to the left. Note that in performing such gestures the limb usually needs to flex and/or extend.

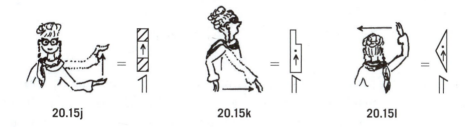

20.15j   20.15k   20.15l

As we know, traveling for the body-as-a-whole is shown with a path sign, as in 20.15m. Thus, it can be seen that a straight pathway and the direction of progression are, in fact, the same basic movement idea. A path sign could therefore be chosen to express the motion of such direction of progression gestures. Example 20.15n illustrates a sideward horizontal gesture for the right arm. In 20.15o this is written as a sideward direction of progression. This movement could also be thought of as a sideward horizontal path, 20.15p. Either is correct but 20.15o is often easier to read.

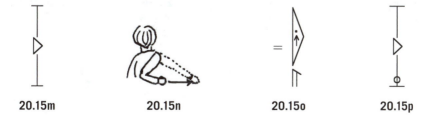

20.15m   20.15n   20.15o   20.15p

READING EXAMPLES

Examples 20.16a–20.16f show several pantomimic gestures for everyday actions which make use of direction of progression; palm facing is also indicated. The starting positions are all understood to be destinational positions. Note that a general cancellation is indicated by a very small "away" sign, stating that the previous result is no longer in effect.

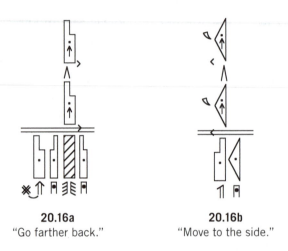

20.16a
"Go farther back."

20.16b
"Move to the side."

For the next examples a new sign, a diamond, needs to be introduced. This sign, 20.16c, indicates a spatial retention, it is generally called a "space hold." It states that the previous direction is to be maintained despite other related movement. In 20.16d, the palm remains facing up as the arm rises; in 20.16e and 20.16f, the palm continues to face down during the arm movement.

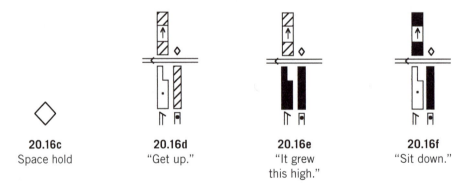

20.16c
Space hold

20.16d
"Get up."

20.16e
"It grew
this high."

20.16f
"Sit down."

READING PRACTICE U (NO MUSIC)

DIRECTION OF PROGRESSION

A Direction of Progression gesture indicates no distance; whether only a little space is covered or a great deal is left open to the performer. Indication of the limb being flexed or extended can provide some guidance, but exactness is not expected nor usually desired. Find a distance suitable for the context of each example. In F, all movements are direction of progression; in G the hand is holding a baton.

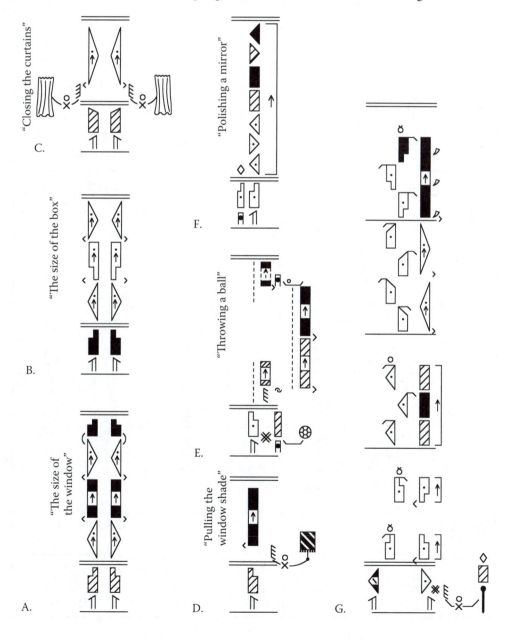

REVIEW FOR CHAPTER TWENTY

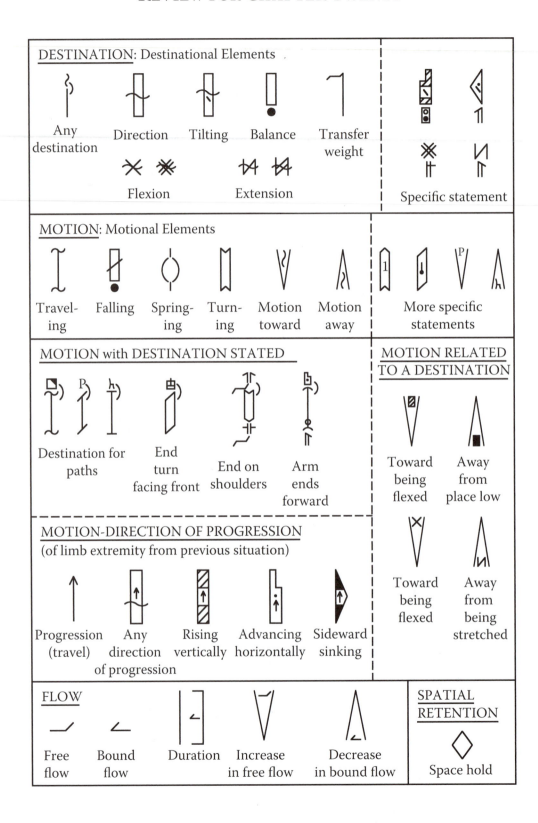

DESTINATION: Destinational Elements

Any destination | Direction | Tilting | Balance | Transfer weight

Flexion | Extension

Specific statement

MOTION: Motional Elements

Travel-ing | Falling | Spring-ing | Turn-ing | Motion toward | Motion away

More specific statements

MOTION with DESTINATION STATED

Destination for paths | End turn facing front | End on shoulders | Arm ends forward

MOTION RELATED TO A DESTINATION

Toward being flexed | Away from place low

Toward being flexed | Away from being stretched

MOTION-DIRECTION OF PROGRESSION
(of limb extremity from previous situation)

Progression (travel) | Any direction of progression | Rising vertically | Advancing horizontally | Sideward sinking

FLOW

Free flow | Bound flow | Duration | Increase in free flow | Decrease in bound flow

SPATIAL RETENTION

Space hold

CHAPTER TWENTY-ONE
Direction:
Systems of Reference

INTRODUCTION

When a directional action is requested, for example "Leg forward" or "Arm up," to what do the words "forward" and "up" refer? There is more than one possible interpretation. The following pages present the main systems of directional reference in daily use. It is interesting to note that most dance notation systems take directional reference from the body build; highly developed systems provide a choice.

In many movement activities, no matter what form, verbal instructions tend to switch from one system of reference to another without the speaker or listener being aware of a change. Within one exercise, reference might change from one system to another, a fact that often does not strike either teacher or student; such switching is common and occurs because it serves a purpose. There is nothing wrong in such change of reference, but one needs to realize it is taking place and that "forward" or "up" now refers to a different system of reference. Because the desired movement is usually demonstrated and a visual impression given, the spoken words have only a secondary value and often are not heard, let alone questioned. But terminology is vital for full, clear communication and so it is imperative that the precise meaning of such words be pinned down.

DIRECTION—THE STANDARD KEY: ✛

Our concept of direction is habitually affected by our image of the vertical, upright standing or sitting position. Up is toward the ceiling; it is also past our head. When we are standing, down is toward the floor; it is also toward our feet. Up and down, therefore, directly relate to the line of gravity. In Motif and Structured Description (Labanotation), the Standard Key is the most common reference used, it is the understood, the default key unless another is specified. Right and left directions are established by the right and left sides of the body when we are standing. Forward and backward are determined by where the front and back surfaces of the body are facing in the normal, untwisted standing position. We are aware of where our personal front is; thus the direction forward is easily determined. When a turn of the whole body takes place, the direction forward is carried with us. Since the pull of gravity is constant, up and down remain constant.

The key for the Standard System of Reference is based on the sign of 21.1a, representing the vertical line of gravity, and the sign for a cross of directions, 21.1b, together they produce the Standard Key of 21.1c. When looking at this sign as if from a bird's eye view, the black circle represents the missing third (vertical) dimension in the cross. Thus the Standard System has a constant gravity-based up and down.

21.1a
Vertical line
of gravity

21.1b
Cross of direction

21.1c
Standard Key

UPRIGHT SITUATION

Example 21.2a shows the right arm and right leg forward horizontal. Although in 21.2b the body has turned, this direction for the limbs remains the same in relation to the body. In 21.2c, the right arm and leg are right side middle, and no amount of turning will change this direction.

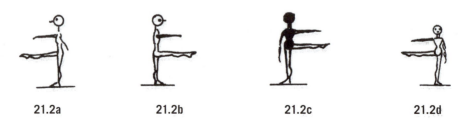

21.2a　　　　**21.2b**　　　　**21.2c**　　　　**21.2d**

This system of reference is called the **Standard Key** because it is the most commonly used. When the body is upright, there is no question about the location of the various directions. However, when the torso tilts off the vertical, the body's physical "up" and the line of gravity "up" are no longer the same. In the Standard Cross of Directions the line of gravity remains constant and it is the directions stated for the torso and limbs that are adjusted. These are illustrated in the diagrams, in the following section that show some typical examples of this spatial adjustment.

TORSO OFF THE VERTICAL

Examples 21.3a–21.3d illustrate a progression in lowering to the ground indicating how the direction forward horizontal is maintained despite the change in torso direction and change in support. For many types of movement there is a strong need to relate to the Standard Directions in such situations.

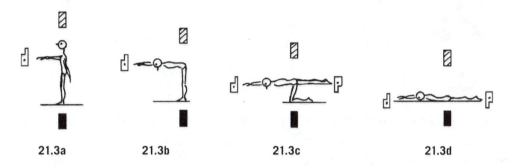

| 21.3a | 21.3b | 21.3c | 21.3d |

Examples 21.3e–21.3h follow the same progression but show the sideward horizontal direction.

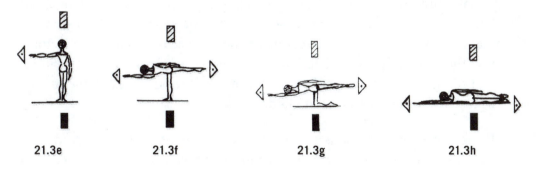

| 21.3e | 21.3f | 21.3g | 21.3h |

DIRECTION—THE STANDARD STANCE KEY: ◈

Many forms of dance include strong twisting actions in the torso with the result that the upper and lower parts have different fronts, a condition known as **"divided front."** In 21.4a, the chest has twisted to the right so that forward for the arms is into a different room direction from forward for the pelvis and legs. In this twisting action the front of the chest clearly establishes the forward direction for the arms. Such twists may occur to give greater spatial scope to arm gestures without any sense of abandoning the previously established forward direction. This established forward direction is called **Stance**, a term familiar from a golfer's stance, the front established before body twist occurs. In the illustration of 21.4b, it is the feet, knee, and pelvis that establish the Stance direction. There may be a considerable change in the shoulder line without a sense of a new forward direction having been established. As with the Standard Key, up and down still relate to gravity, it is the divided front from Stance or the previously established Front that makes this key useful.

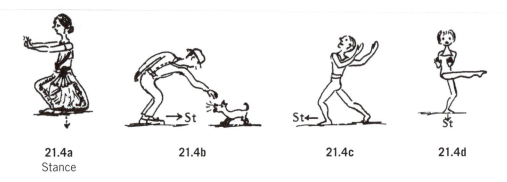

21.4a
Stance   **21.4b**   **21.4c**   **21.4d**

In 21.4b, a twist in the upper body has resulted from the inclusion of the body in the man's gesture reaching forward to touch the dog. Note the use of "St" in these illustrations to indicate the direction of Stance. Example 21.4c shows a chest twist in a stylized movement in which the arms are carried backward from Stance; Stance being retained by the feet. In the next example, the chest and one foot retain Front, establishing Stance, while the pelvis rotates taking the right leg with it, 21.4d. The direction of Stance can be maintained by either the upper or lower body while the other part twists into a new direction. The head is often an important factor in retaining the previously established Front; usually the eyes project into the Stance direction so that Stance is held at both extremities of the body, i.e., by the support and the focus of the head, such as in 21.4d.

The sign for Stance directions is a combination of the Key for the Standard Cross of Directions, 21.4e, combined with the sign for retention in space, 21.4f, producing the Stance Key of 21.4g.

21.4e   **21.4f**   **21.4g**
Standard   Retention in space   Stance Key
Cross of Directions

DEFINITION OF STANCE

Stance is the personal front, the forward direction established by the body-as-a-whole prior to a twisted state. When parts of the body twist away from that front, the part that does not twist (usually the feet or a foot) retains the original Front, the forward direction. In some dance forms, the lower part of the body twists away while the upper part retains the front direction of Stance. Example 21.5a illustrates the legs and hips twisting away while the chest, arms, and head retain Stance (in this case the direction facing the reader); 21.5b is a similar example.

21.5a   21.5b

Since direction for arm gestures is judged from the front of the chest (the shoulder line) and leg gestures from the front of the pelvis, we need the Stance Key to state that, despite twists in the torso, forward is to be taken from the direction of Stance.

Example 21.5c illustrates use of the Stance key. The general body twist to the left is accompanied by a general forward movement. Forward is understood to be toward stage right since this was the basic facing direction for the body-as-a-whole at the start. One possible interpretation is shown in 21.5d.

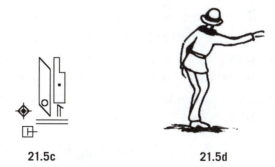

21.5c   21.5d

DIRECTION—THE BODY KEY:

The understanding of directions based on the build of the body is often the one most people easily relate to, though it is not always the one used. While people are aware of gravity, when the torso tilts away from the vertical, the direction "up" for the arm is still thought of as in line with the spine, i.e., "overhead." In the illustration of 21.6a, the left arm is up, the left leg is down, and the right arm and leg are both directed to right side middle. Although this figure subsequently rotates to varying degrees so that it appears to be lying on its side, upside down, etc., the configuration of the limbs in relation to the torso remains constant. In the Body Key, changes in placement of the limbs (inclining the head, tilting the chest, etc.), are all related to the line of the spine established at the base of the pelvis.

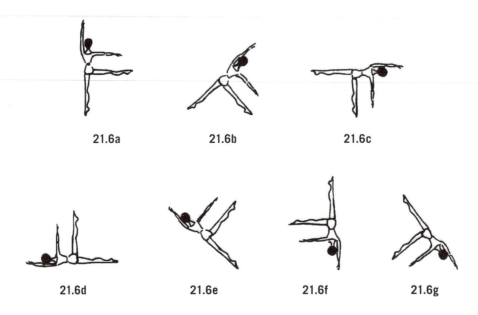

21.6a   21.6b   21.6c

21.6d   21.6e   21.6f   21.6g

A directional reference to the **Body Cross of Axes** is based on the body build; there is no concern with outside points of reference, neither with the pull of gravity (a constant "down") nor with a front established by a stage or classroom. In this key, up is toward the top of the spine and down is toward the base of the spine; forward is determined by the facing of the front of the body, a situation which astronauts experience when in the zero-gravity state. On earth we do not face this extreme since gravity is always with us; but there are many actions for which we find reference to directions according to the build of the body more convenient or more appropriate than reference to any other system.

The key for this system of reference is based on the idea of a circle representing aspects of the body, 21.6h, combined with a cross of directions, 21.6i, producing the Body Key, 21.6j. Example 21.6k is the notation for 21.6d.

When is this system used? In general, this key is most often used for the arms, head, and chest when the torso tilts away from the vertical. When one is lying down,

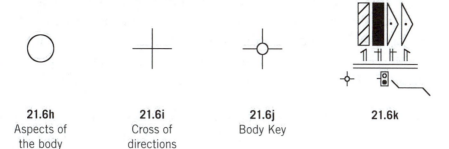

21.6h	**21.6i**	**21.6j**	**21.6k**
Aspects of the body	Cross of directions	Body Key	

or upside-down, the legs may also be described from this key. In some forms of dance, the direction of gestures is strongly related to the body; the resulting expressiveness is significantly different from the concept of relating to directions outside the body.

DIRECTION—THE CONSTANT KEY:

In any defined area, it is usual for one side (one wall) to be designated as "Front." On stage this Front is obviously the audience. Whatever the location, once the room Front is set, it remains the Constant Front and all Constant Directions relate to it. This Constant Front neither turns with the performer (as the Standard Directions do) nor does it tilt with the performer (as the Body-Based Directions do). The idea of the **Constant Key** was introduced in Chapter 15, in relation to the Front Signs. Here we are concerned with its use for movement.

The Constant Key can be likened to a compass carried by the performer in which the direction North remains North no matter how much the performer turns or moves around. Similarly, the **center of these Constant Directions lies in the performer** (not in the center of the stage) and travels with the performer. Though he/she may turn, as mentioned before, the Constant Directions do not; thus Constant Forward always remains the same spatial direction in the room. The established Front direction (the audience or other identified Front) is called Constant Forward. In this key, up and down are judged in relation to the line of gravity, that is, levels for gestures are as in the Standard Key, as are also levels for steps.

The sign for the Constant Cross of Directions is based on the sign for an area, 21.7a, combined with the cross representing a cross of directions, 21.7b, creating the Constant Key, 21.7c.

21.7a	**21.7b**	**21.7c**
An area	Cross of directions	Constant Key

Thus the Constant Key represents the directions in an area, usually a room or stage, but it could be any area in which one direction is designated as Front, the Constant Forward direction. This direction is not to be confused with the specific location of the center front **area** of the room or stage. Again, it is important to note that the Constant Directions are centered in each performer.

When and why do movements need to be described in terms of the Constant Directions? There are two main needs. The first relates to a group in which people are facing different directions and hence have different personal fronts. When these performers should all travel in the same room direction, describing this as a Constant Direction avoids having to state different directions for each performer. Similarly, when a comparable group should gesture on parallel lines into the same room direction, this key provides the best description.

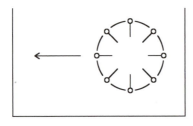

21.7d
A circle of dancers facing in
travels toward stage left

21.7e
Three people facing different
directions, all inclining into
the same Constant Direction

In 21.7d, the whole group travels Constant Left. The actual step direction is different for each person as judged from each individual front.

In 21.7e, three people facing different directions gesture into the same Constant Direction. Another example, 21.7f, shows three men pulling a rope into the same Constant Direction although each is facing a different direction in relation to the rope.

21.7f
Same Constant Direction for three men,
each facing a different direction

For Constant Direction descriptions, levels for steps and gestures are determined as with the Standard Key; all middle level gestures are horizontal, parallel with the floor, high level is slanting upward, low level is slanting downward.

The second need for a Constant Directional description arises when a single person performs gradual turning while traveling, as in 21.7g. The direction traveled remains constant even though the performer's relation to it changes. A similar need arises when a performer is gesturing undeviatingly into a Constant Direction while turning. In 21.7h, while turning to the left the performer's right arm moves steadily toward Constant Left ending in middle level. For such gestures a Standard or Body key description is not satisfactory in that neither directly describes the movement idea.

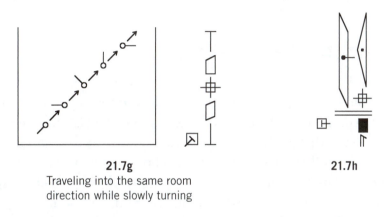

21.7g
Traveling into the same room
direction while slowly turning

21.7h

USE OF CONSTANT CROSS OF DIRECTIONS KEY

By placing the key for the Constant Cross before a direction symbol (using it like a pre-sign) we indicate how that particular direction is to be interpreted. In 21.8a, the instruction is to travel on the Constant Right Forward direction; this means that, no matter where the performers are facing, all will move on parallel paths into the same Constant Direction, as illustrated in 21.8b. Each performer will be stepping into a different direction judged from the personal front.

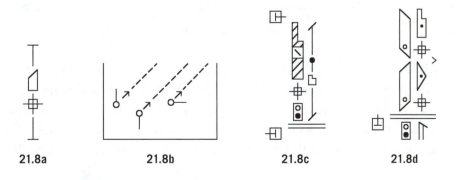

21.8a   **21.8b**   **21.8c**   **21.8d**

As an example of a gesture using a Constant Key description, 21.8c shows the torso tilting to Constant Forward while the performer travels on a half circular path. Physically the torso will start tilting to the performer's right, then progress through a forward tilt and end tilted to the left; but the movement intent is to have the torso tilting constantly toward the audience. The notation of 21.8c describes this intention simply and clearly. In 21.8d, two torso twists of no specified degree occur, first to the right, then to the left. During the first twist the right arm gestures toward Constant Side Right, then to Constant Forward as the twist to the left occurs. Because degree of twist is not stated and a clear directional result for the arm is desired, a Constant description is the most practical. In jazz dance where many twists in the body occur, because degree of twist may vary slightly among individual performers, spatial clarity and uniformity for the group will result from use of Constant Directions.

DETERMINING CHOICE OF KEY

How does one determine which system of reference to use at any particular time? Observation and experience indicate that **the decision is based on recognition of clearly defined directions**. On looking at the destination of a limb, the mind immediately latches onto what is visually clear and so chooses the description that is most strongly perceived. When there is no dictated choice of key; whatever visually "hits home" is chosen. The eye is impressed by directions which register as dimensional directions or into 45° intermediate directions according to Standard Key, Body Key, or Constant Key. Usually, the mind instinctively rejects descriptions which involve subtle intermediate directions. Let us take some examples. What descriptions would you give to the movement destinations for the right arm in 21.9a–21.9f?

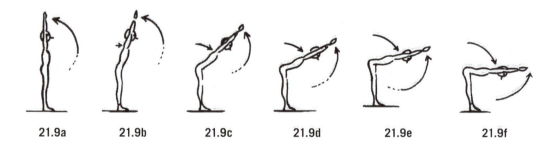

| 21.9a | 21.9b | 21.9c | 21.9d | 21.9e | 21.9f |

In 21.9a, the torso is vertical and the arm arrives up. There is no question about how to describe direction here; it is the same for Body Key and Standard Key. In 21.9b, the eye will see the torso slightly forward and the arm ending up from Body Key, the line of the spine, so this reference will come to mind. In 21.9c, the torso and arm are clearly forward high from Standard Key. But, in 21.9d and 21.9e, the

torso is at intermediate points; therefore the arm will be seen to end up from Body Key. If the torso is forward horizontal, as in 21.9f, the eye will likely revert again to judging the direction from Standard Key, though some people might be conscious of the body alignment and call the direction up from Body Key; either would be acceptable with the correct direction and level identified by each key.

Examples 21.9a through 21.9f illustrate that the eye looks for clear spatial lines and that perception switches between seeing directions in relation to the space around the body, or directions in relation to the body itself. In several cases the clear line existed only in the Body Key; thus Body reference for directions came first to mind.

| 21.9g | 21.9h | 21.9i | 21.9j | 21.9k | 21.9l |

Consider the series in 21.9g–21.9l. The right arm changes its relationship to the torso with each example. In 21.9g, like 21.9a, the arm ends up from both Body and Standard Keys. As the torso tilts, there is no clear simple body line for the arm until 21.9l. Even 21.9k, which could be written as arm ending side high in the Body Key, is unlikely to be so described. What hits the eye is the Standard Key vertical line; thus this key will probably be the choice for all these examples.

Examples 21.9m–21.9r, seen as from bird's-eye view, illustrate determining choice of description in the forward direction.

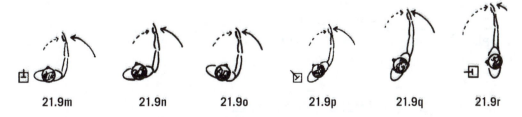

| 21.9m | 21.9n | 21.9o | 21.9p | 21.9q | 21.9r |

In 21.9m, the performer is facing Constant Front and the right arm ends forward from Standard Key, Body Key, and also from Constant Key. In 21.9n and 21.9o, the slight change of front for the chest to one side or the other, produces an intermediate arm direction which is awkward to describe in relation to the Standard or Body Keys

but from Constant Key is the clear-cut direction of forward middle. In 21.9p, the arm is diagonal from both Standard Key and Body Key, but forward from Constant Key. Therefore, this last may be the first choice, depending on the sense, i.e., the idea in the movement context. Forward from Constant Key is the clear direction for 21.9q. In 21.9r, the description is clearly the sideward direction from both the Standard and Body Keys. There would need to be a particular reason for preferring to call this destination forward from Constant Key, i.e., Constant Forward.

The examples given above have purposely been put into a series to illustrate the point. A far better test is to meet isolated examples with no related previous reference. It is important to become familiar with the four main keys and to be able to refer to them as needed. The Standard Key is the one that is commonly preferred when circumstances do not demand another description and hence another key. Consistent use of one system of reference facilitates quick giving and receiving of information; but if this system is not serviceable, then it is better to switch to another, using the key as an adjective as in "Body" up, "Constant" forward, and so on. In the classroom, physical demonstration of a desired direction makes such adjectives superfluous. The eye sees, but no mental note is made as to what reference is being used and how this reference can affect the idea or intention of the movement. Improved movement education must include full awareness of how space is being used and perceived and for what purpose. How directions are determined and named should be part of every performer's knowledge.

PLACEMENT OF KEYS

The appropriate key for a system of reference may be applied in six ways:

1. used as a pre-sign before a direction symbol
2. placed next to a direction symbol
3. placed in an addition bracket
4. placed next to the starting position
5. placed at the left of the staff during a score
6. pre-score Key Signature statement

As a Pre-Sign to a Direction Symbol

The key may be placed immediately before the direction symbol it modifies, as illustrated in 21.10a: on count 1 the right arm is "overhead" in line with the spine; on count 2 there is a return to the Standard Key.

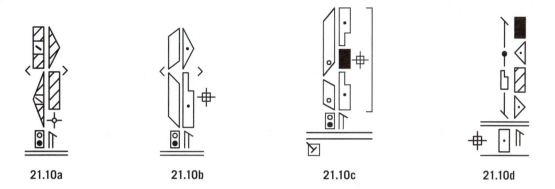

| 21.10a | 21.10b | 21.10c | 21.10d |

Next to a Direction Symbol

Related to the example above, but written in a different way, the key may be placed next to the direction symbol it modifies, as in 21.10b below. After the Constant forward gesture, the arm moves to Standard side middle.

In a Vertical Bracket

When a key refers briefly to two or more movement indications, the key is placed alongside the symbols in a vertical angular addition bracket, as in 21.10c. Movement after the bracket will return to the previous key.

In a Starting Position

A key, other than the default Standard Key, is written at the left of the starting position, 21.10d. It is in effect until another key is indicated. In 21.10d, the right arm gestures to Constant right and left while circling.

At the Left of the Staff during a Score

A change of key, placed outside the staff on the left, will apply to all directional indications as in 21.10e until it is cancelled by another key, as in 21.10f.

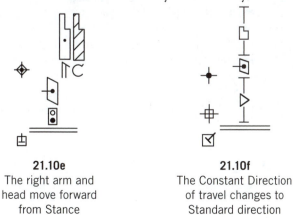

21.10e
The right arm and
head move forward
from Stance

21.10f
The Constant Direction
of travel changes to
Standard direction

Pre-Score Statement

Just as in music, for which a key signature stated at the start of a music score is to be in effect until a change is indicated, so in a movement score a particular Key Signature can be stated before the starting position in a movement score. The Pre-score Key is written before the starting position and is separated from it.

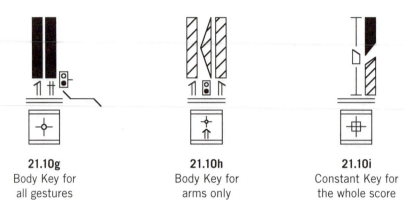

21.10g	21.10h	21.10i
Body Key for all gestures	Body Key for arms only	Constant Key for the whole score

In 21.10g, the Body system of reference is indicated for the piece that follows. Example 21.10h states that the Body Key will refer only to the arms. Example 21.10i shows the Constant Key established for the whole score. Remember that **when nothing is stated the Standard Key is automatically understood.** A key is cancelled by an indication of a change to another key. In Reading Study No. 64, the Body Key is cancelled in measure 5, but is again in effect for the arms in measure 6. The chart in this section lists constants and variables for each of the keys.

NAME	KEY	SPATIAL UP & DOWN	FRONT	BODY UP & DOWN
Constant Key		Constant line of gravity	Constant established Front	Same as Spatial Up & Down
Standard Key		Constant line of gravity	Changes as performer turns	Same as Spatial Up & Down
Stance Key		Constant line of gravity	Established front retained despite divided front	Same as Spatial Up & Down
Body Key		Changes when performer is off the vertical	Changes as performer turns	Tilts with performer, hence bodily constant

Reading Practice V (no music)

BODY, STANDARD, AND STANCE KEYS

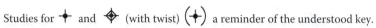

Studies for ✛ and ◈ (with twist) (✛) a reminder of the understood key.

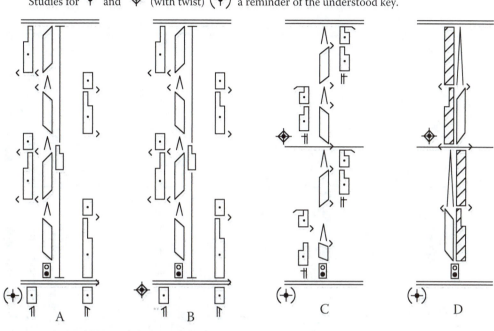

Studies for ✛ and ✛ (with tilt)
Perform each with understood standard key ✛, then in body keys ✛.

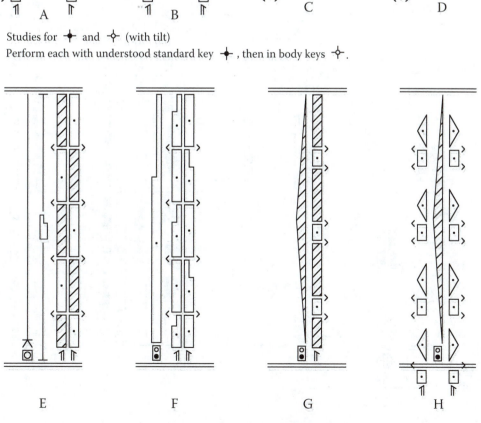

READING STUDY NO. 64

SYSTEMS OF REFERENCE

Note the change of key given to the left of the staff.

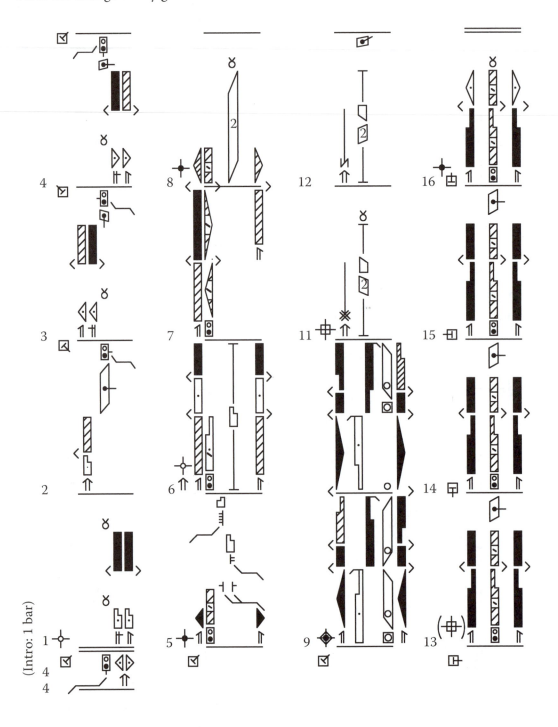

Review for Chapter Twenty-One

__SYSTEMS OF REFERENCE__

Symbol	Location	Travels	Front	Vertical line
Constant cross	Centered in performer	Travels with performer	Constant established Front does not turn	Constant line of gravity
Standard cross (understood key)	Centered in performer	Travels with performer	Turns with performer	Constant line of gravity
Stance key	Centered in performer	Travels with performer	Previous untwisted front retained for steps, gestures	Constant line of gravity
Body cross	Centered in performer	Travels with performer	Turns with performer	Tilts with performer

Note: Torso directions must always relate to ✛.

__THE SIX WAYS KEYS ARE USED:__

Pre-staff statement for whole piece

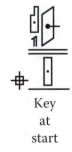

Key at start

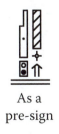

As a pre-sign

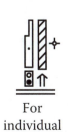

For individual symbol

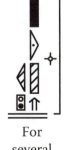

For several symbols

Change of key

Timing; Phrasing; Dynamics—Recapitulation

TIMING

Timing is a major element in how it affects the performance of a movement sequence. In dance training it is a rarity to explore subtle changes in timing in a movement pattern. While focus in this book has not been on specific timing, certain movements require some extension in time to be satisfactorily accomplished; examples of this are meandering and spiral paths. However, specific timing has been incorporated into some of the Reading Studies, particularly those where stepping or landing from a spring needs to be on a specific beat in the accompanying music. Such structured musical timing will now be investigated here.

A Basic Beat and Its Subdivisions

In Chapter 1 we looked at the organization of beats into measures enclosed between bar lines; producing 2/4, 3/4, and 4/4 meters. Now we will consider the beat itself and its subdivisions. A beat in music is usually easily felt and identified. How in movement do we use the subdivisions of a beat? Example 22.1a illustrates two beats, one following the other, as would occur in a 2/4 meter in music. The first beat is called "1," the second "2." In 22.1a an action occurs on each beat, taking the full duration of each beat. Dividing the beat in half is shown in 22.1b. Each count retains its own number, while the half beat is called "and," often shown as "&." As can be seen from the notation, these duple subdivisions are even in timing. Example 22.1c shows a step-hop pattern using this timing, the take-off step leading into the air on 1 and the hop landing on the "&" of count 1. A series of such step-hops is typical of American Indian dances, an earth-bound, plodding pattern.

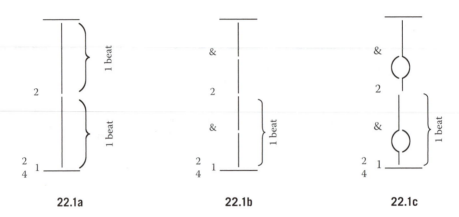

22.1a   22.1b   22.1c

Each basic beat can be subdivided into three—a triple subdivision, thus producing triplets, 22.1d. Such subdivision does not make use of the "&" (the halfway mark), and therefore a special verbal indication has been established for the subdivisions. The appropriate sounds are "1-a-da 2-a-da." It should be noted that these are not the identifications generally used by dance teachers and choreographers. The habitual terminology is to use the "&" word even though it is not the equal (half) subdivision of the beat that is being used. Clear, logical use of terms allows a verbal reinforcement of the rhythmic patterns, so useful in conveying timing facts when teaching movement. In 22.1e a triplet skip is shown, the step being on count 1, up in the air on the "a" and landing on the "da." This same division of time occurs in a fast waltz where, of course, the counting can be "1-a-da 2-a-da 3-a-da 4," and so on.

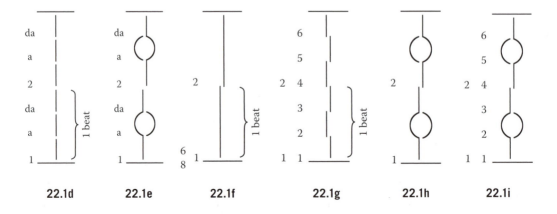

22.1d   22.1e   22.1f   22.1g   22.1h   22.1i

This same time division occurs in a fast 6/8 meter, illustrated in 22.1f–22.1i. Here there are basically two beats in the measure (bar), but each is subdivided into three, the 1/8 note value being used. Example 22.1f shows the two main beats in a 6/8 measure, these being counted "1-2." Giving each of the subdivision beats a number, as in 22.1g, can be helpful, count 4 marking the beginning of the second half. In 22.1h a skip in 6/8 meter is shown, the main counts being given. In 22.1i the subdivisions are counted. The quality of such 6/8 skips is obviously very different from that of 22.1c; the full subdivision count in the air produces a lighter, more airborne skip. These are called "ternary skips."

Next, the subdivision of a beat into four parts is presented. Each count receives its proper number and the halfway mark will again be called "&." The other two subdivisions are called "y," pronounced as the "y" in "any," and "u," as said in "up." What is important here is that subdivisions of different values are not given the same name. Example 22.1j illustrates the subdivisions into four with their names. The stepping pattern, shown in 22.1k, visually indicates one slower step followed by a much quicker one which occurs on the "u" subdivision. Such a quick step is sometimes called a "catch step" and used to return at the last minute (so to speak) to the same foot again. In 22.1l a skip is shown using this timing. The take-off step is longer and the time in the air is short, providing a more earth-bound skip.

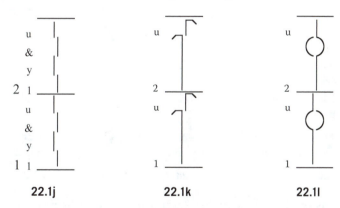

22.1j   22.1k   22.1l

The binary rhythm is typical of a child skipping down the road; it is also often used in folk dances. A ternary skip, such as in 22.1h, allows time for a gesture of the free leg in the air, whereas the timing of 22.1l is often used more for traveling, covering ground.

TIMING BETWEEN ACTIONS

Timing between actions can affect the flow of the movement sequence. It is one thing to read and execute a series of movements; it is another to produce a sequence which has cohesion, kinetic logic, and expression. When one movement follows another, are they related? Is there a link or is the second action a separate "thought," in no way a development of what went before? Timing can give some indication; a definite break in the movement flow usually means a new start, a new idea. Let us investigate a simple movement sequence to discover the possibilities.

As explained in Chapter 1, action indications which follow one another without a break represent continuous movement. Example 22.2a shows three such actions; the visual gap, the break between the action strokes is just enough to make clear that there are three separate symbols rather than just one action. In 22.2b, three general directional actions are shown in the same timing. The break between actions in 22.2c can be more clearly seen. In the directional sequence of 22.2d, the performance will require a brief establishment of the arrival at each direction before continuing to the next. This brief "showing" of the arrival is familiar and usually comfortable, indeed, performers often have difficulty in making 22.2b a truly continuous legato movement from one direction to the next. In 22.2e, pausing at the arrival point is more marked, as indicated by the larger gap, i.e., more time before moving to the next action. As this space increases, the movement becomes more separated. In 22.2f only the first half of each beat is used, in the second half (the "and" count) there is absence of movement. Distinctly staccato actions are illustrated in 22.2g.

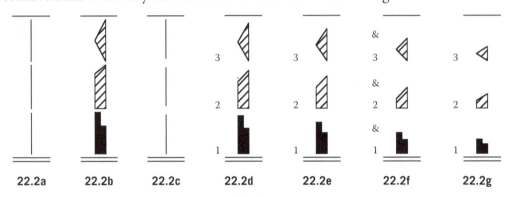

| 22.2a | 22.2b | 22.2c | 22.2d | 22.2e | 22.2f | 22.2g |

What happens during the gaps in 22.2f and 22.2g? Absence of symbols means absence of movement, no change. Should it be a static retaining of the point of arrival, or could it be an active stillness? To be registered clearly, stillness needs a little time. If the music is slow enough, there could be expressive stillnesses for 22.2g, as indicated in 22.2h. A static holding of each arrival could also occur, 22.2i. This "holding" energy pattern is familiar from "making statues," in that statues have to hold still, whereas stillness requires inner motion in the sense of extending the energy, the "vibrating sound" of the movement lingering on. A better movement example featuring stillness is 22.2j, here the swifter movement to forward low becomes slower as it moves to diagonal high and ends in stillness.

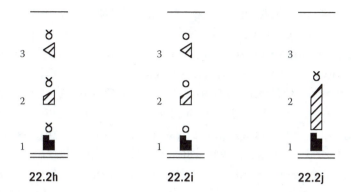

PHRASING OF MOVEMENT SEQUENCES

In 22.3a turning is followed by a circular path in the same direction; moving into the circular path flows easily out of the turning action, an example which was explored at the end of Chapter 3. As we saw, this simple sequence can be interpreted as the turning action around one's center enlarging spatially into becoming a circular path. In contrast, turning to the right in 22.3b is followed by a circular path to the left. This requires a "braking" action at the end of the turn (probably in use of the foot and the center of weight) to prepare to circle into the other direction. The choice of step direction for the circling in 22.3b can change the dynamic and probably the form of the "braking" action. For example, the backward steps in 22.3c will require a different transition and hence produce a different effect.

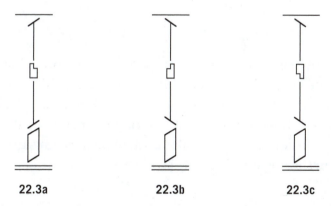

Experiment with a straight path following a turning action, sense the difference between use of forward, sideward, or backward steps for the straight path.

MAJOR OR MINOR MOVEMENTS

What is the value, the sense, the intent of a particular movement? The duration used or placement of the movement in the sequence can affect how it is "handled."

Take first a simple example involving a turn. In 22.4a, before the step forward on count 1, there is a quick 1/4 turn to face right front. What is the function of this turn? It usually has no importance, it serves merely to produce the new Front for the step which follows; it is the step which is important. At the end of count 3 a similar quick turn occurs for the same purpose. Compare this with 22.4b. Here the turn is on count 1 and is slower, in addition, it is followed by a stillness. This turn should be performed with importance, the physical action of turning is the focus to be enjoyed. On count 3 there is a forward step which, in this placement in the measure, suggests it is unimportant, and serves as a preparation for the turn which follows. If this step were on the "&" count its lack of importance would be increased.

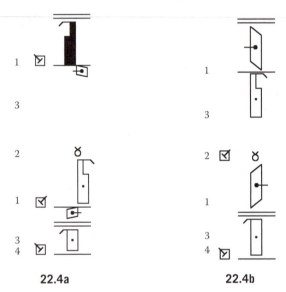

22.4a   22.4b

The above can be embellished by arm and/or torso gestures, but, by themselves, these simple statements give us much information concerning manner of performance. Of course a change to a sharp, dynamic use of energy for the quick turn in 22.4a can give it importance, and a lowering of energy for the slower turn in 22.4b can make it of less importance. But without such playing around with level of energy, the plain statement provides its own message.

KINETIC LOGIC

As mentioned before, each kind of movement has its own kinetic logic. There must be a line of development for a movement phrase to have such logic. The germ, the seed of, or feeling for, the next movement must already be there within the body by the end of the previous action. This germinating of a new idea is a small dynamic change which takes place usually in the center of the body, the torso. We do not want to spell out how to achieve this development; it takes place within—organically. It is sensed by the performer and may not be evident to an observer. In the early stages of being physically aware, it is best for these functional minor dynamic changes to be obvious, to be performed visibly; subtlety can come later.

Example 22.5a is composed of material similar to 22.3a, 22.3b, and 22.3c. Traveling forward is followed by a slow turning and then the sideward traveling that ends with a quick 1/4 turn, allows the sequence to be repeated from the same facing direction. The movement is continuous. In 22.5b, gaps between the actions show enough of a pause to break the thread of the "movement thought." Each action has its own start, each is a new "idea." Each must overcome the moment of inertia which preceded it. Such a kinetic pattern, three separate thoughts, may be just what is wanted. It is important that the timing differences be clear in movement as well as in the notation, which is merely the expression of the movement ideas on paper.

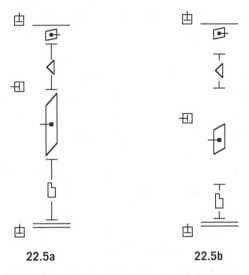

22.5a   22.5b

What do we mean by "one movement thought related to or growing out of the previous one"? Let us take a verbal sentence to draw a parallel. "I enjoy writing poetry as a gift for your birthday." This statement carries the message that the pleasure of writing the poetry springs from the fact that it is to be a gift. This thought progression is missing in the following: "I enjoy writing poetry. I plan to give you a gift for your birthday." Movement has a comparable logic in its progression from one movement event to another. One cannot easily put into words just how or why one action grows out of another. The physical kinetic sense needs to be developed. The resulting performance will be subtly different for each person. Herein lies the delight in dance—the individual interpretation of the same material.

Complete separation, isolation of movement ideas can be intentional in a movement composition; this is particularly true of contemporary choreography. Just as modern music, poetry, and prose may juxtapose unusual, unexpected sounds and words to achieve a particular effect, so contemporary choreography often juxta-poses unusual, non sequitur movements for a similar reason. In any study, it is wise to master the traditional forms, to progress from the physically more familiar to the unknown. First discover fully the simple forms, the usual, logical transitions and make them your own, then embark on being adventurous and find links, kinetic reasons when dealing with unrelated material. Take the challenge!

SIMPLE MOVEMENT PHRASING

Phrases may be of different lengths; in music they often encompass several measures. Within a long phrase there may be sub-phrases. Such usage can be related to punctua-tion in speech. In Language of Dance®, we follow the usage in music in understand-ing what is meant by "a phrase": "A short section of a work into which the music seems naturally to fall. In dance and folk music it is frequently four measures. A performer's phrasing is often instinctive, a feature by which a supreme artist can be distinguished."[*] However, in our first investigation here, we start with a two-part movement "figure" (the term used in music) to explore how in a very simple way the emphasis, the meaning of the movement can be changed. In music, phrasing marks are long horizontal bows encompassing a series of notes. In Motif Notation similar bows are used, but placed vertically, linking the symbols to which they relate.

In 22.6a, the right arm moves up and lowers in even timing, without any pause. There is no break in the movement, there is no emphasis to mark one direction as more significant or expressive than another. A phrasing bow has been added in 22.6b indicating a linking in the relationship of the first two movements; this "up-down" pattern is then repeated. In 22.6c, the different placement of the phrasing bow pro-duces a "down-up" pattern. Instinctively the performer will change the quality to express this difference. It may be a slight change in energy, or in timing, or in both. Such variation can be spelled out in detailed notation, but this would pin it down to a specific performance, an interpretation which may not be desirable. The artistry of the performer is revealed through how such variations in phrasing are handled.

Examples 22.6d, 22.6e, and 22.6f continue this exploration but with a different space pattern.

In 22.6d, a three-dimensional pattern covering four directions is shown as one phrase. It is broken up in 22.5e into two shorter phrases. In 22.6f, the phrasing indication starts after passing through the forward middle point; this division produces a very different effect. Each of these possibilities needs to be physically

---

[*] *The New Oxford Companion to Music*; Oxford University Press, 1984.

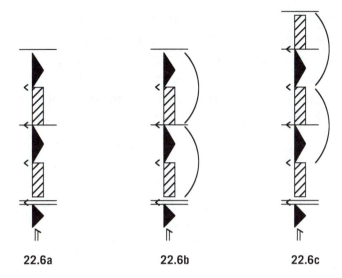

22.6a   22.6b   22.6c

explored until a kinetically meaningful result emerges. It can be helpful to hum to oneself while trying each variation. Such inner sounds may not be heard but they help support the movement. From famous performers, we learn that they often hum their personal movement rhythm (in contrast to the accompanying music) and also talk to themselves (inaudibly) describing what they are in the process of doing, e.g., "Now, lengthen more, a bit more, now prepare to bend down," and so on.

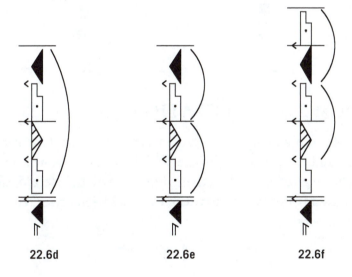

22.6d   22.6e   22.6f

WITH MINOR MOVEMENTS

The timing of minor movements, indicated by minor direction pins, is often made more understandable through the addition of a phrasing bow. Between each pin, a gap provides visual clarity; this gap is not intended to have time significance.

In 22.7a the right index finger starts pointing down. Three small clockwise circles are performed, starting with a sideward right displacement. With the pins evenly placed and nothing stated, an even, almost "monotone" performance will result. The addition of phrasing, 22.7b, makes the sequence more interesting. From the displacement to the right, the first phrase encompasses the backward, sideward, and forward displacements which follow. Next, another three-pin phrase takes place from side right, over back to side left. The last, longer phrase starts and ends forward. Subtle changes in manner of performance apply also to larger movements.

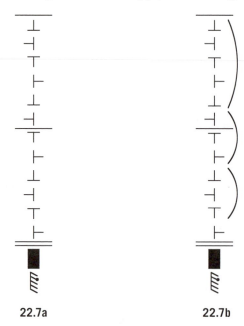

22.7a   22.7b

DYNAMICS: RECAPITULATION

In the course of this book, aspects of dynamics in movement have been introduced, both the ideas and the signs. In the chart of these signs, shown on page 521, the various aspects are given a number; these numbers will be referred to as we explore again the various possibilities. A survey of what has been presented in the previous chapters is given here.

ACCENTS

Accents are a well-known feature of music. They are equally applicable to movement. A quick movement can be performed without an accent, 22.8a, with a slight accent, a slight increase in energy, 22.8b, or with a strong accent, a greater increase in energy, 22.8c. Accents are always brief—after occurring, their energy disappears. With a movement of longer duration, an accent can occur at the start, 22.8d, in the middle, 22.8e, or at the end, 22.8f. The energy used for the accent is short lived, it is dissipated immediately, except in the case of an accent at the end, the impact, where the energy may be held. A movement of sufficient duration may have more than one accent, as in 22.8g, here four accents take place in the course of the gesture.

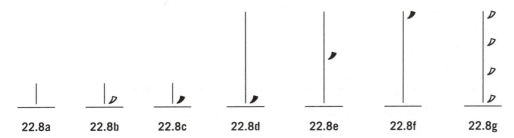

In the Dynamics Chart at the end of this chapter, the first items listed are the accents—a slight accent, or a strong accent. To produce an accent there must be a rise in the energy level of the movement, above what is normally used for that action. An accent is always quick, but a rise in energy level can be sustained, sustained increasing to that level, or sustained in maintaining that level.

ENERGY LEVEL—THE CONCEPT OF "PAR"

Despite noticeable differences between people and how they naturally move, a certain "normal," a "standard" level of energy for each person can be experienced by the mover and discerned by others. It is the average, the neutral level when nothing has occurred to lower that level or to heighten it. The need to run, perhaps for a bus, raises the energy level; your muscles need strength for the sprint. The relief when the bus is caught and you sink into your seat, expressing "Whew!" is manifest by a drop in energy level, a relaxing of the body's muscles below par. Just the effort of standing requires energy, but this is so usual, so normal, we do not even think about it. This level of energy needed for ordinary activities is called "par." As explained in Chapter 4, par is represented by an imaginary horizontal line, 22.9a; a rise in energy is shown by an upward curving bow, 22.9b; a drop in the normal energy level is shown by a downward curving bow, 22.9c. At par level is shown by the sign of 22.9d. Degree of such increase or decrease is shown by addition of a white circle for a slight amount, 22.9e, by a black circle for a greater amount, 22.9f. These degrees are just general indications, no precise system of measurement has been found necessary.

Par					
22.9a Line of "Par"	**22.9b** Rise in energy	**22.9c** Drop in energy	**22.9d** Sign for par	**22.9e** Slight amount	**22.9f** Greater amount

INDICATION OF FORCE

Force deals with the amount of muscular engagement involved.

The following numbers refer to those on the Dynamics Chart.

No. 1. A slight accent
No. 2. A strong accent
No. 3. A slight rise in energy, alert, gentle (22.10a)
No. 4. A greater increase in energy, strong, forceful (22.10b)
No. 5. A slight drop in energy, relaxed, drooping (22.10c)
No. 6. A greater drop in energy, flop, collapse (22.10d)

| 22.10a | 22.10b | 22.10c | 22.10d |

EMPHASIZED, UNEMPHASIZED

An accent in movement is a form of emphasis, however, emphasis may be of greater duration. In speaking, words to be emphasized are often spoken more loudly, there may also be a modification of timing, usually a slowing down. In movement, as investigated in Chapter 7, such rise in energy and subtle change in timing also occur. There may also be a slight spatial modification. There is no set pattern, it is up to the individual and depends very much on the type of movement involved. The reverse is a de-emphasis of a movement, the usual energy level is dropped or minimized so that the action is less noticeable. It may be intentional that the observer does not notice a particular gesture; a good example is a return to normal or standard carriage for a part of the body when another action is featured. After a significant bending of the upper body, the return to upright is often unnoticeable, in contrast to a clear, active, return to the vertical situation. It is the minimizing or lack of the usual energy level which produces such unemphasized movement. Indication of emphasis in movement will vary between individuals, it is not the aim at this point to spell out exact details of performance, rather to provide the means of indicating such addition of emphasis as well as intentionally unemphasized actions.

The sign for a slight emphasis, 22.11a, is related to the sign for a slight rise in energy, 22.11b. The white circle is given a "tail" which points in toward the symbol to which it refers. The sign for a marked emphasis, 22.11c, the one more commonly used, has the black circle, and is related to the sign for strong, 22.11d. Similarly, unemphasized, 22.11e, is related to the sign for weak, relaxed, 22.11f, the circle end of the sign pointing in toward the symbol to be so modified. The possibility for very unemphasized, 22.11g, is related to that indicating limp, complete lack of energy, 22.11h. This degree is seldom needed.

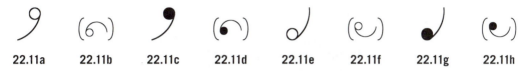

| 22.11a | 22.11b | 22.11c | 22.11d | 22.11e | 22.11f | 22.11g | 22.11h |

No. 7. Slight emphasis (22.11a)
No. 8. Marked emphasis (22.11c)
No. 9. Unemphasized (22.11e)
No. 10. Much unemphasized (22.11g)

RELATIONSHIP TO GRAVITY

An imaginary vertical line, representing the vertical line of gravity, is at the center of the curved bows that state a rise or fall in energy, 22.12a. Placement of the white and black circles on this center vertical line indicates relationship to gravity. Thus a rise in energy or a drop in energy is shown to relate specifically to gravity.

| 22.12a | 22.12b | 22.12c | 22.12d | 22.12e |
| Line of gravity | Resisting gravity | Fighting gravity | Giving in to gravity | Using Gravity |

No. 11. Uplift, resistance to gravity (22.12b)
No. 12. Strong uplift, fighting gravity (22.12c)
No. 13. Weighty, giving in to gravity thus sensing the weight of the limbs (22.12d)
No. 14. Heavy, using gravity's pull to feel and express heaviness in the body, torso (22.12e)

ELEMENT OF FLOW—BOUND OR FREE

Flow is the manner in which a movement progresses, either it is controlled, guided, restrained, contained, indicated by the symbol of 22.14a, or the movement energy is allowed to expel freely, in an outpouring and unfettered way, as it moves through space, 22.14b. In Chapter 20 we looked at how free and bound flow relate to motion and destination. The signs used here are the same as those in Laban's Effort graph.

22.13a	**22.13b**
Bound flow	Free flow

In the Dynamics Chart these are:

No. 31. Controlled, guided, using restraint (22.13a)
No. 32. Free flowing, uninhibited (22.13b)

PHYSICAL EXERTION; EMOTIONAL INTENSITY

As explored in previous chapters, a rise or lowering of energy may occur for practical reasons, perhaps the muscles are engaged to achieve a particular result, the
hauling of a rope (physical force), the lifting of one's weight in fighting, resisting
gravity. Or the reverse may occur, the letting go of muscular tension in a swaying
action or the relaxation needed to mimic underwater plants. To indicate duration, a
vertical bracket is used, 22.14a. In dance performance, expressive movements may
require intensity (or lack of it), resulting from a dramatic situation; for this energy is
expended in expressing feeling. What causes a rise or a drop in feeling, emotion may
vary considerably; the notation does not state the cause, only the existence of such
strong or weak emotion. A curved vertical bracket, 22.14b, is used to specify that the
dynamic indication inside refers to feeling, emotion. As explained in Chapter 18,
this curved bracket was derived from the symbol for a heart.

22.14a	**22.14b**

Examples 22.14c–22.14j compare physical and emotional counterparts. The
numbers refer to those on the chart.

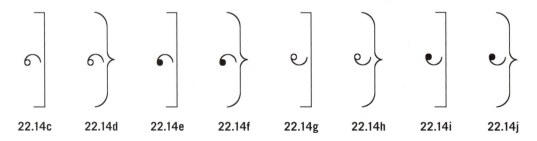

| **22.14c** | **22.14d** | **22.14e** | **22.14f** | **22.14g** | **22.14h** | **22.14i** | **22.14j** |

No. 15. Rise in physical energy, alive, alert, physically ready (22.14c)

No. 16. Rise in emotional feeling, awareness, sensitivity (22.14d)

No. 17. Physically strong, a powerful stance or gesture (22.14e)

No. 18. Emotional intensity, strong feelings (positive or negative) (22.14f)

No. 19. A drop in physical energy, weak, relaxed (22.14g)

No. 20. A drop in emotional feeling, indifferent (22.14h)

No. 21. Lack of energy, as in flopping, fainting (22.14i)

No. 22. Without feeling, moving as an automaton, as if in a daze (22.14j)

The next sets are concerned with relationship to gravity, the physical use in contrast to the emotional.

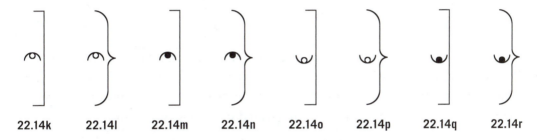

22.14k   22.14l   22.14m   22.14n   22.14o   22.14p   22.14q   22.14r

No. 23. Uplift, lifting the body away from gravity (22.14k)

No. 24. Feeling hopeful, able to cope, on top of things (22.14l)

No. 25. Buoyant, strongly resisting gravity, energy for big jumps (22.14m)

No. 26. High spirits, exhilarated, bounding joy, able to take on the world (22.14n)

No. 27. Using gravity to feel the weight of the limbs, as in a swing (22.14o)

No. 28. Dejected, sad, dispirited, losing heart (22.14p)

No. 29. Increased giving into gravity, heavy, lowering the body weight (22.14q)

No. 30. Despairing, giving up the fight, totally hopeless (22.14r)

TIMING OF DYNAMIC INDICATIONS

Any dynamic marking can be placed at the point in an action when that quality occurs. This could be at the beginning, in the middle, or at the end, as illustrated in Examples 22.15a, 22.15b, and 22.15c, these being a repeat of those given in Chapter 4.

22.15a   22.15b   22.15c

Duration of Dynamic Indications

How long a dynamic quality is maintained is shown by the length of the angular or curved vertical bracket in which it is placed. Within this bracket the stated dynamic will be constant. In 22.16a and 22.16b a brief duration is shown; in 22.16c and 22.16d it is maintained for a longer time.

| 22.16a | 22.16b | 22.16c | 22.16d |

The length of the increase or decrease sign indicates how long the stated quality should grow or diminish, i.e., become established or fade away. Example 22.16e shows a short duration; in 22.16f it is longer. These indications apply to both physical and emotional aspects, the latter illustrated in 22.16g and 22.16h.

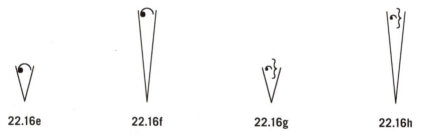

| 22.16e | 22.16f | 22.16g | 22.16h |

Cancellation

When no dynamic indication is given, the performance is expected to be at the level of par appropriate for that particular kind of action. Cancellation of a dynamic indication occurs when another dynamic aspect is indicated, as in 22.17a. After a statement in a vertical bracket, 22.17b, a return to neutral, to par is understood when another movement happens. Use can be made of the par symbol to indicate a return to that state; in 22.17c, a return to par is shown to occur quickly. The return to par is of a longer duration in 22.17d.

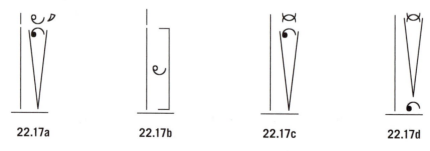

| 22.17a | 22.17b | 22.17c | 22.17d |

REVIEW FOR CHAPTER TWENTY-TWO

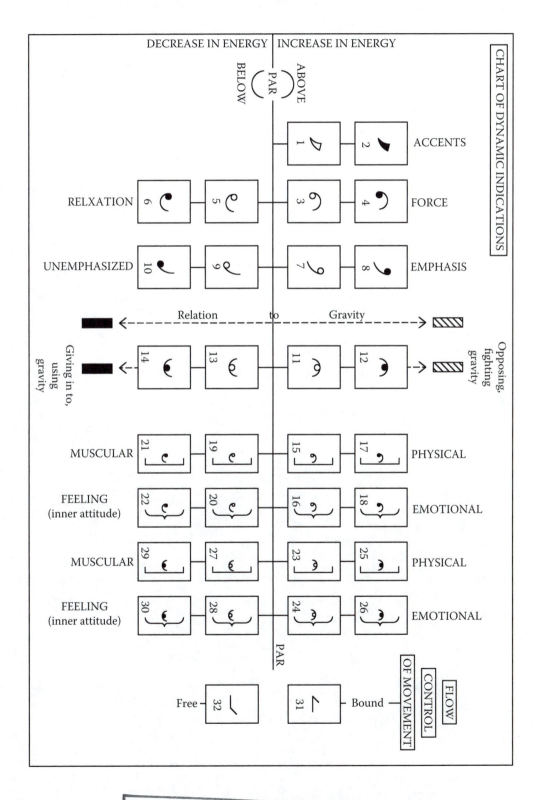

Conclusion

It is not enough to see movement; one must know how to understand it, what to look for when observing and what to aim for when moving. One needs to know what are the component parts of movement and be able to recognize and be aware of which of these are being used or are particularly featured in any composite movement. Separation of the material of movement into its elements means recognizing those elements and naming them through use of a practical, universal terminology.

During the process of exploring and experiencing movement in the course of this book we have progressed from the most general concept and indication of a movement to a range of specific uses. No single type of movement study, no one style of dance has been favored; examples presented have been as general and open to individual interpretation as possible. This book leads comfortably into specific forms of movement study aimed at mastering physical and expressive techniques.

The Movement Family Tree of Verbs, on pages 561–562, illustrates in an organized form the raw material with which we have been dealing. Our main focus has been on the actions themselves; thus it is the "verbs" we have explored. "Nouns" are the parts of the body, parts of the room, a partner, and any objects (props) in use. "Adverbs," which are the "how" in movement performance, include certain specific uses of time, of dynamics, of minor spatial variations, and of the manner in which parts of the body initiate a movement. Some of these have been included in this book.

As has been evident from the material investigated in these chapters, many of our movement concerns are focused on the aim or outcome of a movement. Thus we have needed to state directly the result of an action when this result is of greater importance than the movement that caused it.

The mechanics of movement may be analyzed in many ways—the sequence of muscle action, the degree of the angles produced by limb segments, at the joints, and so on. The specific need dictates the form that the investigation (the analysis) will take. For the student mastering movement as an expression of the human condition or in order to gain specific movement skills, a balance between an objective analysis of movement structure and a comprehension of the content or intent of the movement is essential. It is hoped that for those who are new to movement studies, the explanations and progressions in this book will have provided a basis on which to build and for those with previous movement training, a new insight into movement itself.

APPENDIX A
Validity; Organization of the Notation

Motif Description has very few rules. The main rule that needs to be known at once is that of validity, i.e., how long the result of a previous movement indication is to be in effect.

VALIDITY; CANCELLATION RULE

Motif Description is concerned with movement; a full awareness of and involvement in a specified action. Because concentration is on each new movement in a sequence, importance is placed on the new material to be expressed, however, the result of the previous movement may or may not be retained, the choice is open. If cancellation is specifically required, it must be stated through use of the "away" cancellation sign. If retention is desired, the hold sign must be indicated, and subsequently cancelled.

RETENTION OF A STATE

If a state, such as a twist, an extension, a flexion, or a relationship is to be retained, continued, maintained, this is indicated by placing the sign for retention, A1a, immediately after the movement indication. The result of this movement will then be retained until a cancellation sign appears. For a retained relationship, a release sign, A1b, is placed above the bow or active part. To cancel any other state, use the "go away" sign, A1c, placed vertically above the indication it is to cancel. This sign has the general meaning of "give up," "forget about it," "let it disappear." The timing of this cancellation can be fast, as in A1d, or slow, as in A1e. The length of the sign indicates duration, the time it takes for cancellation to be achieved.

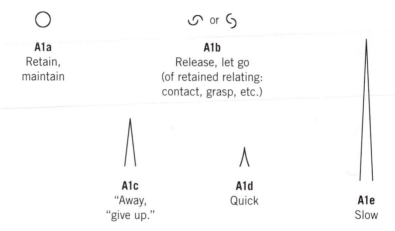

A1a
Retain,
maintain

A1b
Release, let go
(of retained relating:
contact, grasp, etc.)

A1c
"Away,
"give up."

A1d
Quick

A1e
Slow

VALIDITY WITH ACCOMPANYING MOVEMENTS

In A2a, a twist accompanies the start of traveling backward. As no retention sign is indicated, the performer may choose whether to retain the twist or let it go away while traveling. In A2b, the twist to the right is specifically indicated to be retained while the performer is traveling backward, but it is cancelled by the "away" cancellation sign when sinking starts. The twist, which starts at the beginning of traveling backward, is immediately cancelled in A2c. Retained states are also automatically cancelled by indication of the opposite kind of movement. In A2d, the twist, which is held during the traveling, is cancelled by the twist in the opposite direction with the downward action.

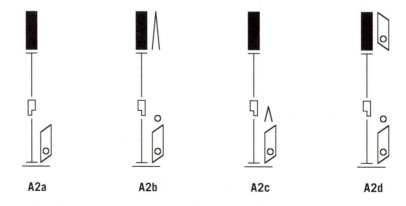

A2a　　　　**A2b**　　　　**A2c**　　　　**A2d**

PLACEMENT OF INFORMATION

Motif Description usually involves comparatively few indications. However, as we have seen, when two or more movement ideas occur at the same time, a clear organization of the material facilitates reading. To avoid ambiguity, certain basic guidelines need to be followed. One indication, the main activity, is centered on the staff. Example A3a indicates one action, a turn. When more than one piece of movement information needs to be stated, the question arises as to how the symbols should be arranged. In A3b, extending occurs at the same time as turning. The two actions are placed side by side. It does not matter which is placed on the right and which on the left, the meaning is the same.

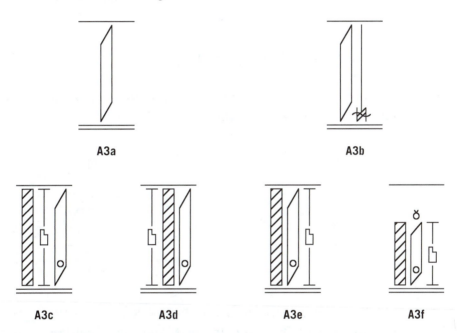

A3a   A3b

A3c   A3d   A3e   A3f

In A3c, three main actions are shown: traveling, rising, and twisting. There is no difference if these are arranged as in A3c, as in A3d, or as in A3e. When stillness occurs after combined actions, its indication is usually centered, as in A3f.

After two simultaneous actions a single action is usually centered, as in A3g. However, placement of the symbols as in A3h would be quite clear. A3i illustrates three simultaneous actions followed by two actions. Here again, it would not matter if the two subsequent actions were placed slightly differently. The writer has only to be concerned with what seems logical and what facilitates reading.

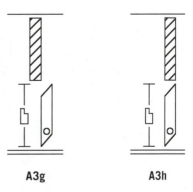

A3g   A3h

The turning sign in A3i logically follows after the twist into the same direction, just as in A3j the general movement down is placed above the previous movement up. Thus, for placement on the page, actions of the same category—flexion/extension, turning, directional actions, paths—would logically follow one another in vertical placement. In arranging symbols, placements which are "reader-friendly" is a good rule to follow.

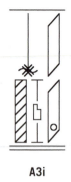

A3i

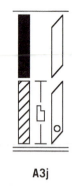

A3j

RIGHT AND LEFT SIDES

Addition of the center line to indicate use of right or left side of the body poses the question of where other information should be placed. Example A4a shows a simple statement of a sideward action for the right side of the body. In A4b, a path traveling forward is added; the spacing makes the instructions clear.

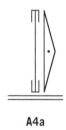

A4a

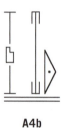

A4b

Example A4c illustrates a sideward action for the left side of the body during a turn to the right. Because of the "left" and "right" natures of these actions, there is a natural tendency to put them on the appropriate side. Example A4d shows turning to the right while upward and downward actions occur for the left and right sides of the body.

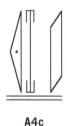

A4c

A4d

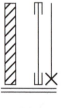

A4e

A4f

A4g

Actions that do not relate to the center line should be placed apart, leaving enough space so that it is clear that a separate, independent statement, not related to the center line, is being made. Example A4e shows a general rising movement accompanied by a contraction on the right side of the body. In A4f, use has been made of a small horizontal curved bow to tie the indication of contracting to the center line. In A4g, both the rising and the contracting are tied to the center line indication; stating clearly that, while the right side contracts, the left side is performing an upward movement. Use of this small horizontal linking bow clarifies two simultaneous indications that belong together. However, use of a separation, as in A4e, is visually helpful.

LIMBS, PARTS OF THE BODY

Main actions for the body as a whole are centered; actions for specific parts of the body (additional features) are placed adjacent on the right or left. Once certain placements have been established, it is more practical for subsequent reading to keep indications of one kind vertically one above the other, rather than switch placements. The degree to which this can be done may depend on what comes next. If an action of a limb is the main movement, it is centered on the staff. In A5a, a limb moves up.

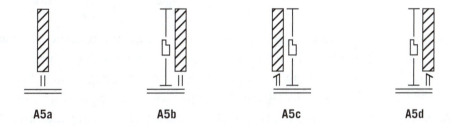

A5a	**A5b**	**A5c**	**A5d**

If there is a main general action, such as traveling, this is centered and the limb indication is placed alongside, A5b. In such cases right or left placement does not mean right or left limb; which side of the body is involved is still open. In A5c, the limb is stated to be the left arm; in A5d, it is the right arm. Limbs for the right side of the body are placed on the right, A5d, those for the left side on the left.

In A5e, two main actions, a twist and a lowering, occur in addition to the arm gesture. Traveling forward in A5f begins with a twist to the right as both arms move across to the opposite sides.

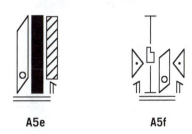

A5e	**A5f**

When both limbs perform the same action, their signs may be placed next to each other to facilitate reading, as in A5g. In the case of indications for arm and leg of the same side, the arm is placed further out, as in A5h where, during the turn, the right leg is sideward and the right arm up.

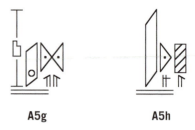

A5g   **A5h**

AREAS OF THE BODY

In the use of body parts, central parts such as the trunk (torso) and its parts, are placed closer to the center, while more peripheral parts (limbs, hands, and head) are placed outside on the right or left. Indications for the whole torso are usually placed on the left of center, those for the chest on the right.

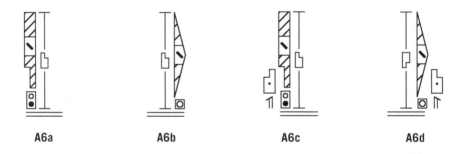

A6a   **A6b**   **A6c**   **A6d**

Example A6a illustrates traveling with a torso tilt; in A6b it is the chest which is tilting. In A6c, the left arm starts forward as traveling and torso tilting begins. Example A6d indicates the right arm moving forward at the beginning of traveling backward combined with chest tilting. For Structured Description of movement, placement of the various pieces of information is carefully organized on the three-line staff to provide ease in reading and in locating any particular movement detail. This can be seen in Appendix B.

SIGNS FOR PARTS OF THE BODY

Standard practice is to place the sign for a part of the body before the movement indication as a pre-sign.

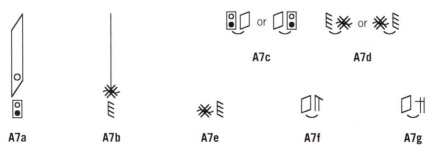

A7a   **A7b**   **A7e**   **A7f**   **A7g**

Thus A7a states: "whole torso twists to the right." Example A7b states: "right hand flexes" and so on. One knows at once the body part involved and then the kind of action it is to do. If the action is very quick the two indications can be placed side by side, as in A7c and A7d, but then they must be tied together with a small curved horizontal bow. Without the bow, as in A7e, the statement would be of some kind of flexion for the body-as-a-whole, the meaning of the hand symbol would not be clear—it appears that a movement indication for the hand has been omitted by mistake. Example A7f shows a quick turn for the right arm, while in A7g there is a quick inward rotation for the left leg.

LEG ROTATION, WHOLE BODY ROTATION

Exact use of leg rotations belongs more to Structured Description, where it is important to record any slight change in the rotational state. In Motif Description, leg rotations are usually the focal point of an action, rather than an additional, subordinate factor.

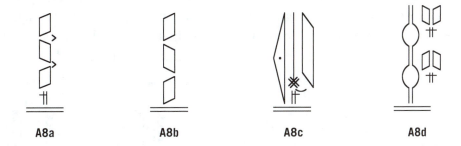

A8a   **A8b**   **A8c**   **A8d**

Concerning leg rotations, it is important to observe that the action of A8a is quite a separate movement from a rotation (turn) of the body as a whole, A8b. For a turn of the whole body, the performer is usually supporting on one or both feet, or may be sitting, while turning. Rotation of the free leg in or out (or even the supporting leg in or out) exists quite separately from a pivot turn. In A8c, a general sideward movement to the left is accompanied by a turning in and flexing of the right leg. We presume the right leg to be gesturing. Such flexion and rotation could, however, occur for a supporting leg; but if these two actions are to be featured, a gesture is more appropriate. In A8d, two consecutive jumps occur. The first lands with legs turned in, the second with legs turned out.

SUPPORTS

The length of an action stroke which terminates in a new support gives the time during which the transference of weight is to be achieved. It is only at the end that weight is fully on the new support, A9a. In A9b, there is a change of support during a lowering action. This very open statement allows the weight to be taken on any part of the body you wish. Because of the accompanying downward action it is likely that certain parts will be chosen in preference to others; however, the change of support could even be onto the shoulders.

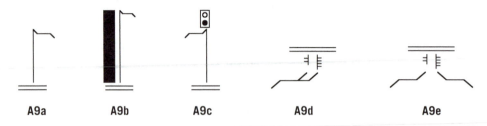

When we write changes of support, which involve use of a specific body part (foot, knee, hip, etc.), indication for the part taking over the weight is placed at the end of the action stroke. Example A9c states a slow action at the end of which you are lying down (supporting on the whole torso). In A9d, the starting position is supporting on one foot and one knee. This support could also be written as A9e. As this notation is of a starting position (note placement of the double horizontal line), it is understood that timing is not shown, only the appropriate body signs and support bows. These bows may be drawn to the right or to the left, choice rests on what is visually clearer in a given context, the meaning is not changed.

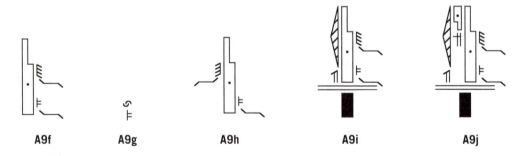

In A9f, a forward action is accompanied by supporting first on the right knee, then on the right hand. It is expected that the knee support will remain until other movement indications cause it to be replaced, or until a specific indication to release the knee support is given, as in A9g. Example A9h is similar but weight is taken on the left hand, the sign logically being placed on the left side. Example A9i illustrates the movement of A9f with the addition of a starting position and an upward gesture for the left arm. In A9j, a backward leg gesture has also been added. It is clear that the forward movement must be of the torso and head. Gradually, the action is becoming more structured, although there is still much leeway for interpretation.

The pathway forward in A9k is achieved by supporting on the knees, right, left, right, and left. Placement of the signs on their appropriate sides facilitates reading, though A9l clearly indicates the same thing and has the advantage of being more compact on the page.

A9k   A9l

PLACEMENT OF SUPPORTING BOW

Some leeway is possible in placement of the supporting bow when specific timing is not required. It is also possible to use the other forms of the bow; A10a, is applicable when lying on the ground. When supporting on a particular surface of the torso, let us say the front, A10b, the supporting bow can be written as in A10c or A10d. It is not necessary to connect the bow to the "tick" which marks the front surface; the torso sign with indication of the desired surface is a unit and thus A10e or A10f would also provide the same message.

A10a   A10b   A10c   A10d   A10e   A10f

Even though gaining writing skills is not the focus in the exploration of movement covered in this book, certain questions will arise concerning how movements are to be expressed on paper. When recording a movement sequence one usually aims at getting the information, the facts down first and then, with the next copy, arranging the indication logically to make reading easier.

DERIVATION OF THE "ANY SPRING" SIGN

The sign for "a spring" is derived from the general form a jump takes in Structured Description. Action strokes in the central support columns indicate weight on the ground; strokes in the next columns, the leg gesture columns, indicate both legs are free of weight—the body is in the air. Action strokes again placed in the support columns indicate a return to supporting on the ground. The spelling of A11a is extracted from the three-line staff to produce A11b. As this looks like six separate actions, the outer two strokes are curved to connect with the "supporting" strokes, and the two supporting lines at start and finish are reduced to one line to produce the basic sign for any form of spring. Thus the composite sign of A11c expresses the basic action of a spring.

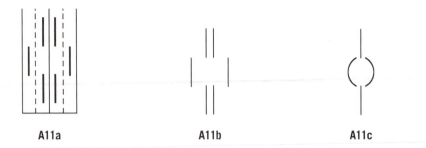

A11a   **A11b**   **A11c**

DIRECTIONAL AREAS—TIMING

Movements related to directional areas may start in that particular area, or take time to arrive in that area. These timing distinctions are shown by where the area sign is placed on the direction symbol. Example A12a describes movement **within any area**. In A12b, the gesture starts in the upward area, having arrived there without emphasis. Gestures are in that area for the duration of the symbol movement. It is appropriate while standing to explore such areas with both arms or with one arm alone, or with the head. A movement may take time to arrive in a directional area, in this case the area sign is placed later on in the direction symbol. In A12c, half of the movement time is spent on the way to the area, the other half of the duration is movement in that area. In A12d, the entire duration of the movement is spent on the way to arriving at some destination in that area. This arrival statement could as well be expressed as a movement to any high level destination, A12e.

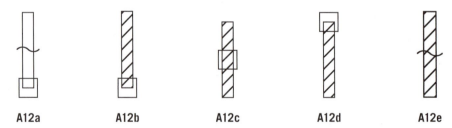

A12a   **A12b**   **A12c**   **A12d**   **A12e**

APPLICATION OF DIRECTIONAL AREAS

While exploration of the areas of directions is educationally valuable, most dance techniques and choreography use clearly defined spatial destinations; it has not been common for vagueness to be a desired feature. However, in contemporary choreography it is becoming more frequent for vagueness to be a desired feature. The need to devise a sign to specify movement within an area came from Ghanaian dance. In this dance form, certain movements emanate from an impulse in the torso that results in a arm gesture toward, say, the forward-right low direction. Each time the movement was performed, the arm might arrive at a different point, but all ended in the same main area; arrival at an exact point is not the object of the movement and therefore it could not be described as such.

Transition from Motif to Structured Description

The following pages are designed to illustrate the transition in writing rules and placement of symbols that occurs in progressing from Motif Description (MD) to the Structured Description (SD) of Labanotation.

STAFF

The basic staff, B1a, to which is added identification of right and left sides of the body, B1b, becomes the three-line staff of B1c. This staff provides vertical columns for the main parts of the body, the movement indications being placed in the appropriate columns.

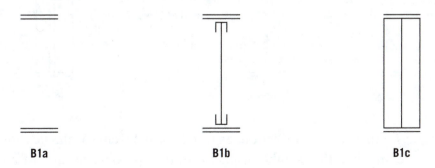

B1a   B1b   B1c

Example B1d shows the full staff with identification of the columns. The dotted lines, marked here for explanatory purposes, are not usually included; for visual clarity only the three vertical lines are used. Within the three-line staff are columns for supports (steps) and leg gestures. Outside the three lines are placed indications for body, arms, and head. Note that the head is always separated by a blank column from other indications.

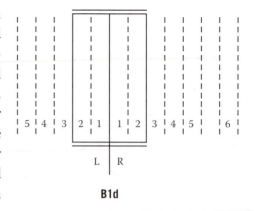

B1d

The center line divides right and left. Use of the columns:

1 supports (usually on the feet)
2 leg gestures (not taking weight)
3 body (torso, etc.)
4 arms
5 hands
6 head (placed away from other indications).

STEPS

Stepping, an action ending in a new support on right or left foot, was written in Motif Notation as B2a or the abbreviation of B2b. This is now shown in the full staff by indications in the right and left center columns, B2c. These center columns are for supports on the feet unless otherwise indicated.

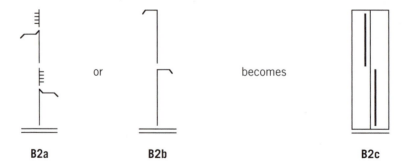

B2a   or   **B2b**   becomes   **B2c**

For steps into a specific direction, as in B2d which states right step forward, left step side, the direction symbol is placed in the appropriate support column, as B2e.

B2d   becomes   **B2e**

TRAVELING

Direction of traveling is shown by the direction of the steps in the support column. If traveling starts with the right foot, then B3a and B3b could become B3c and B3d. The number and level of steps used, not stated in the notation of B3a or B3b, needs to be specified in SD.

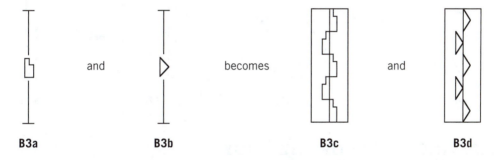

B3a   and   **B3b**   becomes   **B3c**   and   **B3d**

For circular paths the direction of the traveling is shown in the support column, the pathway for circling being placed outside, alongside the steps. Example B3e becomes B3f.

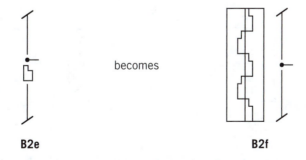

B2e   becomes   **B2f**

TURNING

General turning, pivoting, B4a, becomes specific by the placement of the turn sign in the appropriate support column according to where the weight is placed, i.e., on the right foot, B4b, on the left, B4c, or on both feet, B4d.

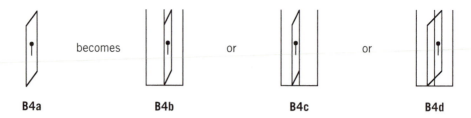

B4a **B4b** **B4c** **B4d**

Turning on the spot through steps in place, B4e, may be shown by placing the turn sign outside the staff to refer to the body as a whole, B4f, or a circular path sign may be used, as in B4g, the logic being that the feet are making a circle, even though a very small one. Should it not be clear that the turn sign refers to the whole body and not to some other recently indicated part, the sign for the body-as-a-whole can be used for identification, B4h. The need for its use is rare.

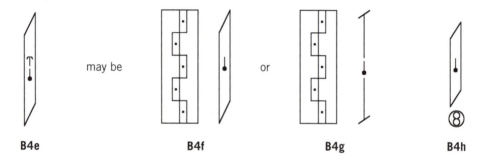

B4e **B4f** **B4g** **B4h**

TURNING: PARTS OF THE BODY

In SD, rotations and twists of the areas and limbs of the body are placed in the appropriate columns. Arms and legs have their own columns; thus B5a becomes B5b, and B5c becomes B5d.

B5a **B5b** **B5c** **B5d**

The parts of the torso are identified and placed in the body columns. Thus, B5e becomes B5f; B5g becomes B5h. In SD it is clear from placement within the gesture columns that a turn sign is not a turn for the body-as-a-whole; therefore, addition of the hold sign within the turn sign to show twist of a limb, i.e., a gesture, is not needed. Unit rotation for the torso, B5i, requires addition of the equal sign when

placed in the appropriate column, B5j. The same is true for the arms and legs, B5k, when unit rotation is required, B5l.

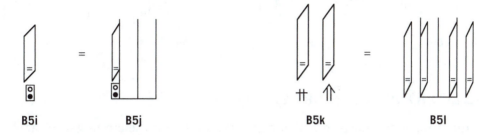

In MD, the combined (composite) turn sign, B5m, gives the choice of turning left or right. In SD, this sign in the support column means the same thing, B5n. When used in a gesture column in SD, this sign indicates a parallel state for that body part, i.e., neither rotated in or out, B5o and B5p.

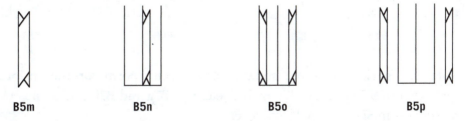

AERIAL STEPS

For the general indication of "any spring into the air" no form exists in SD; the general statement must become specific. Examples B6a–B6i show the specific forms, shown first with no direction indicated.

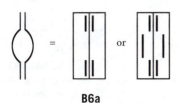

B6a

In SD, a gap (space) in the support column means that there is no support; you go into the air, i.e., a spring. Leg gestures are indicated with action strokes.

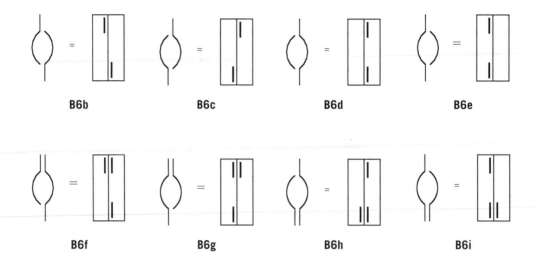

B6b   B6c   B6d   B6e

B6f   B6g   B6h   B6i

DIRECTIONS FOR AERIAL STEPS

Specific directions shown in MD for the take-off or for the landing are translated directly into the support column in SD. The same is true for directions indicated for the legs while in the air.

B7a   B7b   B7c   B7d   B7e

Note that as B7a does not indicate any specific form for the spring, the interpretation in SD could be B7b or B7c, etc. B7f, B7g and B7h give some possible interpretations in SD of the MD examples.

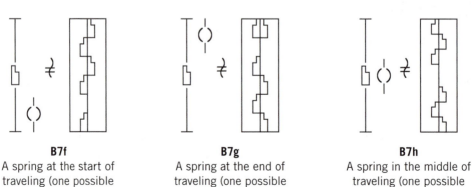

B7f
A spring at the start of traveling (one possible interpretation)

B7g
A spring at the end of traveling (one possible interpretation)

B7h
A spring in the middle of traveling (one possible interpretation)

TILTING, TAKING A DIRECTION

Tilting indications for specific parts of the body are placed in the appropriate column. For the torso and its parts, the specific body sign is still used. Example B8a becomes B8b, B8c becomes B8d, B8e becomes B8f. The tilting (inclining) indication: \ is no longer needed.

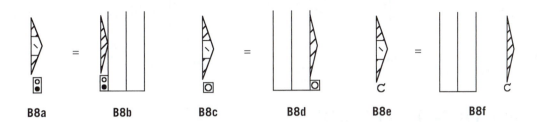

Gestures of limbs to a directional destination are written by placing the required direction symbol in the appropriate column. Thus B8g becomes B8h, B8i becomes B8j, and so on.

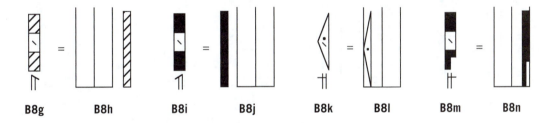

SHIFTING

In SD, the freedom of stating "any level" for shifting movements is not expected, the notation needs to be specific; therefore the shifting sign without a level is taken to be middle level.

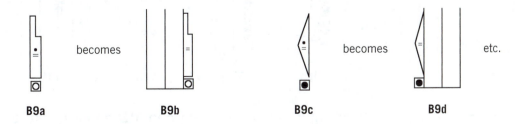

DIRECTION OF PROGRESSION

For the direction of progression, the statement is placed in the appropriate column on the staff. The indication of levels is identical in SD.

B10a   becomes   **B10b**

FLEXION, EXTENSION

Flexion and extension of the limbs and trunk are written in the appropriate columns. This is true of all forms of flexion and extension. For the arms, B11b is the SD of B11a; for the legs B11c becomes B11d.

B11a   **B11b**   **B11c**   **B11d**

Flexion and extension actions that occur at the same time as a directional change are combined in SD, the flexion and or extension indication being placed before the directional symbol as a pre-sign in the same column. Example B11e becomes B11f, and B11g becomes B11h.

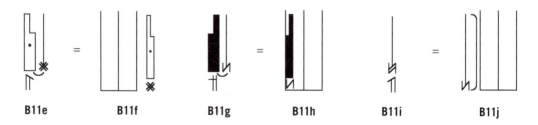

B11e   **B11f**   **B11g**   **B11h**   **B11i**   **B11j**

The double sign for stretching the limbs, B11i, which in MD means reaching out into space, pulling away from the body, is not used in SD. Such reaching out is shown as an arm or leg gesture which includes the body, hence use of an inclusion bow into the body column, as in B11j.

SITTING, LYING, ETC.

Supporting on a body part, e.g., lying on the torso, B12a, is written by placing the appropriate body sign in the support column, B12b. The angular supporting line is not needed when the support column is used.

B12a   =   B12b

PATHS FOR LIMBS

Straight and circular paths for the limbs are placed in the appropriate column. Because it is clear that it is an action of a limb and not of the body-as-a-whole, the hold sign at the base of the path sign is no longer needed. Example B13a becomes B13b.

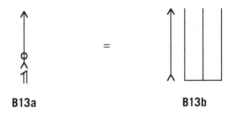

B13a   =   B13b

This survey of the transition from Motif to Structured Description reveals the logical relationship between the broad intentions stated in MD and specific identification of the movement, which is the function of SD. For a fuller exposition of SD consult the textbook *Labanotation* by Ann Hutchinson Guest, published by Routledge, New York.

APPENDIX C
Flexion and Extension— Additional Material

SPECIFIC DIRECTIONS FOR CONTRACTIONS

Chapter 17 presents many aspects concerning specific forms of flexion and extension. Here we delve into some specific details not readily understood. These are: contraction over surfaces, sagittal and horizontal joining and separating, and indications for any degree of the various forms of flexion and extensions.

When the contraction sign is used for a body part, it is generally understood that the contraction occurs over the inner, volar (palm, sole) surface. For the torso, this surface is the front. Since the torso has possibilities for contracting over other surfaces, a short line representing the performer, similar to the meeting line, is used to state the specific direction of the contraction. This line is placed adjacent to the contraction sign to indicate over which body surface (i.e., in which body direction) the contraction should occur. Think of the line as being you.

The sign for open choice, i.e., use of any surface, is shown in C1a. The possibilities for C1b–C1e are illustrated in C1f–C1i with the torso upright.

C1a	**C1b**	**C1c**	**C1d**	**C1e**
Over any surface	Over the front	Over the back	Over the left side	Over the right side

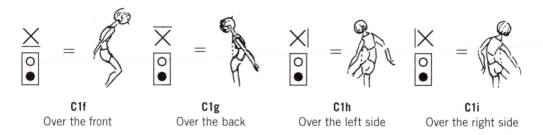

C1f
Over the front

C1g
Over the back

C1h
Over the left side

C1i
Over the right side

Diagonal contractions for the torso and its parts, can also be shown by combining two lines, as shown in C1j–C1m.

C1j
Over the right
front surface

C1k
Over the right
back surface

C1l
Over the left
front surface

C1m
Over the left
back surface

SAGITTAL JOINING, SEPARATING

Two other dimensions provide possibilities for gestures of joining and separating—the sagittal and horizontal. These will now be investigated.

The sagittal dimension provides the possibilities for spreading, opening away from the body (the center line) or closing in to it again. Because of the narrower build of the hips, the legs can experience such relating to each other while in the air or supporting on different parts of the body. The arms can relate to each other sagittally as well as to the torso, although the awareness is less strong than in the lateral dimension.

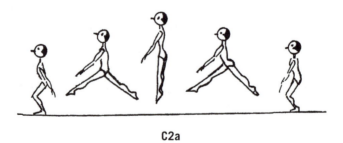

C2a

Example C2a illustrates separating and joining the legs in the sagittal plane. The legs start together, separate, join again in the air, then separate once more before landing with feet together. Many possibilities exist for the legs while one is lying down or performing a shoulder or head stand, not to mention in such special situations as swimming, diving, parachuting, suspending from aerial wires, or a high spring from a trampoline—each of which provides opportunity for the legs to move freely without being concerned with weight-bearing.

Signs for Sagittal Joining, Separating

The general signs for sagittal spreading and joining, C3a–C3d, relate to those for the lateral activities of this kind; the signs are doubled for the greater degree.

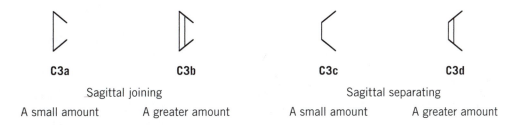

C3a	C3b	C3c	C3d
Sagittal joining		Sagittal separating	
A small amount	A greater amount	A small amount	A greater amount

However, interpretation is open when sagittal separating or closing is involved. How should C3e be interpreted? Which arm would separate in the forward direction, which backward? What movement would logically result from C3f? Would the right arm move away in the forward direction, or to the back? The choice is open, an additional indication is needed to specify within.

C3e   C3f

For sagittal actions of joining and separating, thickening one end of the sign indicates when a forward or backward sagittal action is to occur. In C3g, a sagittal forward separating would be performed, while C3h shows a backward sagittal separating. To indicate specifically that both forward and backward separating should occur, both ends are thickened, as in C3i. This same logic is applied to indications for sagittal joining. What is not stated here is which limb moves forward, which backward; this is left open to choice.

C3g	C3h	C3i
Forward	Backward	Forward
sagittal active	sagittal active	and backward

USE WITH SPECIFIC BODY PARTS

Examples C4a–C4i explore some specific instances in using sagittal separating and joining. In C4a, the choice is open as to whether the right arm will spread sagittally forward or backward. In C4b, the forward separating is clearly stated for the left arm. The right arm separates sagittally backward in C4c. In C4d, which arm to use and which direction is left open to choice. Which arm to use is also left open in C4e for separating sagittally forward.

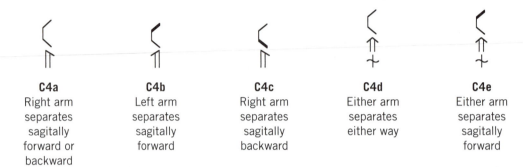

C4a	C4b	C4c	C4d	C4e
Right arm separates sagitally forward or backward	Left arm separates sagitally forward	Right arm separates sagitally backward	Either arm separates either way	Either arm separates sagitally forward

Joining sagittally from the back is shown for the left leg in C4f and from the front for the right leg in C4g. Example C4h represents both legs actively separating sagittally. Example C4i clearly states which leg opens forward and which backward. If the sense of the center line of the body can be retained, two limbs could give the sensation of spreading in the same forward or backward direction from the center line, in contrast to relating to each other.

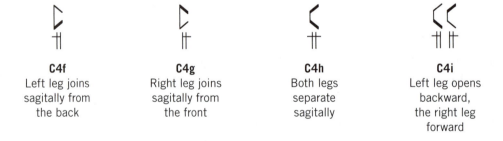

C4f	C4g	C4h	C4i
Left leg joins sagitally from the back	Right leg joins sagitally from the front	Both legs separate sagitally	Left leg opens backward, the right leg forward

DURATION OF SAGITTAL SEPARATING, JOINING

The duration line is attached to the top of the symbol; the longer the line, the slower the movement.

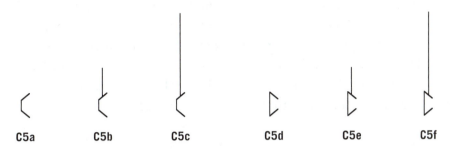

| C5a | C5b | C5c | C5d | C5e | C5f |

HORIZONTAL SEPARATING, JOINING

Lateral separating and joining is easily understood; sagittal separating and joining fall into place, but what of horizontal separating and joining? This is a question that comes up. Horizontal joining and separating are less frequent but are also possible. If the arms start out to the side, they can join in the forward direction and separate by returning to the open side, as illustrated in the bird's-eye view of C6a. For the legs, such horizontal actions are best experienced while sitting on the floor. With legs extended forward, they can open to the sides and then return, C6b. As can be seen, such actions in the horizontal plane are more limited, largely because of the build of the body.

The sign for such horizontal opening and closing is based on the lateral sign, but with indication of the vertical line through use of the white circle representing the place high direction, thus establishing the "seen from above" bird's-eye point of view, C6c.

C6a   C6b   C6c   C6d   C6e   C6f

Example C6c indicates horizontal opening, while C6d is horizontal closing. Indication of one-sided action also applies to these horizontal actions. In C6e, it is the right side that opens; in C6f, the right side closes horizontally.

TERMINOLOGY

The terms "opening" and "closing" are in common use and can as well be applied to three-dimensional contraction and extension, to folding and unfolding, and also to gathering and scattering. For separating and joining of the legs, as in C7, many people would just say "open" and "close" the legs. But separating and joining indicate an awareness of the other part, a relationship different from general opening and closing. The word "widening" is especially applicable to lateral spreading (abducting), as is "narrowing" to the closing in (adducting). The words lateral spreading and narrowing and their signs can also be applied to the chest.

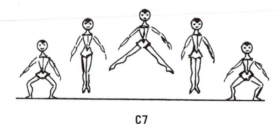

C7

FORMS OF FLEXION, EXTENSION: ANY DEGREE

For all these specific forms of flexion and extension only two general degrees of each have been given in this book. In the detailed Labanotation descriptions, six specific degrees are provided in the standard 6/6 scale; an 8/8 scale is also available. In Motif Description, to allow total freedom with regard to the degree for each of these actions, the vertical ad lib. sign is used; this was introduced in Chapter 17, 17.4h and 17.4i, and also 17.5e, repeated here as C8a and C8e. As a duration line may be added, the small ad lib. sign is placed at the base of the symbol.

CONTRACTION AND ELONGATION

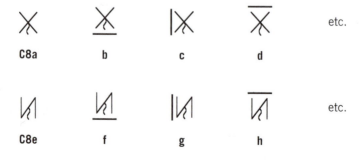

The reason for such placement of this vertical ad lib. sign derives from the location of the dots for specific degrees in Labanotation usage. When the basic symbol for folding, unfolding, and separating, joining, needs to be rotated, the placement of the ad lib. sign changes accordingly.

Folding, Unfolding

Note the indication for any degree of unfolding in C8m; the sign by itself always means total unfolding.

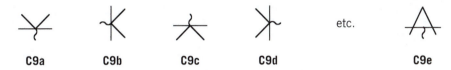

| C9a | C9b | C9c | C9d | etc. | C9e |

Separating, Joining

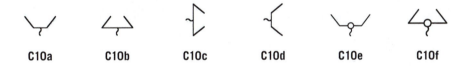

| C10a | C10b | C10c | C10d | C10e | C10f |

APPENDIX D
Terminology

This list is intended to clarify the meaning of certain words used in the analysis of movement in *Your Move*, terms which may not be familiar to all or not so defined in other fields of movement study.

AN ACTION—a movement of a particular type or with a particular purpose or content.

ANY ACTION—freedom to choose any movement, determined by performer.

ANATOMICAL TERMS—terminology used in the study of anatomy.

ASPECTS OF MOVEMENT—the different "sides," "views" of movement on which attention may be focused or which may be particularly featured.

AXIAL MOVEMENT—movement around the body's center (in contrast to locomotor movement).

BREATH PAUSE—a fleeting interruption of the flow of movement comparable to a singer taking a breath during an aria.

CONCEPTS OF MOVEMENT—ideas and comprehensions of movement from which actions are "conceived" and viewed.

CONTRACTION—the form of flexion concerned specifically with drawing in a limb toward the center, the extremity approaching the base of the limb on a straight path. The term is used in its anatomical sense and does not refer to the stylized movement of the torso met in certain contemporary dance techniques.

DORSAL—anatomical term for the back, the back surface.

EXTENSION—this "parent" term includes actions of lengthening (elongating, stretching), unfolding, and separating (abducting). It is not used in the sense of meaning given to it in anatomical terminology.

FACTOR—one of the elements or influences that contribute to produce a result, a component part.

FLEXION—the "parent" term for the actions of contracting, folding, and joining (adducting).

FORM—the shape, type, kind, or category to which a movement belongs. In general parlance the word "form" is applied in many ways. Forms of movement may be gymnastics, games, dance, etc. Forms of dance may be ballet, Spanish, Javanese, etc. Forms of locomotion can be running, skipping, sliding. Forms of flexion are contracting, folding, joining (closing in laterally or sagittally), and so on.

GESTURE—a non-weight-bearing movement. Gestures are usually of the limbs but may also be of the head, torso, and its parts.

HOLD—the retention of a state or situation.

HORIZONTAL PLANE—the plane that is parallel with the floor when one is standing and which divides the body into upper and lower halves (also called the "table" plane).

KINESPHERE—the sphere within which we move, its boundaries being defined by "reach space," i.e., the distance limbs can reach without any traveling occurring.

LANGUAGE OF DANCE®—the means through which dance is communicated, not only by performance of the movement itself—the act of dancing—but through a thorough understanding and analysis of the movement content, the presentation and communication of which is facilitated by a universally based terminology supported by written representation in Motif Notation of the facts and motivations.

LATERAL—pertaining to the sideward directions.

LATERAL PLANE—the lateral-vertical plane in the body dividing front and back (also called the frontal plane, or "door" plane).

LOCOMOTOR—movement which produces traveling of one form or another, usually on the feet.

MOTIF DESCRIPTION—provides a general statement concerning the theme or most salient feature of a movement. It also pinpoints the motivation of a movement, its idea, aim, or intent. The Motif Notation may be kept simple or may be made increasingly detailed leading toward a fully structured description.

MOVEMENT—motion of any kind. In this book this word is used as a general term when no specific action or particular content is intended, but just a general change of some kind.

PERSONAL SPACE—space within the kinesphere surrounding each person which is psychologically their personal "property."

PRIME ACTIONS—the elements of movement, the root actions. Like prime numbers, these actions cannot be further reduced into component parts.

RETAIN—the maintaining of a state (as in a touch) or of an activity (as in continuous sliding).

ROTATION —a turning as a unit of the body-as-a-whole or of a part of the body.

SAGITTAL—pertaining to the forward-backward body directions.

SAGITTAL PLANE—the sagittal-vertical plane dividing the body into right and left halves (also called the "wheel" plane).

SHIFT—direction of displacement of the center of gravity or of a body part where free and fixed end move equally.

SIGN, SYMBOL—indications on paper representing the many component parts of movement. Major indications are usually termed symbols, minor indications called signs.

STILLNESS—absence of change in which the expression, the "feel," the "reverberation" of the previous movement is continued, or stillness may have its own intent.

STRUCTURED DESCRIPTION—the term "Structured" is given to movement described in clearly defined and measurable terms. Such description, the most commonly used for Labanotation, expresses movement in terms of:
The Body—the specific parts that move
Space—the specific direction, level, distance, or degree of motion
Time—meter and duration, measured time and relative time
Dynamics—the quality or "texture" of the movement

TAKING A DIRECTION—the line of the torso or limb that embodies the stated direction and level.

THE BODY—the specific parts that move.

TILT—inclining the body or part of the body away from the vertical line, where the free end moves further in space than the parts closer to the base.

TURN(ING)—the general term used for parts of the body when the specific form (rotation in one piece or twisting) is not important or need not be stated.

TWIST—a turning of the body or part of the body in which the extremity (the free end) produces a greater degree of turn than the base.

UNIT ROTATION—a turn of a body part as a unit, i.e., in one piece.

VOLAR—anatomical term for the palm, sole, but also referring to the inner surface of a body part, e.g., back of leg.

APPENDIX E
The Family Tree of Verbs

The Prime Actions (the raw material of movement) with which we have been dealing are like "parents" in that the subdivisions and variations of each are like "children" and "grandchildren." To illustrate this and show the relationship between various subdivisions, a chart is provided in this appendix. This "Movement Family Tree" is concerned with movement "words of action," i.e., the "verbs." Two other charts, the Family Tree of Nouns ("what" is being moved or is involved in a movement) and the Family Tree of Adverbs ("how" an action is performed, the quality, dynamics) are not included in this book. Their value relates more directly to Structured Description.

The Movement Alphabet, given on pages xxxix–xl, indicates the Prime Actions and Concepts of which movement is comprised. This alphabet provides a basic reference for the material to come. The chart of Verbs, presented here, leads on from the Movement Alphabet. Numbers in the corner of key boxes in the Family Tree of Verbs refer to the items so numbered in the Movement Alphabet. Once the Prime actions have been explored, reference to the Verbs chart is a valuable guide and an aid to clarification in teaching the material covered in *Your Move*. As details on the various forms of movement are presented, the chart is a help in providing perspective on how new material relates to what has gone before. Many people like to know the extent of the material under investigation and to have a clear idea of the relationship of the individual parts. The Family Tree of Verbs is a visual aid in mentally organizing and thus better understanding the many movement facts and ideas.

Some items on the Verbs chart may be met more frequently in Structured Description rather than Motif Description. Although they may not be explored in this book, knowledge of their existence is helpful in obtaining a total picture.

The Movement Family Tree of Verbs progresses from the simplest indication—an action of some kind—to the more sophisticated concepts of filling a shape or penetrating space. The concept of destination in contrast to motion is listed before specific forms of movement are introduced. Anatomical possibilities are then considered, the different forms of flexion, extension, and rotation made possible by the nature of the joints of the body. These physical actions produce spatial changes in placement of the limbs and body parts. How we move in and travel through space is a "multicolored" category. Concern with support and the placement of weight is essential in almost all movement description; transference of weight and balance are important considerations. The chart ends with indication of the results of actions, the many forms of relationship and concerns with visual design.

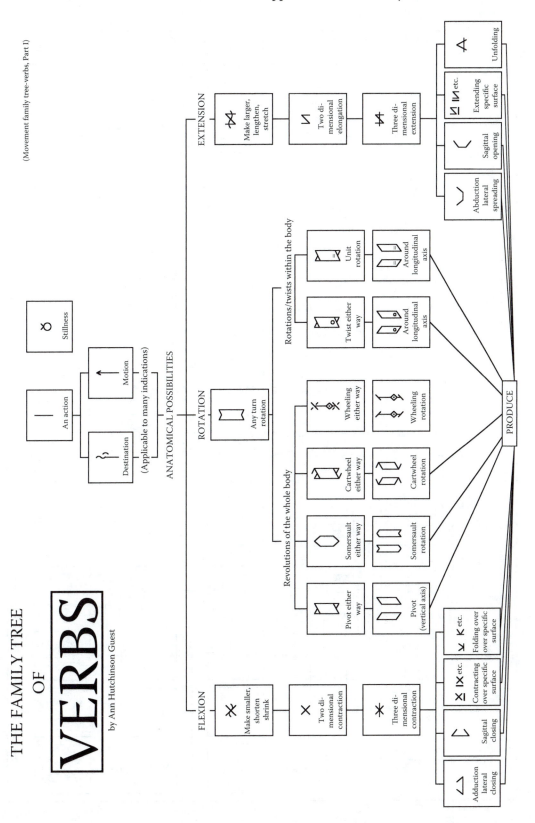

(Movement family tree-verbs, Part I)

THE FAMILY TREE OF **VERBS**
by Ann Hutchinson Guest

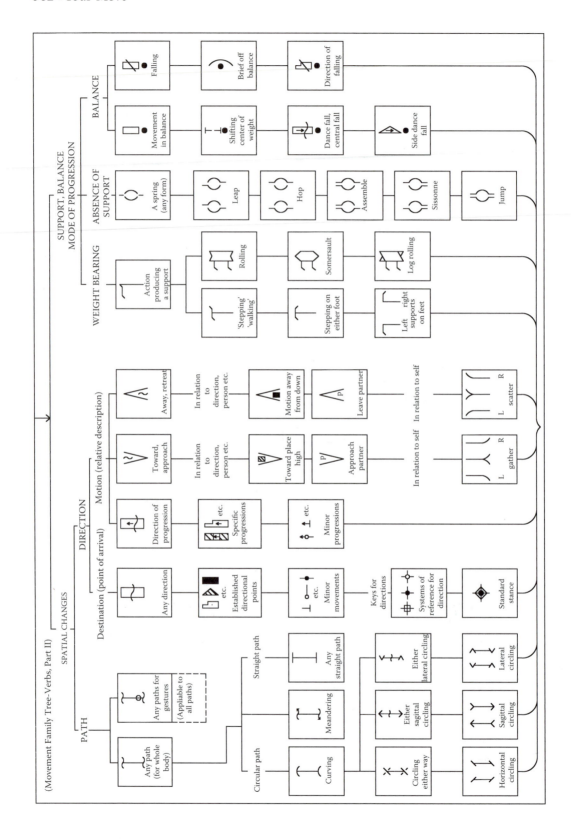

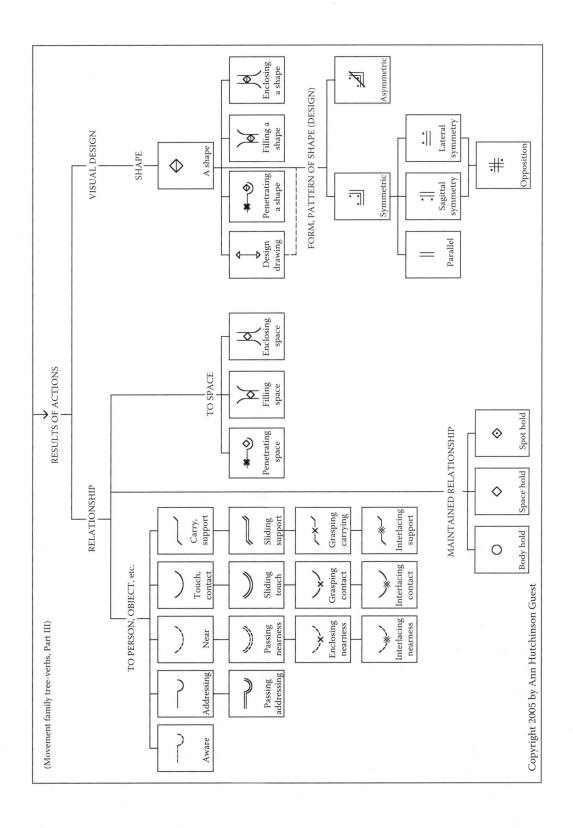

(Movement family tree-verbs, Part III)

RESULTS OF ACTIONS

VISUAL DESIGN

RELATIONSHIP

SHAPE

A shape

Design drawing

Penetrating a shape

Filling a shape

Enclosing a shape

FORM, PATTERN OF SHAPE (DESIGN)

Symmetric

Asymmetric

Parallel

Sagittal symmetry

Lateral symmetry

Opposition

TO SPACE

Penetrating space

Filling space

Enclosing space

TO PERSON, OBJECT, etc.

Aware

Addressing

Near

Touch, contact

Carry, support

Passing addressing

Passing nearness

Sliding touch

Sliding support

Enclosing nearness

Grasping contact

Grasping carrying

Interlacing nearness

Interlacing contact

Interlacing support

MAINTAINED RELATIONSHIP

Body hold

Space hold

Spot hold

Index

M

T

X

Y

Z